POLICE CO-OPERATION IN EUROPE:
AN INVESTIGATION

Other CSPO Publications

Occasional Paper 1: Disadvantage, Politics and Disorder £4.50
by J Benyon ISBN 1 874493 70 7

Occasional Paper 2: Realising the Public World Order £4.50
by S Johnston ISBN 1 874493 65 0

Research Paper 1: Crime on Holiday £4.50
by M Gill ISBN 1 774493 15 4

Research Paper 2: Civilian Staff in the Police Force £4.50
by B Loveday ISBN 1 874493 40 5

The Roots of Urban Unrest £18.50
edited by J Benyon and J Solomos ISBN 0 08 035839-X

Scarman and After £13.50
edited by J Benyon ISBN 0 08 030218

Tackling Racial Attacks £8.50
edited by P Francis and R Matthews ISBN 1 874493 20 0

African Caribbean People in Leicestershire £6.00
by J Benyon and B Dauda (Colour Brochure) ISBN 1 874493 00 6

African Caribbean People in Leicestershire: First Interim Report £12.50
edited by J Benyon and B Dauda ISBN 1 874493 05 7

African Caribbean People in Leicestershire: Experiences and Opinions £11.50
by J Benyon, B Dauda, J Garland, S Lyle and M Rowe ISBN 1 874493 75 8

The Terrorist Threat to Safe Shopping £11.00
by A Beck and A Willis ISBN 1 874493 55 3

Available from:

**Centre for the Study of Public Order, University of Leicester
6 Salisbury Road, Leicester LE1 7QR, UK**

Tel: (0) 533 522458 Fax: (0) 533 523944

POLICE CO-OPERATION IN EUROPE: *AN INVESTIGATION*

John Benyon
Lynne Turnbull
Andrew Willis
Rachel Woodward
Adrian Beck

University of Leicester
Centre for the Study of Public Order

November 1993

ISBN 1 874493 30 8

Published by the Centre for the Study of Public Order
University of Leicester, 6 Salisbury Road, Leicester LE1 7QR, UK

Tel: (0) 533 523942 Fax: (0) 533 523944

First published November 1993

Copyright © Benyon, Turnbull, Willis, Woodward and Beck 1993.

British Library Cataloguing in Publication Data
A catalogue record for this book is available from the British Library

ISBN 1 874493 30 8

Copies of this report may be obtained from the Centre for the Study of Public Order at the above address. Price £47.50 per copy, including postage and packaging. Cheques should be made payable to the University of Leicester. It is possible to invoice organisations for which the total price is £55.50.

Printed by R & G Design Ltd., Humberstone Lane, Leicester.

CONTENTS

LIST OF FIGURES AND TABLES

Figures

Tables

PREFACE

On 1st November 1993 the European Union was born after a long period of gestation. Originally conceived by the founders of the EEC, European Union was given impetus by the Single European Act of 1986, which set the aim of creating an 'area without internal frontiers'. The commitment to establish a European Union was finally made in the Maastricht Treaty which was signed on 7th February 1992. After a number of difficulties, the Treaty was eventually ratified by the end of October 1993.

The Treaty on European Union is in many respects a remarkable document and an impressive achievement. It sets out to build on the foundations of the European Community in order to promote economic and social progress and convergence. The Preamble to the Treaty reaffirms the importance of ending the division of the European continent and stresses the need to deepen the solidarity between the peoples of Europe, while respecting their history, culture and traditions. It confirms the 12 member states' attachment to the principles of liberty, democracy and respect for human rights and fundamental freedoms and the rule of law, and pledges them to enhance further the democratic and efficient functioning of European institutions.

The objectives of the European Union include economic, social and political progress and cohesion. An important aim is to strengthen the protection of the rights and interests of the people by introducing citizenship of the Union. Another important step is the commitment to implement a common foreign and security policy 'which might in time lead to a common defence'. This constitutes the second 'pillar' of the Union. The third pillar is concerned with close co-operation on justice and home affairs to meet the objective of facilitating the free movement of persons, while ensuring their safety and security.

The provisions under Title VI (Article K) of the Treaty on European Union deal with co-operation in the fields of justice and home affairs. Their implementation during the next few years is likely to have a significant impact on the broad area of law enforcement co-operation within Europe. The K4 Co-ordinating Committee, and its subsidiary structure, will bring together within one institutional framework the activities of various groups, such as the *Ad Hoc* Group on Immigration, the customs' group MAG 92, and the different working groups of Trevi. With the decision on 29th October 1993 to locate the EDU/Europol in The Hague, further progress may be anticipated with this initiative and with the proposed European Information System.

However, during the second half of 1993 the Schengen Group forged ahead with its own information system (SIS) and its own rapid communications infrastructure (SIReNE). Six of the Schengen countries confirmed that they would remove their remaining common internal border controls on 1st February 1994. In 1993, there was also evidence of increased activity amongst some of the many different specialist groups and networks which facilitate different types of cross-national police co-operation. Of course, the basic, proven mechanism for information exchange remains Interpol, which itself has undergone considerable changes and improvements during the recent past. It is clearly a period of considerable change and development in the policing arrangements for the European Union.

This Report is, thus, being published at a crucial time for European police co-operation. However, the structures in place today, and planned for tomorrow, cannot be understood without examining their context and historical development. The Report is intended as a broad introduction to the crime and policing issues facing the 'new Europe' and to the structures for law enforcement co-operation that have developed. It provides a snap-shot of the position as it exists in November 1993.

Whilst every effort has been made to ensure that the contents of the Report are accurate, with such an extensive research field and rapid changes it is inevitable that some material may be out-of-date or inaccurate and the authors invite readers to contact the research team with criticisms and comments.

The Report is based on work undertaken by the CSPO's *Police, Crime & Justice in Europe* Research Team between 1990 and 1993. A good deal of the original material was collected during interviews and visits to key respondents and much of the fieldwork, during the early phase of the research, was carried out by Pamela Davies, who is now a Lecturer in the Department of Economics and Government, University of Northumberland. The present researchers wish to acknowledge warmly the considerable contribution that Pamela Davies has made to the project.

It is not possible to name more than a few of the collaborators and respondents who have supported the project, although the research team would like to thank all those who have provided information and assistance. Particular thanks are due to the following: David Allan, Adrian Appleby, Peter Bal, Didier Bigo, Carl-Heinz Blessmann, Dick Bos, Mary Busbridge Wheeler, Heiner Busch, Nicholas Busch, Monica den Boer, Elisabeth Calatayd i Bassols and the library staff at the Catalonia Police School, Stuart Cameron-Waller, Della Cannings, Clare Checksfield, Neil Collins, Fernand Diederich, Tom Dorrant, Bryan Drew, Luise Drüke, Francisco Javier Elorza Cavengt, Charles Elsen, Thomas Feltes, Michael Fenton, Kevin Fitzpatrick, Val Flyn and Adrian Fortescue.

The research team also wishes to express particular appreciation to: Frank Gallagher, Mara Goldstein, Frank Gregory, Anne Harrison, Carlos Otero Hidalgo, Merle Hoefman, Herr von Hutte, Jorgen Jepsen, Herr Kayser, Raymond Kendall, Philippe Keraudren, Helmut Koetzsche, Professer Kühne, Steve Lister, Maurizio Marinelli, Tony Moore, Fans-Jan Mulschlegel, David O'Keefe, Tom O'Reilly, Jonathan Potts, Georges Rauchs, Piet van Reenen, Jean-Claude Salomon, Herr Scheefeld, Suzanne Scheller, Christina Soreiro, Tove Steen Sorensen, Paul Swallow, Jim Taylor, Maggie Thorne, M. Vanderijd, Jaap Verraes, Peter Vowé, Neil Walker, Denis Walton, Herr Welter, Georges Wohlfart and Herr Wolters.

The authors also wish to thank colleagues at the CSPO and elsewhere in the University of Leicester for their support, help and encouragement in the preparation of this Report. In particular, deep thanks are due to: Michael Chadwick, Peter Francis, Jon Garland, Sue Goodyear, Katherine Hackett, Bernadette Hayes, Mike King, Gonzalo Saenz de Miera, Sheridan Morris, Paul Newman and Peter Savigear.

Peter Savigear provided great encouragement to the project, undertook the fieldwork in Corsica which is reported in Chapter 5, and read through and commented on the first drafts of the Report. His death in 1992, at a tragically early age, robbed us of a valued friend and colleague and we dedicate this Report to the memory of a committed and enthusiastic European.

The ratification of the Treaty on European Union marks the beginning of a new stage in the process of European integration. One vital dimension is increased co-operation in the broad field of crime prevention and police co-operation. The commitments to the principles of liberty, democracy and respect for human rights in the Treaty are to be welcomed, but as yet there is much to be done to apply such principles to the decision-making structures established under the third pillar. There is, indeed, a worrying lack of accountability and scrutiny of many of the institutions and groups which currently exist to promote European police co-operation.

There is also much to be done to develop a more solid base of knowledge and understanding upon which to build effective and accountable procedures and institutions. There is an alarming lack of information about crime and its extent, the different police organisations, and the myriad of specialist networks and groups. Police co-operation between the countries of Europe is most likely to succeed if it develops by structured evolution, but such a process requires detailed knowledge and evaluation. This Report seeks to make a contribution to this task and to the vital challenge of developing appropriate policing structures in the new European Union.

John Benyon, Lynne Turnbull, Andrew Willis,
Rachel Woodward, Adrian Beck

Leicester, 1st November 1993

ABBREVIATIONS

AC	Assistant Commissioner
ACC	Assistant Chief Constable
ACIU	Analytical Criminal Intelligence Unit
ACPO	Association of Chief Police Officers
AFR	Automatic Fingerprint Recognition
AHWGE	*Ad Hoc* Working Group on Europol
AHGI	*Ad Hoc* Group on Immigration
AHWGIOC	*Ad Hoc* Working Group on International Organised Crime
AMSS	Automatic Message Switching System
ASF	Automated Search Facility
ASP	Anti-Smuggling Project 1993
BKA	*Bundeskriminalamt*
BVS	*Bundesverfassungsschutz*
CCBE	Council of the Bars & Law Societies of the EC
CCC	Customs Co-operation Council
CEDOCPOL	European Police Documentation Network
CELAD	*Comité Européen pour la Lutte Anti-Drogue*
CEPT	*Conférence Européene des Postes et Télécommunications*
CGI-SIT	*Comisaria General de Informacion Servicio de Informacion*
CID	Criminal Investigation Department
CIREA	Centre for Information, Discussion and Exchange on Asylum
CIREFI	Centre for Information, Reflection and Exchange on Frontiers and Immigration
CIS	Commonwealth of Independent States
CIS (Interpol)	Criminal Information System
CIS (Customs)	Customs Information System
CG	Central Group
CNP	*Cuerpo Nacional de Policia*
COLPOFER	European Railway Police Organisation
CPS	Crown Prosecution Service
CPSA	Civil & Public Servants Association
CRI	*Centrale Recherche Informatiedienst*
CRS	*Compagnie Républicaine de Sécurité*
CSIS	Central Schengen Information System
CSPO	Centre for the Study of Public Order
CVP	*Christelijke VolksPartiJ*
DAC	Deputy Assistant Commissioner
DB	*Deutsche Bundesbahn*
DCCB	*Direccao Central de Cambate Ao Banditismo*
DCPP	*Direzione Centrale Della Polizia Di Prevenzione*
DLO	Drugs Liaison Officer
DST	*Directorte de la Surveillance du Territoire*
EAS	Electronic Archive System
EC	European Community
ECCD	European Committee to Combat Drugs
ECJ	European Court of Justice

EDIU	European Drugs Intelligence Unit
EDU	European Drugs Unit
EFS	European Fraud Squad
EFTA	European Free Trade Area
EIS	European Information System
EKAM	Greek Anti-Terrorist Squad
ELS	European Liaison Section
ENP	European Network of Policewomen
ENS	European Nervous System
EOD	European Observatory on Drugs
EPU	European Police University
ETA	*Euzkadi Ta Askatasuna*
ETSI	European Telecommunications Standards Institute
EU	European Union
EUROSTAT	Statistical Office of the EC Commission
FASTs	Flexible Anti-Smuggling Teams
FBI	Federal Bureau of Investigation
GC	*Guarda Civil*
GIA	*Groupe Interforces Anti-terroriste*
GIP	*Group d'Intervention de la Police*
GN	*Gendarmerie Nationale*
GNR	*Guarda Nacional Republicana*
GSM	*Groupe Special Mobile*
HOLMES	Home Office Large Major Enquiry System
ibid.	'in the same place'
ICAO	International Civil Aviation Organisation
ICPC	International Criminal Police Commission
ICPO	International Criminal Police Organisation
ICPR	International Criminal Police Review
IHESI	*Institute des Hautes Études de la Sécurité Intérieure*
IRA	Irish Republican Army
JCWG	Judicial Co-operation Working Group on Criminal Matters
KGT	*Koordinierungsgruppe Terrorismusbekämpfung*
KLPD	*Korps Laudelijke Politie Diensten*
LKA	*Landeskriminalamt*
MAG 92	Mutual Assistance Group 1992
MEP	Member of the European Parliament
MPD	Metropolitan Police District
MPSB	Metropolitan Police Special Branch
MRRB	Message Research and Response Branch
NATO	North Atlantic Treaty Organisation
NCB	National Central Bureau(x)
NCIS	National Criminal Intelligence Service
NDIU	National Drugs Intelligence Unit
NFIU	National Football Intelligence Unit
NSIS	National Schengen Information System
NUCPS	National Union of Civil & Public Servants
ORSIS	Orientation Schengen Information System
PAF	*Police de l'Air et des Frontières*
pers. comm.	Personal communication
PET	*Politiets Efterentningstjeneste*
PGE	Project Group Europol
PIRA	Provisional Irish Republican Army

PJ	*Police Judiciare*
PN	*Police Nationale*
PNC	Police National Computer
POT	*Politiets Overrankingstjeneste*
PRL	*Parti Reformateur Liberal*
PS	*Parti Socialiste* (Belgium and France)
PS	*Polizia di Stato* (Italy)
PSC	*Parti Social Chretien*
PSP	*Polizia de Seguranca Publica*
PTA	Prevention of Terrorism (Temporary Provisions) Act 1989
PU	*Police Urbaine*
PWGOT	Police Working Group on Terrorism
RG	*Renseignements Généraux*
RPR	*Rassemblement pour la République*
RPS	*Rikspolisstyreisen*
RUC	Royal Ulster Constabulary
SCENT	System Customs Enforcement Network
SEA	Single European Act
SEF	Aliens Police (Portugal)
SEM	Single European Market
SIReNE	Supplementary Information Request at the National Entry
SIS	Schengen Information System
SP	*Socialistische Partij*
SRPS	*Service Regional de Police Secours*
St.Gb	*Strafgesetzbuch*
St.Po	*Strafprozessordnung*
SUPO	*Suojelpolisi*
TCCE	Technical Committee for Co-operation in Europe
TSG	Territorial Support Group
UCL AT	*Unité de Coodination pour la Lutte Anti-Terroriste*
UCLAF	*Unité de Coordination pour la Lutte Anti-Fraude*
UDF	*Union pour la Démocratie Française*
UFF	Ulster Freedom Fighters
UISP	*Union Internationale des Syndicats de Police*
UNESCO	United Nations Education, Scientific and Cultural Organisation
UK	United Kingdom
USSR	United States of Soviet Russia
VU	*Volksunie*

PART I

INVESTIGATING POLICE CO-OPERATION IN EUROPE

Gradually the vision of the founders of the European Communities has come nearer to reality. Progress has been slow, some would say painfully so, but this was always inevitable. As Robert Schuman said in 1950, 'Europe will not be made all at once or according to a single general plan. It will be built through concrete achievements, which first create a *de facto* solidarity' (Office for Official Publications of the European Community 1990).

It was almost a decade ago that the European Commission published the White Paper which pointed Europe along the road to '1992'. To the surprise of many, agreement on the list of measures was reached later in 1985 at the Luxembourg Heads of Government Conference. Some countries were rather quicker than others to embark on the journey, but it became clear that the idea of 'Europe without frontiers' captivated people throughout the twelve EC countries. As a result, the integration of Europe has taken a further step forward with the establishment of the European Union.

However, it is evident that many people and their political leaders are concerned about the effects that an open Europe will have on crime, illegal immigration and social stability, and doubts have been expressed about whether the law enforcement agencies are sufficiently prepared for the challenge.

This Report is one of the first results of a preliminary study into police co-operation in the European Union, taking particular account of the potential impact of open borders on policing functions. It should be stressed that it is a preparatory investigation and it is evident that a great deal more research is needed.

In Chapter 1 some of the thinking behind the research study is outlined and a number of the key issues are identified. In addition, the chapter suggests an approach which may help to focus attention on the different levels of policing and criminal justice questions which arise. Chapter 1 also outlines in brief the structure of the rest of the Report.

CHAPTER 1

EUROPE WITHOUT FRONTIERS:
THE POLICING ISSUES

Understanding police co-operation in Europe means understanding a number of complex realities, including European Union, crime, policing and immigration. These issues are introduced in this first chapter, with a brief discussion highlighting the major themes covered in the rest of the Report. An explanation of the background to this study and the methodology behind the research follows.

1.1   European Union

1.1.1   1993 – A Critical Time

This Report is being produced at a crucial stage in the process of European integration. Debates on the future form and functions of European institutions are taking place in response to the agreements constructing European Union which have been reached over the past few years. One important debate concerns the policing of the new Europe, and this subject forms the focus for this research.

1993 is a critical year for the policing of the new Europe. Many of the structures and agreements relating to police co-operation are being drafted, finalised and put into practice. In particular the implementation of the Treaty on European Union (the Maastricht Treaty) presents many new and challenging opportunities in this field. The co-operative procedures that will help in policing Europe in the coming years are being established, consolidated and finalised now. Others are on the horizon.

With this in mind, the Centre for the Study of Public Order has undertaken preliminary research into this area and this Report is the product of that investigation.

1.1.2   The Context: A Brief History of the European Union

The historical and political background to the establishment of the European Community is given in detail elsewhere (Owen and Dynes 1989; Pinder 1991) but a brief introduction is necessary here in order to clarify some of the legislative agreements that are important to the following examination of policing and associated issues.

The signing of the Treaty of Rome in 1957, by Belgium, France, Germany, Italy, Luxembourg and the Netherlands established the European Economic Community. The Treaty of Rome contains basic provisions for closer co-operation in economic matters for the member states of the Community. Ireland, Denmark and the UK subsequently joined the EEC in 1973, followed by Greece in 1981, and Spain and Portugal in 1986.

3

The Single European Act (SEA) of 1986 provided for the establishment of a European Community without internal frontiers by 1st January 1993. The SEA moved the EC's competence beyond economic issues and into the social realm. It was the Single European Act which established the four freedoms of movement – for people, services, goods and capital.

The Treaty on European Union (the Maastricht Treaty), signed on 7th February 1992, was finally ratified by all the states in October 1993 after Germany's Constitutional Court in Karlsruhe gave the go-ahead. The Treaty came into effect on 1st November 1993.

The Treaty consolidates and extends the provisions of the previous agreements. Debates over the Maastricht Treaty have illustrated the nature of the common ground but also the differences and tensions between the member states over the question of European Union. The terms of the Maastricht Treaty establish a framework for European police co-operation under the third pillar on justice and home affairs. Policing remains a sovereign issue but certain areas (for example, judicial co-operation in criminal matters) are now deemed to be matters of 'common interest'. The objectives of co-operation are set out in the Treaty, including the involvement of some Community institutions (with the exception of the Court of Justice at this stage).

1.1.3   Political Changes in Europe

Over the past three years, monumental changes have taken place in the former Soviet Bloc countries – the Soviet Union, Poland, Hungary, Czechoslovakia, Yugoslavia, Romania, Bulgaria – and also in Albania. The removal of communist regimes and the emergence of new political formations – and conflicts – has (again) brought changes to the social, economic and political geography of eastern and central Europe. New nation states have been born – Lithuania, Latvia, Estonia, the Czech Republic, Slovakia and Slovenia. At the time of writing the former Yugoslavia is in the midst of civil war as national identities are asserted and defended.

These major political changes to the east of the European Union are ongoing. Little can be said about their consequences beyond the certainty that the future of the EU is intimately related to the economic, social and political development of the rest of Europe. It is clear, for example, that the changes in central and eastern Europe have resulted in much more permeable borders. It is now considerably easier for people to cross the frontiers as immigrants and for stolen or prohibited items to pass in either direction across the European Union boundary. Since 1990 the proposed 'ring of steel' to the east has looked increasingly vulnerable. Simplistic as it may sound, recognition of these developments and of the increased interdependency between east and west is fundamental to any discussion of policing in the European Union.

1.1.4   The Future Expansion of the European Union

The European Union is surely set to grow further in the coming years. Eight countries have already formally applied for EC/EU membership, namely Turkey (1987), Austria (1989), Cyprus (1990), Malta (1990), Sweden (1991), Finland (1992), Switzerland (1992) and Norway (1992). The application by Switzerland was subsequently withdrawn following a referendum in December 1992 which reversed the decision to apply for membership of the European Economic Area. This had the

4

effect of suspending the application to join the EC/EU, although the long-term intention is still to seek membership. Other countries have announced that they either intend to apply for membership in the future, or that they are currently considering the possibility of application. These are Iceland, Liechtenstein, the Czech and Slovak Republics, Poland, Hungary, Estonia, Latvia, Lithuania, Bulgaria, Romania and Albania.

Whatever the current crime levels in the European Union, any enlargement of the Union will broaden the problem (by definition); and it may well deepen the problem, particularly as new criminal opportunities present themselves. For example, the proximity of new member states to international drugs trafficking routes, or the potential for abuse in international exchange-rate mechanisms, especially where EC grants, loans and subsidies are involved, will offer new opportunities for crime. In turn, policing the European Union becomes more complex and demanding – and crucial.

1.1.5   Frontiers, Boundaries and Borders

The establishment of the Single European Market (SEM) allowing for freedom of movement for people, goods, capital and services has required the removal of internal borders. The practical realisation of this is discussed throughout the Report.

One of the biggest changes has been with regard to what is commonly termed the 'external border' of the Union. This is as much a conceptual term as it is a geographical one, referring not only to obvious and visible land and sea borders, but also to borders placed at points of entry to the European Union, such as sea ports and airports.

There is currently much debate about the so-called external border or 'ring of steel'. Some see the establishment of tight controls as essential for internal public security. Others are highly critical of the establishment of an introspective, defensive EU or 'Fortress Europe' shutting out migrants, asylum seekers and refugees from other European states and elsewhere. Throughout 1992 and 1993 the debate over stricter controls on immigration intensified in the wake of growing political and social concern about racial attacks. France and Germany have both taken stringent action to limit the immigration of ethnic minorities and further Union-wide curbs are likely. How such a policy can effectively be enforced is a central question.

1.2   Crime in Europe

1.2.1   The European Position

According to national police figures, crime rates have increased in every major industrialised country except Japan in the past three decades. Criminal victimisation has become a feature of everyday life in urban settings, and anxieties are routinely reflected in public opinion polls (van Dijk and Mayhew 1993).

It is notoriously difficult to measure the real incidence of crime in any one country, let alone make valid international comparisons. Police statistics are an incomplete and imperfect measure. Crime 'rates' depend on the perceptions of the victims that an offence has occurred, their propensity to report the offence and the willingness of the police to record an offence. In addition, different legal definitions of crime make cross-national comparisons difficult. Finally, official crime figures disproportionately reflect crimes against property and crimes against the person – those where there is a readily identifiable victim who sees it as in his or her interest to claim victim status.

Many of the crimes of most interest in this study, especially those which have a pan-European character, are difficult if not impossible to identify from official figures. For example, high-value crimes such as the theft of machinery or plant, or of antiques, are routinely coded under a generic heading of 'theft' – with no specific information readily available about the nature or the value of the goods stolen. Drugs-related crime may well be recorded separately, but limited information is available on the 'street' value of seizures, or on those responsible (minor couriers or major trafficker-organisers). Finally, any one set of national figures will obliterate the 'international' character of some crime – a major focus of this Report. A single 'seizure' figure in Amsterdam or London gives little indication of drug routes which may traverse international boundaries, sometimes many times, both within and outside the European Union.

It is, however, possible to offer a broad-brush picture of crime in the European Union. If the UK figure of 5 million officially recorded crimes a year is taken as a benchmark, then the total within the EU can be estimated at approximately 30 million recorded offences a year, mostly offences against property (burglary or theft) and relatively minor offences against the person. This figure assumes a roughly even distribution of crime throughout the European Union.

This 'guesstimate' is a starting point only. It ignores the number of offences which are not reported. Estimates from the UK (Hough and Mayhew, 1983) based on a representative sample of the population, suggest that the real figure is some four times greater. To the extent this UK shortfall reflects the European picture, the EU crime total is approaching 120 million offences a year.

In addition, these figures do not include some of the most injurious criminal actions, including terrorist activities where the size of the problem is not viewed in the limited number of completed operations (explosions and shootings) but in the steady undercurrent of operations which pose a constant threat. Similarly, drugs trafficking is seldom reported and poorly detected, and 'seizures' offer only a hazy image of the real problem.

Official figures point to 35 million crimes a year in the European Union; estimates suggest that the 'real' figure is 150 million offences; and neither offers valid and reliable data on some of the most serious, life-threatening offences.

1.2.2   The Costs of Crime

Crime brings with it social, economic and political costs. Victimisation, and the perceived likelihood of victimisation, creates fear and uncertainty. This in turn impinges on individual freedoms of movement and social interaction. Experiences and fears of crime impoverish social and communal life.

It hardly needs pointing out that crime has enormous economic costs. Industrial and commercial enterprises can be the target of criminal activity such as theft, fraud, public disorder, vandalism and criminal damage. Public institutions suffer in the same way. The financial costs to households and individual citizens are cumulatively very high.

1.2.3   *Rising Levels of Crime in Europe*

In general terms, the rates for most types of crime appear to be rising in the EU member states. There are of course exceptions to this, but the general pattern implies increasing crime levels. Some caution is, however, necessary. Rising official figures only represent changes in recorded crime. These may reflect a genuine upturn in criminal activities, or an increased willingness on the part of victims to report crime, or more effective police methods leading to improved detection rates, or a combination of these factors.

1.3   Police Co-operation in Europe

1.3.1   *The Diversity of Police Arrangements Within the EU*

Law enforcement agencies play the key role in crime prevention and detection. They are publicly and judicially sanctioned to perform this task and are thus critical in controlling crime levels in Europe. It is for this reason that an understanding of their structures, operations and strategies is important.

The strategies for policing in the twelve EU member states are diverse in many fundamental ways. As the evidence in Chapter 3 indicates, some countries have single forces organised nationally. Others have two or more forces with separate roles and responsibilities.

The diversity of policing arrangements goes much further than merely the superficial differences implied by the different numbers of forces in each state. National policing is organised on a different basis across member states, with major differences in legal and judicial systems, operational structures and 'traditions' of policing. This diversity will not be removed in the foreseeable future. The research for this Report did, however, indicate that even basic knowledge about this differentiation was lacking, sometimes to an alarming degree.

There has to date been no comprehensive analysis of the police forces of the European Union, using a conceptually sound comparative framework. This Report offers a preliminary contribution through its brief assessment of the forces within the EU. Although the details in Chapter 3 are necessarily brief, they constitute a first step towards a larger research project which, in conjunction with colleagues throughout Europe, will map out the police forces of the European Union. There is much to be gained through an understanding of different policing strategies and organisations, and this Report is in part a response to demands for information from the police and other interested parties.

1.3.2   *Political Sovereignty: A Key Issue*

Law enforcement agencies are symbolic of a state's sovereignty. Such agencies operate in defined territories or spaces, which either singly or in combination constitute the nation state.

Neither the Single European Act nor the Treaty on European Union grants the Commission powers of control over the police forces and law enforcement agencies of the member states. This power remains exclusive to each national government. Although, in practice, as this Report concludes, police co-operation has a long history in Europe, in principle questions of police co-operation are often politically contentious because they touch on issues of political sovereignty.

A key argument may be that whatever impetus there is for improved police co-operation across borders any state will prove to be reluctant to cede operational autonomy in police matters to a neighbouring state. This is because within each nation state the police have a near monopoly on the use of legitimate force in order to protect both public tranquillity and, more specifically, the interests of the state itself (Marenin 1982). The irony (or even paradox) is that where demands for co-operation are at their greatest, for example, with respect to terrorism, these are precisely the spheres which are so intimately bound to the sovereignty of any individual nation that there may be the greatest disincentive to trans-national policing (Den Boer and Walker 1993).

This may help to explain why progress has been so slow towards a federal European police force, and even on slightly less contentious issues, for example the problem of 'hot pursuit' across national borders.

1.4 Undertaking the Investigation

1.4.1 A Preliminary Investigation of the Issues

The issues outlined above are complex. In combination they raise a host of further questions for research. These issues include: debate on the effects of borders in controlling crime, and the consequences of their removal; debates over levels of crime in Europe; confusion over the organisation of police forces in the member states; concern about the efficacy of various formal structures for police co-operation; questions about the precise role of informal agreements and networks; uncertainties over the use of communications and information technology; and major questions of political accountability and legitimacy.

These matters are of interest and concern to many people, including law enforcement officers, legislators, lawyers, civil servants, journalists, academics and 'ordinary people'. An encouraging feature of this research has been the interest and enthusiasm expressed by a variety of people in the work being undertaken.

This Report has no specific target readership. It has been written and structured to be accessible to a broad readership, and for this reason ignores some academic conventions which might make it less readable. The Report is intended to provide an overview of the most important issues relating to police co-operation in Europe. Some points may seem obvious to the *cognoscenti* but require restating for the wider audience. Obviously, there is a limit to the number of topics that can be covered in one publication, and to the amount of detail that can be provided on each topic. This is a preliminary Report and seeks to provide a comprehensive overview of the issues.

1.4.2 The Centre for the Study of Public Order

The Centre for the Study of Public Order (CSPO) is well placed to undertake this research. Established at the University of Leicester, England, in 1987, the CSPO has built its research reputation around studies of policing, crime and justice issues.

The Centre has close collaborative links with research institutes world-wide, and has been fortunate in being able to consult a number of European-based colleagues about this research. It has been able to develop good working relationships with many different organisations, and is in a position to open dialogue between groups whose interests have often been opposed. A conference programme has been particularly important in bringing together academics and police officers in order to discuss issues arising out of the research.

The CSPO was able to initiate research into European policing issues because of its areas of research expertise and its network of contacts. Funding for the first stage of this research was received from a number of sources, including the European Commission and various other sources including private companies.

The CSPO has made a long-term commitment to the study of policing, crime and justice issues in Europe. The publication of this Report marks the end of the first phase of the research. Further publications on particular aspects of the subject are planned.

1.5   Research Methodology

1.5.1   The Research Team

Initial planning for this research started in 1989. Phase I of the project commenced in May 1990 with the establishment of the research team, comprising Professor John Benyon (Director of the CSPO), Mike King (Lecturer in Comparative Policing at the CSPO), Andrew Willis (Senior Lecturer in Criminology, University of Leicester), and Pamela Davies (full-time research officer at the CSPO). Following the departure of Pamela Davies, in September 1992 Lynne Turnbull and Rachel Woodward joined the team as full-time researchers for Phase II of the project. The research team has been assisted by other colleagues, whose contributions are acknowledged in the Preface.

The members of the project team all have backgrounds in social science research, and the diversity of these backgrounds has been a major asset to the study. The disciplines of politics, criminology, sociology, penology, law, and geography all inform the investigation. The interests of the staff include human rights issues, European policing, crime prevention, race and ethnic relations, geographies of crime, police–public relations, public disorder and political and social change.

The researchers work in a Centre renowned for its research into policing issues. In addition, members of the team have regular contact with police officers who study for postgraduate degrees at the CSPO or are involved in in-service police training. This allows the team to combine familiarity with policing (research and training) with academic objectivity. Indeed, the research team welcomes further contact with police officers wishing to contribute to the research and the continuing debate on policing in the European Union.

1.5.2   Documentary Sources

One of the two principal sources for this research has been written material. A large amount of the team's documentation was collected during Phase I of the research, much of this in the course of study visits discussed below. In addition, an invitation for documentation made in December 1992 to contacts throughout Europe produced further written material and reports. This provided the team with additional information updating the initial collection. The collection and collation of documentary sources is an on-going research objective. The CSPO is currently one of the primary UK repositories of documentary material on pan-European policing.

Documentation on policing organisation and activities was collected from all twelve EU member states. Research papers and academic journal articles were received or obtained. Magazines proved a particularly fruitful source of information, and conference papers provided much in the way of critical comment. The research team is extremely grateful for the efforts of our collaborators in providing us with such an array of valuable written materials.

In addition, an archive of press cuttings has been established at the Centre. Cuttings from national and European newspapers have been obtained and filed. An exhaustive search was made through back-copies of the British newspaper *The Guardian* between 1990 and the present, and this has allowed the project team to build up a comprehensive picture of the political and social events over this period which have affected the overall context of crime and policing in Europe.

It must be noted that some reports and documents have not been made available to the research team. Access to confidential or classified material not in the public domain has been refused on a number of occasions when requested. This was unfortunate. The research team has accepted this as an inevitable part of the research process, but in some cases the refusal to supply documentation has appeared to be the result of excessive secrecy.

The organisation, structures and context of police co-operation in Europe are changing rapidly which means that much of the documentation collected by the research team quickly becomes out of date. Obtaining up-to-date information has been a primary objective in compiling this Report. The research team has made every effort to ensure the accuracy of the information, but inevitably with such a complex and fast-changing field there may be some errors or misunderstandings. We would be delighted to receive comments, criticisms and corrections from readers throughout Europe.

1.5.3   A European Network of Respondents and Collaborators

People have been the other main resource for this research. Over a number of years the research team has established contact, throughout Europe and further afield, with a very wide range of people with expertise and an interest in police co-operation. These include police and law enforcement officers of different ranks and backgrounds, academics, lawyers, human and civil rights workers, and journalists.

A number of respondents from each of the twelve EU countries was interviewed during Phase I of this research and these interviews have been a crucial source of information. This research could not have proceeded successfully without their co-operation. The research team would like to record their deep appreciation of the efforts of those who have given freely of their time and knowledge. All interviews were structured around a schedule focused on an individual respondent's particular expertise and experience. Full notes or recordings were taken.

Less formally, the team has benefited through discussion of many of the issues with contacts and colleagues at informal meetings, conferences and seminars. Although comments have not been attributed to individuals in such cases, the research team should emphasise how useful these discussions have been in informing its thinking and analysis.

The development of a network of researchers and practitioners in this field is a continuing priority for the research project. This network has been extremely useful for the research, and has also been used to establish contact between third parties. It is proving invaluable. Many contacts have been provided by other researchers, and the research team wishes to stress the importance it attaches to these links. The Centre has welcomed a large number of visitors with an interest in European policing and hopes to continue this practice as the research develops. The research team is part of the European Police Documentation Network for European police research institutions (CEDOCPOL), and is intending to consolidate such links.

1.5.4   *The Bibliography*

A select bibliography containing the references to all the books and papers cited or used in the study is presented in Appendix III. The research team has a wider collection of sources, including material from most of the European Union countries, much of which is in the original language. This has been catalogued in an extensive bibliography which is available for consultation at the Centre for the Study of Public Order by other interested researchers. The research team welcomes further written material for inclusion in this collection.

1.6   A Framework for the Study of Police Co-operation

1.6.1   *Three Levels of Police Co-operation*

In order to examine and understand structures for police co-operation in Europe, frameworks for analysis are required. A series of unconnected items of raw data would not in themselves have intellectual coherence. They would be a catalogue of unrelated facts. It has been found to be helpful to look at three inter-related levels of police co-operation in Europe. Each level generates different questions and raises different responses, but each of the levels is important if effective co-operation is to be fostered. The three levels should not be seen as indicating priorities. Rather, they should be viewed as a heuristic device for understanding the complexities of police co-operation. They are set out in Figure 1.1:

Figure 1.1 Three Levels of Police Co-operation

	Level:	Concerned with:
1.	**Macro**	Constitutional and international legal agreements; harmonisation of national laws and regulations.
2.	**Meso**	Police (and other law enforcement) operational structures, practices, procedures and technology.
3.	**Micro**	The prevention and detection of particular offences and crime problems.

1.6.2   The Macro Level

The macro level is concerned primarily with constitutional questions and international legal agreements and the harmonisation of national legislation and regulations. It is the level at which governments and senior officials debate and resolve fundamental issues, and where major, far-reaching decisions are taken.

Some of the issues at this level would include visa agreements, asylum policy and extradition procedures. These are fundamental questions of rights of entry and rules of exit. Also at the macro level there are legal questions concerning police powers, especially relating to arrest, detention and interrogation. Any progress towards harmonisation in these areas can only take place at the highest level.

Another example would be firearms control. Member states have different policies, procedures and traditions concerning the carrying, handling and use of weapons. Harmonisation is simply not possible without high-level agreements, which may be painfully slow in appearing. A further issue at this level is identity cards, which may well facilitate day-to-day policing in an open Europe, but to which there is considerable opposition to what is seen as a civil liberties issue in the Netherlands and Britain.

Whatever the spirit of goodwill and co-operation, these sorts of issues are not settled on an inter-personal basis. They require a constitutional and legislative framework.

1.6.3   The Meso Level

The meso level is primarily concerned with operational police structures, practices and procedures – and those of other law enforcement agencies. This is the formal framework within which day-to-day operational policing occurs.

One important area is that of communication between police forces. A number of issues arise under this heading, including police information systems, common databases, co-ordination and access to information such as criminal intelligence. The rapid growth in advanced information technology and the police use of computers make this area all the more important.

A central feature in enhanced European police communication is language. Besides the obvious need to speak a common language, when necessary, there are also problems of technical language and terminologies which vary between countries. Both direct attention to language training for police officers and others, such as customs officials. The latter also directs attention to compatibility between computer systems and software.

An important feature of meso-level co-operation is face-to-face contact between middle-ranking officers from different countries. Findings from this study show that police officers themselves see these contacts as very valuable – perhaps because they share a common, professional culture with a mutual interest in criminal investigations.

There are considerable opportunities for meso-level initiatives, including the establishment of a European Drugs Unit (the first stage of Europol) to formalise and expand the contribution already made by liaison officers and national units. The trans-national nature of fraud and business-related crime could be seen as an ideal 'target' for a meso-level European-wide fraud squad.

1.6.4   The Micro Level

The micro level is concerned with the investigation of specific offences and the prevention and control of particular forms of crime.

To take one example, problems of public disorder tend to vary between different countries and regions. Distinctive cultures and traditions may give rise to different forms of behaviour which need different forms of policing. Micro-level co-operation can be effective in certain circumstances as was seen, for example, during the World Cup in Italy in 1990 when police from different countries offered information and assistance to their Italian counterparts.

Liaison officers who are seconded from one country to work with their counterparts in another country, especially in the fields of terrorism, drugs and football hooliganism, are good examples of micro-level co-operation.

There are considerable opportunities for micro-level initiatives, and some examples of these networks are described in Chapter 5. But successful networks themselves tend to be established at the meso level, and indeed many micro-level instances of co-operation do depend on effective meso-level arrangements. Equally, meso-level arrangements may evolve from micro-level initiatives. Both may depend, in the first instance, on macro-level agreements.

1.6.5   A Typology for Understanding Police Co-operation

The three levels outlined above are intended to assist understanding of police co-operation. They are not offered as a blueprint, but rather as a guide or an aid to clearer thinking. Police activities will not necessarily fit perfectly within any one level. There will be overlap and sometimes the boundaries will be blurred. The categories are not mutually exclusive.

The typology was presented in evidence to the UK House of Commons Select Committee on Home Affairs investigation into *Practical Police Co-operation in the European Community.* The Committee found the model 'very useful' (House of Commons 1990a, p. xvi). Police officers have also commented on its utility. With this reassurance, the three levels of possible police co-operation are referred to on occasions throughout this Report, as appropriate (see Benyon 1992).

1.7   Police Co-operation in Europe: An Investigation

There are two main parts in this Report – Part II on crime and policing and Part III on the major structures for promoting police co-operation.

Part II examines the context for police co-operation in Europe. In Chapter 2, perceptions of crime and fears of crime are examined with a particular emphasis on the likely effects of Europe 'without frontiers' on EU crime levels. An introductory account of the structure and organisation of police forces of the countries in the European Union is given in Chapter 3.

In Part III, the Report examines the structures and arrangements which exist for promoting police co-operation in Europe. Chapter 4 discusses the major structures for police co-operation. Chapter 5 looks at the informal networks and associations which allow co-operation to occur at a meso and micro level. Chapter 6 then examines communications and information exchange procedures which assist the police in the EU and in the wider European region.

Part IV then summarises the major findings of the Report, drawing together the major themes and presenting the overall conclusions. In addition, specific proposals are made to promote the development of police co-operation in Europe, including areas which require new or additional research.

As previously indicated, change in the field of European policing is occurring rapidly. It is difficult for any one group to keep abreast of all the developments. The worrying possibility is of *ad hoc*, ill-considered incremental change which fails to address the real needs, but proceeds in an arcane fashion, alienating key opinion leaders and thereby losing public confidence and consent.

What is required, as a first step, is a clearer understanding of the need for improved police co-operation in Europe. This will include an appreciation of the real threats posed by cross-border crime, together with comprehensive information about current policing arrangements in each member state. The Report turns to these issues in Part II.

PART II

POLICE CO-OPERATION IN EUROPE: THE CONTEXT

The results of a Gallup poll, announced in July 1990, revealed that public opinion in the UK was more positive about the European Community than ever before. However, the same poll showed that there was concern about crime and the removal of the border controls. Asked about drawbacks of the '1992' developments, the largest proportion of respondents pointed to 'drugs, terrorism and disease as a result of less border controls'.

This part of the Report examines the extent to which such fears are justified, or indeed whether there is evidence upon which to form a sound view. It explores the context in which police co-operation in Europe in the coming years will take place, and includes an outline of the police forces and law enforcement agencies which currently exist in each country in the European Union.

Chapter 2 looks at the ways in which the problems of crime in Europe after 1992 are being viewed and presented, considers the impact of open borders on European crime, and on other areas of law enforcement co-operation, and concludes that many of the more alarmist views are without foundation. However, crimes such as fraud are already serious in Europe and the position may deteriorate further in the future.

During the last few years, the political leaders of Europe have increasingly stressed the need to limit immigration into the member states. As a result, there has been growing emphasis on strengthening the external borders, and this has led to the perception of 'fortress Europe' surrounded by a 'ring of steel'. Chapter 2 examines these issues and associated policies on visas, asylum and clandestine immigration.

At the forefront of the EU Ministers' declared intention to combat international crime are the police forces of the individual nations in Europe. Chapter 3 outlines the law enforcement agencies in each of the 12 European Union countries and also briefly summarises their judicial systems.

It is clearly of considerable importance to understand the differences between the police forces of Europe, as well as the changing context within which they operate, if effective and appropriate co-operative arrangements are to be established.

CHAPTER 2

CRIME, BORDER CONTROLS AND IMMIGRATION

This chapter explores the range of issues surrounding crime and its relationship to border controls in the European Union. It also examines the growing significance of questions surrounding immigration to the European Union. The chapter first introduces some international research on criminal victimisation rates in Europe. It then examines the consequences for crime of the freedom of movement of goods, people, services and capital. Terrorism, drugs, mobile offending, the movement of stolen goods, movements of capital, international fraud and environmental crime are all discussed, as well as non-criminal victimisation such as rabies and motor vehicle safety.

The strengthening of external borders is then considered with respect to the movement of people. These changes have far-reaching implications for migrants, asylum seekers and those involved in extradition cases. It is clear that immigration, and particularly clandestine immigration, is of growing importance in persuading EU countries of the need to strengthen borders, often referred to as the 'hard outer shell'.

The chapter concludes by arguing that fears of increased crime rates as a result of removing internal border controls in the European Union have generated something of a 'moral panic' for which there is little evidence. There is, however, a major problem of crime in European countries and there is evidence of increasing levels of crime across the borders with the former communist states of eastern Europe. The removal of *internal* frontier checks seems unlikely to effect levels of crime markedly, but the continuing rise in crime in EU states itself merits greater co-operation between different police forces.

2.1　　　Crime in the European Union

2.1.1　　　*The Establishment of the European Union*

The Single European Act (SEA) of 1986 began the process of creating an economic area with no internal barriers to freedom of movement. Article 8A of the Treaty of Rome states that:

> The internal market shall comprise an area without internal frontiers in which the free movement of goods, persons, services and capital is ensured in accordance with the provision of this Treaty.

As a result of this agreement, consolidated by the Treaty on European Union of 1992, one of the largest markets without internal frontiers in the world is being created – serving a population in excess of 344 million people. With respect to goods, services, capital and people there is a developing integrated market.

a)   The Appeal of Europe Without Frontiers

One objective of the Single Market was to develop the European Community's economic strength within a common framework, including competitive industry, high productivity and significant innovation. This has led to the European Union.

There is a strong economic and psychological rationale for the removal of physical barriers between member states. Without border formalities industry will reduce its costs and increase its international competitiveness, particularly with respect to transport and handling charges (Commission of the European Communities 1989, Ch.1).

There is also a political justification for removing border controls. The continued existence of internal frontiers, with immigration controls and customs checks, would be a constant reminder of the way the European Union remained divided. The removal of these barriers constitutes one of the most direct and visible signs of a 'Union of the European people'.

The abolition of frontier controls is as rich in symbolic power as it is an economic necessity. This has probably been one of the principal appeals of '1992' to ordinary citizens. It implies genuine freedom of movement (Crossick 1988). In a survey published in June 1992 by *Eurobarometer*, 76 per cent of Europeans were in favour of efforts to unify western Europe and 65 per cent thought that EC membership was 'a good thing' (Commission of the European Communities 1992).

b)   Lingering Doubts

In contrast, the dismantling of internal border controls can generate negative reactions. As Alan Butt Philip noted:

> [...] symbols of national identity are in question, challenges to the authority
> of the Community in this sphere are made, and concerns about the possible
> abuses of the new freedom to move around Europe are raised. (Butt Philip
> 1989, p.1).

The removal of internal border controls is a politically contentious issue because it raises questions of sovereignty and also leads to speculation about the impact of new freedoms of movement on crime levels within the European Union. The member states of the EC in fact included in the General Declaration on Articles 13–19 of the Single European Act the statement that:

> Nothing in these provisions shall affect the right of member states to take
> such measures as they consider necessary for the purpose of controlling
> immigration from third countries, and to combat terrorism, crime, the traffic
> in drugs and illicit trading in works of art and antiques.

The statement indicated the perception held by governments that the removal of border controls would lead to an increase in crime. Whether this will in fact be the case has been the subject of considerable debate and speculation.

c)   Towards the Future

One of the responses to this perception may be found in the Treaty on European Union (the Maastricht Treaty) at Title VI *Provisions on Co-operation in the Fields of*

Justice and Home Affairs. Article K sets out provisions for achieving the objectives of European Union, especially those relating to the free movement of persons. A number of areas are designated as matters of 'common interest', perhaps the most important of which is police co-operation, although all might be described as relating to crime prevention and crime detection in some way or another. The succeeding sections of Article K provide further ways in which co-operation is to be effected. Title VI and the Maastricht Treaty are discussed in more detail in Chapter 4.

2.1.2   Indications of European Crime Levels

a)   Paucity of Data

Very little data are available about the extent of cross-border crime in Europe. There is a clear 'information deficit'. The clearest statement is:

> There is very little hard information available about the numbers of cross-border crimes for gain in Europe, nor about their economic costs to individual nations or to the EC as a whole. Because police forces and national governments define their responsibilities in terms of recording crimes occurring within their own jurisdictions, and because most existing European victimization surveys exclude crimes against organizations and do not specify the social or geographical origins of offenders, no data are collated routinely. Nor are there any specific research studies which demonstrate (accurately) the proportion of crimes across the board which posses a cross-border dimension, even as regards *recorded*, still less unrecorded, crime. (Levi 1993, p.60).

This is a fierce indictment. The concern about crime is real enough as is the fear of crime but these appear to be inversely related to the knowledge of the scale of the problem. Almost any data which purport to be 'authoritative' tend to be seized on by the media and politicians alike and there is seldom any serious attempt to deconstruct the method by which the statistics were compiled. This counsels caution in interpreting any available data but it also makes the search for valid and reliable crime information all the more important.

b)   Trends in Crime

Police figures of registered crimes cannot be used for comparative purposes because of well known difficulties in legal definitions of crime, reporting rates and recording rates, but official statistics offer some information about general trends over time. Most European countries have experienced a sharp rise in recorded crime since the second World War.

During the 1950s the officially recorded crime rate (all offences) for five European countries (England and Wales, France, Germany, the Netherlands and Sweden) was approximately 2,000 registered crimes per 100,000 inhabitants. The crime rate for all countries rose substantially from the early 1960s and by the early 1980s had risen to some 7,000 registered crimes per 100,000 population – an increase of some 250 per cent. There was some indication of stable or falling crime rates during the 1980s, but by the beginning of the 1990s the overall crime rates were showing a new upward trend (van Dijk 1993). The rate of recorded crime was particularly high in England and Wales and Sweden relative to the other three countries.

c)   The 1989 International Crime Survey

There have to date been few serious attempts to conduct European-wide surveys of crime levels (Heidensohn and Farrell 1991). However, some research data are available which start to indicate crime levels in Europe. Early in 1989, fourteen European and non-European countries joined together to conduct a unique victimisation survey, using tightly standardised methods to ensure comparable results. The survey involved interviewing one person aged 16 years or more in 2,000 households about their experience of eleven forms of victimisation (Mayhew 1990; van Dijk, Mayhew and Killias 1990).

The participating countries were Australia, Belgium, Canada, Finland, France, West Germany (that is, the Federal Republic, pre-unification), the Netherlands, Norway, Spain, Switzerland, England and Wales (statistics for which were counted together), Northern Ireland, Scotland and the United States of America. In total, six separate EU member states participated in the study.

The survey data, which avoided the difficulties of comparing police statistics on crime (because of definitional and recording differences, and potential differences in reporting rates), enable countries to see how they are faring in comparison with other countries in rates of criminal victimisation. The survey was confined to counting crime, primarily household property crime and crimes against the person, against clearly identifiable individuals, excluding children. It could not address organisational victims, victimless crimes such as drug abuse, or very infrequent serious offences such as terrorist attacks.

The rates of victimisation were calculated as personal prevalence rates for 1988 – the percentage of those interviewed who experienced a specific form of crime once or more in the year. Some interesting differences emerged (Mayhew 1990; van Dijk, Mayhew and Killias 1990).

i)   Burglary

There were few differences between the European countries in the survey, with a prevalence rate of 2.0 to 2.4 per cent for Scotland, England and Wales, Belgium, the Netherlands and France. These rates were well below those for Australia (4.4 per cent), USA (3.8 per cent) and Canada (3.0 per cent), but well above those for Spain (1.7 per cent) and Germany (1.3 per cent). The European Union Nordic neighbours of Norway (0.8 per cent) and Finland (0.6 per cent) were the least subject to burglary.

ii)   Robbery

Spain topped the league table for the prevalence of robbery (2.8 per cent) ahead of the USA (1.9 per cent) with an average of 1.0 per cent for western Europe as a whole. France had the lowest rate of all countries (0.4 per cent).

iii)   Sexual Incidents

The 1988 prevalence victimisation rate for sexual offences against women was highest in Australia (7.3 per cent), USA (4.5 per cent) and Canada (4.0 per cent) with West Germany next (2.8 per cent), closely followed by the Netherlands (2.6 per cent). England and Wales had a low rate (1.2 per cent) as did Finland (0.6 per cent). The western European average was 1.9 per cent.

20

iv)   *Motor Vehicle Crime*

France headed the league for car theft (2.8 per cent), a rate six times as great as that in the Netherlands or West Germany and three times the rate of car theft in Belgium. With respect to thefts from motor vehicles, Spain had by far the highest rate (14.6 per cent), with twice the rate of western Europe as a whole. Finally, for criminal damage or vandalism to cars, West Germany and the Netherlands experienced the greatest victimisation.

d)   The 1992 International Crime Survey

A repeat survey in 1992 (van Dijk and Mayhew 1993) generated broadly similar results in some 20 countries, offering the potential for comparisons over time as well as comparisons between countries. The most recent survey offers two important findings which relate to pan-European police co-operation.

First, the two ex-communist countries in the survey (Poland and the former Czechoslovakia) had much higher levels of crime than indicated by police-recorded crime figures. This may be a function of victims' unwillingness to report offences to the police, or to a general rise in crime in east European countries (Kury 1992; Dashko 1992).

Secondly, a tentative interpretation was offered that property crime rates were partly determined by crime-specific opportunity structures, so that vehicle crime related to the supply of available targets and burglary rates reflected the number of semi-detached and detached houses.

When these points are taken together, there are grounds to suppose that if the European Union expands to take in former communist countries, and as affluence increases, the downside of economic prosperity may well be increased crime in these states. This real increase will be all the greater if reporting rates also rise.

e)   Criminal Victimisation in Europe

The data from the two surveys were combined to offer a prevalence rate expressed as a percentage of persons aged 16 years and over who had been victimised in 1988 or 1991 at least once by one or more of the eleven types of crime covered in the surveys (van Dijk 1993).

For the 20 different countries the overall victimisation rate was about 20 per cent, as was the average victimisation rate for all European countries. Germany and Sweden had an average rate.

Many of the European countries in the surveys had a higher than average victimisation rate: England and Wales, Czechoslovakia, Italy and Spain (22 – 25 per cent); Poland and Estonia (25 – 27 per cent); and the Netherlands (28 per cent).

In contrast, some European countries had a lower than average victimisation rate: Belgium, Finland, France and Scotland (18 – 20 per cent); and Northern Ireland, Norway and Switzerland (18 per cent or lower).

For non-European countries, Australia, Canada, New Zealand and the USA had very high victimisation rates (28 per cent or more), whilst Japan had the lowest rate of criminal victimisation (under 12 per cent).

21

These figures offer a crude indicator of the crime problem in different European countries, but they do not reflect the average seriousness of crimes committed against property and the person.

2.1.3   *Criminal Statistics and Policing*

It would be imprudent to infer too much from a brief summary of the principal findings of international surveys, but two preliminary observations can be made.

First, although the methodology used in the victimisation surveys was probably that most suited to a cross-national comparison of crime, no method is ideal. In addition to the general lack of research and data on crime levels in Europe, one should also note the difficulties associated with data collection on crime and comparative research (see Hantrais, Mangen and O'Brien 1992).

Secondly, and more importantly, there are significant differences in crime levels between the European Union member states. On the one hand, there are marked differences by type of crime: Spain has the highest rate for robbery and thefts from motor vehicles; France, the Netherlands and Belgium seem burglary prone; and Germany has the highest rate of sexual victimisation. On the other hand, there are marked differences by country (for all crimes combined): England and Wales, Italy, the Netherlands and Spain have above average victimisation rates; Germany has average victimisation rates; and Belgium, France, Northern Ireland and Scotland have below average victimisation rates.

The point to note here is that the geographical variations in rates of crime between EU member states need to be studied. More detailed information would allow the full implications for practical police co-operation to emerge. It would also allow resources to be targeted where required and allow for the development of appropriate policing practices and procedures.

Both official criminal statistics and data derived from victimisation surveys are imperfect and incomplete measures of crime, although they both offer some indication of the level and extent of criminal activity. Developments in European-wide policing policy and co-ordinated cross-frontier police action will need to be predicated on solid empirical research on crime levels in Europe. More research on the extent and seriousness of crime in Europe, as well as trends over time, can be seen as a necessary condition for police co-operation.

2.2   International Terrorism

2.2.1   *The Nature of the Terrorist Threat in Europe*

Whether border controls have a role in deterring terrorist activity is hotly debated. The international nature of much terrorist activity must be emphasised at the outset. For example, in the case of the murder of two Australian tourists in the Dutch town of Roermond in May 1990, the killing took place in the Netherlands, the get-away car was found in Belgium, the assailants were Irish, and their intended targets were British soldiers based in Germany. Of the four persons charged in connection with this incident only one was convicted. He was released on appeal but on return to Ireland he was arrested and charged with firearms offences. Germany requested the extradition of the other three persons whom the police wished to question in connection with assorted terrorist offences.

The nature of the terrorist threat in Europe should not be underestimated. Recent sources of terrorism in the European Union have included threats from internal nationalist movements, such as the Provisional Irish Republican Army (PIRA) and the Basque separatist movement *Euzkadi Ta Askatasuna* (ETA), ideologically-based groups such as the Italian Red Brigades, the German Baader-Meinhof Group and Red Army Faction, and the French *Action Directe*, and externally-based groups based mainly in the Middle East (Latter 1990, p.12; Alexander and Myers 1982).

Terrorism is an emotive subject. An examination of the language and vocabularies used when discussing the presumed threat of increased terrorist activity indicates this. One commentator, for example, warned that any 'slackening off' in police efforts and controls would lead to Basque or *Action Directe* terrorists operating in Britain with impunity (Robertson 1992). However, he was unable to offer any evidence to substantiate this claim.

Another was typically forthright in his view that with the introduction of the Single European Market 'the speed and irreversibility of the changes create a nightmare of additional security problems' making it 'an obvious necessity for us to ensure that national security against the growing international scourge of terrorism is in no way weakened' (Wilkinson 1990, p.12).

2.2.2 Border Controls and Terrorists

There is some evidence that border controls can stop terrorists. For example, two PIRA terrorists were apprehended by a German customs official on the frontier with the Netherlands in September 1988 (Crossick 1988). German authorities were however reported as saying that this was entirely fortuitous.

The Police Federation of England and Wales, Superintendents Association and ACPO, in a memorandum to the House of Commons Home Affairs Committee, were adamant that on the basis of their experience border controls were essential:

> The prospect of terrorists being detected after an attack would be severely hampered by reducing the police capacity to effect deterrents at the ports. The 'All Ports Warning System' has proved invaluable over many years in the apprehension of wanted persons seeking to leave the UK. [...] the first opportunity for prevention and the last chance of detection remains at our ports. (*Police* 1992b, p.28).

Similar remarks have been made by Denmark's National Commissioner of Police, Ivan Boye:

> Although it may be argued that the checks present no real hindrance, they do provide the facility for surveillance of known or suspected terrorists crossing borders and the collation of that intelligence. The terrorist perception of the risk of his interception at the borders cannot be ignored and the absence of systematic checks can only increase his confidence and undoubtedly increase his cross-frontier activity. (Boye 1990, p.16).

2.2.3 Terrorists' Ability to Circumvent Border Controls

As with so many issues relating to the future for policing and crime in a Europe without borders, the role of frontier controls is hotly debated. There are groups and individuals who argue that border controls constitute little or no deterrent to terrorists. The House of Commons Home Affairs Committee took the view that terrorists are clearly not going to be deterred by land borders (House of Commons 1990a, p. xii). They cited evidence that border checks in Spain had done little to deter or apprehend terrorists.

They also quoted evidence from the Northern Ireland Office that the land border between Northern Ireland and the Republic of Ireland was actually 'a strategic resource to terrorists'. Moreover, even when large numbers of persons were stopped by the German Border Police *(Bundesgrenzschutz)*, the largest number of incidents related to passport irregularities and offences against the Aliens Act.

As Alan Butt Philip pointed out, some of the most audacious feats by terrorist groups have occurred in the midst of heavy security provision, for example, the shipping by the IRA of arms from Libya to Ireland (Butt Philip 1989, p.21).

2.2.4 An Increased Role for Police Intelligence

The major implication of the removal of internal border controls within the European Union for controlling terrorism appears to be an increased role for police intelligence. Many would argue that the apprehension of terrorists at borders is incidental, and that police intelligence has a far greater role to play in anti-terrorist activities:

> Under the 1992 process [...] the apprehension of criminals and terrorists is provided for through the strengthening of external frontiers, European-wide police intelligence co-operation, and common visa and immigration policies on the grounds that most arrests do not, in any case, take place at air or seaports or border crossings. Where they do, the criminals have often in reality been tracked for miles through police co-operation (for example, from Spain or Italy to a Channel port) and the frontier is simply a convenient location for a police or customs operation. (Owen and Dynes 1989, p.63).

Committed international criminals are not noted for their respect of borders. They are as enterprising as they are determined, and their containment is arguably more likely from international police intelligence and associated activities than by isolated measures at borders (Alderson 1989; Latter 1991, p.5). Most successes against terrorists derive from effective intelligence and targeted counter-intelligence operations, rather than as a result of checks at borders (Latter 1990, pp.11-12), although border controls constitute a convenient location for the apprehension of suspects.

Of course, this increased reliance on police intelligence in tracking and intercepting terrorists depends in turn on adequate mechanisms for co-operation of activities and suitable communications networks. Tom King MP, whilst he was British Defence Secretary, welcomed the capture of suspected PIRA terrorists by the Dutch police following active co-operation between Belgian and Dutch authorities. He saw this as 'a good sign of international co-operation in Europe in the fight against terrorism' (King 1990, p.1). The structures in place for this are discussed in following chapters.

2.3   Drugs Trafficking

2.3.1   *Perceptions of the 'Drugs Threat'*

Drugs trafficking and drugs-related crimes pose a considerable threat within the European Union. As the European Parliament observed in its recent inquiry into drugs trafficking:

> The power of the criminal organizations which control the drugs traffic is growing at an alarming rate. It is having increasingly serious effects on society and on the political institutions of the member states. It is undermining the foundations of the legitimate economy and threatening the stability of the states of the Community. The financial gains to be made from drugs trafficking enables the criminal organizations involved to contaminate and corrupt the structures of the state at all levels. (European Parliament 1992, p.4).

Drugs trafficking is an emotive and politically important issue. Indeed, it is the potential threat of increases in drugs-related crime which have produced the most comment by police and politicians. As the quotations below illustrate, graphic language is often deployed to give additional emphasis to the serious nature of the drugs threat.

a)   Evil Trade

For example, Sir Leon Brittan, a former British Home Secretary and currently a European Commissioner, whilst speaking to a National Drugs Conference in Preston, UK, stated that:

> As a former Home Secretary, I can have no illusions about the quantity of drugs flowing into Britain from other Community countries. This is an evil trade which destroys the lives of many young and vulnerable people. It is imperative that we should maintain and, indeed, step up the fight against trafficking. (Brittan 1990, p.18).

The vocabulary used in this statement demonstrates how language can be used in order to construct a 'moral panic'. Using his status as an acknowledged expert – an ex-British Home Secretary – he builds up a specific image and speaks of drugs 'flowing into Britain'. There is a moral condemnation of the 'evil trade' and the country's youth are deemed to be at risk. As a consequence, there is a clear imperative to 'step up the fight' against drugs trafficking. The speech is emotively laden – there is nothing surprising about this. Sir Leon did not, however, produce empirical evidence to substantiate his claim.

b)   Drugs Menace

Similar rhetoric can be seen in statements on the same theme by the Chair of the Police Federation of England and Wales. This is the body which represents the interests of police officers up to the rank of Chief Inspector, and the views of Alan Eastwood, then its Chairman, echoed those of Sir Leon Brittan:

> No one here, and no one in any position of authority, can have any doubts about the menace of a Columbian export drive in heroin and cocaine. It is

now a cliché to say that the USA is saturated and that the South American drug barons are looking for other markets. A Single European Market without boundaries and without a consistent policing policy would be an open invitation to them. (Eastwood 1989, p.26).

Again, a position of authority is used to promote the idea of an omnipresent menace, to which the relaxation of border controls in the European Union would constitute an invitation. Again, whilst not doubting the serious nature of the consequences of drugs trafficking, rhetorical statements such as this can often mislead. Policing strategies based on perceptions of a threat, rather than on empirical evidence, risk being ill-directed and ineffective, although it is recognised that perceptions and fears of crime do need to be addressed by the police.

c)   Worldwide Turnover of Drugs

Sir Jack Stewart-Clark, MEP, spelt out his perception of the danger:

> The drugs traffickers have been winning the battle; they are organising an increasingly efficient network for the distribution of cocaine across western Europe; their resources are mounting relentlessly. The worldwide turnover of drugs at street-level prices is approaching £250,000 million per annum. This is twelve times greater than the European Community budget and is more than the combined turnovers of General Motors, Ford and IBM. (Stewart-Clark 1989, p.23).

This quotation uses defeatist militaristic imagery and implies that the drugs traffickers have already succeeded in establishing very substantial markets within Europe. This opinion tallies with information received by the project on the existence of drugs trafficking networks. The figures he quotes are, however, unattributable and highly speculative, and do little to increase our knowledge of potential rises of crime with the relaxation of internal border controls within the European Union.

d)   Mind Corrosive Substances

The House of Commons Home Affairs Committee shared these concerns, pointing to drugs trafficking as 'a major international criminal activity involving a significant degree of organisation' with 'the grave potential of escalating in importance' (House of Commons 1990a, p. vii). However, the only evidence referred to was a successful police operation in Galicia, north-west Spain, involving 350 officers and resulting in 18 arrests.

These alarmist views on the dangers posed by drugs trafficking are not unique to the UK. In Greece, a country with an extended coastline and innumerable islands, there are, perhaps, near ideal conditions for the illegal trans-shipment of drugs. This may explain the great concern about the effects of illegal drugs voiced by Brigadier Alexandros Kondogiannis of the Hellenic Police:

> These mind corrosive substances demoralise societies, western manpower reserves and destroy the youngsters which are the future of our countries. Narcotics can undoubtedly be awarded first prize in the 'best disguised assassin' competition. (Kondogiannis 1990, p.6).

The paper, presented to a conference of European police chiefs, is strong in imagery but empty of detail. Brigadier Kondogiannis presents no data on narcotics, trans-shipment or policing, leaving an emotive statement unsubstantiated by empirical evidence. This, again, could be judged as contributing to a moral panic on the rise of crime in an EU without internal border controls.

2.3.2 Levels of Drugs Trafficking in Europe

Accurate figures on the quantities of drugs reaching the European Union, and circulating within it, are of course impossible to compile. The two UK customs officers' unions, the National Union of Civil and Public Servants (NUCPS) and the Civil and Public Services Association (CPSA) have stated, quite simply, that:

> There is no sure way of knowing what quantities of drugs are imported into this country. (NUCPS and CPSA 1992, p.2).

Similarly, the House of Commons Home Affairs Committee noted that:

> Quantifying the extent of an illicit activity such as drugs trafficking is notoriously difficult. (House of Commons 1989, p. v).

The overall volume can only be inferred from the quantities of drugs seized by customs authorities (Clark and Sanctuary 1992). The following tables give some indication of the amounts of drugs seized.

These figures give an indication of the scale of the threat faced by the member states of the European Union. To the extent that there are many illegal trans-shipments of drugs which are not seized by the authorities, the figures offer an underestimate of the size of the problem. Clearly, further research is required to establish the precise scale of the problem and the most appropriate way in which resources can be targeted to tackle it effectively.

Table 2.1   Drugs Seized by UK Customs and Other Authorities, 1987–1990

Year	Drug	UK Customs seizures (Kg)	Other UK seizures (Kg)
1987	Heroin	190	46
	Cocaine	362	44
1988	Heroin	231	24
	Cocaine	283	60
1989	Heroin	331	16
	Cocaine	424	113
1990	Heroin	588	21
	Cocaine	561	44

(Source: NUCPS and CPSA 1992, p.4)

There is certainly evidence of a substantial increase in seizures of heroin and cocaine. From Table 2.1 it can be seen that the total of these drugs seized by UK authorities rose from 642 kilos in 1987 to 1,214 kilos in 1990 – an increase of 89 per cent. Similarly, Table 2.2 shows that the total amount of cocaine seized in nine European countries rose from 6,001 kilos in 1989 to 12,811 kilos in 1990 – an increase of 113 per cent. These figures point strongly in the same direction, although they may reflect increased or more effective customs activities, a 'real' rise in drugs trafficking, or both.

Table 2.2　　Seizures of Cocaine in Nine European Countries, 1989–1990

| Country | Seizures | | | | | |
	Quantity (Kg)		Number		Traffickers involved	
	1989	1990	1989	1990	1989	1990
Spain	1,164	4,054	143	203	295	405
Netherlands	783	4,021	84	154	149	234
Germany	1,284	2,076	146	197	301	388
Italy	466	678	163	143	393	294
Belgium	83	517	32	46	53	79
France	839	479	126	150	235	264
UK	455	470	84	132	149	196
Portugal	681	287	52	32	84	57
Switzerland	246	229	56	87	104	145
Total	6,001	12,811	886	1,144	1,763	2,062

(Source: European Parliament 1992, p.22)

Between 1988 and 1993 the customs authorities alone in the UK seized 200,000 kgs of prohibited drugs with a street value of over £1 billion. Over 60 per cent of these seizures were of drugs coming from or through the European Community. This figure does not include seizures made by other agencies (a further 50,000 kgs), nor does it include seizures made in other countries where the UK authorities provided assistance or intelligence (Russell 1993).

In Europe, the total of heroin seized rose from 1,850 kilos in 1985 to 6,100 kilos in 1990. The proportion of the seized heroin which was being trans-shipped through the Balkan route (from Turkey through Greece or Bulgaria and Yugoslavia) rose from 35 to 80 per cent, partly reflecting the opening up of eastern Europe (Levi 1993).

2.3.3　　*What Difference Do Borders Make?*

Do border controls have a role to play in preventing the movement of drugs and traffickers? There are, again, two conflicting schools of thought.

a)   **The Need for Border Controls**

There are powerful arguments that border controls are essential. For example, and not surprisingly, the UK customs officers' unions have stated:

> We believe that the task of stemming the tide of drugs coming into the country is enormous. With the advent of the European Single Market we believe that the risks will be even greater if the public, including drug smugglers and potential drug smugglers, see fewer uniformed Customs officers on duty. (NUCPS and CPSA 1992, p.8).

The European Parliamentary Labour Party also made this point:

> After 1992 Europe will face a major challenge from drugs traffickers exploiting the newly opened market between the 12 member states of the EC. Already organised crime is strengthening its hold on European markets – despite an array of laws in each EC country designed to crack down on drugs and drug traffickers. (European Parliamentary Labour Party 1991).

b)   **Border Controls Make No Difference**

However, many with policing and border control responsibilities have argued that the removal of border controls will make no difference to the movement of criminals involved in organised crime and drugs trafficking. As Sir Peter Imbert noted, when Commissioner of the Metropolitan Police in London, such offenders generally have considerable money and are in a position to make full use of the travel and communication facilities of the modern world (Imbert 1989). They are unlikely to be hindered by border controls on persons. They have financial resources and a large measure of audacity.

Similarly, Merle Hoefman of the CRI in The Hague, argued against the presumption of a sudden upsurge in international activities by organised criminals. She pointed out that of 159 targeted groups of suspected offenders in the Netherlands as many as 57 per cent were already operating internationally. The removal of the internal borders would make no difference. As far as internal barriers are concerned, Hoefman thought that a border check may just act as a deterrent to a 'small fry' criminal, perhaps dissuading somebody from taking two or three grammes of cannabis from the Netherlands to Germany. There was, perhaps, a 'psychological barrier'. If so, a modest increase in low-level crime might follow in the wake of 1992. For the 'big time' offender, the border made no difference before or after the removal of frontier checks (Merle Hoefman 1990, personal interview).

More recent reports from the UK Customs and Excise confirm that casual frontier checks often only result in small seizures. Again, intelligence operations were responsible for the seizure of larger consignments. Similar conclusions were drawn by a former European Commissioner, who, working from first principles, argued:

> If, for example, you were considering how to deal with the drug problem and assumed that you had no frontiers to start with, would you end up by saying that the right solution to the drug problem was the creation of national frontiers? I very much doubt whether you would. (Lord Cockfield, quoted in Owens and Dynes 1989, p.65).

These arguments suggest that the removal of border controls is unlikely of itself to produce a sudden increase in drugs trafficking.

c)   Border Controls are Irrelevant

There is a strong argument that the abolition of internal border controls will enhance the opportunties for drugs traffickers is fundamentally flawed:

> Professional drug entrepreneurs have never been that much impressed by border controls as to be frightened out of business. Given a certain market demand, stricter border controls have usually only served to increase consumer prices which meant a higher net profit per unit for the trafficker. (van Duyne 1993, p.12).

This was certainly the outcome of the USA's 'war on drugs' after the intensified policy of interdiction and eradication during the 1980s. There is no reason to suppose that the same is not true for Europe in the 1990s. The drugs market is open, irregular and flexible where developments appear to be primarily determined not by the unification of the member states of the European Union but by market demand and the expected profits.

2.3.4   *The Removal of Border Controls: New Opportunities?*

If there is an increase in the drugs problem in Europe in the next few years, it is more likely to come from the increases in freedom of movement in eastern Europe, rather than from the abolition of the EU internal frontiers. The overall decline in the enforcement of law and order in the former communist countries of central and eastern Europe, and the concomitant growth in organised crime and corruption, is allegedly leading to new routes and opportunities for drugs trafficking into the European Union.

This view was expressed by the EC Ministers' meeting in Dublin in June 1990. Serious consideration was given to extending the policing of drugs trafficking to include eastern Europe. There was some anxiety that new opportunities for travel would create new drug routes from India, Afghanistan and Pakistan (Castle and Sutton 1990). But, if so, this would be a result of the disintegration of the eastern bloc, not the creation of the Single Market in the European Union. As a set of briefing notes for police officers in Surrey, UK, noted:

> The political and social upheaval in the east European bloc will bring opportunities for increased regional drugs trafficking and abuse, with rival ethnic groups using drugs as a source of income with which to purchase arms for local conflicts. These countries already have people involved in the black market which will not be as profitable in an open economy. Such groups will become increasingly involved in the drugs trade. (Surrey Constabulary 1992, p.10).

A UK Government Minister has also made this claim:

> Since the revolutions in central and eastern Europe there has been a massive increase in the flow of goods and people across borders. This freedom of movement, while very welcome in itself, has provided greater opportunities for drugs traffickers. (John Patten, quoted in *The Independent on Sunday* 21st April 1991).

It has also been suggested that the disintegration of the former communist states will cause organised crime groups from eastern Europe to spread aggressively into the EU, particularly in the fields of drugs trafficking, the theft of machine tools and plant, 'black marketeering' and the distribution of counterfeit merchandise and stolen property (Gregory 1993, p.21).

Of course, fundamentally any increase in drugs trafficking will be the result of increased *demand* in EU countries and any real solution to the problem needs to address the social and cultural reasons for this demand. The whole field of the use of psychoactive drugs, the reasons for their use, and the policies which European Union countries have adopted merits detailed investigation. As experience in the United States between 1919 and 1933 revealed all too clearly, if there is a real demand for prohibited drugs there is an opportunity for organised crime to make huge profits by supplying the demand. In such circumstances, criminals will find ways to circumvent controls, including bribery, corruption, extortion and violence, and the law enforcement agencies will be left largely plugging the holes. The critical factor is understanding and tackling the demand, and the introduction of discerning policies and legislation.

2.4　Offender Mobility

2.4.1　An Increase in Offender Mobility

Although a sudden upsurge in terrorist activity and organised crime and drugs trafficking is most unlikely to occur as a consequence of the removal of internal border controls, it has been argued that, with an increase in personal mobility, levels of acquisitive crime will rise due to increased opportunities for travel within the European Union. This possibility merits further serious investigation.

2.4.2　Less Serious But More Frequent Criminality

Increased mobility amongst offenders may possibly spawn an increase in certain types of offences. Some of the obvious examples would include hawkers, pedlars and door-to-door salespersons plying an illegal trade and doing so in a rapid succession of locations, including different member states. The sale of fraudulent lottery tickets is one possibility, whilst others would include everything from selling bogus insurance to non-existent holidays.

These sorts of activities could also take place trans-nationally by mail. It is arguably the case that these types of criminal victimisation, although less harmful than terrorist attacks, are much more likely to impinge directly on the everyday lives of European Union citizens.

2.4.3　Criminals Abroad

Respondents interviewed in the course of the preliminary study in 1990 could point to evidence of 'travelling' offenders. Police officers in Devon and Cornwall in England, for example, voiced concern about offenders taking the ferry from Plymouth to Roscoff in order to commit burglaries in French caravan sites.

There are probably three inter-related reasons for this type of development: a simple urge to travel; a perception (or misperception) of a higher return on crime on the continent; and, because the offender abroad would probably be unknown to local police, he or she would calculate that this would significantly lower the chances of detection.

2.4.4   *Crimes Against Property*

At a lower level again, in terms of the perceived threat to the security of the state or to the fabric of society, there is a numerically large class of less serious offences. This category includes crimes against property (theft and burglary), which accounts for 70 per cent or more of recorded crime in European Union member states. It has already been noted that about two in every 100 households in EU member states will be burgled in the course of a single year.

There has been a feeling that the removal of internal barriers was likely to facilitate 'ordinary crime' in much the same sort of way that it would promote commerce or tourism, simply because travel would be made easier. It would be unreasonable to suppose that non-offenders have a monopoly on the urge to travel.

It would be equally unreasonable, however, to suppose that the period after the removal of border controls would witness a qualitative shift in criminality away from traditional property crime and towards the very serious crimes of drugs trafficking or terrorism. It was always more likely that there would be more of the same type of crime, but perhaps in different locations.

2.5   Free Movement of Goods

2.5.1   *The Movement of Stolen Goods*

The abolition of internal frontiers also has implications for crime in relation to the movement of goods.

One possibility is that major criminals may turn increasingly to enterprises which have the potential for a large, quick and secure profit. This will direct them to high-value, easily transportable commodities with restricted supply and high demand (Imbert 1989, p.1174).

2.5.2   *High-Value Easily Transportable Goods*

Part of the justification for a Europe without frontier checks is to ease restrictions on trade and commerce, so it would be wrong to suppose that the ethic of the 'marketplace' does not also apply to crime. In practice, this may have a number of important consequences.

High-value, portable goods are likely to be stolen in one country, quickly transported to another and then realised as cash. The criminal may well reason that the increased risks incurred by transporting goods are more than compensated for by the switch from one criminal jurisdiction – and police intelligence network – to another. It will probably follow that ease of transportation becomes an important variable in the planning and execution of offences against property.

2.5.3   *Geographical Distribution of Crime*

It also follows, given that crime is more urban than rural in nature, that there may be a change in the geographical distribution of crime. European cities which are close geographically, or close in transport terms but located in different countries, may become a focus for regular crime involving the theft and movement of goods.

Ironically, those countries with the greatest investment in transport infrastructure may inadvertently place themselves on a pan-European crime axis. Good transportation networks will facilitate the easy movement of stolen goods.

2.5.4   *Motor Vehicle Theft*

Among the sorts of goods which are the most readily transportable are motor vehicles themselves. In rough terms, about one-third of all crime relates in some way to motor vehicles and the removal of the frontiers may well have direct implications for auto-crime. Data from one provincial British police force indicate that 20 per cent of stolen vehicles are never seen or heard of again. The same is true of over one-half of the motorcycles taken, and two-thirds of the lorries.

The British police service supports arguments for dedicated stolen motor vehicle liaison officers operating throughout Europe, pointing to some 389 recovered vehicles valued at £4.5 million which were stolen from the UK and transported for sale in other EC countries in 1988–89 (House of Commons 1990b, p.25). Traditionally, theft of motor vehicles has been a 'local' affair – joyriders stealing cars for immediate, short-term use or gangs taking cars to be sold locally with new identities. This now appears to be changing.

a)   **International Motor Vehicle Theft**

There is increasing evidence of motor vehicle theft taking on international dimensions. For example, in Germany between 1990 and 1991 there was a 45 per cent increase in the theft of motor vehicles, and in 1992 there were in excess of 173,000 motor vehicle thefts (Hadfield 1993). Only one-quarter of these vehicles were recovered. The Auto Crime Unit of the UK's Kent Police recovered vehicles worth £1.25 million in 1991 which were passing through the port of Dover *en route* to mainland Europe. In another example, two thieves drove from the UK to Turkey in a pair of Ford Sierra Cosworths, worth £24,000 apiece, which they then sold for less than 10 per cent of their list price (Heard 1990). Finally, Imbert (1989, p.1174) gives the example of a high-value motor car stolen in Milan, driven over land to England and packed into a container ready for shipment to Australia.

A joint survey by the Association of British Insurers and their European counterparts in 8 European countries in 1990 revealed that Germany, Switzerland and the UK appear to be net exporters of stolen vehicles whilst Italy and Spain are net importers. A significant proportion of the stolen vehicles pass through other European countries which act as a conduit for final destinations outside Europe (Levi 1993).

b)   Organised Motor Vehicle Theft

Such thefts are increasingly understood to be the work of organised criminal groups operating internationally to supply cars to a growing market in the eastern European countries and in the Middle East and further afield. In 1993 a £45 million 'car racket' was investigated by the Metropolitan Police Stolen Vehicle Squad involving the theft of Mercedes cars which were being sold as legitimate vehicles in Malaysia at three times their British sale value (Gregory 1993, p.79). Luxury models like Porsches, BMWs and Mercedes are stolen to order to supply a healthy illegal market in Africa and the Middle East.

2.5.5   *Theft of Art and Antiques*

a)   The European Union Dimension

Theft of works of art and antiques is a recognised concern within the European Union and is often linked to other types of international organised crime, for example, drugs trafficking and money laundering. London has been described as the 'smuggling capital of the art world' (Roberts 1993). The highly transportable nature of these items, and the relatively few export and import restrictions in some countries, coupled with their relatively high value, makes them an attractive target for international criminals.

Although London has been singled out as a particularly 'soft spot' it should be noted that other EU states have extremely strict export restrictions. Greece and Italy, for example, impose such tight conditions that the legal export of art is almost impossible. Relatively little is known about the art thieves themselves and there is an equal lack of knowledge about the dealers who give false provenance to what are in fact stolen art and antiquities.

b)   Scale of the Problem

The theft of art and antiques is an under-researched topic, but it is clear that a serious problem exists. This was highlighted nearly 30 years ago by Milton Esterow (1967) in his book *The Art Stealers* and subsequently by Keith Middlemass (1975) in *The Double Market: Art Theft and Art Thieves*. In 1985, J. Wright presented a paper on the subject to the Cross Channel Intelligence Conference and he reported: 'Increasingly we are experiencing high-value burglaries in dwellings when antiques and objects of fine art are stolen. Little is ever recovered. What we have discovered, however, is an increasing international connection within the criminal fraternity linking the burglar through various receivers to the continental market'.

A number of examples of cases of thefts of art and antiques and their transport across European borders are known. In 1991 a London art dealer was arrested in Italy, as a result of co-operation between police in the UK and the *Carabinieri*, and was found to be in possession of stolen items (*The Times* 11th April 1991). In the same year, over 500 items stolen in Yorkshire, valued at over £1 million, were recovered in Italy. In 1990, two valuable Scottish landscape paintings stolen in London were found in Amsterdam. The existence of border controls were easily circumvented in these and similar cases.

c)   Responding to the Problem

Although art and antiques will no longer be subject to checks at the internal borders of the European Union, they are given special surveillance. An EC Regulation which came into effect in early 1993 deals with the export of works of art to non-Union countries and provides that authorisation of the member state from which they are to be exported is required. In addition to this a Directive was adopted in March 1993 (to take effect in 1994) which provides for co-operation between national authorities to help ensure that any 'national treasures' which have been illegally exported are returned (*Frontier-free Europe* 1993, p.2).

2.6   Movement of Capital and International Fraud

2.6.1   *Possibilities for European Fraud*

The European Commission's objective with the establishment of the Single European Market is the complete liberalisation of all financial transactions and services within the European Union. Both are subsumed under the free market banner of fair conditions for competition, together with adequate saver and investor protection (Commission of the European Communities 1989, pp.42–43).

a)   Financial Regulation

The relaxation of controls within the EC on financial transactions and services is of course broadening the possibilities for fraud. Yet in *Europe without Frontiers* (Commission of the European Communities 1989, pp.42–45) the sections on 'Free movement of capital' and 'Financial services' contain not a single reference to policing. Financial regulation is seen as necessary, but it is referred to solely in terms of 'harmonisation', 'prudential practice' and 'mutual recognition'. Such self-regulation will not dissuade the committed criminal entrepreneur.

b)   New Opportunities for Fraud

Merle Hoefman of the CRI in The Hague argued in 1990 that fraud would be *the* menace of the Single Market:

> If there is one sort of crime which will probably prosper [...] which might be stimulated [...] it is fraud. (Merle Hoefman 1990, personal interview).

The hard-core offender, the organised criminal and business people alike will all see new opportunities and some will seize them. White-collar crime is characterised by relative invisibility, complexity and a lack of publicity. These factors conspire to keep it at a 'safe distance' from official scrutiny.

c)   Fraud in a National Context

In contrast, there is an argument that a significant proportion of all fraud is relatively small-scale and takes place within a national context. Much of cheque and credit-card fraud, bogus insurance claims, mortgage fraud, procurement fraud or 'backhanders' and employee dishonesty all occur within national jurisdictions (Clarke 1993). Moreover, there is little or no benefit in relocating the fraud abroad. The potential fraudster would be at a disadvantage because of a lack of familiarity with the business culture and the financial systems of the new jurisdiction.

2.6.2   *International Cross-Border Commercial Crime*

Collecting data on international fraud is not easy; financial institutions and fraud investigators are often unwilling to release information on fraud on the grounds that such data could assist further criminal activities. Additionally, disclosing fraud victimisation may be seen as a commercial embarrassment. There is, however, evidence for significant cross-border commercial crime.

a)   The International Dimension

For example, the City of London is a major international centre of banking and financial services and, by implication, the City of London Police has a special interest and expertise in dealing with commercial crime. In a powerful statement on international cross-border commercial crime, the force commented that:

> Many of the major frauds [...] have an international element [...] and it is an area of criminal activity which requires effective co-operation of the police forces of the countries involved. [...] The incidence of major fraud is increasing. [...] It is anticipated that the increasing use of computers by banking institutions [...] will present further opportunities for the international criminal. (House of Commons 1990b, p.28).

b)   European Examples

There have been various examples of European fraud during recent years. It is arguable that there are few major international commercial frauds in Europe without equally important interests on the other side of the Atlantic or in the far east, or in various 'tax havens' throughout the world.

A group of Germans executed a fraudulent operation for some years from an office in London. They advertised commodity investment in Europe, mainly in Germany, and simply took the money which was sent in which amounted to some £400 million (Levi 1987).

There is growing evidence of 'long firm' fraud whereby a person visits the stand of a supplier at an international trade exhibition and orders goods to be delivered in another European country. These are then moved on from the address, often to an empty industrial unit, leaving the supplier without payment and without the means to trace the fraudster (Collier 1993, p.96).

In the UK notable cases such as Guinness and Poly Peck involved international fraud. The murder of two Russians in London in early 1993 was linked to a £1 million fraud of German business interests over the sale of raw materials (Gregory 1993, p.22).

In September 1993, several months of co-operation between Benelux, French and Italian law enforcement agencies resulted in the exposure of major cross-border fraud by a sugar-trafficking criminal gang. Co-ordinated raids took place after 160 25-tonne truck-loads of sugar were monitored. These left Rotterdam bound for eastern European countries but travelled back through France to Italy where the sugar was sold. The criminals were thought to have embezzled over ecu 2.25 million in export subsidies.

c)   Money-Laundering

The greater the extent of business crime the greater the need for criminal enterprises to have access to money-laundering mechanisms. As competition increases within the illegitimate sphere of business crime, and as law enforcement improves, only those groups with the highest organisational and informational skills in dealing with 'hot money' will survive. The process of money-laundering can be divided into three phases: *placement* or the physical disposal of bulk cash profits in a secure place; *layering* or the piling on of layers of complex financial transactions to conceal the illicit source of the income; and *integration* or the provision of legitimate-looking explanations for the appearance of new wealth (Savona 1993). The major conclusion from a study of the impact of the new Italian legislation on money-laundering and the Mafia was:

> The boundaries between different kinds of money may become extremely blurred as time passes. The mob bosses may become financial speculators, while financial speculators may use organised crime services to launder the money. (Savona 1993, p.51).

In effect, the links between organised crime and economic crime are likely to become closer as there is freer circulation of capital funds across borders and greater international investment opportunities. The boundaries between 'legitimate' money and 'hot' money will become increasingly blurred. In the case of the Mafia, the recent investigations by the Palermo prosecutors and the revelations of high-level political corruption will drive money-laundering in an international direction.

The most urgent priorities in dealing with the problem include solving the political problems of persuading reluctant countries to open-up their banking and financial systems, the enforcement of money-laundering legislation and developing co-operation in the investigation and prosecution of offences.

2.6.3   *The High Cost of Fraud*

Victimisation in commercial crime is less visible than other types of crime. Physical violence and stolen motor vehicles are singularly easier to 'see' than many instances of fraud or illegal credit transactions, or most computer-related crime.

a)   Calculating the Costs of Fraud

There is an unknown number of crimes which do not come to light – although the available figures are awesome. For example, in 1985 the City of London and Metropolitan Police Fraud Squads alone dealt with frauds valued in excess of £1.3 billion, and nationally for England and Wales the police-recorded frauds totalled £2.1 billion, with a further estimated £5 billion worth of income tax fraud (Levi 1987, Ch.2). The cost of fraud in 1990 for the two London police force areas alone was reported to be some £4 billion (Collier 1993, p.43).

More significantly, in England and Wales the losses from fraud were far in excess of the costs incurred in other, more conventional, crimes. The cost in 1985 of burglary in dwellings was £221 million, the cost of non-residential burglary was £157 million and the cost of all auto theft was £443 million – a total of just over £800 million. This huge total was estimated to be just 10 per cent of the estimated value of frauds in the same period (Levi 1987, Ch.2).

Even these figures do not begin to address the 'hidden' costs of fraud, for example, the loss of commercial confidence and the social and political impact of fraud. John Wood, whilst Director of the Serious Fraud Office, London, with an annual budget of £11 million to investigate complex fraud cases, admitted that he had failed to 'clean up' the City of London (Wood 1990).

b)   Fraud in the Member States of the European Union

The international data, even when they are clearly incomplete, point to the high cost of fraud throughout Europe. The European Community Information Technology Task Force (1984) discovered 40 cases of theft and embezzlement via computers. The cases originated in the United Kingdom, France, West Germany, Belgium, Italy and Switzerland. In 10 per cent of them the individual losses were greater than £5 million.

A conservative 'guesstimate' of the scale of economic crime in the mid 1980s in West Germany was DM50 billion or £15 billion sterling a year (Tiedemann 1985, p.101). For France, in 1975 offences against the Exchequer were estimated to cost up to 40 million francs or £4 billion sterling, or about 17 per cent of the budget expenditure (Levi 1987, p.32). Finally, some years ago in Italy the 'underground economy' was reported to account for up to 50 per cent of the gross national product (Mattera 1985, p.84).

2.6.4   Credit Card Fraud

There are problems in identifying the extent of credit-card fraud as the banks and other organisations which issue cards are reluctant to discuss their losses. The Association of Payment Clearing Services (APACS) recently established a major anti-fraud initiative and estimated that credit-card fraud amounted to £160 million in 1991 in the UK – a rise of 126 per cent since 1988.

Of the 80 million cards issued in the UK each year some 2 million are lost or stolen (*Police Review* 13th March 1992). Some of these are given to young, unemployed people who are taken in groups to European countries where they use the cards to make purchases of goods (Collier 1993, p.96). Others find their way to lorry drivers who use them to make illegal purchases of fuel and other goods during journeys through Europe.

The FBI European Chapter is of the view that there is a developing market for forged credit cards with the best forgeries being produced in Hong Kong and Taiwan.

It is extremely difficult to estimate the costs of credit-card fraud. At one extreme, a commentator noted that 'Mastercard' was closed down in Romania because the level of fraud exceeded that of legitimate transactions (Clarke 1993). In contrast, another commentator suggested that cheque and credit-card fraud accounts for roughly one per cent of turnover of all transactions – a cost passed on to the customer (Levi 1987, pp.42–43).

During 1991, fraud on UK-issued cards occurred in 103 countries, but three-quarters of the fraud by value took place in just 8 countries and 68 per cent within Europe. Italy was the top fraud-producing country, accounting for 17 per cent of UK overseas fraud, France was second (16%), Spain was third (12%), Hong Kong was fourth (8%) and the Netherlands and Germany were in joint fifth place (6%) (Levi 1993).

It is clear that credit-card fraud is a major problem in European countries. It is particularly difficult to prevent when a stolen card is used to make a large number of relatively small transactions in another country. With greater mobility in Europe this problem may be expected to grow unless preventative measures are introduced.

2.6.5   *Fraud and the European Commission*

The defrauding of the EC itself is a major problem. The Commission's fourth report on EC fraud, published in April 1993, pointed to a sharp increase in reported cases from the previous year. In the twelve month period up to April 1993, 1,850 cases accounting for around 270 million ECUs were discovered and notified to the Commission. The main area for fraud was the Agricultural Guarantee and Guidance Fund. The report noted that the level of fraud against the EC was probably far higher than that detected, and also pointed out that only around 10 per cent of funds received fraudulently are ever recovered (Commission of the European Communities 1993a).

One of the most forceful and authoritative statements on the extent of fraud against the EC referred to it as a 'public scandal' and there have been estimates that as much as 10 per cent of the total EC budget is affected by fraudulent practices, including figures from the European Parliament and the British House of Lords (Ruimschotel 1993).

The existence of the EC's Common Agricultural Policy (CAP) has been described as a 'charter for fraudsters' on the grounds that the system itself facilitates fraud and that those with an opportunity would be 'foolish' not to avail themselves of it (Clarke 1993). The European Court of Auditors is regularly critical of CAP fraud in its annual reports.

A Court of Auditors' Report, published in November 1993, was critical of the continuing level of fraud against the EC, which was estimated to amount to almost 10 per cent of the annual budget of ecu 66 billion. Cataloguing a series of swindles, the Report drew attention to poor management of the ecu 45 billion Common Agricultural Policy. Between 1971 and 1992 over 7,000 cases of farm fraud were discovered with half of them in the period since 1987. Despite the introduction of more stringent controls, and a new computerised system to monitor payments, fraud continues to rise. The Court of Auditors also uncovered 820 cases of fraud against tax and customs duty in 1992 worth more than ecu 152 million.

The European Commission has established a Unit for the Co-ordination of Fraud Prevention (*Unite pour la Co-ordination de la Lutte Anti-Fraude* or UCLAF) and set aside £50 million in the 1990 budget for fraud prevention activities (House of Commons 1990a, pp. viii-ix; see also Reinke, 1992). In 1993 the total budget for fraud prevention was ecu 73.2 million, or approximately £56 million (Commission of the European Communities 1993a, Annex 4.2).

UCLAF claims to have had increasing success in the last year in tracking down fraud, but the deputy head of the Unit, Siegfried Reinke, said in September 1993:

'We cannot do as much as we would like. We have less than 100 people and we need more.' Mr Reinke said UCLAF needed more investigators but did not have the necessary funding. It would appear to be money well spent, for in the first nine months of 1993 fraud worth ecu 160 million was uncovered and yet the total cost of the Unit is only ecu 3 million per year.

2.6.6   *The Hidden World of Business Crime*

Business crime is far more complex and therefore more difficult to understand than conventional crime. Few ordinary people have a working knowledge of the European market or a ready grasp of commercial fraud. Criminological and social policy and criminal justice attention is directed away from the crime-in-the-suites to crime-in-the-streets.

a)   Relative Invisibility

White-collar crime is difficult to identify because, within the established practice of the business community, illegal activities may not be seen to be crime at all – the most obvious examples being expense account 'fiddles' and offering 'sweeteners', these being private expressions for 'fraud' and 'bribes', respectively. Some crime known to be illegal, may be seen as acceptable and regarded as a necessary condition for business to take place.

There is also the question of publicity relating to commercial crime. Generally, public interest and media concern are largely reserved for crimes which pose an immediate threat to personal safety or to the security of property (Hough and Mayhew 1985). One survey found that respondents considered senior business executives taking money from a client's account to be less serious than predatory street-crime but more serious than vandalism or burglary in a private dwelling (Levi 1986).

It is possible that calculations about the likelihood of victimisation inform these judgements, with the perception of white-collar crime being reassuringly remote for most ordinary people. Alternatively, for members of the business community there may be powerful forces at work which seek to 'deny' both the incidence and seriousness of victimisation. It may not make commercial sense for banks to acknowledge or to pursue large-scale losses through computer fraud. The costs, in terms of damage to a commercial reputation or in investigating offences, may be more than offset by profits elsewhere. Either way, there are disincentives to giving white-collar crime publicity.

b)   Preconditions for Business Crime

It is difficult to give a quantitative answer on the extent to which the legitimate business market in the European Union is penetrated by organised business crime. It is, however, possible to identify the three preconditions which may further the development and continuity of business crime enterprises (van Duyne 1993). First, there must be a stable demand which allows the crime enterprise to develop its market place. With increased competition and legitimate entrepreneurs 'fighting for survival' there is every opportunity for criminal entrepreneurs to establish themselves by exploiting opportunities on the wrong side of 'cut throat' competition. Secondly, there needs to be a low complaint rate either because of the invisibility of the crime in the first place or the tendency for law enforcement agencies to shy away from investigating complicated white collar crime. Thirdly, where there are under-developed mechanisms for control (for example, special fraud investigation units) illegitimate entrepreneurs can operate with impunity. It is difficult to think of any large-scale business operation where these three preconditions are not met.

2.6.7   Tax Avoidance

The removal of fiscal barriers also raises questions about fraudulent activity. Without frontier controls customs officials will have to find new ways of ensuring that taxes on goods are paid when and where they are due. The temptation will be for private individuals and traders alike to travel to low-taxed countries, buy goods and to take them back for onward sale at a higher price.

In the UK, following the 1993 relaxation of duty payable on imported goods (alcohol, in particular) there is already anecdotal evidence of large quantities of wines and spirits being imported supposedly for 'personal consumption', but in fact being sold in both legal and illegal retail outlets. HM Customs and Excise has had to adapt to this new form of criminal activity.

These sorts of offences lead both to a loss of VAT revenue for the authorities and to a distortion of legitimate trade. One study points to massive VAT and excise fraud throughout the 1980s in the seemingly innocuous fields of consumer electronics and the mineral oil industry (petrol). Because taxes create a kind of 'price wedge' beween the cost price and the delivery price, the business crime entrepreneur can take his or her 'profit' by failing to pay the legal duty (van Duyne 1993).

The long-term solution to this problem is the pan-European harmonisation of indirect taxes, even if, in the first instance, this has to be approached by means of two tiers of 'approximated' rates of VAT: 14–20 per cent standard rate and 4–9 per cent for the reduced rate (Commission of the European Communities 1989, pp.51–56).

With stolen goods the position is worse. There are double costs – the direct costs of the thefts, and the indirect or consequential losses as stolen goods are moved from a 'low tax' to a 'high tax' area to be sold.

Tax avoidance is both a political and policing matter. In the short term its control is a function of improved law enforcement. In the long term the solution is tax harmonisation not law enforcement. To the extent that the EU member states fail to move in this direction, or are slow to do so, they (unwittingly perhaps) make a contribution to crime.

2.7   Environmental Crime

One area of increasing concern in many European countries is environmental crime. Very little research has been undertaken to date, and it is only within the past year that attempts have been made at an official level (that is, Trevi Group level) to map out the extent of criminal activities in this area and formulate effective strategies to combat them.

Environmental crimes include illegal trafficking and transportation of hazardous, toxic and nuclear waste, illegal tipping and dumping of waste, and pollution offences.

Figures made available to the CSPO research team for environmental offences in Germany in the first quarter of 1992 showed 17,000 cases of illegal depositing of waste and 6,100 cases of water pollution. A Dutch example involved a Dutch transport company dumping waste containing the dangerous chemical PCB in Belgium. Before crossing the border the waste was covered with a thin layer of earth described as 'loose earth from market gardening'. This was dumped on the Belgian site at lower cost than if it had been properly described. There was also the cost of environmental pollution (Levi 1993).

A high-level meeting involving six European Union countries was held on 7th – 8th September 1993 in the Netherlands to discuss environmental crime. The results of the discussions, between representatives of Belgium, Denmark, France, Italy, the Netherlands and Spain, were due to be presented to the next meeting of Trevi Working Group III. It was reported that an illegal market in waste disposal had developed which involved criminal organisations being paid to remove toxic waste which was then illegally dumped on land or at sea causing serious pollution.

This is clearly an area where preliminary research needs to be undertaken, as very few figures are available. Most commentators regard environmental crime as likely to increase with the relaxation of border controls allowing greater freedom of movement of goods.

2.8 Non-Criminal Victimisation

2.8.1 Rabies

La rage is a killer, with a mortality rate of 100 per cent when no prophylactic measures have been taken. One-quarter of the European Union population live in areas where rabies is endemic in foxes. In 1987, there were 16,690 known cases of rabies in mainland Europe, overwhelmingly confined to wild foxes, although in the same year there were 279 fatalities amongst domestic cats and dogs in mainland Europe. Since 1958 28 animals have died from rabies in quarantine in the UK. There have been no human fatalities from rabies contracted in the EC since 1985 (Joint ACPO/Metropolitan Police European Unit 1989).

Concern has been expressed about the possible spread of rabies into Britain, and the spread from the former eastern bloc into the European Union with the removal of the more stringent border controls that existed there. Yet whilst the fear must be addressed, there are no strong grounds for believing rabies to be a genuine threat.

There are concerns and risks associated with the Channel Tunnel and the possible passage of rabies to Britain. There is the risk of rats moving through the three passages. On the other hand, and probably more dangerous, there is the prospect of ordinary citizens unwittingly transmitting rabies by concealing family pets in their motor vehicles in order to avoid strict quarantine regulations. It is unlikely that the UK Government will relax quarantine regulations for the present time.

2.8.2 Motor Vehicle Safety

The sheer number of motor vehicles in Europe will create a specific problem. With the Commission's proposal for a regulation to abolish entirely technical controls on vehicles at borders, safety on the roads might be at stake. For example, an average of 135,000 vehicles a year crossing the German borders are found to be violating some technical standards on the basis of spot checks.

There is already a significant number of regulations governing common transport policy in the EC which impact on road safety. The areas they cover are diverse, ranging from harmonisation on agricultural vehicles to type approval of motor vehicles. Some of the legislation is specifically directed at road safety, for example the Directives on the minimum depth of tyre treads on vehicles or, even more obviously, the Directives on the wearing of seat belts and restraint systems for children. Two Directives concerning driver behaviour are currently at the proposal stage; fixing speed limits for goods vehicles and buses, and fixing the maximum blood alcohol concentration levels for drivers. A Community data bank to hold information centrally has also been proposed. This would contain road accident statistics and a documentary file on road safety (Commission of the European Communities 1993b).

It is clear now that the EC has begun to take action in this area and has given it priority, but there is much more that could be done to harmonise road safety standards across the European Union.

2.9   Extradition

In principle, taking down the internal borders in Europe could allow criminals of all kinds to take refuge in another member state. Changing country and criminal jurisdiction may prevent an offender being brought to justice. According to some authorities, suitable extradition arrangements are therefore a necessary condition for the abolition of border controls (Stein undated).

The European Convention on Extradition (1957) is the mechanism for bringing offenders to justice across European frontiers. The United Kingdom ratified the European Convention on 14th May 1991. This allows extradition simply on the basis of a formal request, an arrest warrant, a statement of facts and evidence of law and identity. A *prima facie* case will no longer need to be established. This now leaves Belgium as the sole European Union member state yet to ratify the European Convention on Extradition (House of Commons 1990a, p. xxxi).

There are three obstacles to extradition. First, with respect to terrorist offences, the Convention contains a 'political offence' exception. Suspected terrorists need only to claim that their actions were politically motivated to secure a defence against extradition. Ironically, this prevents extradition in those cases where it is valued most. The European Convention on the Suppression of Terrorism (1977) suffers from the same defect.

Secondly, the Convention on Extradition requires extraditable offences to be pursuable under the laws of both countries (the principle of double incrimination), and to carry a minimum sentence of one year's imprisonment in the state requesting extradition. This inhibits the extradition of minor offenders.

Thirdly, the principle of *aut dedere aut judicare*, permits signatory states to refuse the extradition of their own nationals, provided they try the subject of extradition under their own law. In practice, refusal to extradite is only made in very serious circumstances. Only Belgium, Greece and Germany will not extradite their own nationals.

2.10   The External Frontiers of Europe

2.10.1   *Removing the Internal Frontiers*

a)   Background

Martin Bangemann, a European Commissioner and Vice President of the Commission of the European Communities, saw a Europe 'unhampered by internal frontiers' as the gateway to Europe's economic, cultural and political future (Commission of the European Communities 1989, p.7). There was an overriding political imperative to open up the internal market.

In order to accomplish the open border policy the European Community has given a correspondingly high priority to tightening controls at external frontiers, especially through increased international co-operation (Commission of the European Communities, 1988). The fact that the newly created Single European Market was to have a reinforced external frontier initially eluded attention (Lodge 1991, p.23). Many commentators have, however, commented that a strengthened 'ring of steel' is a logical consequence of the abolition of internal frontiers in order to compensate for the loss of internal checks made on non-Union nationals (Birch 1989, p.918).

Incidentally, the research team have tried to discover the origins of the terms 'ring of steel' and 'fortress Europe', for they have a certain currency in discussions over border controls, and a powerful associative imagery. The origins of the terms are still unclear.

b)   The Schengen Group

In October 1993, nine EU member states reaffirmed their agreement to abolish formal border controls through their commitment to the Schengen agreements (see Chapter 4) and the Single European Act. In April 1993, the newly-elected government in France had announced a return of border controls, despite their relaxation in recent years and France's ratification of the Schengen Implementing Convention. The French had, in effect, suspended their agreement to Schengen whilst they considered the perceived problem of illegal immigration.

However, on 30th June 1993, the Schengen Group of countries agreed to press ahead as soon as possible with proposals to remove identity checks at borders. On 18th October 1993, Belgium, France, Germany, Luxembourg, the Netherlands and Spain announced that remaining frontier controls would be removed from 1st February 1994 and Portugal would follow suit as soon as practicable. It was thought that Greece and Italy would not be in a position to remove their remaining internal frontier checks until late 1994 or 1995 at the earliest.

c)   Opposition to Schengen

The UK, Denmark and Ireland intend to maintain some border controls. The logic for this, for the UK and Ireland, lies with the geography of these states. As the British Home Secretary said in response to a question about frontiers:

It would be absurd if we were to throw away the natural advantages we have from being an island. (House of Commons 1990b, p.157).

Denmark's position within the Nordic Union would be compromised if it were to commit itself to the Schengen Agreements.

2.10.2 Policing the Outer Limits of the European Union

Given the absolute commitment to the free and faster movement of people and goods within Europe, it follows that once inside the Union any traveller – subversive, terrorist, professional crook or honest citizen – will be able to move about more readily than in the past. 'Getting in', or being prevented from so doing, assumes crucial significance. An inevitable consequence of the open market is the opportunity for people to enter the Union at points of their choosing, or points of perceived weakness, and then move through EU countries at will. The potential for abuse is substantial.

The European Commission's handbook for '1992' contains not a single reference to the defence of the external frontiers, nor does it contain any practical proposals for policing the outer limits of Europe (Commission of the European Communities 1989, Ch.3). The focus is exclusively on completing the internal market.

2.10.3 Illegal Immigration

Illegal immigrants are a mixed group – gypsies from eastern Europe facing renewed persecution, economic refugees from former communist states and others from further afield (Africa, the Middle East, Pakistan, India and China).

It is disconcerting that many arguments against immigration are couched in nationalistic, xenophobic or racist terms, and fail to draw any distinction between legal and illegal immigration. Again, some sort of 'moral panic' is detectable in statements about the potential increase in immigration with the creation of a European Union without frontiers.

The problem of illegal immigration cannot be wholly divorced from the fact that very large numbers of people (the vast majority travelling legitimately) cross national boundaries in the course of a year. According to one authority, in 1991–1992 in excess of 110 million persons crossed the borders into Germany (Blessmann 1993). Among this number there was evidence of illegal immigrants from Asia routed through Romania and Bulgaria, as well as increasing numbers of illegal immigrants from the far east coming to Germany via Prague and Moscow. In many cases these illegal immigrants were paying substantial sums to be smuggled to the German border and beyond.

As one senior officer from the *Gendarmerie* in Luxembourg put it the overriding imperative for police co-operation in Europe in general, and for the Schengen arrangements in particular, is in 'fighting clandestine immigration' (Diederich 1993).

The issue of illegal immigration, however, does raise at least six central concerns in relation to the adequacy or otherwise of external border controls.

45

a)   Inadequate Border Controls

The first dimension of illegal immigration concerns the permeability of external borders and the slackness of border controls. In recent years quite explicit fears have been voiced about the inability of some EU member states to stop the entry of illegal immigrants. In particular, Spain, Italy, Greece and Portugal have been criticised for failing to stop illegal immigration from North African and Middle Eastern countries (Bethell 1990a; van Reenen 1990, personal interview). These countries however are all now signatories of the Schengen agreements and have made commitments to stop illegal immigration.

b)   Bilateral Agreements

The second factor concerns the permeability of external borders through bilateral agreements between EU and non-Union states. Germany has an agreement with Austria, which in turn has agreements with Poland, the Czech Republic and Slovakia. There is some suggestion that Austria intends to seek observer status in the Schengen Group in early 1994. There are also arrangements between Belgium and the Nordic states of Sweden, Norway and Denmark which control rights of entry. Step-by-step entry into the Union is possible. It is, therefore, incorrect to speak in terms of secure external frontiers for Europe. As one commentator told the research team, 'the external borders of the European Union are as permeable as a sponge'.

c)   Disintegration in the East

The third aspect relates to the re-unification of Germany and the disintegration of the communist bloc countries. The economic prosperity of western Europe relative to the new nation states in the east will inevitably draw labour (legal and illegal) to the more prosperous regions. The existing patterns of labour mobility (from North Africa to France, from Turkey to Germany and from Albania to Greece) all suggest that a powerful employment-income 'magnet' is attracting unskilled workers into Europe. The scale of both legal and illegal immigration is likely to rise. Some commentators hold that the eastern borders of Germany are the 'prime sites' for both legal and illegal immigration from former communist states and other countries (Blessmann 1993).

It is arguably the case that too little attention is being paid to the relation between these large-scale demographic changes and their crime potential. As van Duyne (1993) points out there is a huge human reservoir of discontent and, by implication, a substantial potential for criminality in the large number of 'luck hungry' refugees who can expect only 'dead-end situations' on their entry to Europe. The position is similar to the second half of the 19th century in the United States. Instead of being alarmed about the rising crime rate, the more sensible question might be to ask why there is not even more crime.

d)   Immigrants and Crime

The fourth point is that some illegal immigrants are forced to turn to crime to pay off the fees charged by those who engineer their passage from one country to another (in German, the *Schleppers*), or to pay an exorbitant price for the return of their passports. In addition, some illegal immigrants allegedly turn to 'predatory' street crime (theft and robbery) for basic subsistence.

e)   Extent of Illegal Immigration

The fifth point is that EUROSTAT, the EC statistical office, suggests that there are approximately 10 million legal immigrants in the European Union. Germany is home to almost one-half of this number (43 per cent) (*The Guardian* 22nd June 1993). Many estimates have been made of the number of illegal immigrants who are resident in the EU. In fact, of course, the number of illegal immigrants living in EU member states is not known and estimates vary widely. Data from the Council of Europe and the International Labour Organisation are seemingly amongst the best informed, although the figures are derived from few and isolated sources, and their validity and reliability may be questionable – but an informed 'guesstimate' is better than no estimate at all. In its 1990 *Report on the New Countries of Immigration* (Document 6211), the Council of Europe estimated that there was a total of 1.3 to 1.5 million illegal migrants living in Greece, Italy, Portugal and Spain. The other European Union states were believed to have much smaller numbers.

More recently, in June 1993, the International Labour Organisation estimated that there were 2.5 million illegal immigrants living in EU countries, with evidence of a growth in clandestine migrants as the legal ways of gaining entry became more difficult. Some other commentators believe that the figure of 2.5 million is too conservative (Marshall 1993).

f)   Regulating Immigration

Finally, as far as the EC is concerned, the regulation of immigration remains a matter for the individual member states. However, the Maastricht Treaty makes specific reference to immigration policy as an area of 'common interest'. In doing so, the Treaty effectively brings Union immigration policy within the bounds of intergovernmental concern, although each member state retains the prerogative to act independently. It remains unclear where the balance will lie between an individual state's autonomy and the 'common interest' or European Union-wide policies on immigration. The Maastricht Treaty gives impetus to the latter, but ultimately these matters remain the prerogative of each member state. However, a state the immigration policy of which varies substantially from others is likely to come under considerable pressure to bring its policy into line with those of the remainder of the European Union states.

2.10.4   Asylum

The spirit which continues to open up borders inside the European Union will make entry at the perimeter more difficult. Whilst the EU is becoming more liberal towards internal travel of its own citizens, the attitude towards those without citizenship is visibly and dramatically hardening. Of most concern is the fact that little differentiation seems to be made between the legal and the illegal groups of immigrants, and thus both are generally subject to exclusion.

The position of asylum seekers is particularly acute. At one and the same time asylum seekers may be those with the greatest need to be afforded protected status within the Union, and yet are also presumed to be those most likely to circumvent immigration controls in order to enter the European Union illegally. The net effect is that the most 'needy' are seen to be the least 'acceptable'. When immigration (legal and illegal) and asylum are horribly conflated, and where xenophobic nationalism gives rise to racist attacks (which then aggravate misgivings about the scale of entry to the EU), policing immigration, policing racism and policing asylum become inextricably linked.

a)   Numbers and Destinations of Asylum Seekers

The number of asylum seekers arriving in the European Community rose sharply during the late 1980s and early 1990s. In 1992, 556,947 people entered the EC and declared themselves as asylum seekers, compared with 420,150 in the previous year.

Germany alone experienced a sharp increase of 71 per cent in applications for asylum with a total of 438,000 applicants in 1992, whilst other member states saw the numbers of applicants decrease by 50,000. In addition, Germany had almost 4 in 5 of the total number of asylum seekers in the EC in 1992 (78%). These figures offer startling evidence of the 'pressure' on Germany to absorb refugees. France had 26,852 applications, followed by the UK with 24,610 applications. The remaining states had the following number of applications: Belgium (17,643), the Netherlands (17,148), Denmark (13,855), Spain (12,655), Italy (2,493), Greece (1,965), Luxembourg (1,158) and Portugal (599) (Carvel 1993b). Figures for Ireland are not available.

The proportion of asylum seekers of European origin has increased. For example, 64 per cent of asylum seekers were from other European countries in 1992 compared with 44 per cent in 1991, mainly from the former Yugoslavia, Romania and Bulgaria. In total 356,720 applicants for asylum came from Europe, 103,758 from Africa, 64,148 from Asia, 25,422 from the Middle East and 6,899 from the Americas (Carvel 1993b).

In addition, many asylum seekers arrived in countries which have close ties with the European Community. According to figures from the London-based European Consultation on Refugees in Exile, in 1992 Austria received 16,000 applications, Finland received 3,625 asylum requests and Norway was the subject of 5,238 applications. The largest number of asylum seekers applied to Sweden (83,200) and Switzerland (18,000).

b)   'Fortress Europe' and Asylum Seekers

Asylum seekers have been subject to an increasing level of hostility over the past five years. The language of those critical of the policies allowing asylum seekers refuge in the European Union can sometimes be viewed as incorporating racist undertones. For example, Rudolf Krause, a German Interior Minister speaking about racial attacks, commented that:

> One must admit that there are asylum seekers who do not behave according to local customs or in a manner befitting our cultural level. (*New Statesman & Society* 1992, p.5).

When such sentiments are coupled with politicians' perceptions of generally unfavourable public attitudes towards over-liberal asylum legislation, a likely consequence is a restriction of the criteria for asylum applications. There is evidence to support this view. The UK and Germany have recently changed their legislation and changes are pending in France, possibly reflecting a resurgence of support for the *Front National.*

Recent information from the United Nations High Commissioner for Refugees (Drüke 1993) showed that the vast majority of asylum seekers have their applications turned down. In 1992, the recognition rate was below 10 per cent in the following countries: Belgium (8%), Spain (6%), Italy (5%), Germany (4%), UK (3%) and Ireland (3%). In non-Union countries the rate of recognition was also low: Austria (10%), Sweden (5%), Switzerland (5%), Norway (2%) and Finland (1%). The recognition rate was much higher only in France (28%) and the Netherlands (14%).

The overall rate of granting asylum applications in EC countries in 1992 was only 9.2 per cent. Out of a total of 556,947 requests for asylum some 506,000 people had their requests turned down.

Under the terms of the 1990 Schengen Implementing Convention and the Dublin Convention of 1990, which are examined in more detail in Chapter 4, the 'external ring' of the European Union is being fortified to reduce the number of applicants for asylum, as well as grants of residence qualification for successful applicants. Applicants will only be able to apply for asylum in one EU country; the first at which they arrive on fleeing their country of origin. The Schengen Information System (SIS) will be crucial in recording applications.

These developments may be seen as a compensatory device of strict 'gate keeping' in order to offset any disadvantages caused by the relaxation of internal controls. However, the effect of these developments will be to restrict entry of non-EU nationals to the Union. It is at odds with the overall EU policy of openness and free movement, and it is wholly at odds with the Declaration which the Trevi Group of ministers made in Paris on 15th December 1989 (see Chapter 4). It is seen by some as ironic that as eastern Europe is 'opening up' in a remarkable way, there is some evidence that western Europe is closing ranks, particularly with respect to developing countries. EU policies towards asylum seekers highlight the 'fortification' of Europe.

c)   **Causes for Concern**

Although the European Union member states guarantee to comply with their obligations under the 1951 Geneva Convention Relating to the Status of Refugees, as well as continuing to allow persons to stay in their territory for 'other compelling reasons', the considerable increase in asylum applications in Europe are giving increasing cause for concern. The United Nations High Commissioner for Refugees is anxious about the high number of claimants who are deemed not to qualify for refugee status or who do not fulfil the criteria to be allowed to stay in EU member states on other compelling grounds (Drüke 1993). There appear to be a number of particular problems.

Perhaps as a function of the increasing number of claimants and the pressure on decision-making mechanisms, there is evidence of a tendency to treat some applications as 'manifestly unfounded' and to use 'accelerated procedures' for decision making, especially in cases of deliberate deception or abuse of the asylum procedures. The UNHCR takes the view that decisions on manifestly unfounded applications may fail to do justice to their inherently complex nature, and that in cases of asylum applicants who give false statements to the authorities this does not in itself vitiate an asylum application. In addition, most states in Europe deny entry to asylum applicants if they come from a so-called 'safe third country' (that is, country of first asylum) where it is deemed to be reasonable to return the applicant on the presumption that there will be access to a fair procedure in that third country.

The UNHCR offers the example of Germany which sees all of its neighbouring countries as 'safe countries' and is concerned that there is an increasing tendency to return asylum seekers to a country through which they passed *en route* to their preferred destination, and is worried that the new German asylum procedures will have a 'domino effect' on other European states. Two court decisions in late 1993, however, suggested that both Greece (in the case of an Iraqi asylum seeker passing through Turkey and Greece before reaching Germany) and the Czech Republic could not be considered as safe countries. To some extent these decisions throw the basis of the new German asylum legislation into question.

The position in France is that the Constitutional Council declared on 13th August 1993 that the new French law on immigration of July 1993 does not conform to the Constitution, specifically the provisions which would deny entry at the border. The Court ruled that an asylum applicant which has been rejected in another European country may have his or her case examined in France. By implication this means that the Schengen Convention provisions of 'one chance' only applications are non-applicable in France, and this necessitates a constitutional change which is expected to be approved by the end of 1993.

2.10.5   *Visas for Entry to EC Countries*

The strengthening of the external border of the European Union is also involving changes to visa policies. A common visa will be introduced for all EC countries under Article 100c of the Treaty Establishing the European Community (the EC Treaty), now that the Treaty on European Union (the Maastricht Treaty) has been ratified. This is discussed further in Chapter 4.

For the Schengen partners, agreement has been reached on uniform conditions for entry including the introduction of a common visa valid for all contracting states for a period not exceeding three months. Any visa issued for a period exceeding three months will continue to be a national visa. The nationals of other states will only be allowed to enter Schengen countries if they possess a valid travel document, if they have sufficient means for their stay, and if they are not listed as undesirable aliens or considered to be a danger to public order or security.

In December 1992 the ministers and secretaries of state with responsibility for these matters agreed a series of measures including the basic criteria to determine which states are on the visa list, and the adoption of a proposal for a uniform visa stamp valid for three months. The common approach was confirmed at the first meeting of the Schengen Executive Committee on 18th October 1993.

Three lists have been drawn up by the Schengen working group responsible for visas. The first is a list of approximately 20 countries from which nationals do not require a visa to enter the Schengen territory. The second is a list of countries (123 countries by October 1993) the nationals of which require visas to enter the Schengen states. The third is a list of countries where one Schengen state will require visas from visiting nationals who will only be allowed to enter that particular Schengen state. This last category is known as the 'grey list'. The various Schengen lists will almost certainly provide the basis for the EC-wide scheme of common visas to be implemented under the new Article 100c in the EC Treaty.

The harmonisation of visa policies is possibly a euphemism for the introduction of visa obligations for nationals from many developing countries. Only citizens from countries with a predominantly white population or a rich population will be allowed to visit western Europe without a visa (Groenendijk 1989). All the countries on the 'negative list' (where visas are required by all Schengen countries) are in Africa, Asia, South and Central America, as well as countries in eastern Europe.

Again, it appears that the policy of securing the external frontier of the European Union will help create a fortified EU in which the nationals of poorer nations will not be welcome, even if only to visit.

2.10.6   The Role of Customs

The role of customs must not be neglected in a discussion of the attempts to tighten controls at the external frontiers of the European Union. Customs checks at border crossings, as discussed earlier, have had an impact in controlling the import of narcotics and other items.   British data show that HM Customs and Excise seize only 14 per cent of total UK drug seizures *by number* but as much as 93 per cent *by weight* (House of Commons 1990b, p.173). A senior member of HM Customs and Excise pointed out to the research team that customs controls are essential because at the point of importation the traffickers are at their weakest. In addition, drugs seized at this point are often at their highest purity, as well as affording customs the maximum scope for intelligence on trafficking operations.

Spot checks will continue to be carried out by customs officials in the UK regardless of whether the border is internal or external. As the UK HM Customs and Excise Department argued:

> The single market will bring a host of real and evident changes for travellers from 1 January 1993. No more routine and irksome Customs formalities and no more complaining that your allowance of duty paid goods will not last five minutes! But these advantages would soon appear quite trivial if the UK were to be flooded with drugs, child pornography, weapons, rabies and the like after 1 January 1993. Customs are committed to protecting society against such threats and this is why they will continue to carry out some spot checks. (*Customs News* 1992, p.3).

Figures for 1989–90 indicate that UK Customs also seized 1,546 live animals and birds and 188 plants, all from endangered species; over 32,000 obscene or indecent items; 1,600 guns; and other items of strategic importance such as nuclear triggers and parts of the alleged Iraqi 'supergun'. In the first quarter of 1992 eleven cases of suspected illegal movements of nuclear materials had been discovered in seven countries (Austria, Bulgaria, the former CIS, Hungary, Italy, Norway and Switzerland).

Customs controls therefore have an important role in policing Europe's external frontier and are discussed in further detail in Chapter 5. In addition, it is worth noting that increased co-operation between customs, police and intelligence services in many member states has become more necessary because of the consequences of the removal of internal border controls.

2.10.7   The External Frontiers Policy

There is sufficient evidence to confirm that strengthening the external perimeter of Europe is something of a compensatory device for opening up its internal frontiers. This has a superficial plausibility, as well as a certain political attraction.

Whatever its attraction it does not appear to be a wholly feasible option. There is no single external boundary to be patrolled. There are many points of exit and entry out of and into the Union, ranging in type from coastlines and rivers to land borders and airports. Bilateral agreements between member states and countries outside the European Union also undermine the idea of a tight external border – and some of these countries have declared they are not going to dispense with their own bilateral agreements with non-Union states. The 'hard outer shell' may have some political currency, but it is impossible to operationalise fully. It is only as strong as its weakest link.

In addition, whether or not the strengthened external border functions successfully it certainly has significant political credibility – and this alone has real consequences. The principal effects are likely to be a clamp down on illegal immigration, restrictions on legal immigration, toughened criteria for asylum seekers and more targeted visa policies. Perhaps inadvertently, the price being paid for freedom of movement within Europe is that getting into Europe becomes correspondingly more difficult.

It is clear that the idea of Europe without frontiers was driven essentially by economic liberalism, and it is therefore ironic that one consequence (fortress Europe) is seen as a threat by other liberals who view civil liberties, particularly for non-European Union nationals, as being in danger from the new arrangements.

2.11   Assessment: A Case of Misplaced Fears?

Questions about the implications and effects of the removal of border controls for policing in Europe are not easily answered. The debate has been continuing for many years and opinion – of police personnel, politicians, civil servants, journalists, academics and of course the 344 million citizens of Europe – is much divided. There seems little consensus on the implications of open frontiers for crime and policing. Whilst this might be a source of frustration for those wanting an instant answer, the uncertainty makes the debate all the more relevant and important.

The central question is whether the benefits of the removal of internal border controls in the European Union outweigh the costs in terms of increased crime and criminal activity.

2.11.1   *An Increase in Criminal Activity?*

a)   **Rising Crime**

Many fears have been expressed about a possible increase in criminal activities in Europe without frontiers, particularly with respect to international organised crime, terrorism and drugs trafficking. As Sir Roger Birch, former Chief Constable of the UK's Sussex Police and Chairman of the International Advisory Committee of the Association of Chief Police Officers (ACPO), commented:

> [...] it is my belief that there are many good class criminals who will be encouraged to expand their activities across internal boundaries in the belief that 1st January 1993 will produce a sudden relaxation in police and customs activity. (Birch 1992a, p.4).

Birch was not alone in this view. Representatives of the police services in the UK (ACPO, ACPO (Scotland), the Superintendents' Association and the Police

Federation), in their submission of evidence to the 1990 UK House of Commons Home Affairs Committee enquiry into Practical Police Co-operation in the European Community, gave the following response to a question on the extent of cross-border crime following the removal of internal border controls:

> It is reasonable to assume that the relaxation of frontier controls will enable criminals and fugitives to move more freely throughout Europe than has previously been the case and displacement of crime may acquire an international dimension. (House of Commons 1990b, p.18).

The evidence then went on to outline the areas where crime could increase as a result of the relaxation of border controls. In their view, the British police anticipated that 'organised crime and the numbers of travelling criminals will increase, with terrorism and illegal drugs trafficking being major concerns' (ibid.). Although no hard evidence was given, a large increase in international crime was predicted with the establishment of the Single Market. According to another view:

> Maintaining effective policing and security in the face of the vicious tide of European and international crime, terrorism and drugs trafficking will remain a central consideration in the Government's attitude to 1992. (Scottish Home and Health Department 1990b, p.10).

In Britain, a House of Lords European Communities Select Committee Report on 1992 and border controls summarised the various misgivings about the free movement of persons as follows:

> There is genuine fear that abolition of border control of people will lead to an enormous increase in drug smuggling, organised crime, terrorist attacks and to uncontrolled movement of immigrants. (House of Lords 1989).

These statements certainly reflect genuine anxieties about post-1992 European crime levels but two important points should be made.

First, there is an inverse relationship between the rhetoric in the statements and the evidence offered to support them. Secondly, no attempt is made to differentiate between the fear of crime and the actual risks of criminal victimisation. The fears may be genuine, but they are almost certainly misplaced. Abolishing controls at the frontiers will add little or nothing to the scope for international crime of a serious nature. It is understandable that some politicians engage in such polemics not least because they cannot afford not to, especially when they are aided and abetted by news media in search of a good story.

b)   No Major Impact

Although the fear of an explosive 'crime wave' in Europe following the abolition of internal borders may be real, there is very little evidence to support this conclusion. The weight of the data points in the opposite direction, namely that the borders make little or no difference to the overall levels of crime.

i)   Germany

An analysis of the border-defence statistics in Germany for the period 1980 to 1989 suggested that the rate of arrest at borders was 2.9 arrests per 100,000 border crossings (Kühne 1993). The implication of this finding is that, even in the period prior to the formal abolition of border controls, the contribution of checks at the western border of Germany to the maintenance of internal security was marginal. The borders were never a 'serious obstacle' to the committed criminal. Kühne's view was that border controls only allow the authorities to 'catch the little stupid offenders', that is those whose demeanour and bearing offer *prima facie* evidence of criminal activities. Border controls may impress the casual delinquent, but for the more accomplished offender, one with a tactical awareness of border controls, the intelligent option was (and remains) to cross the 'green border' or a point on the frontier known not to be subject to checks. The abolition of internal frontiers will not, therefore, add to the 'border deficit', not least because they were permeable in the first place – at least with respect to offenders who operated in a premeditated and purposeful manner.

ii)   Switzerland

A similar study in Switzerland suggested that of 400,000 offences each year registered by the police at the federal level as many as 20 per cent of offenders known to the police had no legal residence in Switzerland. If these offenders had been stopped at the frontier it would have required some 80,000 successful checks out of a total of 75 million legal and unproblematic passages of the border (Killias 1993). It would be impossible to target these offenders without unduly harassing millions of travellers who would not warrant being stopped.

iii)   Abolition of Frontiers

An important general point has been made by a criminologist from the University of Lausanne in Switzerland, namely that 'it may not be an exaggeration that criminal organisations abolished national boundaries long ago' (Killias 1993, p.9). Most senior police and customs respondents would agree with this conclusion. It may well be the case that the border is more of a handicap for the police and prosecution authorities than for the offenders. It does, however, have an interesting implication for crime control. Paradoxically, and contrary to popular opinion, it may not be the crime trade which will take advantage of the open borders within the European Union but the law enforcement agencies for whom barriers against fruitful co-operation are gradually being removed (van Duyne 1993).

2.11.2   An Increase in Opportunities?

Whilst some commentators have asserted an automatic increase in crime in Europe with the removal of internal border controls, others have been more cautious in their assessment, pointing instead to an increase in opportunities for crime.

For example, evidence submitted by the CSPO to the Home Affairs Committee in 1990 suggested that 'the opportunities for increased crime [...] must surely be a significant consideration' (House of Commons 1990b, p.181). Similarly, Sir John Dellow, Deputy Commissioner of the Metropolitan Police, commented that 'the opportunity to commit crime is increasing' (ibid, p.105).

Notes from a briefing paper written for members of the Surrey Constabulary in southern England expanded on these sentiments:

> Much has been written about the impact of the Single European State. [...] Although there is no clear evidence to suggest a dramatic overnight effect on policing in Surrey, the Force must be proactive to prevent being overtaken by events without adequate realisation of the extent of the potential for change. (Surrey Constabulary 1992, p.3).

The emphasis, here and elsewhere in the document, is that changes will be substantial, but gradual. Rather than speculating wildly about the consequences of the removal of internal border controls, this more cautious approach points towards more slow-paced change – for both criminals and the police.

This view was echoed elsewhere in interviews with respondents to this study. In Germany, *Inspektor der Bereitschaftspolizeien der Länder*, Gilbert Welter and Herr Scheefeld, *Polizei Direktor*, thought that there was something of a problem, but that through Schengen there were improved opportunities to counteract crime (1990, personal interviews). Herr Kayser and Herr Wolters of the *Bundeskriminalamt* predicted some increase in crime, principally because of less deterrence, but no sudden upsurge or 'tidal wave' (1990, personal interviews).

Similarly, Tove Steen Sorensen of the Copenhagen Police was reluctant to predict a sudden increase in criminality (1990, personal interview). Lieutenant-Colonel Georges Rauchs, *Directeur Adjoint de la Police Luxembourgeoise*, supposed that there would not be a significant increase in crime (1990, personal interview). Organised crime is already organised, and border checks do not affect these criminal networks.

Heiner Busch, of the Free University of Berlin, did not predict a sudden upsurge in crime or a significant change in the type of crime after 1992 (1990, personal interview). Piet van Reenen, then Director of the Police Academy, Netherlands, considered that a Europe without internal frontiers would see 'no difference' in the types and levels of crime (1990, personal interview).

On the other hand, J. Peek, Deputy Director of Police, Ministry of Justice for the Netherlands, saw traditional crime, especially bank robbery, as increasing in post-1992 Europe, but also anticipated a significant increase in money laundering (1990, personal interview).

It is almost impossible to predict accurately the effect of the removal of internal border controls on crime levels in Europe. The commentaries show wide variation – from a 'tidal wave' of very serious crime (for example, terrorism and drugs trafficking) at one extreme, to little or no change at the other extreme. It is interesting to note that in general it is the politicians who incline to the former (alarmist view), whilst the majority of police respondents tend to offer the latter (less alarmist) opinion.

The view of the research team is that increased offender mobility may bring a change in the ways in which offenders operationalise their criminality. At its most basic level, the removal of internal frontiers will facilitate some criminal activity in a choice of jurisdictions (Imbert 1989, p.1174). The removal of border controls in themselves will not produce an automatic increase in rates of serious crime, such as terrorist activity, organised crime and drugs trafficking.

2.11.3   Crime in Central and Eastern Europe

The recent fundamental political and social changes in central and eastern Europe have implications for crime in the European Union. As the countries in the former communist bloc have shifted to a market economy, in the rush to adopt a capitalist ethic there has been widespread unemployment and (officially recognised) rapid inflation. In Russia, for example, the average purchasing power is plummeting and the average Russian family must spend 80 per cent or more of its income on basic subsistence. In addition, the life savings of many have been wiped out by inflation. These substantial economic changes have knock-on effects on the provision of social welfare, health and education (Joutsen 1993).

The increasing problems of day-to-day survival have had an enormous impact on crime, particularly the rise in organised crime through profiteering and speculation – essentially unauthorised free enterprise. There are two illegal markets. The so-called 'black market' is entirely illegal and deals mainly in smuggled goods, foreign currency, pornography and drugs. The 'grey market' provides goods and services in competition with the state-controlled market, but at free market prices. These forms of illegal activities will expand as the number of suitable targets for crime increases and as the number of motivated offenders gets larger. The problem will worsen as the law enforcement authorities become more stretched.

The extent to which the real growth in organised crime in central and eastern Europe will begin to cross the borders from the east into the European Union is not yet clear. To date it has occurred only on a small scale, principally in relation to organised theft, drugs trafficking and the illegal sale of firearms. This may be because there is a lack of suitable international criminal contacts, or due to the fact that sufficient criminal opportunities are available in the domestic market. In addition, operating in the west may be problematic because it is more expensive and there may well be competition from local organised crime, as well as more efficient law enforcement agencies.

Conversely, the 'economic magnet' of the EU for organised criminal activities may prove to be more powerful than the domestic market in eastern Europe because of the size of the potential rewards, irrespective of the increased risk and self evident disincentives. It would be naïve not to treat the potential of imported crime from the east as a new and significant factor in policing the European Union.

2.12   The Need for Further Research

The lack of data on European crime levels is recognised as a major problem by many working in the field. Merle Hoefman, from the Dutch police's CRI Europe Unit in The Hague, was unambiguous and forthright in her view that the greatest problem facing co-operative police efforts was the 'almost total lack of high quality research'. Basic information on crime and trends in crime, together with data on the structure, organisation and training of police officers throughout Europe, was not available. There were isolated pockets of information but nothing of sufficient quality to inform European-wide co-operative efforts. The starting point had to be basic information (1990, personal interview).

Similarly, a recent European Parliament Report on the links between drugs trafficking and organised crime noted:

> Independent scientific research is necessary in those areas where insight is a prerequisite for taking action and decisions, of which the negative consequences are incalculable and of which the results are more disadvantageous than the small successes of the investigation force (e.g. the legal admissibility of methods to combat drugs). (European Parliament 1992, p.6).

The Report continued:

> The EC should also induce research into the correlation between organized crime and rising business crime on the one hand, and their direct detrimental

effects on the social situation of the people as well as on the environment on the other hand, so that the awareness of the fact that such crime is a clear infringement of human rights will be sharpened. This way the tendency to trivialise particularly business crime could be reduced and persons involved could more easily be charged and condemned.

In a similar vein, the meeting of justice and interior ministers resolved at their meeting on 6th – 7th May 1993 that the systematic collection and analysis of information should be undertaken periodically to assess the threat and spread of organised crime. The ministers were reported as emphasising the point that an in-depth knowledge of the extent of the problem was essential for the development of appropriate strategies to combat organised crime (Danish Ministry of Justice Press Release, 7th May 1993).

This Report supports these and other calls for further research into the levels and nature of crime (of all types) in the European Union, as a contribution towards the development of effective, co-operative police strategies.

It is only with the advent of the Maastricht Treaty, and the plans for greater co-ordination of policing policy in the European Union, that the European Commission has been prompted to start collecting the relevant crime statistics. Their first reports are expected in the autumn of 1993. An initial problem was the lack of expertise within the Commission's EUROSTAT division for compiling and analysing crime statistics.

It is manifestly unsatisfactory that many of the arguments for greater police co-operation in Europe are asserted in the absence of concrete data on crime. The fears of serious crime may be genuine, as indeed might the risks, but well-informed policing policies need to be underpinned by a much clearer knowledge and understanding of the extent of crime.

Valid and reliable data are required, and they are needed on a European-wide basis. This Report supports the idea of a European Centre for Crime Research, partly in order to act as a conduit for disseminating existing national crime data throughout the member states, but also in order to generate new data on a pan-European basis using a common statistical and analytical framework. This is a substantial undertaking, as the analysts at EUROSTAT have realised.

2.13　Misplaced Fears, Moral Panics and Crime Policy

2.13.1　The Construction of a Moral Panic: All at Sea

From this brief review of statements and commentaries on the likely levels of serious crime in the European Union, with the relaxation of border controls, a key point must be made about language used in the construction of the arguments.

The quotations have a high rhetorical content and are rich in symbolic power. They are often strong on sentiment but lacking in substance. The commentators frequently use a specific set of images, often relating to the sea; they talk of rising tides, tidal waves and inexorable forces. The commentators also use a militaristic vocabulary when describing the appropriate response to such threats; they talk of 'fighting back'. Emotive language like this can reinforce ideas about an escalation of crime. A consequence is that it establishes the threat as real. Whilst this may be unintended, it is still problematic, as Busch points out:

> In order to gain public acceptance for 'crime control' policies, use is made of the demagogical trilogism of drugs, organized crime and immigration, thereby provoking irrational feelings of fear and rejection. (Busch 1992, p.1).

2.13.2   Moral Panics and Crime Policy

It is possible to detect some sort of 'moral panic' when looking at statements predicting future European crime levels. The term moral panic refers to a 'public fear of crime, deviance and disorder; it implies that such fear is exaggerated and out of proportion to the real threat offered' (Muncie 1987, p.42). The notion of a moral panic about the possible crime levels facing the European Union in the absence of hard data is not a view unique to this Report. As Jepson has suggested, what this amounts to, at an ideological level, is a resort to 'magic thinking' about crime (Jepson 1986; 1990 personal interview). It is underpinned by the use of crude moral sentiments rather than hard data, and such scaremongering offers a non-factual basis for crime control. The worries and concerns may be real enough, but in themselves they do not justify social policy responses.

The constant parade of emotive language about the inexorable rising tide of lawlessness, in the public discourse of politicians and professionals, creates what Bigo (1992) calls an 'internal security continuum' – the perception of an indivisible security deficit across the borderless new Europe. In turn, the idea of a pan-European security field becomes embedded in the rhetoric, and perhaps the institutions, of the frontierless Europe (Den Boer and Walker 1993).

The absence of research and genuine crime data means that there is a missing link between concern and crime policy. Nevertheless, this combination of well-intentioned 'crime-fighting' sentiment with a sense of high moral purpose is often sufficient to produce real and rapid changes in criminal justice practices. There are two key points to be made about the likely consequences of this. Both are crucial to the future of police co-operation in Europe.

a)   Promoting Police Co-operation

First, constructing a 'moral panic' around serious crime is likely to prove effective in the promotion of international police co-operation. Statements such as those given above can easily influence public perceptions of the likelihood of a large and sudden increase in serious crime in Europe. A call by the public, politicians and law enforcement agencies for increased European police action and co-operation, in the light of this threat, makes complete sense. As Dorn notes, it is also functional for police agencies:

> The hypothesis that the free movement in the Single Market of 1993 will stimulate a big increase in large-scale, organised crime definitely has popular appeal. It fits in with the resurgence of nationalistic feelings in Europe and eastern Europe, and with suspicion of all things 'foreign'. Also, it may be said to be functional for police agencies, since the European-wide wave of concern over major crime, including large-scale drugs trafficking, helps to release financial resources for policing, and also has helped legitimise the creation of new police powers in several countries. (Dorn 1992, p.7).

A fear of crime manufactured in the fashion outlined in this chapter might thus be viewed as an argument for increased resources and powers for the police forces of Europe.

The creation of a fear of a European crime wave is also functional in consolidating moves towards practical police co-operation in Europe. The *Union Internationale des Syndicats de Police* (UISP – a federation of European police unions) noted that:

> The complete transformation undergone in eastern and south eastern Europe has led – on account of the explosive growth in criminality – to the necessity of intensifying collaboration with the police forces of these countries. (UISP 1992, p.1).

Monica Den Boer, a researcher on an Edinburgh University project investigating a system for European Police Co-operation in 1992, sums up the situation when she writes:

> The burden of international crime has therefore been with us for years, but despite the fact that it has been closely monitored by professionals (police, academics) for some time now, one still creates the impression as if this is a recent phenomenon. Although the vigour with which international crime strikes should be far from underestimated, this justification resembles the act of taking an old bunny out of a hat to legitimise the intensification of European police co-operation. International crime does not establish a greater threat to the internal security of EC Member States than a decade ago. Perhaps an admission that one was slow to react would be more appropriate. (Den Boer 1992a, p.14).

However old the 'bunny' in the conjurer's trick might be, and however dangerous, the magic worked by a moral panic may be a powerful variable in stimulating both the perceived need for greater police co-operation and, in turn, the actual development of collaborative mechanisms.

b)   Creating Repressive Social Policies

Secondly, the upsurge of interest in combating crime may generate repressive social policies out of all proportion to the size and nature of the problem. Criminal justice could become based increasingly on measures which are more expressive of moral sentiment than instruments for social reform. As a number of commentators have warned, 'moral panics' have been instrumental in creating demands for tougher modes of state control (Cohen 1972; Hall *et al* 1978; Jepson 1986, p.1).

For example, if police actions aimed at stopping illegal drugs trafficking were to involve, say, compulsory identity cards, super-secure external frontiers, random 'stops and searches', increased police powers, ease of prosecution and, ultimately, tougher penalties, there are some who would argue that the costs involved would outweigh the advantages to the police and the state. Indeed, the European Parliament has explored this trade-off, pointing to the possibility that the 'costs' of securing convictions may be out of proportion to the crime control 'benefits' (European Parliament 1992, p.6).

This argument is being used increasingly by commentators on the process and progress of European Union, particularly with regard to the implications for civil liberties of formal structures for police co-operation such as the Schengen Information System (details of which are found in Chapter 6). As Busch argues:

'Crime Control' is the most cherished slogan of the adepts of the security state. Crime must be combatted even before it can be committed. Potential threats to public order must be detected before they can become reality. From such a point of view even the most harmless citizen must be seen as a potential future criminal and thus deserves preventive police surveillance. (Busch 1992, p.1).

This is a serious issue, although it is one often dismissed by politicians and law enforcement agencies. Den Boer quotes the views of Sir James Hopkins:

The open frontier system could not be better for the terrorist or for the drug cartel and to counteract them we need more and more exchanges of information. Crimes are now worldwide, let alone European-wide and the spreading of data is a vital way of combating them. There are those who say that this impinges on civil rights. That is not my view. (Den Boer 1992a, p.15).

2.14 Summary of Findings

2.14.1 There is a serious lack of knowledge and understanding about the extent and type of crime in Europe:

- The lack of data is recognised to be a major problem by many working in the field.

- The ignorance of the facts of crime is impeding the development of appropriate structures and strategies to combat crime in Europe.

- The vacuum is being filled with some wild and frightening predictions about the rising tide of crime in the new Europe.

2.14.2 It is difficult to predict with any certainty the likely effects on the levels of crime of a Europe without frontiers, but the following conclusions seem supported by the small amount of available evidence:

- International terrorism will neither increase nor decrease as a consequence of the open borders policy but increased co-operation on intelligence matters will continue to be essential.

- The relaxation of internal border controls is unlikely to see the pattern of organised drugs trafficking within the European Union change significantly, although the increased smuggling of smaller quantities of drugs is more likely. The potential for an increase in drugs trafficking from eastern Europe should not be underestimated.

- Lower-level crime, particularly acquisitive crime, is likely to increase because of greater freedom of movement.

- This is likely to be particularly true of thefts of motor vehicles.

- There is an increasing market for stolen precious art and antiques. Open borders facilitate crime involving high-value easily transportable goods.

- The free movement of capital, together with a common market for financial services, is likely to stimulate fraud and other business-related crime. Informed sources suggest that if there is one sort of crime which will probably prosper, and which might be stimulated, in an open Europe, it is fraud. Although victimisation in commercial crime is less visible than other types of crime, the extent of fraud in the European Union is substantial, including significant cross-border commercial crime, abuse of financial regulations, cheque-card and credit-card fraud and fraud against the EC itself.

- Environmental crime poses great long-term risks to the environment and ecology of the European Union.

2.14.3   The notion of a secure 'ring of steel' around the external frontiers of the European Union is not a wholly feasible proposition:

- There is no agreement as to what constitutes an internal and external boundary. For example, an airport may be both.

- Even with previously existing frontiers, there was already significant penetration by illegal immigration, although estimates about the precise figure vary wildly. Legal immigration is estimated to be around 10 million persons in the European Union. Illegal immigration is estimated to be in excess of 1.5 million persons.

- There are particular concerns about the permeability of the external borders and the near-impossibility of securing the external frontiers, although the nine signatories to the Schengen Agreements are optimistic that the 'ring of steel' can be made secure.

- Bilateral agreements between EU countries and non-EU states make step-by-step entry more probable.

- The disintegration of the former USSR and communist bloc countries is causing large-scale illegal immigration, particularly into Germany. Illegal immigrants may turn to crime to pay for their 'passage' into the European Union or to support themselves once they have entered.

- Extradition arrangements are in place in the European Union. Most of the states are signatories to the European Convention on Extradition although this cannot be described as a wholly effective instrument for judicial co-operation. Obstacles to extradition may be presented which are not covered by the Convention.

- Customs controls will change as a consequence of the relaxation of internal border controls and a tightening of external border controls. The use of surveillance and intelligence by customs services will increase.

2.14.4 **The Schengen Group countries have agreed uniform conditions for entry to the nine states, which will have far-reaching implications for non-Schengen nationals from outside the European Union:**

- Visa requirements will restrict the entry of non-EU nationals especially from developing countries.

- Asylum will be made more difficult, and the tightening of procedures for dealing with applicants for asylum may result in the criminalisation of asylum seekers.

- The spirit which continues to open up borders inside the European Union will make entry at the perimeter more difficult. Whilst the EU is becoming more liberal towards internal travel of its own citizens, the attitude towards those without citizenship is visibly and dramatically hardening. Of most concern is the fact that little differentiation seems to be made between the legal and the illegal groups of immigrants, and thus both are generally subject to exclusion.

- Article 100c in the EC Treaty provides for the introduction of an EC-wide scheme of visas, following ratification of the Maastricht Treaty.

2.14.5 **A consequence of speculation about the effects of the removal of internal border controls on the levels of crime in Europe has been:**

- A 'moral panic' about the level of crime, exaggerating the threat posed by the removal of internal border controls.

- Worry and concern about repressive policies as part of an over reaction to the perceived threat of crime.

2.15 Proposals

2.15.1 **Research and discussion on crime in Europe needs to move beyond predictable concerns about terrorism and drugs trafficking. In addition, new research should concentrate on acquisitive crimes related to the free movement of people and also investigate business crime related to the free movement of capital, especially fraud.**

Too much attention has been given to the crimes which cause most anxiety but where the risk of victimisation is low, and too little attention has been paid to offences which receive little publicity but where the risks are real and the harm considerable. There is an imbalance which needs rectifying. For example, much more attention could be paid to firearms control and availability. There are differences between the European Union states which will remain until a recent EC Directive takes effect.

2.15.2 **Consideration should be given, as a matter of priority, to the establishment of a European unit for the co-ordination of activities against fraud and the policing of fraud.**

This would need to have operational capabilities. There are enormous difficulties in tracking down international business crime and divorcing 'intelligence' and 'operations' will be counter-productive. This may need legislation and will certainly need resourcing properly. This unit should be developed with the benefit of the experience of UCLAF.

2.15.3 **Environmental crime threatens the health of the European Union's ecosystem, and research is urgently needed into the levels and implications of environmental crime.**

Environmental crime threatens everyone, including those who perpetrate it. It poses great risks to the health of the planet, and the long-term costs are incalculable.

2.15.4 **Europe as a whole, and at the highest level, needs to re-think its position with respect to conditions of entry for non-European Union nationals. There is evidence of an inner-Europe excluding non-Union nationals.**

The price of freedom of movement within Europe may be to restrict the right of entry for people from outside Europe. This would seem incompatible with the spirit of 'open borders', although some degree of control is essential. There is a subtle balance to be struck.

2.15.5 **Policing policies must not be made in the absence of high-quality research. Fear of crime is easily generated by unsubstantiated claims from so-called experts. A consequence of this may be repressive social policies.**

Policing the European Union needs to be well-organised, but the structure of collaborative efforts needs to be based on fact not scaremongering fantasy. Policy makers should pay attention to the warnings of the civil liberties lobby on the dangers of a policing policy constructed on the basis of moral panics.

2.15.6 **In order for high-quality research to be undertaken a European Centre for Research into Crime should be established.**

Such a Centre would need to be adequately funded. Contributions could come from European Union governments or from EC institutions. The research undertaken should be European in nature and benefit from the wealth of experience available across Europe. Academics and practitioners from all European countries should be actively involved in the programme.

A pan-European, strategic approach to police co-operation can only be effective if it is premised on high-quality information about types and levels of crime, and trends in crime over time. These point to the need for a European Centre for Research into Crime. To avoid disagreement over its location the Centre should be federal in nature with one or two sites in each European Union country.

CHAPTER 3

POLICE FORCES IN THE
EUROPEAN UNION

The law enforcement agencies which operate in the twelve countries of the European Union are outlined in this chapter. It concentrates on the various police organisations, but mentions in passing other law enforcement agencies which have powers in some countries, such as customs and excise.

The chapter adopts a common approach for each country. First, some general background information is given, noting in particular the country's administrative structure as this often affects police operational organisation and accountability. Secondly, each country's judicial system is outlined in brief. Thirdly, the organisation and operation of the country's police are described and any unusual or interesting points noted. The chapter concludes with a discussion of training initiatives for police within the European Union.

3.1 Comparing the Police Forces in the European Union

3.1.1 Lack of Published Sources

There appears to be a paucity of comparative accounts of different European policing organisations and structures in English. Although some reference guides to the law enforcement agencies in the world do exist (Andrade 1985; Kurian 1989) the accuracy of such accounts is sometimes doubtful. The French *Institute des Hautes Études de la Sécurité Intérieure* (IHESI) has published (in French) a comparative account of six EC countries (Erbes *et al* 1992). No full, comparative and up-to-date account of the policing systems in the 12 European Union countries exists in the English language.

3.1.2 Research Difficulties

In researching background information on the police forces of the 12 member states, it soon became clear that it was in fact difficult to obtain accurate information on policing in each country. Some forces in the EU produce reports and brochures detailing their activities, but by no means all. Critical comment is obviously absent from such accounts. In this study, much of the most valuable information came from interviews with key respondents who were often able to present a more accurate picture.

One major problem proved to be finding figures on the numbers of police in each European Union country. The figures found by the researchers, from different sources, often varied greatly, and no one source seemed to have the monopoly on reliability. Table 3.1 and Figure 3.1 present figures which are indicative of the numbers of police officers in each force in each European Union country.

3.1.3   Definitions of Police

Definitions of police and policing vary between countries. One view, which would command widespread support, is that policing:

> [...] is about the regulation of social conflict and the representation of social authority. (Reiner 1993, p. ii).

Another view, which may command less support, is that police officers are:

> [...] people authorized by a group to regulate interpersonal relations within the group through the application of physical force. (Bayley 1985, p.7).

These broad definitions cover all the forces discussed in this Report. Some definitions and inclusions may seem strange to police from other countries; the strategy here has been to include as police all those whose work is defined as such in their own country.

3.1.4   Towards a Comparative Framework

As yet, no suitable comparative framework has been produced to assist a comparison of policing systems in the European Union, although steps have been taken in that direction (Mawby 1992).

This is a task for a separate book, and research for this is under way at the CSPO. In this chapter discussion is confined to mapping out in brief the organisational structure and operational duties of the police forces in each country. Some general background on each country is included, as is a brief description of the judicial systems in operation. Certain aspects of policing are not included in this brief survey, either because of lack of space in this Report, or lack of information at the time of going to press. These include accounts of the historical development of policing in each country, detailed discussions of recruitment and training practices, discussions of codes of conduct for each force, and an account of the cultures of policing in each force.

The UK police forces are described in greater detail here than other forces. This is not only because information on these forces is more readily available to the research team, but also, and more importantly, because the level of detail given indicates the amount of information that the research team would wish to see available on all the forces in the European Union, for comparative purposes.

Table 3.1 Principal Police Forces in the European Union

Country	Police Force		Number of Police	Population (millions)	Number of Population Per Police Officer
Belgium	*Gendarmerie*		15,647		
	Police Communale		15,704		
	Police Judiciare		1,340		
		Sub total	**32,691**	9.97	305
Denmark	*Rigspolititiet*				
		Sub total	**10,300**	5.14	499
France	*Police Nationale*		116,300		
	Gendarmerie Nationale		96,313		
	Police Municipale		15,000		
		Sub total	**227,613**	56.18	247
Germany	*Landespolizeien*		255,047		
	Bundpolizei		27,700		
		Sub total	**282,747**	79.50	281
Greece	Hellenic Police				
		Sub total	**38,783**	10.14	261
Ireland	*Garda Siochana*				
		Sub total	**10,500**	3.54	337
Italy	*Arma dei Carabinieri*		104,211		
	Polizei de Stato		96,178		
	Guardia di Financia		57,181		
	Vigili Urbani		25,922		
	Others		18,000		
		Sub total	**301,492**	57.60	191
Luxembourg	National Police		500		
	Gendarmerie		600		
		Sub total	**1,100**	0.39	355
Netherlands	25 Regional Forces and 1 Central Force				
		Sub total	**49,500**	14.89	301
Portugal	*Policia de Seguranca Publica*		18,641		
	Guarda Nacional Republicana		17,212		
	Guarda Fiscal		7,795		
	Policia Judiciara		1,921		
	Policia Maritima		500		
	Aliens Police		700		
		Sub total	**46,769**	10.30	220
Spain	*Cuerpo Nacional de Policia*		51,109		
	Guarda Civil		75,346		
	Policia Autonomica		15,000		
	Municipal Police Corps		40,000		
		Sub total	**181,455**	38.96	215
United Kingdom	52 Semi-Autonomous Forces				
		Sub total	**154,738**	57.60	372
European Union			**1,337,688**	**344.21**	**257**

Figure 3.1 Number of Population Per Police Officer by European Union State, 1993

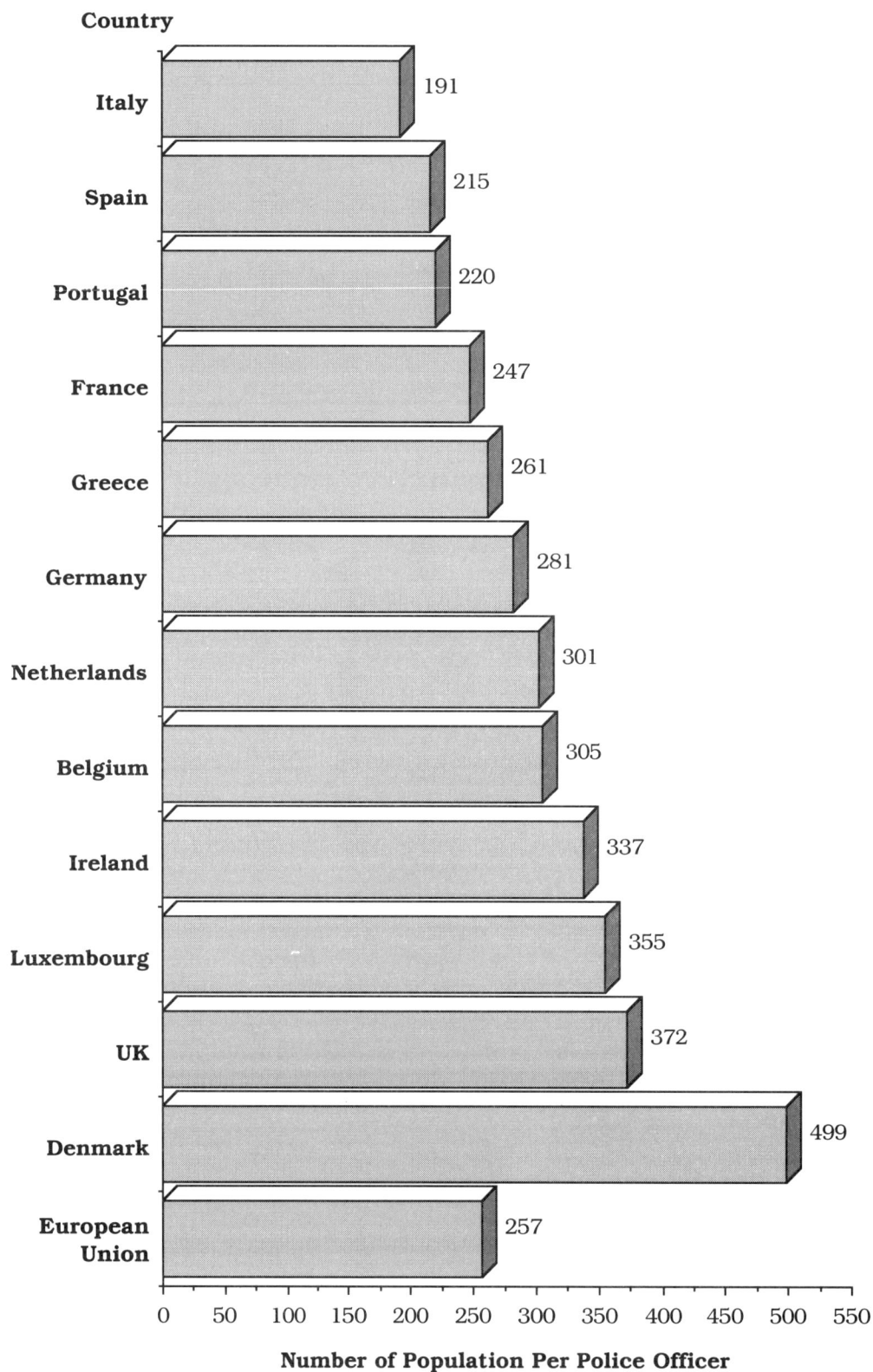

Country

Country	Number of Population Per Police Officer
Italy	191
Spain	215
Portugal	220
France	247
Greece	261
Germany	281
Netherlands	301
Belgium	305
Ireland	337
Luxembourg	355
UK	372
Denmark	499
European Union	257

Number of Population Per Police Officer

3.2   Belgium

3.2.1   *Background*

a)   Politics and Administration

The Kingdom of Belgium has a population of 9.97 million (1991) living in an area of some 30,518 square kilometres, giving a population density of 327 people per square kilometre. The capital is the increasingly important administrative city of Brussels, which requires special policing arrangements. The population is divided between the Flemings (58 per cent) who speak Flemish, and the Walloons (42 per cent) who speak a dialect of French.

Belgium is a constitutional monarchy. Its Constitution (1831, rewritten 1971) allocates legislative power to the bicameral Parliament, made up of the Chamber of Representatives and the Senate, and the King. Executive power resides in the Cabinet led by the Prime Minister. Political power is decentralised. The country is divided into nine provinces, each with a governor and provincial council, and they are divided into administrative districts (*arrondissements*) which are then divided into *communes* headed by a *burgomaster* or mayor. In mid-1993 Beglium began moves towards a more federalist structure.

Elections for the national Parliament and provincial councils take place every four years. There are some 20 active parties but only a few have sufficient seats in the Parliament to enable them to compete for government. The major political parties are the *Christelijke Volkspartij* (CVP), the Flemish-speaking Social Christian Party; the *Parti Socialiste* (PS), the French-speaking Socialist Party; the *Socialistische Partij* (SP), the Flemish-speaking Socialist Party; the *Vlaamse Liberale en Democratische Partij* (VLD), the Flemish-speaking Liberal Party; the *Parti Reformateur Liberal* (PRL), the French-speaking Liberal Reform Party; the *Parti Social Chretien* (PSC), the French-speaking Social Christian Party; and the *Volksunie* (VU), the Flemish People's Party.

Belgium has extensive state provision of welfare, education and other social services. It is strongly committed to freedom and liberal values. For example, opposition to censorship is embodied in the Constitution.

b)   The Benelux Economic Union

After the Second World War, during which Belgium was noted for its strong resistance movement, it joined with Luxembourg and the Netherlands to form the Benelux Economic Union (1947). This was consolidated by the Treaty of the Benelux Economic Union in February 1958 which came into effect in 1960.

The objective was the promotion of economic integration by the co-ordination of policies and the abolition of border controls, which finally took effect in 1970. The Benelux Agreement is supervised by the Committee of Ministers and the Council of Economic Union. Day-to-day administration is under the Secretary General.

3.2.2 Judicial System

The Belgian legal system is based on a mixture of French, Dutch and local law. The judicial system is still principally regulated by the Law of 10th October 1967.

At the lowest level, criminal cases are heard by police tribunals, while civil cases are heard in Justice of the Peace Courts. This division of case-load is fundamental and continues throughout the court system. Criminal cases can only be heard in police courts. At the next level of the court system are the Courts of First Instance, divided into criminal, civil and juvenile courts, and commercial and industrial tribunals. The next tier comprises the Courts of Appeal, Industrial Courts and Courts of Assize. The highest court is the Court of Cassation.

Belgium is divided into 26 judicial districts, each of which has a Court of First Instance, a Commercial Court, an Industrial Court and a District Court. The sub-divisions of the districts are called cantons, of which there are over 200. Each of these has a Justice of the Peace Court. This court has to serve a dual role in smaller cantons, being both the Justice of the Peace Court and the Police Court. Each of the nine Belgian provinces has an Assize Court, composed of three judges and a jury, which tries serious criminal cases. There are five Courts of Appeal, and five Labour Courts of Appeal. The Court of Cassation is based in Brussels. It has three divisions which deal with civil and commercial, criminal and labour law.

3.2.3 Organisation of the Police

There are some 32,691 police officers (ENP 1992a), which is approximately one officer for every 305 inhabitants. Policing in Belgium is carried out by three main policing bodies: *La Gendarmerie*, *La Police Communale* and *La Police Judiciare*. The organisational structure for the police in Belgium appears to result in some conflict over jurisdiction and competence, although reorganisation plans brought into effect in 1992 may have led to improvements.

a) La Gendarmerie

Until 1992 the *Gendarmerie* (*Rijkswacht* in Flemish) was a military-style, armed force responsible for the internal defence of national territory. Both the Minister of Defence and the Minister of Justice exercised some jurisdiction over the functions of the police. However, the law of 18th July 1991 following a Parliamentary Commission of Enquiry removed the military character of the *Gendarmerie*, rendering it a general police service which has competence throughout the whole of Belgium. This law came into effect on the 1st of January 1992. Despite the demilitarisation of the *Gendarmerie* it retains responsibility for a number of functions relating to the armed forces, notably the military police. The Minister of the Interior is now wholly responsible for the functions of the *Gendarmerie*.

There is a total of 15,647 officers in the *Gendarmerie*. The officers are divided into brigades of not less than six persons (depending on the services each brigade is required to provide). The 427 brigades are dispersed across the whole of the Belgian territory. Several brigades comprise a district, of which there are 52. The final grouping of the *Gendarmerie* is in regions. There are five regions with a headquarters situated in Brussels, Ghent, Antwerp, Liège and Charleroi.

The *Gendarmerie* is responsible for investigating offences, and additionally is concerned with the enforcement of law, maintaining public order, traffic services and military police functions.

b)   La Police Communale

La Police Communale (*Gemeentepolitie* in Flemish), the Communal or Municipal Police, is a civil force which like the *Gendarmerie* has responsibilities for general policing, including maintenance of order, traffic, and preventive policing, and also has judicial policing functions, such as the investigation of specific offences. As each commune has its own local force, the Communal Police exercise a kind of administrative police function. However, after their initial investigations, they pass the case on to the Judicial Police.

The Communal Police, of which there are 589 local forces with a total of 15,704 officers (ENP 1992a), is responsible to the *Burgomaster* of each commune for general policing, but the forces' judicial function is under the jurisdiction of the procurators. In the larger towns the Communal Police is commanded by a *Commissaire* of Police, who is an officer of the Judicial Police.

The authority of each local force is limited to that commune, although a force can be authorised to operate in an adjacent area if circumstances so require. The Communal Police is also responsible for certain regulatory functions such as the issue of licences for the sale of alcoholic drinks, aliens' registration and the issue of taxi-drivers' permits.

c)   La Police Judiciare

La Police Judiciare (*Gerechtlijke Politie* in Flemish) or Judicial Police is solely concerned with judicial functions and law enforcement. This is primarily a reactive role with no competence in a preventative or administrative function. It acts as a detective and investigative body for the procurators, collating evidence and bringing the accused before the courts. Cases assigned to the Judicial Police are usually of an important or delicate nature. Often the other police forces have already been involved in the case since the forces all exercise some judicial function to a limited extent.

The Judicial Police is under the authority of the *Procureurs du Roi*, and under the surveillance of the *Procureur Generaux*. The Minister of Justice is ultimately responsible for this force. The Judicial Police, of which there are 1,340 officers, is divided into 22 brigades, dispersed throughout the whole of Belgium and covering the 27 judicial districts. Each brigade is commanded by the Chief Commissionaire. Most of the brigades work only in their own district, but some cover more than one district. The brigade based in Brussels is the central office of the Judicial Police where the national and international data centres are located and this is the organisation through which contact is maintained with overseas forces and Interpol.

d)   Other Policing

Besides these three police forces in Belgium, there are other ministries which have powers over specific policing activities. There are sixty special police units, for example, the state security police (*Landlijke Politie*, sometimes called '*Veldwachters'*), railway police, aeronautical police and those concerned with maritime, health administration, post and telecommunications, and other matters. The Finance Ministry is responsible for customs and excise matters, and rights of entry. There is even a police service under the direction of the Prime Minister, which is responsible for ensuring that public administration is carried out properly and legally. There is also a crisis management centre which takes responsibility for major incidents, for example, The Herald of Free Enterprise disaster and the Heysel stadium disaster.

3.3 Denmark

3.3.1 *Background*

a) Constitutional Arrangements

The Kingdom of Denmark occupies some 43,080 square kilometres, and has a population of 5.14 million (1991), giving a population density of 119 people per square kilometre. Greenland and the Faroe Islands are self-governing dependencies, although policing is the responsibility of the Danish state. Extraordinarily, neither Greenland nor the Faroe Islands are members of the European Community. The standard of living is high and Denmark has a well-developed comprehensive social welfare system.

Denmark is a constitutional monarchy, with a unicameral legislature called the *Folketing*, a Prime Minister and Cabinet. Its 179 members are elected for four years, although the Prime Minister may dissolve the Parliament at any time. Executive functions are undertaken by the State Council. The Faroe Islands and Greenland each send two representatives to the *Folketing*.

b) Politics and Administration

The country is divided into 14 counties and further subdivided into 277 municipalities, each of which is governed by an elected council and an executive council under the mayor (*Borgmester*).

There are a number of different parties which contest local and national elections. The Social Democratic Party is the principal party, whilst others include the Conservative People's Party, the Socialist People's Party and the Liberal Party. Government tends to be by coalition.

3.3.2 *Judicial System*

Danish law is based on Nordic law, local custom and is also influenced by Roman law. The present Criminal Code dates from 1930, when capital punishment was abolished, but has been amended several times since. It deals with crimes against the state, property and people. The local Chief of Police institutes certain prosecutions, usually for petty misdemeanours, while for more serious offences the decision to prosecute is made by the local Public Prosecutor.

Justice is administered by 84 Lower District Courts, two High Courts, which are in Copenhagen and in Viborg, Jutland, and the Supreme Court, situated in

Copenhagen, which consists of a President and fourteen judges. There are also various special courts and administrative tribunals. All courts are presided over by one or more judges appointed by the Crown. Certain cases are tried before a judge sitting with jurors or lay assessors. Most criminal cases are heard before the District Courts in the first instance. More serious cases, requiring a hearing before a jury, will be heard before the High Courts. Appellate procedure generally permits appeal to the court immediately above.

3.3.3 Organisation of the Police

a) Levels of Policing

The Danish police force (*Rigspolitiet*) is a national force under the control of the state which funds the police. The national force is divided into fifty-four districts, each under the command of a *Politimester* (Chief Constable). The districts are organised into seven police regions for the purposes of policing emergencies and major incidents. Each region is headed by a Chief Constable of one of the districts, except in Copenhagen where it is headed by the *Politidirektor* or Commissioner of the Copenhagen Police. Greenland and the Faroe Islands are independent police districts. The local Chief Constables are responsible for both policing and prosecutions. There are some 10,300 officers in the Danish police service (ENP 1992a), which is approximately one officer for every 499 inhabitants.

The supreme police authority is the Minister of Justice. Executive management of the police force is conducted through the National Commissioner of Police (*Rigspolitichefen*), who is responsible for the central management of personnel and finances, the Commissioner of the Copenhagen police and the Chief Constables of each district who are responsible for the management and policing of the districts.

b) Duties of the Police

There is no statutory police law; provisions are dispersed throughout the legislation. The principal provisions for the organisational structure, duties and operational tasks of the police are laid down in the Administration of Justice Act which also stipulates police practices and procedures. The duties of the police are to maintain security, tranquillity and order, to cause laws and regulations to be obeyed, to take necessary steps to prevent crimes and to investigate and prosecute crimes (National Commissioner's Office 1992). Other duties have been allocated to the police, for example the conduct of driving tests and the issue of driving licences.

c) The National Commissioner's Office

The Interpol office, traffic police, fingerprint files, aliens branch and forensic science laboratory are all in the National Commissioner's Office, which is also responsible for recruitment, administration of personnel and police budgets, and equipment and its maintenance. Training, and civil and national security, are other functions of the Office. It is divided into seven departments, one of which is the Police Academy. The police are also responsible for border control and participate in immigration work. There is a separate customs service which operates at the borders, but investigative work is undertaken by the police.

3.4   France

3.4.1   *Background*

a)   Politics and Administration

The French Republic has a population of 56.18 million (1989) living in a country with an area of some 543,965 square kilometres, giving a population density of 103 people per square kilometre.

The Constitution of the Fifth Republic (1958, revised 1962) provides for a bicameral Parliament and vests executive authority in the President, who is arbiter of the Constitution. Final arbitration is task of the *Conseil Constitutionnel.* The President appoints a Prime Minister and Council of Ministers. The legislature is bicameral consisting of the Senate and National Assembly.

The President is elected every seven years, the 321 members of the Senate are indirectly elected to nine-year terms by an electoral college, while the 577 members of the National Assembly are directly elected every five years.

The main political parties are the Socialist Party, the Gaullist Rally for the Republic (RPR) and the Union for French Democracy (UDF). The Communist Party has lost support during the last ten years, while that of the National Front and the Greens has grown. France has a comprehensive social welfare system.

Within the boundaries of France is the small principality of Monaco, with a population of some 27,500 people living in an area of two square kilometres. It is formally independent, although its government is closely related to that of France.

b)   Local Government

The main units of local government are the 21 administrative regions, the districts (*départements)* and the communes. In addition, there are overseas territories. The key level is that of the 96 *départments*, in France and a further four overseas (Guadeloupe, Martinique, French Guiana and Reunion). France also has two overseas collective territories (Mayotte and Saint-Pierre et Miquelon) and four overseas territories (French Polynesia, French Southern and Antarctic Territories, New Caledonia, and the Wallis and Futuna Islands). Corsica is an internal collective territory divided into two *départements* (Haute-Corse and Corse-du-Sud), five *arrondissements*, 52 cantons and 360 communes.

The *départments* are governed by an elected General Council, alongside which the Commissioner of the Republic (formerly the *Préfet)* operates. The communes each elect a municipal council which in turn elects the mayor. He or she is chief executive and, among other things, is responsible for the municipal police and for public order, security and safety. In the Paris conurbation, in which about 16 per cent of the entire population resides, the mayor is also president of the *département.*

3.4.2   *Judicial System*

a)   The Penal Code

The French criminal justice system is based on the inquisitorial rather than the adversarial model. The key responsibility lies with the judges, and particularly the examining magistrates (*Juges d'Instruction*), to conduct a thorough inquiry to find out all the facts. The trial itself is not a contest between the prosecution and the defence, but the final act of investigation.

Criminal laws are set out in a systematic code of regulations known as the *Code de Procédure Penale*. One interesting aspect of the French justice system is the distinction between the judiciary and the administrative judicial system. The former includes trials between private persons and infringements of the Penal Code, while the administrative system settles suits between individuals and between public bodies.

b)   Criminal Courts

In the French criminal justice system there are three types of criminal courts, and where individual cases are tried depends on the gravity of the alleged offence.

(i)   The *Tribunal de Police* deals with the least serious category of offences; those contravening police regulations (*contraventions*). The prosecutor is often a police officer and the court has one magistrate and a clerk. There are 471 such courts in France which handle over 10 million cases a year.

(ii)   The *Tribunal Correctionnel* deals with what could be called misdemeanours (*délits*). There are three judges but no jury. As with the police tribunals, appeals go to the *Cour d'Appel* and the prosecution as well as the defence may appeal. There are 181 correctional courts which handle over 500,000 cases annually.

(iii)   The *Cour d'Assises* deals with grave offences (*crimes*). There is one in each *département*, and cases are heard before three magistrates and a lay jury of nine people.

(iv)   In addition, there are investigative divisions (at the lowest level the *Juges d'Instructions*), from whom appeals go to the *Chambre d'Instruction,* and finally to the *Cour d'Appel.*

c)   Civil and Administrative Cases

Civil cases are heard firstly before the *Tribunaux d'Instance* and then before higher courts, the *Tribunaux de Grandes Instance*. The *Tribunaux de Grandes Instance* have exclusive jurisdiction in certain areas but are also courts of general jurisdiction.

Administrative cases are heard before a separate court system beginning with the *Tribunaux Administratives* and ending with the court of last resort, the *Conseil d'Etat.*

d) Cour de Cassation

All courts are subject to the highest court of appeal, the *Cour de Cassation*. The *Cour de Cassation* may only hear appeals based on points of law. There are several possible avenues of action that it may take. It may reject the appeal, terminate the action, annul the decision which caused the action in the first place, or refer the appeal back to a court of the same level as that which referred the case, but in a different judicial area.

3.4.3 Organisation of the Police

The French police consists of two highly centralised forces, the *Police Nationale* (PN), and the *Gendarmerie Nationale* (GN). There is a further independent local force called the *Police Municipale* (PM). In total there are some 227,613 officers (PN 116,300, GN 96,313, PM 15,000) which is approximately one police officer for every 247 inhabitants. Relations between the two major forces are often described as strained. The municipal police force operates in theory alongside the *Police Nationale* and the *Gendarmerie*. All the French police are armed. Different sections of the police have different powers.

a) La Police Nationale

The *Police Nationale* is considerably larger than the *Gendarmerie* with some 116,300 officers (Monjardet 1992) and is responsible to the Ministry of the Interior. In addition to the uniformed and plain clothes police officers, there are about 10,000 civil support staff.

The *Police Nationale* has executive and administrative functions which are split between the various units and services, for example, suppression of public disorder, road and motorway patrols, intelligence service, border and air control service, VIP security service. Drugs, vice and forensic work are often covered by specialist squads and there is also an anti-terrorist unit.

The *Directorate Général* is in overall charge and within it are specialist sections and 9 divisions for active policing. These include: (i) *Police Urbaines* (ii) *Police Judiciaire* (iii) *Renseignements Généraux* (iv) *Surveillance du Territoire* (v) *Police de l'Air et des Frontières* (vi) *Compagnie Républicaine de Sécurite* (CRS) (vii) *Préfecture de Police*.

(i) Police Urbaines

The Urban Police (PU) operate in the 477 towns with a population of 10,000 or more. Each district is controlled by a *Commissaire* and consists of uniformed officers and a plain clothes detective and administrative division. The tasks of the Urban Police division are to maintain law and order, public safety, security and salubrity, and traffic control.

(ii) Police Judiciaire

The Judicial Police (PJ) is divided into 19 regions under a Central Directorate, which also acts as the French Interpol contact. There are three sub-divisions of the PJ which deal with different types of cases: criminal; financial and economic; and the technical and scientific police. The duties of the Judicial Police are 'to investigate all breaches of the law, to gather evidence and to bring the perpetrators before the tribunals empowered to try them' (*Code de Procédure Penale*, Article 14). It does this under the direction of the magistracy and public prosecutors.

(iii) *Renseignements Généraux*

The *Renseignements Généraux* (RG) is essentially a political police, of approximately 4,000 officers. Their duty is to collect and collate information on individuals or groups who are regarded as constituting a danger to the state, as well as conducting undercover investigations on persons in public life. Its plain clothes officers are empowered to infiltrate organisations, collect information, tap telephones and open mail, subject to warrants. It has rather wide powers and the officers seem to be largely free to act as they wish. In some respects it is similar to the UK Special Branch. It operates throughout France and passes information to the central directorate in Paris.

(iv) *Directorate de la Surveillance du Territoire*

The *Directorate de la Surveillance du Territoire* (DST) is the state security service concerned with the secret activities of foreign states operating in France. Few details are available about its operation. It consists of approximately 1,500 officers.

(v) *Police de l'Air et des Frontières*

The *Police de l'Air et des Frontières* (PAF), numbering roughly 6,000, is responsible for the movement of people across French borders and through airports. It works closely with the Customs Service (*Douanes*), which has responsibility for the supervision of the movement of goods across the frontiers.

(vi) *Compagnie Républicaine de Sécurité*

The *Compagnie Républicaine de Sécurité* (CRS) consists of mobile, highly trained and well-equipped para-military riot police. The 15,750 officers are divided into 63 companies and their main duty is the suppression of disorder although they also assist the Frontier Police (PAF) on occasions and patrol highways.

(vii) *Préfecture de Police*

The *Préfecture de Police* contains a number of specialist units and services, including the drugs squad.

There are two other small forces which form part of the *Police Nationale*; the *Service de Coopération Technique Internationale de Police*; and the *Service des Voyages Officiels et de la Sécurité des Hautes Personnalités.*

b) Gendarmerie Nationale

The *Gendarmerie Nationale* (GN) is a military force, of 96,313 officers (*La Gendarmerie Nationale* 1993), the organisation of which is under the control of the Ministry of Defence. The *Gendarmerie* operates throughout France, in the rural areas and towns with less than 10,000 population, and also has some responsibilities at frontiers. They are in fact responsible for about 90 per cent of the territory, although this comprises only 50 per cent of the population. Being a military force, its officers are not permitted to operate in plain clothes or to undertake undercover work, although, it appears that this is carried out unofficially (Anderson 1991, p.12).

The *Gendarmerie* has two major divisions:

(i) The *Gendarmerie Départementale* carries out judicial police work and ordinary policing functions. It is divided into territorial brigades. Theoretically there is one brigade per 'canton', but in actual fact there are some 3,653 brigades. Each of the territorial units has a particular task. There are, for example, traffic patrols, mountain units, and the airborne section. They patrol and investigate offences, and collect information which is passed to their documentation centre at Rosny-sous-Bois. This central data bank is estimated to hold over 220 million entries.

(ii) The *Gendarmerie Mobile* do not undertake judicial work but are able to move to reinforce other police or to undertake special duties. Their principal duty is to maintain order. There are over 20,000 mobile Gendarmerie officers and they are well trained and equipped for riot control as well as for diplomatic protection, disaster rescues and control of strikes and crowds.

c)   Police Municipale

The *Police Municipale* (PM) is a force independent of both the *Gendarmerie* and the *Police Nationale*. It is under the control of the Minister of the Interior. The estimated number ranges between 9,000 and 25,000 officers, with consensus around the figure of 15,000 officers. The variation arises because many of those who are considered to be *Police Municipale* are often only *Agents Champêtres* (rural police), that is persons who direct traffic outside schools and undertake other such tasks.

There is no special police statute governing the *Police Municipale*. They are responsible for daily urban policing covering all criminal and public order matters within their urban boundaries. Approximately one-half of the officers are sworn agents and carry arms, but many of the others are merely municipal agents. Training is not mandatory and as a result tends to be rather haphazard. Some may attend the private training school which is situated in Orange, but others receive only the standard training for municipal employees.

3.5   Germany

3.5.1   *Background*

a)   Constitutional Arrangements

The Federal Republic of Germany (including the former German Democratic Republic) covers an area of 356,957 square kilometres. It has a population of 79.5 million (1991), giving a population density of 223 people per square kilometre. This includes 4.8 million *Gastarbeiter* ('guest-workers'), who constitute 6.5 per cent of the labour force, and other foreign-born immigrants (Layton Henry 1992, p.217). Germany has a high standard of living with a comprehensive social welfare system.

The Federal Republic of Germany is a parliamentary democracy. The 1949 Constitution provides for a federal structure in which political authority is divided between the federal government and the *Länder* or states. There are now, since reunification, 16 *Länder* (Baden-Württemberg, Bayern, Bremen, Hamburg, Hessen, Niedersachsen, Nordrhein-Westfalen, Rheinland-Pfalz, Saarland, Schleswig-Holstein, Berlin, Brandenburg, Mecklenburg-Vorpommern, Sachsen, Sachsen-Anhalt and Thüringen). Each *Land* exists as an autonomous entity with its own constitution and administration. The Treaty on Unification of the German Democratic Republic and the Federal Republic of Germany provides that on the accession of the GDR the rules of the Basic Law apply to the new *Länder*, except where the terms of the Unification Treaty specifically amend the Basic Law (Article 3).

b) Federal Government

The bicameral federal Parliament is made up of the *Bundesrat*, the Federal Council, and the National Assembly or *Bundestag*. The latter comprised between 496 and 499 deputies pre-unification (fluctuating according to constituency wins) and 22 representatives from West Berlin who had observer status. In October 1990 a further 144 delegates from the East German *Volkshammer* were added to this number, bringing the chamber total to 662. They continue to be elected for four years. The 45 members of the *Bundesrat*, which increased to 68 after unification, are appointed by the *Länder* and the government. The two principal parties are the Social Democratic Party and the Christian Democratic Union.

The Federal Chancellor, who is head of the executive, is selected by the *Bundestag*. The federal government is responsible for defence and foreign relations, finance and some economic functions, migration and customs and other matters.

3.5.2 *Judicial System*

The German judicial system is based on the federal structure and is divided into different jurisdictions. Civil and criminal cases are heard before the ordinary courts, and there are also administrative courts, labour courts, tax courts, social courts and constitutional courts.

The first action that every court must take is a review of the jurisdiction. The court must decide whether the proceedings may validly continue before that court or whether they have to be referred to the courts of another jurisdiction. Jurisdiction is determined by the rules on subject matter. These determine which court in the court system may hear any given case. Ordinary court jurisdiction is determined by the value of the matter in the proceedings (civil cases), or the seriousness of the crime (criminal cases). The more minor cases are heard before the District Courts (*Amtsgerichte*), and more serious cases by the Regional Courts (*Landgerichte*). Only in the ordinary courts are there different courts of first instance; other types of jurisdiction have only one court. In addition, the domicile of the defendant (civil cases) or the place where the offence was committed (criminal cases) has a bearing on which court may hear the proceedings. The most superior court in the hierarchy of the ordinary courts is the Federal High Court (*Bundesgerichtshof*).

The judicial system places less importance on formal rules of evidence than in common law countries and lays more emphasis on determining the facts. Judges tend to play an active role in proceedings, which are not based on the adversarial approach. As the German criminal justice system is based on the 'inquisitorial' model the trial represents the final act of investigation. Judges are very much in control and have wide-ranging powers to carry out their enquiries and to build up a file of information about the case on which the ultimate decision is based.

Laws are set out in a systematic code of regulations known as the *Strafgesetzbuch* (St.Gb), the Penal Code. Similarly, procedural rules are collected together in the *Strafprozessordnung* (St.Po), the Criminal Procedural Code. Justice is based on two principles: total legal protection and far-reaching specialisation.

3.5.3   Organisation of the Police

Policing in the Federal Republic of Germany is undertaken at both the federal and *Land* level. Pre-unification there were approximately 195,000 police officers in total – 171,382 from the *Länder* and 23,500 federal police (Marinelli pers. comm. 1992). This generated approximately one police officer for every 407 inhabitants. Post-unification there are 282,747 established police posts, although the actual man power figure is slightly less (Feltes pers. comm. 1993). These more up-to-date figures show one police officer for every 281 head of population, a considerable increase in the number of police per head of population since reunification. According to the Constitution, sovereignty in most police matters rests with the *Länder*, although federal powers exist to promote co-operation and provide central facilities for information, communications and criminal investigation.

a)   The Police Forces of the Länder (Die Landespolizeien)

Most policing is carried out at the state or *Land* level. Police forces in each *Land* are responsible to the respective Minister of the Interior, apart from the city states of Berlin, Hamburg and Bremen where police forces are responsible to the Senator for the Interior. Each *Land* has its own police regulations and codes and each force is divided into four branches: (i) the *Schutzpolizei* (ii) the *Kriminalpolizei* (iii) the *Bereitschaftspolizei* (iv) the *Wasserschutzpolizei*.

(i)   The *Schutzpolizei* or 'Schupo' is the uniformed constabulary with approximately 187,972 officers. It has a mainly preventive role in maintaining law and order and also deals with minor crimes. It is usually organised into sectors and districts. Approximately three-quarters of each state's police are in this branch.

(ii)   The *Kriminalpolizei* or 'Kripo', with approximately 42,075 officers, is the criminal investigation branch which is divided into units dealing with fraud, vice, general crime and criminal intelligence. Criminal intelligence is gathered centrally by the *Landeskriminalämter* or LKA (State Offices of Criminal Investigation) and the *Bundeskriminalamt* or BKA (Federal Criminal Office) at Wiesbaden, which is discussed further below.

(iii)   The *Bereitschaftspolizei* or 'Bepo' or stand-by police (Cullen 1992, p.20), with approximately 25,000, support police operations when a significant presence is required, for example when there is civil disorder. It is basically an emergency police unit, although it also plays an important part in police training.

(iv)   The *Wasserschutzpolizei* are the river police, responsible for policing waterways and coastal areas.

The police of the *Länder* include the traffic police and they also have a great many administrative duties including issuing certain types of licences.

The police forces of the *Länder* are under the jurisdiction of the states' ministers of the interior who hold regular conferences to ensure co-operation, at which the Federal Interior Minister is also present. The country's Constitution provides that there shall be mutual assistance between the two levels of police.

b) The Federal Police (Die Bundpolizei)

The tasks of the Federal Police (*Bundpolizei*) are split into three main areas:

(i) The *Bundeskriminalamt* (BKA), or Federal Criminal Investigation Department, is established under a constitutional provision. It consists of some 3,700 officers based at Wiesbaden. It is the centre for co-operation between federal and state law enforcement agencies and it gathers and evaluates information and documentation for combating crime, and handles serious criminal investigations relating to narcotics, currency counterfeiting and offences involving arms and explosives. Anti-terrorist activities are co-ordinated under the *Koordinierungsgruppe Terrorismusbekämpfung* (KGT), under the BKA. The BKA is the National Central Bureau for Interpol.

(ii) The Federal Border Police (*Bundesgrenzschutz*), is a force of some 24,000 officers and is responsible to the Federal Minister of the Interior. It is a para-military force the main task of which is to control the Federal Republic's external borders. Its position with the removal of internal border controls is unclear. Reunification has already brought changes to this force (Cullen 1992, p.43). Checks are made on incoming and outgoing traffic, and it deals with any disturbances in the frontier regions and with emergencies. Immigration and customs duties are dealt with by a separate branch of the Border Police known as the Individual Services. Customs officers and the Customs Investigation Branch come under the jurisdiction of the Federal Minister of Finance. The *Deutsche Bundesbahn* (DB), the German Railways, had its own police, responsible for the protection of company property and installations against disruptions and damage, and the investigation of criminal acts against them. The former railway police are now part of the *Bundesgrenzschutz*.

(iii) The *Bundesverfassungsschutz* or BVS is the Federal Office for the Protection of the Constitution. It is an information-gathering force, and not an executive police force, and has no law-enforcement authority.

Reunification has brought changes to the policing of what was the German Democratic Republic. The former *Volkspolizei* or ('People's Police Force') was re-established as a civilian force on the Federal Republic's model. The influence of the former *Staatsicherheitsdienst* or 'Stasi' (the secret police) was all-pervasive and a widespread process of 'de-Stasification' is currently taking place (Cullen 1992, pp.6–11).

3.6 Greece

3.6.1 *Background*

a) Constitutional Arrangements

The Hellenic Republic covers an area of some 131,990 square kilometres and has a population of 10.14 million (1990). It has a population density of some 77 people per square kilometre. A notable feature is the number of islands, perhaps as many as 2,000, of which Crete is the largest. Greece has extensive sea, mountain and river frontiers which bring policing problems unique to the country.

Greece is a parliamentary democracy. The 1975 Constitution (amended in 1986) established a unicameral Parliament (*Vouli*) and it exercises legislative power in conjunction with the President. Executive functions are divided between the President and the Prime Minister, who is head of government. The 300 deputies in the Parliament are directly elected for four years. The major political parties are the New Democracy Party and the Pan-Hellenic Socialist Movement (PASOK).

b) Local Government

The country is divided into thirteen administrative provinces which are further subdivided into 51 *nomoi* or prefectures. Each of these is administered by a *nomarch* who is appointed by the Minister of the Interior. The country also has elected mayors and urban and rural councils.

3.6.2 *Judicial System*

a) The Penal Code

The criminal justice procedures are similar to the French system, although there are no judicial police. As in many other European countries there is a distinct separation of the competence of ordinary courts and the administrative courts. The Penal Code, which is based on Roman law modified by the Napoleonic Code, defines three categories of crime: felonies, misdemeanours and petty offences.

An investigating magistrate examines the evidence and questions witnesses and, if he is satisfied there is a substantive case to answer, the case will then be referred to the public prosecutor, who decides whether charges should be preferred.

b) The Courts System

Throughout Greece there are Justice of the Peace Courts which handle petty criminal offences and civil cases. Above these are Courts of First Instance, which also hear civil and criminal cases (misdemeanours). Exclusive jurisdiction for civil hearings is attached to the Single Judge Court. Courts with a panel of judges deal with cases which the Justice of the Peace Courts are not competent to handle. Both the Justice of the Peace and the Courts of First Instance have separate divisions which deal with criminal cases only. These are called Petty Offences Courts and Misdemeanour Courts. Alongside these are other criminal and juvenile courts, and a number of towns also have administrative (tax) courts. The more serious criminal cases (felonies) are tried in the Jury Court, which consists of three judges and a jury of four.

Appeals from the Court of First Instance go to the Court of Appeal, and from there if there remain any disputes over points of law the Supreme Court (*Arios Pagos*) will make a ruling.

3.6.3 Organisation of the Police

a) Structure of the Police

There is a single national police force, known as the Hellenic Police, which is administered by the Ministry of Public Order and headed by the Chief of Police (*Anistratigos Astynomikos*). The total number of officers in 1989 was 38,783, which was approximately one police officer for every 261 inhabitants. The Hellenic Police was formed in 1984 by an amalgamation of the municipal police and the Gendarmerie and it undertakes policing throughout the whole country, except for the limited areas which are the responsibility of the Ports Police.

The organisation of the Hellenic Police is based on the administrative division of Greece into 51 prefectures. Each prefecture constitutes a police district, apart from Attica (Athens) which is subdivided into three police districts, bringing the total number of police districts to 53 (ENP 1992a, p.67).

Each police district has a police department which exercises all powers provided for it by the state law, within its local jurisdiction, and is responsible to the Ministry of Public Order. A Police Director heads each police department.

Athens and Thessalonica each have a General Police Department under the directorship of a Major General or Brigadier General. These two areas also have special police services for narcotics control. Supervision and co-ordination of the work of the police departments is undertaken by eight district inspectors and three general inspectors who are responsible to the Chief of Police.

The general duties of the police include ensuring public security and order, the protection of the state and the democratic system, suppression and prevention of crime and law enforcement in general.

b) Specialist Policing Operations

At the regional level there are specialist police who handle public security, drugs and serious criminal investigations. Crime prevention, smuggling, theft of antiques and works of art, and missing persons are dealt with centrally by the Ministry of Public Order. There is a special anti-terrorist unit (EKAM) and a central Criminal Services Directorate which is the National Central Bureau for Interpol.

There are other specialised police forces in Greece, including the Ports Police, who act as coast guard and are under the control of the Ministry of the Merchant Navy, the Customs Guards and the Forest Police.

3.7   Ireland

3.7.1   *Background*

a)   Constitutional Arrangements

The Republic of Ireland covers an area of 70,285 square kilometres and has a population of 3.54 million people (1988), giving a population density of 50 people per square kilometre.

Ireland is a parliamentary democracy with a Constitution passed in 1937. The President, elected by direct vote for seven years, is head of state. The head of government is the *Taoiseach* or Prime Minister who chairs the Cabinet and consults for certain purposes with the advisory Council of State.

The Irish Parliament (*Oireachtas*) has two houses. The *Dail* has 166 members, elected at least once every five years, while the *Seanad* or Senate members are selected by various groups to represent economic, cultural and vocational interests. The major political parties are *Fianna Fail*, *Fine Gael*, the Progressive Democrats and the Labour Party.

b)   Local Government

The system of local government is based on county and borough councils, directly elected at regular intervals. They are responsible for various services, such as planning, health, highways and water, but their functions do not include education or policing. Administration is the responsibility of county and city managers.

3.7.2   *Judicial System*

Irish law is based on common law modified by statute. The lowest courts in the Irish judicial system are the 23 district courts, each presided over by a District Justice without a jury. They have jurisdiction in summary criminal cases. Above these are 7 circuit courts, with a judge and jury, which have jurisdiction for all serious crimes except murder.

The High Court has jurisdiction in both criminal and civil hearings and consists of a high court judge and jury. In civil cases it is normal for the judge to sit alone. Where the High Court is sitting on criminal cases the judge sits with a jury and the court is then known as the Central Criminal Court. On occasions the High Court is the court of first instance, generally involving serious criminal charges. The Special Criminal Court, established in 1972, tries terrorist offences. Appeals are made to the Court of Criminal Appeal, which consists of three judges: one Supreme Court judge and two High Court judges. The court of last resort in Ireland is the Supreme Court. This may sit as a court of three or five and exercises appellate jurisdiction.

3.7.3   *Organisation of the Police*

a)   Territorial Divisions

There is one police organisation in the Republic of Ireland which operates throughout the whole of the territory. The *Garda Siochana* ('Guardians of the Peace') is headed by the Commissioner who is responsible to the Minister for Justice. The Secretary of the Department of Justice has responsibility for the financial management of the force. Through the Minister of Justice, the Irish Parliament controls the *Garda.* There are approximately 10,500 officers in the *Garda,* of which 8,500 are uniformed police and 1,700 are plain clothes detectives. There are also some 500 civilian employees. The total of 10,500 police personnel gives a ratio of one police officer for every 337 people.

The *Garda* is organised into twenty-three territorial divisions, five of which are in the Dublin Metropolitan area under the control of an Assistant Commissioner. Each division is further sub-divided into districts and each has a traffic corps, a uniformed branch and a District Detective Unit.

A Government-appointed Advisory Committee on Fraud has recently recommended the formation of a National Bureau of Fraud Investigation. This may set a trend towards the formation of national *Garda* units (Rae 1993, p.7).

b)   Policing Duties

The *Garda* has the duty to prevent and detect crimes, to protect persons and property and to maintain public order. Depending on the size of the division, the Chief Superintendent responsible for it may assign specific police functions to designated groups, for example, fraud, drugs, and subversion.

Support services are provided at *Garda* headquarters and these include communications, computer and intelligence services and the technical bureau which deals with forensic and associated support.

The *Garda Siochana* is generally unarmed. Police powers are derived from common law and statute law. Members of the *Garda* can prosecute for the less serious offences, but those which are more serious are prosecuted by the Director of Public Prosecutions.

3.8   Italy

3.8.1   *Background*

a)   Constitutional Arrangements

The Italian Republic occupies an area of 301,263 square kilometres and has a population of 57.6 million (1989). It has a population density of 191 people per square kilometre. Italy has a system of welfare benefits, low-cost health care and free education.

Italy is a parliamentary democracy based on the 1948 Constitution which is upheld by the Constitutional Court of 15 judges. The bicameral Parliament consists of the Senate and the Chamber of Deputies. The members of both houses are directly elected for five-year terms (with the exception of five Senators who are appointed for life). Deputies and Senators have enjoyed immunity from arrest, search and criminal trial, although the 1993 corruption scandals may change this in the future.

The head of state is the President, who is elected for seven years by the Parliament together with some 60 regional representatives. The President has a number of special powers, including the power to dissolve Parliament, and he is head of the armed forces.

The head of government is the President (Prime Minister) of the Council of Ministers, all of whom are answerable to the Parliament. The principal parties are the Christian Democratic Party, the Communist Party, the Socialist Party, the Social Democrats, the Liberal Party, the Social Movement and the Republican Party.

b)   Regional and Local Government

Italy is divided into 15 ordinary regions and another 5 special regions (Sicily, Sardinia, Valle d'Aosta, Friuli-Venezia Giulia and Trentino-Alto Adige) which have greater autonomy. The regions are able to legislate on certain matters, and can collect various taxes. Each region is governed by an executive body, the *Giunta*, with its own president and laws are passed by the regional council. Disagreements between the regions and the national government may go to the Constitutional Court for adjudication.

Below the regions are 95 provinces and below these are approximately 8,000 communes. Each level elects a council which in turn elects a *Giunta* and president or, in the case of the communes, a mayor. The communes collect certain local taxes, organise their own police and undertake services such as public transport and public health.

Within the Italian boundaries are two semi-sovereign states: the Vatican City State (Temporal State of the Bishop of Rome) and San Marino (Most Serene Republic of San Marino). Each is a self-governing country, but neither is formally a member of the European Community. Their combined population is less than 23,000 people.

3.8.2   *Judicial System*

Under the Constitution the Italian judiciary is fully independent of the executive and legislature and is supervised by the Superior Council of the Judiciary. Italian law is fundamentally based on Roman law and is largely codified although the law has been modified by statute.

The Italian judicial system is divided into three separate areas of jurisdiction, these being the ordinary (further sub-divided into civil and criminal) jurisdiction, the administrative and the fiscal jurisdictions.

At the lowest level of the 'ordinary' courts there are several different courts. In civil cases the lowest of these is the court of the *Guidice Conciliatore* which hears disputes up to the value of Lir.1,000,000. Above this is the *Pretore*, a court with a single judge which has competence in cases involving values up to Lir.5,000,000. A *Pretore* is present in the major town of every district of Italy. The *Tribunale* is a three panel court dealing with matters above the competence of the *Pretore*, and acting in some instances as an appellate court from the *Pretore* decisions. The next level in the hierarchy of the civil courts is the *Corte d'Apello* which hears appeals from the *Tribunale*. Finally the *Corte de Cassazione* will determine appeals on points of law.

Criminal cases follow a separate hierarchy of courts. The *Corte d'Assis di Primo Grado* deals with serious crimes. The *Pretore* in its competence as a criminal court deals with cases where a maximum sentence of four years imprisonment or a fine may be imposed. The *Tribunale* is a general criminal court dealing with all cases which do not fall into the jurisdiction of either of the other two courts at this level. Appellate courts are the *Corte d'Appello* hearing cases referred from the *Pretore* and the *Tribunale*, and the separate *Corte d'Assise d'Appello* competent to hear appeals from the *Corte d'Assises di Primo Grado*. The supreme criminal court is the *Corte di Cassazione* determining appeals on points of law.

The administrative courts have two tiers, the *Tribunale Amministrativo* and the *Consiglio di Stato*. Fiscal courts are based on three tiers. The lowest is the *Commissione Tributaria di Primo Grado*, the next tier is the *Commissione Tributaria di Secondo Grado*, and final appeals are heard by the *Commissione Tributaria Centrale*.

Prosecutions are initiated and carried out by the *Pubblico Ministero* (Public Prosecutor) on behalf of the state. He or she is charged with safeguarding the public interest and is entitled to initiate any investigations considered necessary to collect evidence – assisted by the police, which may be members of the *Carabinieri*, the *Polizia di Stato*, the *Guardia di Finanza*, or the Corps of Prison Warders.

3.8.3 Organisation of the Police

There are four separate police systems in Italy: *L'Arma dei Carabinieri*; the *Polizia di Stato*, which are the public security police; the *Guardia di Finanza*, which are the treasury police; and the *Vigili Urbani*, who are the local community police. In addition there are the Corps of Prison Warders and the Corps of Foresters, the latter responsible for the protection of forestry and the environment. In total there are some 301,492 police officers, giving 1 officer for every 191 members of the population.

The Italian police all come under the authority of the Minister of the Interior who co-ordinates the activities of law enforcement agencies. The Minister is responsible for the maintenance of public order and safety and the services of the Public Security Department are employed to enforce this authority. This department in turn is sub-divided into various departments and agencies headed by the Chief of the Italian Police (*Direttore General della PS*).

a) Arma dei Carabinieri

The *Carabinieri* is a national force of 104,211 officers (Marinelli 1992, pers. comm.), which has both military and civilian policing duties. Its military operations, which come under the direction of the Ministry of Defence, include military policing, protection of military establishments and special escorts. For other duties the *Carabinieri* are either under the control of the Ministry of Internal Affairs or the judicial authorities (Agelink *et al* 1990).

The regular policing duties of the *Carabinieri* include ensuring that laws and regulations are observed, combating all forms of crime, assisting with disasters, maintaining public order, providing prisoner surveillance and a guard service at court hearings. The *Carabinieri* also undertakes diplomatic protection. When conducting criminal investigations the force is responsible to the judicial authorities. Units of *Carabinieri* judicial police are attached to the courts of appeal and lower courts under the direction of the judges and prosecutors.

The headquarters of the *Carabinieri* contains intelligence data and a sophisticated forensic laboratory. Under the command of General Headquarters, the *Carabinieri* is divided for organisation purposes into training, territorial, military police, mobile police, special branch and welfare and leisure branches (Borghini 1992, p.109). The territorial branch is organised in a hierarchy with 3 divisions, 9 brigades, 24 legions and 100 groups which generally coincide with the provincial levels of local government. Below these are 499 companies and 4,608 stations which are the basic operational units of the force.

The *Carabinieri* also maintains various specialist units, such as the *Squadriglie* which fight organised crime, notably the Mafia, and are provided with helicopters and special communications equipment. In addition there is the Special Branch, which includes the naval service for coastal patrols and the drugs squad. It also includes units subordinated to other ministries, the duties of which include the location of stolen works of art, the prevention of food adulteration, enforcement of labour legislation, providing security for diplomatic missions and preventing crimes which cause damage to the environment.

b)   Polizia di Stato

The *Polizia di Stato* (PS) or State Police is responsible to the Ministry of the Interior and has responsibilities which include maintenance of public order, protection of life and property and investigation of offences. The PS is directed by the General Director of the National Police. This force, formerly the *Corpo delle Guardia di Pubblica Sicurezza*, was demilitarised in 1981 (Andrade 1985, p.101).

There are 96,178 officers in the PS (Marinelli 1992, pers. comm.). The State Police has the general policing task of enforcing law and order, maintaining public security and carrying out the Interpol liaison function within the Criminal Police Department (*Criminalpol*). The PS has a complex national organisation. Tasks are divided between a number of departments, each responsible for one particular policing function (Agelink *et al* 1990, p.46). The departments are the Office for Co-ordination and Planning, the Office for Central Inspection, the Criminal Police Department, the Office for Crime Prevention, the Department of Traffic, Rail, Border and Postal Police, the Education and Training Department, the Department for Technical Affairs and the Accountancy Office.

The Minister of the Interior has overall responsibility for law and order and co-ordinates law enforcement through the Public Security Authority (*Amministrazione di PS*). The Department of Public Security, which is directed by the head of the Italian Police (*Direttore General della P.S.*), has overall charge of the administration and supervision of the police.

In each Italian province, the *Prefetto* is charged with the maintenance of law and order and public security and co-ordinates the policing activities. In each province the *Questore* is responsible for public order in respect of technical and co-operative matters, and liaises closely with the *Prefetto*. In those communes that are not also provincial capitals, but which are seats of the commisariat of the PS, the director of that office is the local authority of the PS. In the communes where there is no commisariat the local police authority is the mayor.

One important section of the police in Italy in respect of European policing is the special police which polices the frontiers. It is responsible directly to the Central Office for Highway, Railway, Border and Postal Police in the Department of Public Security. These police officers work closely with customs officers and with the *Guardia di Finanza* to ensure that customs and excise regulations are properly observed.

c)   Guardia di Finanza

The prevention and investigation of smuggling, illegal immigration and tax evasion are the functions of the *Guardia di Finanza*, or Treasury Police, which are under the control of the Ministry of Finance. There are some 57,181 Treasury Police officers. They perform customs and excise, and also coastguard tasks.

d)   Vigili Urbani

The community police (*Vigili Urbani*) of about 26,000 officers are directed by the mayors of the communes. They undertake traffic duties and regulate local activities such as taxis, public health and markets.

e)   Other Police

There are various other police agencies in Italy including the Harbour Police, of about 1,000 officers responsible for ports, the Corps of Prison Guards (of about 14,000 officers) and the Forestry Police (of about 3,000 police), under the control of the Ministry of Agriculture and Forestry, responsible for combating environmental offences.

3.9   Luxembourg

3.9.1   *Background*

The Grand Duchy of Luxembourg covers an area of 2,586 square kilometres and has a population of 389,800 (1992), giving a density of 151 people per square kilometre. Per capita income in Luxembourg is one of the world's highest, and there is a comprehensive social welfare system.

Luxembourg is a constitutional monarchy. Under its Constitution of 1868, revised in 1919 and 1956, legislative power resides in the unicameral legislature, the Chamber of Deputies, the 64 members of which are directly elected to serve for five years. There is also an appointed Council of State (21 members) which must examine all draft legislation before it may be enacted, except in cases of urgency. The head of government is the Prime Minister. The main political parties are the Christian Social Party, the Luxembourg Socialist Workers' Party and the Democratic Party.

3.9.2   Judicial System

The legal system of Luxembourg is based on the French and German models. At the most local level are the Justice of the Peace courts, in which a single judge presides over civil, commercial, industrial and minor criminal cases. The Justice of the Peace may only hear cases where the value in dispute does not exceed LUF100,000. No appeal is possible if the disputed sum is less than LUF15,000. From the Justice of the Peace appeal lies to the Court of First Instance (except in industrial cases where appeal is immediately moved to the Court of Appeal).

The Courts of First Instance, of which there are two, are composed of three judges. They are competent to hear civil, commercial, criminal and appeal actions. If they are dealing with a criminal case they sit as either a *Tribunal Correctionnel* or as a *Chambre Criminelle.*

The Court of Appeal is the next level of the court system. This sits as a court with three judges, except when hearing appeals from the *Chambre Criminelle* of the Court of First Instance, in which case five judges hear the appeal.

The court of last resort in Luxembourg, as in France and Belgium, is the *Cour de Cassation* composed of five judges who hear appeals on points of law.

In addition, there is a separate Administrative Court (*Comité du Contentieux du Conseil d'Etat*) which hears disputes concerning the acts or omissions of the public administration. Here, five judges sit in chambers.

3.9.3   Organisation of the Police

Policing in Luxembourg consists of a dual system made up of the *Corps de la Police* (National Police) and the *Gendarmerie.* In total there are about 1,100 police officers, giving one officer for every 355 members of the population.

a)   Corps de la Police

The National Police was originally a local civil police force under the authority of the *Bourgemestre* (mayor). In 1952 the police became a national military force, and in 1968 a new law attached full responsibility for the funding of the police to the government. There are currently about 500 personnel (ENPa1992).

The *Corps de la Police* is commanded by a Director, whose rank is that of Colonel. He is responsible for the organisation of the police, training of the personnel, control of the service and liaison with judicial and governmental authorities.

The police are responsible to three different ministers for different aspects of their work. The *Ministre de la Force Publique* is responsible for organisation, administration, training and discipline, the *Ministre de l'Interieur* is responsible for public order and for matters of public administration, and the *Ministre de la Justice* has responsibility for the *Police Judiciaire* and immigrant control.

The *Police Judiciaire* is a small specialised force, separate from the *Corps de la Police*, with responsibilities for criminal investigations, directed particularly against middle-sized gangs and organised crime.

The National Police are deployed across Luxembourg in areas which have larger population concentrations (over 5,000), divided into nineteen *Commissariats*. The *Commissariats* are the basic units of the police, and in each of the three districts, several of these are grouped together. There are five regional services of *Police-Secours* (SRPS), consisting of 14 *Commissariats*, which cover the more densely populated areas and provide a 24-hour crime and support service.

The police function is to ensure public order and the execution of laws and regulations. Within this definition three areas of the police may be distinguished: the functions of the judicial police; those of the administrative police; and the various other functions they perform.

The basic task of the administrative police is to ensure public order and prevent crime. The Judicial Police record all penal offences, gather evidence and seek the offenders. Their character is essentially reactive, in seeking to investigate all offences that the administrative police were unable to prevent. Other functions of the police also relate to public order, for example, in the areas of patrol and traffic enforcement.

In addition there is the *Groupe d'Intervention de la Police* (GIP), which is responsible for VIP protection, surveillance and special operations.

b)   The Gendarmerie

The *Gendarmerie* is also a national, centralised, military police force. It consists of about 600 personnel who are deployed throughout the whole of the territory (ENP 1992a). It is responsible for policing the rural districts and highways, railways, the airport and borders. It is commanded by a Colonel, with a deputy of the rank Lieutenant-Colonel. The *Gendarmerie* are primarily responsible for patrol, traffic and major criminal investigations.

In each of the three districts of Luxembourg, several brigades are grouped together depending on the population size, the geographical extent of the district, and the tasks it has to carry out. There is a total of 37 brigades. Both the *Gendarmerie* and the *Corps de la Police* are armed.

3.10   Netherlands

3.10.1   *Background*

a)   Constitutional Arrangements

The Kingdom of the Netherlands occupies an area of some 41,864 square kilometres and has a population of 14.89 million (1990), giving a population density of 356 people per square kilometre. The Netherlands has a well-developed social welfare system.

The country is a constitutional monarchy. Legislative authority lies with the government and Parliament. Members of the Second Chamber are directly elected for four years, while those in the First Chamber are elected for six years by the provincial councils. Government is conducted by the Cabinet chaired by the Prime Minister.

There is a large number of political parties, of which the most significant are the Christian Democratic Appeal, the Labour Party, the People's Party for Freedom and Democracy, and Democrats '66.

The Netherlands has two dependencies in the Caribbean. Aruba has a population of some 68,000, while that of the Dutch Antilles is just over 200,000.

b)   Local Government

The Netherlands is divided into 12 provinces each of which has a directly elected council which chooses the members of the executive, the chair or Queen's Commissioner being appointed by the government.

At the local government level the municipalities, of which there are 672, are run by directly elected councils. Each chooses an executive which is chaired by the *Burgemeester* or mayor, appointed by the government.

3.10.2   Judicial System

Responsibility for the administration of justice lies with the independent judiciary. Judges sit in all the courts and trials by jury do not occur. At the lowest level, the 62 Magistrates Courts have jurisdiction over many minor criminal and civil matters. The 19 District Courts handle more serious offences and also hear appeals from the lower courts. Above them are 5 Courts of Appeal and the Supreme Court (*Hoge Raad*) is the final court of appeal.

The Penal Code and Criminal Procedure Code identify crimes and their seriousness. Criminal proceedings are instituted by the public prosecutor. There are, in addition, various tribunals for resolving disputes between citizens and the state.

3.10.3   Organisation of the Police

a)   The Old Structure

The Dutch police forces were comprehensively reorganised in 1992–93 Briefly, there have been three police forces in the Netherlands:

(i)   The *Rijkspolitie* or State Police were responsible to the Minister of Justice and deployed in rural areas and urban areas which did not have their own police. Police functions included patrol, traffic enforcement, water traffic, security and policing at airports, crowd-control and criminal investigation. Personnel numbered around 13,400 in 1992 (ENP 1992a, p.105).

(ii)   The *Gemeentepolitie* or Municipal Police were responsible to the individual local majors, the size of each force being dependent on the size of the community served. There were 148 municipal forces in the Netherlands. Personnel in 1992 numbered around 32,600.

(iii) The *Koninklijke Marechaussee* or Royal Military Police numbered around 3,470 in 1992. The force was responsible to the Ministries of Defence, Justice and Interior, and had responsibility for border controls, including the major airports.

92

b)   The New System

The implementation date set for the reorganisation of the police in the Netherlands was April 1993 (Den Boer 1991; Kuijvenhoven 1992; Kniper 1993). The two ministers who were responsible for the police agreed that the police organisation as it stood was disrupted, inefficient, expensive and could not cope with the increasing incidence of crime. However, despite this date being set and the re-organisation being carried out, implementation has not yet officially occurred at the time of writing. All the preparations are in place, but a new Police Act is still required. It now seems likely that the Act will not be in force before January 1994.

The solution to the problems of the old system was to combine the local and state police to create one totally new police force. This is divided into twenty five geographical regional forces, ranging in size from 450 to 4,500 officers. In addition, a Special Central Police Force has been created. This force contains all the services which support the regional forces in certain aspects of their work. For example, the National Criminal Intelligence Service and the Water Police will be part of the Special Central Police Force. The changes do not affect the role of the Royal Military Police. The total number of police will not change. In effect all that has happened is that the serving police officers have been moved around into new positions. There remain approximately 49,500 officers, or one police officer for every 301 members of the population.

One mayor from each region is now appointed as *Korpsbeheeder* or administrative official over that regional force, and chairs regional committees in which all mayors and the Chief Public Prosecutor participate. This committee is the final decision-maker on financial and organisational matters. Daily operational command is the responsibility of a *Korpschef* or Chief of Police.

The Minister of the Interior is responsible for the financial matters of the police forces, and also sets minimum standards for professional aspects of policing and quality or best practice within the police service.

The Minister of Justice has an expanded role in relation to certain services, under the title *Korps Landelijke Politie Diensten* (KLPD). The services are traffic police on roads and waterways, criminal intelligence and analysis, the protection of the royal family and other VIPs, and national facilities and telecommunications and equipment.

c)   The CRI

The *Centrale Recherche Informatiedienst* (CRI) is the National Criminal Intelligence Service with headquarters in The Hague. It is an independent external service of the Police Directorate, which in turn has responsibility for police matters within the Ministry of Justice. It is involved with data collection and analysis relating to criminal activity, with establishing international police contacts, and with assisting the national police forces with their enquiries. The Interpol National Central Bureau function is incorporated into the CRI's structure. The CRI does not have executive powers of its own (see Den Boer 1991, pp.12–14). Its files contain a comprehensive crime index on types of crime, criminal working methods, fingerprints and other information. It also has a criminal investigation department with specialised branches in narcotics, organised crime, firearms, fraud, counterfeits, arts and antiques, stolen motor vehicles and terrorism.

The Ministry of Justice also runs a number of other common services for the police. They include the Police Communications Service, the Police Supply Service and forensic services.

3.11   Portugal

3.11.1   Background

The Portuguese Republic covers an area of 91,985 square kilometres and has a population of 10.3 million (1988), giving a density of 112 people per square kilometre.

Under the 1976 Constitution (revised in 1982), the legislature is the unicameral Assembly of the Republic, the 250 members of which are directly elected every four years. The head of state is the President who is directly elected for a five-year term. He or she has the right to veto legislation and can dissolve the Assembly. The Council of Ministers is chaired by the Prime Minister.

There are nearly 20 political parties, of which the most important are the Social Democratic Party, the Socialist Party, and the Democratic Renewal Party.

There are two autonomous regions, in the Azores and Madeira, to which significant powers are devolved. Portugal is divided into 22 administrative districts, including three in the Azores and one in Madeira. Each has a governor, responsible to the Ministry of the Interior, who is assisted by a board. The districts are divided into municipalities and parishes with elected councils.

3.11.2   Judicial System

The Portuguese Legal Code is based on Roman law and is regularly revised. The Constitution is considered to be one of the most progressive in terms of the protection that is offered for fundamental rights.

The judicial courts are divided into tiers, with appeals to the next court above. The lowest courts are Courts of First Instance, above these are Courts of Second Instance. The Supreme Court of Justice is the highest judicial authority, except in constitutional affairs where the Constitutional Court has jurisdiction. All the courts have general jurisdiction to hear both civil and criminal cases, and cases from all areas, although the Courts of First Instance do have some specific geographical competence.

In addition to the ordinary courts hearing civil and criminal disputes there is a hierarchy of administrative and tax courts.

3.11.3   Organisation of the Police

There are several different police organisations in Portugal, with a total of 46,769 personnel, or one police officer for every 220 inhabitants. Co-ordination of the Portuguese police forces is the responsibility of a board under the direct jurisdiction of the Prime Minister. This responsibility may be delegated to the Ministry for

Internal Administration, the Ministry of Justice or the Ministry of Defence. Those police organisations responsible to the Ministry of Internal Administration have been undergoing structural change since October 1992. The restructuring measures are not all being taken immediately, but will take place over the course of the next 6 or 7 years.

a)   Policia de Seguranca Publica

The *Policia de Seguranca Publica* (PSP) or Public Security Police are responsible for the maintenance of public order, direction of traffic and criminal investigation. They operate principally in towns with a population of over 10,000 people. The force is under the direction of the Ministry of Internal Administration. In December 1992 there were 18,641 personnel in the *Policia de Seguranca Publica* (Soreiro pers. comm. 1993).

The Headquarters of the PSP is in Lisbon under the control of a commander. Central sections include administration, communications, identification, immigration, information, public security and traffic.

The country is divided into 18 districts within which there are divisions in each major town and sections or squads in smaller towns. There are separate commands for Madeira and the Azores.

The Public Security Police deal with minor offences in their own police courts (*Tribunais de Policia*) but more serious crimes are investigated by the Judicial Police *(Policia Judiciara).*

Traffic duties are undertaken by the Traffic Service (*Servico de Transito da PSP*) which liaises with the Traffic Brigade of the National Guard.

There are three special units within the Public Security Police: a special riot-control unit, the Polica de Intervenção (Intervention Corps): a special anti-terrorist unit or special operations unit: and a bodyguard unit, the Security Division (DS).

The reorganisation of the police structures will affect the PSP. It is intended that PSP super squads will be created in the Greater Lisbon and Greater Oporto areas. This along with different geographical distribution will ensure that the PSP and the *Guarda Nacional Republicana* do not operate in the same areas.

b)   Guarda Nacional Republicana

The *Guarda Nacional Republicana* (GNR) or National Guard patrols the rural areas and border communities. It undertakes internal security duties, traffic policing outside the towns and provides special escorts. As a military force it is responsible to the Ministry of Defence in war time and the Ministry of Internal Administration in peace time. Its structure is also of a military character. The headquarters of the GNR is in Lisbon. There were 17,212 personnel in the *Guarda Nacional Republicana* in December 1992.

In addition to the restructuring of the PSP which will have an effect on the GNR, a new squad is to be added to the GNR. This squad will have responsibility for fiscal affairs, replacing the *Guarda Fiscal* by incorporating the staff from this corps into the GNR. In particular it will be responsible for control of the Portuguese coast. This will include economic matters, criminal investigation and security functions.

c)   Guarda Fiscal

The *Guarda Fiscal* with national headquarters in Lisbon currently polices frontiers and ports of entry. It has 7,795 personnel. It is essentially a customs and tax service and so investigates smuggling, tax evasion and illegal financial transactions. Its officers are to be found in coastal and frontier towns, including Madeira and the Azores, and is under the control of the Ministry of Internal Administration. The *Guarda Fiscal* is, as noted above, to be incorporated into the GNR.

d)   Policia Judiciaria

The *Policia Judiciaria* reports to the Minister of Justice. There are 1,921 personnel within this force. Its duty is to prevent and investigate crime. It undertakes observation of public places and also operates at ports and airports.

It is a national force which operates at both the local and national level. At the local level it is based in towns throughout Portugal and liaises with the courts and prosecutors on whose behalf it carries out investigations. At the national level it carries out investigations into major crime such as subversion, drugs trafficking, theft of art, counterfeiting, terrorism and murder.

The General Directorate provides back-up support for the Judicial Police and includes telecommunications, laboratories and central records, as well as the Interpol National Central Bureau role. There are three central directorates which carry out national functions.

(i)   The *Direccao Central de Cambate Ao Banditismo* (central anti-gang squad) investigates armed robberies, terrorism and similar organised crimes.

(ii)   The central squad investigates crimes of an economic character (DCICFIEF).

(iii)   The central drug traffic investigation squad (DCITE) concentrates on tackling narcotics.

e)   Policia Maritima

The *Policia Maritima* or Maritime Police, of about 500 officers, undertakes harbour patrols. It is a navy service and is therefore responsible to the Ministry of Defence.

f)   Aliens Police and Border Control

The Aliens Police (SEF) is essentially an immigration police. This force of about 700 officers is responsible for the entry and residence of all foreigners in Portugal. They also deal with extradition papers and asylum requests. They operate at all airports, ports and borders and are responsible to the Ministry of Internal Administration.

3.12   Spain

3.12.1   Background

The Kingdom of Spain occupies an area of 504,750 square kilometres, amounting to some 85 per cent of the Iberian Peninsula, and has a population of 38.96 million people (1990). The population density is about 77 people per square kilometre.

Modern Spanish, or Castilian, is spoken throughout the country although there are some local dialects and important linguistic minorities. These include Catalan, Galician and Basque. The only significant ethnic minority is the Gypsies, although some Basques and Andalusians would also claim to be distinct ethnic minorities. The social welfare system includes various benefits.

The semi-sovereign state of Andorra is located between Spain's northern border and that of France. Covering an area of 468 square kilometres it has a population of some 35,000 people. Until 1993 Andorra had no constitution and its government was conducted on a semi-feudal basis under the joint heads of state, the Bishop of Seu d'Urgell in Spain and the President of the French Republic. Parties and unions were illegal. In March 1993, however, a Constitution was approved and Andorra's first ever general election is planned for 12th December 1993.

a)   Constitutional Arrangements

Spain is a parliamentary monarchy.   Under the 1978 Constitution the head of state is the king. He appoints the President of the Government (Prime Minister) who is leader of the majority party in Parliament. This is the bicameral *Cortes Generales*. The members of the Congress of Deputies are elected every four years while the Senate is composed of representatives from the autonomous regions also elected every four years.

The President and the Council of Ministers have executive power. There are four major parties in Spain, these being the Socialist Workers' Party, the Popular Alliance, the Christian Democrats and the Liberal Party. There are also local nationalist parties in Catalonia, Andalusia and the Basque country.

b)   Autonomous Communities

The Constitution recognises the demands for regional autonomy and 'the right to self-government of the nationalities and regions'. Provinces 'with common historic, cultural and economic' ties may form together to create 'autonomous communities' (*Comunidades Autonomas*) with the power to govern themselves, subject to the interests of Spain as a whole. There are some 17 such communities. Each of these regions has its own government, led by a President and a Council of Ministers, with a legislative assembly.

The provinces are made up of groupings of municipalities, and are each governed by a Provincial Delegation. The municipalities themselves are governed by municipal councils, elected by the inhabitants, and each of these elects a mayor as its chairman and chief administrator. The large cities of Madrid and Barcelona have special forms of municipal government. The Canary Islands constitute an autonomous community.

3.12.2   Judicial System

a)   Criminal Code

In common with most European legal systems, the Spanish system is 'inquisitorial'. It is the duty of the examining magistrate or judge to build up a dossier of information. The Criminal Procedure Code lays down the rules for the conduct of proceedings, while the Criminal Code (*Codigo Penal*) specifies the different kinds of offences: *delitos* (serious offences) and *faltas* (minor offences).

b)   Lower Courts

At the lowest level is the *Juzgado de Paz* (Justice of the Peace Court), of which there are over 500, which sit with a single lay Justice. They hear cases of minor civil or criminal misdemeanours.

The *Juzgado de Primera Instancia* (Court of First Instance) sits with a single Judge. They are based in the municipalities and try civil and criminal cases, and are also responsible for the civil registry of local citizens.

The *Juzgado de Instrucción* (Court of Instruction) is the criminal court of first instance. The Instruction Courts sit in the larger cities, where there may be a number of such courts (in Madrid there are 33). They may try some serious offences, but for the most serious prepare a case report which is passed on to one of the 15 Provincial High Courts (*Audiencias Provinciales*).

c)   High Courts

Each of the Provincial Courts (*Audiencias Provincales*) are divided into criminal and administrative divisions. Three judges sit in the Criminal Division, which may also hear appeals from the lower courts. In some more serious criminal matters this functions as the court of first instance. There is also a National High Court (*Audiencia Nacional*) with jurisdiction over the entire country. It hears cases of national interest and thus deals with very serious cases such as terrorism, piracy and complex offences of smuggling or organised crime.

In each of the autonomous communities there is a High Court of Justice (*Tribunales Superiores de Justicia*). These serve as a court of appeal in some cases, and in matters relating expressly to the autonomous communities this is also the court of last resort.

Above all of these is the Supreme Court (*Tribunal Supremo de Justicia*) which has jurisdiction in all cases except constitutional matters throughout the whole of Spain. It has six courts within it – the civil court, the penal court, three courts for administrative litigation, and one for labour issues. Appeals to this court are made on points of law. This may generally be described as the court of last resort, with the exception that hearings involving high public officials would appear before this court in the first instance.

There are also several other courts which merit a brief mention. The first of these is the Constitutional Court (*Tribunal Constitucional*). Technically this is not part of the judicial administration system, but as the supreme referee in matters involving the Constitution, it does play a role in the judicial system. Amongst the various chambers of the Supreme Court there is a labour division which hears appeals from the separate labour courts. Finally, the administrative courts have jurisdiction over government bodies. There are several of this type of court, for example, tax courts and administrative claims courts.

3.12.3 Organisation of the Police

There are two national police organisations in Spain: the National Police Corps and the Civil Guard. In addition there are police forces with a limited territorial role: the Police of the Autonomous Communities and the Municipal Police. In total there are some 181,455 officers or approximately one police officer for every 215 inhabitants.

a) National Police Corps

i) Duties of the National Police

The *Cuerpo Nacional de Policia* (CNP), in which there are 51,109 officers, operates in the provincial capitals and urban areas, with a population of 20,000 people or more. It is an armed civil force (effectively paramilitary police) under the control of the Director General of Police in the Ministry of the Interior.

The National Police has a number of tasks which it carries out in the urban areas under its remit. These include maintenance of public order, protection of people and property, the prevention and investigation of crime and the collection of information and intelligence.

In addition, the National Police has some specific duties which it undertakes throughout Spain. These include issuing identity cards and passports, enforcing laws on foreigners, immigration and asylum, extradition, investigating drugs offences, controlling private security agencies and co-operating with the police in other countries. They also have crowd-control units which are trained to act in instances of urban violence.

ii) Structure of the National Police

The National Police is organised on a regional basis. There are 13 regional headquarters, including those in the Balearics and the Canaries, each commanded by a Regional Chief responsible to the civil governors and to the Director General. Below this is the provincial level, under a Provincial Chief, which is accountable to the Provincial Governor.

The local police stations are the *Comisarias*, of which there is one in each town and several in the larger cities. In each police station there are two different corps of police: the uniformed branch and the detectives. In addition, there are three national support divisions.

- The uniformed branch carry out foot and vehicle patrols, hold accused people in custody, protect VIPs and public buildings, undertake disaster and emergency support and give assistance in criminal investigations.

- *The Cuerpo Superior de Policia* is the plain-clothes detective or investigation branch of the National Police. The largest group is the Judicial Police which undertakes investigations into crime. This is usually carried out at local police

(*Comisario*) level, but there are also Regional Crime Squads. There are two other groups: the Inspection Group, which takes statements and compiles reports, and the Sector Group, which carries out surveillance and information gathering.

- The support divisions of the National Police include training, personnel management, technical support and forensic services. The three most important operational divisions are: the Criminal Investigation (Judicial Police) Division, which co-ordinates the Regional Crime Squads and carries out national investigations, and operates the Central Drugs Brigade; the Intelligence Division (*Comisaria General de Informacion* [CGI]), which is largely involved in anti-terrorist work; and the Documentation Division, which controls borders, foreign nationals and gambling, and issues identity cards and passports, and holds central records. The CGI is the contact point for Interpol.

b) Civil Guard

i) Duties of the Civil Guard

The *Guardia Civil* (GC) operates outside the urban areas throughout the national territory (in towns of less than 20,000 persons) and also polices territorial waters. They have the same general policing responsibilities in the rural areas as the National Police do in the towns. There are 75,346 officers in the Civil Guard (ENP 1992a).

They also have special functions throughout Spain, including the control of weapons, the enforcement of national tax laws, the prevention of smuggling, the protection of communications, the policing of borders, ports, and airports, and the movement of prisoners.

ii) Structure of the Civil Guard

The Civil Guard is an armed military force with civilian responsibilities and it is supervised by the Ministry of the Interior, although internal organisation, discipline and conditions are the responsibility of the Ministry of Defence. The Director General is a Lieutenant General based in the central headquarters in Madrid.

The *Guardia Civil* is organised in a hierarchical structure. It is divided into units which operate in six zones, centred on Madrid, Seville, Valencia, Barcelona, Lograno and Leon, and these are sub-divided into *Comandancias*, each under a Lieutenant Colonel, which correspond with the provinces. These are further divided into companies, lines and posts.

iii) Specialist Units

Each zone has a mobile public order unit and an office which collects information and intelligence. In addition to general policing, there are various specialist units. These include the *Agrupacion de Trafico*, which consists of about 7,000 officers who patrol the motorways, the *Servicio Fiscal*, of around 6,000 officers who investigate fraud, and the maritime service, which polices ports.

At the frontiers, some 6,000 officers are involved in security checks and assisting the Customs (*Aduana*) to combat smuggling. There are also Mountain Units, which operate in the Pyrenees to combat terrorism and smuggling, and 3 companies of the *Grupo Antiterrorista Rural*, which operates primarily in the Basque Country in close co-operation with the National Police and the army.

c)   Police of the Autonomous Communities

The autonomous communities are empowered to establish police forces and three regions have so far done so: the Basque Country, Catalonia and Navarra. The *Policia Autonomica* operates only within its own autonomous community. There are about 15,000 officers.

These police are responsible for protecting public buildings and regulating traffic on trunk roads, for enforcing local legislation and for undertaking general police duties, if necessary in conjunction with the national forces. They are under the control of the relevant autonomous community government.

d)   Municipal Police Corps

The local police operate within their particular municipality. Their main function is traffic control, but they are also specifically responsible for protecting their local authority and public buildings, dealing with accidents, and enforcing local by-laws and administrative orders. There are about 40,000 local or municipal police offciers.

3.13   United Kingdom

3.13.1   Background

a)   Ethnic Groups

The United Kingdom of Great Britain and Northern Ireland occupies an area of 244,100 square kilometres and has a population of 57.6 million (1992). The United Kingdom (UK) consists of England, Scotland, Wales, Northern Ireland and numerous small islands.

English is spoken throughout the UK, although a significant minority in Wales also speak Welsh. Alongside the predominant national group, the English, are the Scots, Welsh and Irish. There are also significant numbers of people of African Caribbean and Asian descent. The UK has a reasonably comprehensive social welfare system.

In addition to the UK Crown dependencies of the Channel Islands and the Isle of Man, which are discussed in section 3.13.9 below, the United Kingdom has 14 dependent territories in various parts of the world. These include Anguilla, Bermuda, the British Virgin Islands, the Cayman Islands, the Falkland Islands, Hong Kong, Montserrat, the Pitcairn Islands, St. Helena, and the Turks and Caicos Islands. The UK government is responsible for internal security and policing in many of these dependencies. The UK dependent territory of Gibraltar is of particular significance as it is also claimed by Spain. Although the UK is responsible for internal security in Gibraltar, most internal affairs are governed by the Council of Ministers drawn from the elected House of Assembly.

b)   Constitutional Arrangements

The United Kingdom is a constitutional monarchy. Unlike any other European country it does not have a written Constitution. It is derived from a number of sources: common law, statute law, judicial precedent, traditions and conventions and works of authority.

The monarch is head of state, but royal powers and prerogatives are exercised on the advice of the head of government, the Prime Minister, who is leader of the Cabinet of ministers and also leader of the majority party in Parliament.

The bi-cameral legislature consists of the House of Lords, the members of which are either appointed for life, or are hereditary, and the House of Commons, the 651 members of which are directly elected at least every five years. The major parties are the Conservative Party and the Labour Party. There are also the Liberal Democratic Party and Scottish and Welsh nationalist parties, and various other parties in Northern Ireland.

c)   Scotland and Wales

Scotland has a distinctive historical and cultural identity and a number of separate institutions. It is administered by a Secretary of State with various responsibilities. Wales, too, has a distinctive identity and like Scotland has a nationalist movement which campaigns for self-government. It is administered by a Secretary of State with fewer responsibilities than his or her Scottish counterpart.

d)   Northern Ireland

Northern Ireland was governed by its own Parliament (Stormont) and government until 1972, but since then it has been governed from Westminster through a Secretary of State. The population of Northern Ireland is divided between Protestants (60 per cent) and Roman Catholics (40 per cent) and has its own distinctive party system.

The unionist parties, primarily supported by Protestants, are in favour of continued attachment to Britain; the Social and Democratic Labour Party (SDLP), supported by some Catholics, is a nationalist party committed to unification of Ireland by peaceful means. Sinn Fein is a republican party, committed to the unification of Ireland, and is described as the 'political wing' of the Provisional Irish Republican Army (PIRA) which has been conducting a terrorist campaign to achieve unification.

Northern Ireland has been the scene of terrorist outrages and serious disorder, called 'The Troubles', since 1968. Terrorism is committed by extreme unionist groups, notably the Ulster Freedom Fighters (UFF), and by the republican Provisional Irish Republican Army (PIRA). The terrorist activities of the PIRA also occur in England and other parts of Europe.

e)   Local Government

Local government in England, Wales and Scotland is based on a two-tier structure, although this is currently under review. In the top tier in Wales and non-metropolitan England are 47 directly-elected county councils (9 regions in Scotland), with responsibilities for education, strategic planning, social services, transport and police and fire services (some of which are run jointly with other county councils), and under these are 333 district councils, with responsibility for local planning, housing, environmental health and other matters.

In the large urban areas in England the top tiers are appointed authorities responsible for police and fire services and public transport, while below them the extensive functions of the 36 metropolitan districts include education, social services, housing and planning.

In London, most local authority functions are carried out by the 32 boroughs and the Corporation of the City of London. There is no local government authority for the whole of London, although there are joint boards for services such as fire and transport. Policing in the capital is not the responsibility of local government.

In the Orkney, Shetland and western islands of Scotland there are 3 all-purpose councils, while in Northern Ireland major services are the responsibility of statutory bodies and the 26 single-tier elected councils undertake a number of minor functions. In mid-1993 the government announced plans to reform local government in Scotland to create a small number of single-tier authorities.

3.13.2   Judicial System

a)   Judges and Magistrates

Justice in England and Wales is administered by judges and magistrates. The former are recruited from practising lawyers whereas magistrates, who try some 90 per cent of all cases, are generally unpaid justices of the peace although there are some paid lawyers who act as stipendiary magistrates. There are 620 Magistrates' Courts. More serious criminal cases pass on to Crown Courts, where they are tried by a judge and jury.

b)   Criminal Proceedings

In England and Wales, the decision to commence criminal proceedings is usually made by the police in consultation with the Crown Prosecution Service (CPS), established in 1986, which is independent of the police forces. The CPS then decides whether to continue proceedings.

Offences generally fall into three categories. First, there are summary offences which are dealt with by magistrates without a jury. Secondly, there are rather more serious offences which may be dealt with by magistrates or may be tried in the Crown Court, depending on whether the defence or prosecution so opts. Thirdly, there are serious offences or indictable offences which can only be tried by the Crown Court.

c)   The High Court

Appeals are heard by the Court of Appeal, which is divided into criminal and civil divisions. Civil cases are heard in County Courts, usually before a single judge, or in the High Court. The Queen's Bench of the High Court also hears some serious criminal cases. Final appeal may be made to the Judicial Committee of the House of Lords, which is the supreme court with jurisdiction in all fields.

d) **The Scottish Legal System**

Within the UK, Scotland has a separate legal system based on customary law and Roman law. The court system is quite different from that in England. Civil cases are heard first in the Sheriff Court. If an appeal is allowed, the case will then move to the Sheriff Principal, or may be remitted directly to the Inner House of the Court of Session. The Outer House of the Court of Session is also a court of first instance where more serious cases are heard initially. From the Court of Session appeals are taken to the House of Lords.

Criminal cases follow a different route. From the District Court, where minor cases are heard, appeals on points of law are remitted to the High Court of Justiciary. Alternatively, where the case is more serious the Sheriff Court is the court of first instance (unless jurisdiction is specifically exclusive to the High Court of Justiciary). Appeals lie to the High Court of Justiciary.

Criminal prosecutions in Scotland are brought by the Procurators Fiscal who operate in each Sheriffdom independently of the police under the overall control of the Lord Advocate. A Procurator may conduct a prosecution, make a preliminary investigation, or inquire into a death. At the preliminary hearing witnesses are not confronted, but rather the Procurator's task is to examine the evidence and prepare a case. In Scotland there remains the unique situation that three verdicts are possible in a criminal prosecution: Guilty, Not Guilty, and Not Proven.

3.13.3 *Organisation of the Police*

a) **Co-ordination Between Separate Forces**

There are 52 police forces in the United Kingdom with a total of 154,738 police officers, or approximately one police officer for every 372 inhabitants. There are eight forces in Scotland (14,007 officers), one in Northern Ireland (8,478 officers, with a reserve of 4,627 officers, of which 3,209 are full-time and 1,418 are part time) and 43 in England and Wales (127,626 officers). In addition, there are various specialist forces, such as the British Transport Police.

Some measure of co-ordination between the different police forces is achieved by the provision of common services, many based in the Metropolitan Police. These include the services co-ordinated by the National Criminal Intelligence Service (NCIS), which was established in 1992. The National Drugs Intelligence Unit, the National Identification Bureau, the National Football Intelligence Unit and the Interpol National Central Bureau functions are all part of the NCIS. In addition, there are five Regional Crime Squads of specialist detectives, under the command of Detective Chief Superintendents who liaise with the National Co-ordinator.

b) **Powers of the Police**

Modern UK policing is normally dated from 1829 when the Metropolitan Police was founded. During the thirty years after 1829 local police forces were established in many different parts of Britain so that by the middle of the century there were some 256 separate forces. There were still 183 separate forces in England and Wales in 1939 but amalgamations have reduced this to the present 43.

The police task is concerned with the prevention and detection of crimes and with the maintenance of public order. The powers of a police officer are derived from common law and statute. Common law powers stem from the office of constable. Every officer must uphold the Queen's Peace without fear or favour. The main statutes on which contemporary policing in England and Wales are founded are the Police Act 1964 and the Police and Criminal Evidence Act 1984.

c)   Police Accountability

There are 43 police forces in England and Wales of which one, the Metropolitan Police, is by far the largest. In total there are around 127,600 police officers in England and Wales. In London, the City of London (the historic financial centre) is policed by its own force.

Each police force is headed by a Chief Constable (a Commissioner in the case of the Metropolitan and the City of London Police) who is responsible for the management and operation of the force. He reports to a police authority, which consists of local councillors and magistrates. Its responsibility is 'to secure the maintenance of an adequate and efficient police force'. The Home Office is the central government department responsible for policing. Police forces are also accountable to Her Majesty's Inspectorate of Constabulary.

d)   Policing Structures

There is considerable variation in the size of the police forces outside London. Some, such as Greater Manchester, West Midlands and South Yorkshire, cover large conurbations and consequently each have a complement of several thousand officers, whereas others operate in predominantly rural areas and so have only 1,500 – 2,000 officers.

Each police force has a headquarters, which includes specialist support services – for example, a central criminal investigation unit, which deals with organised crime, drugs, extortion, commercial fraud and other major crime in the area; and the Special Branch, which collects intelligence on crimes such as subversion and terrorism.

Each force is made up of uniformed officers, detectives in the Criminal Investigation Department (CID) and traffic police. Officers may move between these branches or spend time in more specialised fields. The basic structures for operational policing are divisions and subdivisions which operate from local police stations.

The chief officers are responsible for law enforcement in their force areas. In addition to a Deputy, usually two or more Assistant Chief Constables (ACCs) are appointed. In a large force there may be as many as six ACCs, with special responsibilities in fields such as crime, operations, management and administration, personnel, or similar specialisms. Designated squads may be formed to deal with drugs or fraud investigations.

For the execution of their duty, police officers are usually equipped with wooden truncheons. Firearms are only issued to some authorised units for special operations.

The Sheehy Report and the Report of the Royal Commission on Criminal Justice, both published in July 1993, recommended various changes to police structure and procedures. The government is expected to bring forward firm proposals for change in the autumn of 1993.

3.13.4 *The Metropolitan Police*

a) Policing Structure

The Metropolitan Police ('The Met') was established in 1829 primarily to maintain public order. From its initial complement of some 3,000 officers it has grown to over 28,000. There are also some 14,000 civilian administrative staff. It is under the control of the Commissioner of Police. There is no police authority of local councillors and magistrates, as elsewhere in England and Wales; in London this role is undertaken by the Home Secretary.

The Metropolitan Police District (MPD) covers Greater London, excluding the City of London. Some 6.8 million people live in this area of 787 square miles, and many others travel in and out each working day.

The MPD is divided into eight areas, each of which is subdivided into divisions, the boundaries of which generally coincide with those of the London borough councils. Some divisions are further divided into sub-divisions.

Each Area has its own headquarters and is under the command of a Deputy Assistant Commissioner (DAC). The DACs are in charge of uniformed and CID work in their Area and report to the Assistant Commissioner (Territorial Operations) at New Scotland Yard.

b) The Criminal Investigation Department

The 3,500 detectives who work in the Metropolitan Police Criminal Investigation Department (CID) are divided into two groups: those who work from police stations in the 75 Divisions and 1,500 who work in Scotland Yard. They work in various branches and squads including:

(i) *Major Investigation Reserve* which investigates murders and other serious crimes and conducts enquiries, in Britain or abroad, on behalf of the Director of Public Prosecutions.

(ii) *National Central Office for the Suppression of Counterfeit Currency.*

(iii) *Extradition, Illegal Immigration and Passport Squad.*

(iv) *Central Drugs Squad* which also liaises with HM Customs and Excise.

(v) *Stolen Motor Vehicle Investigation Squad.*

(vi) *Serious and Organised Crime Squad* known popularly as 'The Gang Busters'.

(vii) *Central Robbery Squad* which used to be known as the Flying Squad, or 'The Sweeney'.

(viii)   *Criminal Intelligence Branch* which collects and analyses information on important active criminals.

(ix)   *Fraud Squad* which is staffed by officers from both the Metropolitan Police and the City of London Police.

(x)   *Special Branch* which collects information about subversives and watches the movement of suspected terrorists through air and sea ports.

(xi)   *Anti-Terrorist Branch.*

c)   Other Special Groups

The Metropolitan Police has many other special groups, some for purposes such as royalty and diplomatic protection, or special escorts, others for back-up to other squads or for collating information, such as the Missing Persons Bureau. Traffic control is another responsibility of the Metropolitan Police.

There is a central traffic control in Scotland Yard liaising with Area Traffic Control which uses a computerised system to monitor trouble spots and alter traffic lights accordingly. 700 specially trained traffic police, assisted by 1,800 traffic wardens, patrol the streets to undertake traffic duties.

Each Area has a Territorial Support Group (TSG) which is a flexible, rapid-response unit of police specially trained to deal with crime and public disorder. Each TSG consists of a superintendent, a chief inspector, 5 inspectors, 12 sergeants and 100 constables, divided into four units. The TSGs are trained and equipped to deal with serious outbreaks of disorder, such as riots, but they also undertake other policing duties.

3.13.5   *Scottish Police*

There are 8 separate police forces in Scotland, most of which cover large geographical areas. There are around 14,000 police officers in Scotland. Each force is headed by a Chief Constable who runs the force on a day-to-day basis and reports to a police authority made up of Scottish regional councillors. The Secretary of State for Scotland has the same role in relation to policing as that of the Home Secretary in England and Wales.

The basic organisation and duties of the police in Scotland are the same as in England and Wales. There is a separate police college located in Tulliallan Castle. There is a Scottish Crime Squad and a Scottish Criminal Record Office, both of which are based in Glasgow.

3.13.6   *Royal Ulster Constabulary*

a)   Accountability of the Royal Ulster Constabulary

The Royal Ulster Constabulary (RUC) is responsible to a Police Authority, the members of which are appointed by the Secretary of State for Northern Ireland.

The force is entirely funded by central government. Operational control of the RUC is vested in the Chief Constable, who decides policing priorities and allocation of resources.

The RUC is inspected annually by Her Majesty's Inspector of Constabulary. Investigations into complaints against the police are monitored by the Independent Commission for Police Complaints for Northern Ireland. There were 2,396 complaints made in 1987 of which 26 were upheld.

b)   Duties of the RUC

The priority for policing in Northern Ireland is the eradication of terrorism. Since 1969 when the present 'Troubles' began some 2,135 civilians have been killed by terrorist actions. Deaths among members of the security services caused by terrorism amount to 441 soldiers, 197 members of the Ulster Defence Regiment, 5 members of the Royal Irish Regiment and 290 members of the Royal Ulster Constabulary, including 99 reserve members. Over 6,500 members of the RUC have been injured by terrorists during this period.

Of course, the RUC also has the duty to prevent and detect other crime and judged by the published clear-up rate of 43 per cent, one of the highest in the UK, has a high rate of success. In fact, the reported level of crime in Northern Ireland is the lowest in the UK, although this may be connected with the terrorist situation and the low level of reporting of crime in some areas.

c)   Size of the Force

From its inception in 1922 until the late 1960s the size of the RUC remained at around 3,000 officers. However, with the advent of serious civil disorder and terrorist activity the number of officers has grown to its present strength of 8,474 (1993). In addition there are 4,627 members of the RUC reserve, of whom 3,209 are full-time and 1,418 are part time.

Religion is an important factor in Northern Ireland and currently 10 per cent of the RUC is Roman Catholic. Despite the dangers of policing in Northern Ireland, there is no shortage of applicants: in 1987 some 5,000 people applied for 246 vacancies.

The RUC is divided into uniformed officers, plain clothes detectives and a traffic division. In addition, there are many specialised sections including the Special Branch.

The Royal Ulster Constabulary is the only force in the United Kingdom in which the officers are armed as a matter of course.

d)   The Role of the British Army

Some policing activities are also carried out by the army in Northern Ireland. The army's role is to assist the RUC in maintaining law and order. The army is involved in two respects: regular troops from the British army are posted to Northern Ireland for tours of duty and in addition there were locally-recruited soldiers who served in the Ulster Defence Regiment (UDR). On 1st July 1992 the UDR and the Royal Irish Rangers were amalgamated to become the Royal Irish Regiment, as a result of restructuring in the UK armed services. From September 1993 the Royal Irish

Regiment has consisted of one general service battalion and six home service battalions. In addition there are two territorial army battalions. The general service battalion, as the former UDR, will continue to serve only in Northern Ireland whilst the other battalions may serve in other countries across the world.

3.13.7   Other Police in the UK

There are various other police organisations in the UK with particular responsibilities. These include the British Transport Police, the UK Atomic Energy Authority Constabulary, the Ministry of Defence Police, the Royal Parks Constabulary and an array of Port, Harbour and Tunnel Police.

In the UK, for example, ports and airports are policed by uniformed and Special Branch police and by customs and immigration officers, who have various powers to stop and (in the case of customs) search people and verify documentation. Responsibility for the security of ports and ships, and airports and aircraft, lies with the Secretary of State for Transport. Twelve ports have their own police forces which deal with security and safety of passengers and freight, but local police and Special Branch undertake activities relating to terrorism, major crime and drugs trafficking.

Nine airports are 'designated' under Part III of the Aviation Security Act 1982 which means that the responsibility for policing them is that of the local police force. The police are responsible for crime prevention and detection and also for serious major incidents such as accidents, hi-jacks and terrorist threats. The UK Prevention of Terrorism (Temporary Provisions) Act 1989 (PTA) is also important for the policing of frontier controls. Ports can be 'designated' which allows for police control points. This is the case at London's Heathrow Airport. In other cases, police will be present but behind the scenes.

3.13.8   The Channel Islands and the Isle of Man

a)   The Channel Islands

The Channel Islands in the English Channel consist of four main islands, Jersey, Guernsey, Alderney and Sark, with a number of other smaller islands. The islands are dependencies of the British Crown and are not part of the United Kingdom. The total population of the Channel Islands is some 140,000 people.

The islands are grouped into two bailiwicks, of Guernsey and Jersey, and are administered according to local traditions. In Alderney, the Court of Alderney administers justice, while in Guernsey the Royal Court, presided over by the bailiff with 12 jurats, administers the law which is founded on that of old Normandy amended by local custom. The island is governed by the States of Deliberation.

The judicial system in Jersey is similar to that in Guernsey while justice in Sark is administered by the Court of the Seneschal. There are two local police forces, the States of Jersey Police and the Guernsey Police, each under a Chief Officer.

b)   The Isle of Man

The Isle of Man covers an area of 572 square kilometres in the Irish Sea and has a population of about 65,000 people. It is a Crown possession, under the general administration of the UK Home Office, and is not part of the United Kingdom. There is a large measure of self-government which is conducted by the Lieutenant-Governor, the Upper House and the House of Keys, which together form the Court of Tynwald. The local police force is the Isle of Man Constabulary.

3.13.9   *Customs and Excise*

There are no special border police in Britain. Her Majesty's Customs and Excise have a wide-ranging responsibility for investigating the illegal import of goods liable to forfeiture. These responsibilities are matched by extensive powers of search and confiscation.

Customs officers are able to enter and search premises and to seize and detain. These powers are considerably greater than comparable powers of British police forces. Liaison between the police and customs is increasingly important as both have responsibilities in the fight against drugs trafficking.

3.14   Training Preparations for the Single Market

Training preparations for the Single Market have varied considerably throughout the police forces of Europe. The diversity amongst European law enforcement agencies is reflected in the different approaches that have been taken towards training and education about the Single European Market and the consequences for policing. This section deals first with issues relating to collaborative training between different European police forces. Language training is then discussed. Finally, an assessment is made of training initiatives undertaken to prepare police officers more generally for a new 'European' dimension in their work.

3.14.1   *European Co-operation in Police Training*

The diversity amongst the different European law enforcement agencies is apparent from the information given in this chapter. The forces themselves are different. The judicial systems in which they operate vary greatly. The criteria for entry and minimum training periods also differ considerably. These key points seem to militate against extensive co-operation between member states in police training.

a)   The Provisions of Trevi Working Group II

As detailed in Chapter 4, Working Group II of Trevi has responsibilities for police training. A 1990 statement by that group noted:

> With the object of developing reciprocal information regarding the organisation and methods of police services and on the legislation procedures and regulations of member states, police training schools and colleges shall arrange for regular exchange of students and instructors. (Trevi 1990, para. 7).

Such steps are now being taken by many police training institutions, and this is briefly discussed below. The extent to which these initiatives are inspired by the Trevi declaration is difficult to assess.

The evidence indicates that efforts towards European co-operation over police training will only develop when the Single European Market becomes fully operational. As the Association of Scottish Police Superintendents remarked:

> Until such times as political decisions are taken as to what extent entry controls are to be relaxed and precisely what the implications are going to be for police officers, it is difficult to see how detailed training can go ahead. (House of Commons 1990b, p.51).

Respondents to this study during its second phase in 1992 and 1993 mentioned that Trevi is sponsoring a European Police Studies course at the French training centre in Clermont-Ferrand, the *Services de la Formation des Personnels de Police*. However, further information on this course, though requested, has not yet been made available.

b)   Issues of Professional Self-Regulation and Harmonisation

Two issues seem crucial to discussions on common training arrangements within the European Union police forces. The first lies with professionalism and best practice. The police forces themselves are arguably the agencies most able to define appropriate training standards and programmes. If the development and maintenance of standards of good practice is best undertaken by an organisation itself, then it follows that the police themselves, rather than national governments or the European Commission, should be responsible for developing standards in European training. The police services may be reluctant to do this until clearer evidence has emerged indicating the shape and nature of the new Europe. There is also the problem of which organisations will initiate such developments.

The second issue lies with the harmonisation of standards. Even if there is a willingness to seek uniformity of approach, the harmonisation of professional training is far from straightforward. Although the European Commission is keen to promote harmonisation in general, it has recognised that this is a problematic area:

> For many professions [...] common requirements have still not been agreed, often despite long years of negotiation. Even where progress has been made it has been slow and difficult. A natural pride in national traditions and institutions can often make acceptance of equally meritorious but different systems difficult. (Commission of the European Communities 1989a, p.42).

Given the differences in legal systems, force organisations and traditions of policing in Europe, the goal of a single system of mutual recognition involving standardisation of police training is one which at the very minimum will require concerted effort and political will. This seems unlikely for the time being, given current debates about sovereignty and the position of police forces (see Walker 1992).

c)   Special Courses

The most promising area in which co-operation over training has seen progress is in relation to courses targeted towards specific areas of policing. For example, in

August and September 1992, a 12-day course was run in Brussels and Eindhoven for police and immigration officers on the detection of forged documents. The course was organised by the Belgian *Gendarmerie*, the Dutch CRI and the UK immigration service (*Statewatch* 1992b, p.1).

Other specialist programmes include the European Police Studies courses which are run by the national police academies of Germany, Spain, the UK and France, and the annual police summer course held in the Netherlands. The Trevi sponsored courses at Clermont-Ferrand are understood to be part of this network.

Training for customs officers is also organised under the Mattheus programme, which is discussed in Chapter 6. A more recent initiative under the KAROLUS programme gives customs officials the opportunity to gain experience of other community administrations, shadow their counterparts from other member states and receive general training on the Single Market.

d)　　Assessment

Joint training initiatives are the first step towards long-term harmonisation of standards of police practice, At present these are few and far between, although it is interesting to note that police respondents who had been party to them were unequivocal in their support. Whilst Trevi Working Group II has supported these sorts of initiatives in principle, the Working Group has yet to put their proposals into practice. The structured co-ordination of co-operative efforts in training is likely to develop incrementally – most probably through small scale courses on focused, specialist areas of police work.

3.14.2　*Language Training*

It has long been recognised that language skills amongst police officers will be crucial to effective international co-operation. For example, Interpol's National Central Bureau staff have always included linguists. Language proficiency is an issue discussed here, and three UK initiatives are assessed.

a)　　Varying Standards of Linguistic Proficiency

Proficiency amongst police officers (or any cross section of the population) in the UK in other European languages is notoriously bad. English reticence in this area is blamed on many factors, including the dominance of English globally, and a poor educational system for language training.

In some of the north European states standards of language proficiency are very much higher, with all schoolchildren learning one foreign language and most children studying two other languages.

Consequently, many non-British, north European respondents to this survey considered language training of their forces to be a non-issue, because their educational systems already provided such high standards. As Piet van Reenen, former Director of the Netherlands Police Academy, told the research team, the only exception to this was the top-up language tuition received by Dutch police officers seconded abroad. This point was echoed by Tove Steen Sorensen of the Copenhagen police in Denmark (1990, personal interview).

b)   Hesitancy

In the UK, some senior police officers have been hesitant and unwilling to promote the idea of full language training for the police in the UK. At most it was thought that language training '*might* then be provided for *selected* groups of officers' (House of Commons 1990b, p.23, emphasis added). Objections based on fears of the costs involved were raised, and in addition an argument was put forward that training UK police officers in European languages might jeopardise police relations with minority language groups in the UK.

The Home Office noted that individual forces should adopt a 'targeted' approach, as language training for all officers would not make the best use of scarce resources (House of Commons 1990b, pp.13–14). This again does not present an impression of enthusiasm for language training by any means.

The Scottish Police Federation were more concerned over the lack of language training for police officers, and noted that it was only recently that 'serious consideration had been given to the compulsory learning of a second language [...] but there is little evidence of the police taking this on board' (House of Commons 1990b, pp.56–57).

More recently, some forces such as Surrey Constabulary have recognised a need for language training. As a recent briefing paper noted:

> The increase in Euronationals in this county, who become involved in crime and accidents, whether as victims, witnesses or perpetrators, will result in a demand for police staff with the language skills necessary to be able to cope with the situation. The distress felt by entering a foreign police station to report a crime or loss would be much relieved by finding that there is someone who can speak, if only a limited amount, in one's own language. (Surrey Constabulary 1992, p.15).

c)   Three Initiatives

Initiatives on language training by the Kent Constabulary point to the ways in which language training might proceed. Language training for Kent officers is essential, given the county's geographical position in the south of England. The 'PoliceSpeak' project, run in conjunction with Wolfson College, University of Cambridge, aimed to 'ensure accurate and speedy communication between English and French frontier police when the Channel Tunnel opens in 1993' (Follain 1989). The project was funded by the Home Office Police Research Award Scheme, Kent County Council and British Telecom. The two-year study is now complete and two principal recommendations for the reform of police communications include detailed proposals for standardised voice procedures for radio, and a preliminary lexicon of police terminology, with around 5,500 entries (*Focus* 1992, p.16). (See section 5.9.2 for further information.)

ACPO has also produced a 38-page glossary of policing and legal terms in French, German and Spanish, intended to assist police officers when communicating with European Union counterparts who do not speak or understand English (*Statewatch* 1992a, p.3).

A third initiative involves intensive residential courses in French for Kent police officers, or day-release arrangements for language training (Devon and Cornwall Constabulary 1990; Grundy 1990).

d)   Assessment

Clearly it is costly and impractical for all police officers to receive language training. The Surrey and Kent initiatives do however indicate a possible way forward, through the provision of language training for selected officers whose duties require language proficiency, and through the provision of a reliable network of interpreters when assistance is required.

It is also worth noting that at the UK national level, recent initiatives by the Department of Education to promote foreign language proficiency in schools may gradually improve the language skills of those entering the police forces. Such changes will only happen in the longer term, but must not be dismissed solely on those grounds.

3.14.3   *Educating Police Officers About Europe*

a)   The German Experience

In Germany, the BKA has a well-established international training programme for its officers. The most recent information shows that courses include a standard six-month course for CID investigators; a ten-week narcotics course; a four-week 'scenes-of-crime' course; and a course on securing physical evidence.

b)   The Dutch Experience

In the Netherlands, the initiative is taken by the Police Academy in Apeldoorn. Officers are placed on international secondments throughout the EU member states for a period of one month in their fourth year of training. Additional language tuition is given, if necessary. There are regular contacts with the police throughout Europe, and also links with the USA through the Transpol initiative. This facilitates and arranges placements for police officers in domestic and foreign companies and in police forces abroad. Representatives from the Swedish police force, the Berlin Police (Germany) and the UK Metropolitan Police participate in this initiative, as well as some Canadian and USA forces (Den Boer 1991, p.19).

Contacts between the Police Academy and other European countries outside the European Union are good. For example, contacts exist with Hungary, Poland, Switzerland and Norway. Piet van Reenen, former Director of the Netherlands Police Academy, emphasised to this study that training on international policing issues, including proficiency in other languages, is seen as an integral part of police training, and not as a 'bolt-on' luxury (personal interview).

c)   The UK Experience

In 1990 the English Home Office and the Scottish Police Superintendents Association were both unable to give the House of Commons Home Affairs Committee any concrete information on EC-oriented training for police officers at a force level (House of Commons 1990b, p.12, p.23, p.51).

However, for higher-ranking police officers, training on Europe and the EC is available. For example, at Bramshill, the English and Welsh Police Staff College, students on the Intermediate Command Course study specific aspects of European

Union policing as an integral part of their programme. Those attending the Senior Command Course (Superintendents and Chief Superintendents) visit other European countries as part of their studies. In turn, the Staff College offers reciprocal hospitality to senior officers from the Dutch and German academies for one week every year.

Tulliallan Castle in Scotland houses the Scottish Police Staff Training College. Officers attending training sessions in the Junior Staff and the Detective Sections are given no training on European matters. Officers attending the course in the Senior Division do, however, receive briefings on European policing issues (Jim Taylor 1992, personal interview).

Training on European policing issues only for more senior ranks is most probably a consequence of two beliefs. First, European police training is concentrated on police service managers, who would be in a position to pass on their knowledge and expertise within their forces. Secondly, financial considerations must play a part. The Home Office has indicated that training initiatives in this area are subject to the availability of 'accommodation and other resources'.

There are disadvantages with the concentration of training in senior ranks. The research team learnt of dissatisfaction and feelings of marginalisation amongst some British European Liaison Officers attending a conference in May 1990, hosted by the Devon and Cornwall Constabulary. Officers expressed the view that they had little or no sense of professional purpose or direction, and that they saw themselves as at the margin of 'European policing', with their roles being defined in reactive rather than proactive terms. This was extraordinary given their formal position as European Liaison Officers.

In November 1992, the research team contacted all forty-three police forces in England and Wales to find out the name of each force's European Liaison Officer. Inquiries were made to the Chief Constable's office in each case. The results of this small exercise proved interesting. Twenty eight of the initial telephone calls produced an immediate reply with a name. In the other cases, further inquiries had to be made and the researcher re-contacted. In one instance, the force in question did not have a European Liaison Officer – although an individual was appointed as a result of the telephone call! This limited evidence is useful because it suggests that the full potential for European Liaison Officers in each force is not necessarily being realised. This should not, of course, be read as a criticism of the individuals concerned, but rather as a comment on the organisations in which they work.

d)   Assessment

The evidence available to the research team suggests that, certainly in the UK, there is much that could be done to educate police officers about the European Union, about policing in other EU countries, and about the means and procedures for co-operation. Other evidence suggested that those with specialist policing roles, who required contact with their colleagues in other EU countries, were able to conduct their duties adequately on the basis of the training they had received.

However, the research team also learnt of a great enthusiasm for receiving information and training on matters relating to European policing from officers who did not necessarily have regular contact abroad, or a clear European dimension to their work. In particular, the view was expressed that information would not necessarily 'trickle down' to the lower ranks, despite an expressed interest in European policing issues.

3.15   Summary of Findings

3.15.1   Numbers of Police Officers in the European Union

Table 3.1 and Figure 3.1 at the beginning of this chapter indicate the numbers of police officers in each member state of the European Union. There are around 1.3 million police officers in the European Union. With a total population of about 344 million this means that there is approximately one police officer for every 257 people in the European Union.

However, there is considerable variation between the member states, with an estimated one police officer for every 191 citizens in Italy, and only one officer for every 499 people in Denmark.

There are 105 separate police forces in the EU, excluding agencies with primary responsibilities in areas such as customs and forestry policing. Dividing the 105 forces by the twelve member states gives an average of 8.75 forces per member state. Even if the UK with its 52 forces and the Netherlands with its 26 forces are counted as one force each, this still gives an average of just over 2 forces per member state.

3.15.2   The Need for a Detailed Comparative Study

The policing arrangements for the European Union are complex, given the number of forces with policing responsibilities. Before police co-operation in Europe can be promoted seriously and effectively a detailed comparative study of existing police organisations and other law enforcement agencies must be undertaken.

Without a clear outline and account of existing police structures and organisations and their responsibilities, attempts to promote co-operation are likely to be, to say the least, haphazard and inefficient.

3.15.3   Diversity: A Research Agenda

Even though the information in this chapter is inevitably incomplete, one of the clear features of European policing is its diversity. This diversity is at times frustrating, but it also provides the basis for a research agenda. Areas for consideration in a comparative study of European Union policing systems would include the following:

a)   The Organisational Structures of Policing

The organisational structures of the police vary between EU states. Some forces have a dual structure, with a Gendarmerie and a state police force. Others are regionalised, like the UK and Dutch systems. In Germany, policing is organised at a national and state level. There is little uniformity between the states.

This does not preclude the possibility of conducting comparative work. On the contrary, the variation invites comparison – to tease out common denominators, where they occur; to highlight differences, including the benefits and disadvantages of one organisational structure over another; and, most importantly, to use this analysis to stimulate a more informed debate about the desirability of, and means towards, improved police co-operation across national frontiers.

The research team has been reminded constantly, primarily by senior police personnel throughout Europe, of the need for such a study.

b)   Police Powers

The powers of police officers vary between – and often within – the European Union countries. Successful co-operation between individual officers from different countries is in many ways dependent on an understanding of police powers in different countries. Comparative work which was able to map out the variations in police powers would surely assist co-operative processes.

c)   Police Accountability, Codes of Ethics and Standards of Best Practice

The accountability of law enforcement agencies and officers is of crucial importance in a democratic European Union. Institutional arrangements for ensuring accountability vary between countries. Codes of ethics and standards of best practice also vary between forces. The question *quis custodiet ipsos custodes?* is as valid today as in the past.

This is an area not covered in detail here and a full comparative account of police forces in the EU should undertake a study of these issues.

d)   Special Policing Organisations

Special police organisations exist in many countries, often operating outside the main policing structures. Examples of such police include railway police, forestry police and waterway police, police at sea ports and airports, and customs and excise. These law enforcement agencies sometimes have particular importance for international policing, especially with the continued European development of the transport infrastructure and mobility of persons.

As described in Chapter 5 there are various associations and networks between some of the special policing organisations, but as yet the existence of these special police agencies in Europe is poorly charted. A detailed comparative study will need to take account of these specialist organisations.

e)   Recruitment and Training

Recruitment and training practices vary between forces. This topic needs serious consideration, within a comparative framework, as part of a wider study of European policing agencies. Due to lack of space, and in some cases lack of available information, this topic is not treated in full in this Report. However, this should not be taken as an indication of the unimportance of studying police recruitment and training.

f)   Cultures of Policing

A comparative study of policing in the European Union would be enhanced by an investigation into the culture of policing in the different countries. As other commentators have suggested, common functional roles exist which bind police officers together, creating a police culture (Manning 1977; Muir 1977). There is evidence to suggest that the 'cop cultures' of the police forces in the EU countries share some common features, but also have significant differences. These need elaboration as part of a comparative study.

g)   Legal and Judicial Systems

The legal and judicial systems of European countries vary considerably. Besides the obvious differences between adversarial and inquisitorial systems, some countries rely on statute and case law, others have systematic codes and regulations. Rules of evidence also differ greatly. The proposed study of existing police organisations might usefully include well-researched summaries of key aspects of the legal and judicial systems in the respective European countries.

3.16   Proposal

3.16.1   A comprehensive comparative study of existing police organisations and other law enforcement agencies in European Union member states should be undertaken.

The study should outline key national, administrative and cultural features that bear on policing, describe the legal and judicial systems in each country and its effects on policing, and chart in detail the functions and structures of the police and other law enforcement organisations, including special police agencies.

The investigation should also outline police powers and mechanisms for accountability. The study should not rely solely on police organisations' accounts of their activities, but should consult and interview other knowledgeable sources.

The research should also examine the mechanisms for police recruitment and training, as well as the ways in which 'performance indicators' are used to monitor and evaluate the ways in which police officers discharge their responsibilities.

A conceptually-sound comparative framework would be needed in order to give such a study coherence and credibility.

PART III

PROMOTING POLICE
CO-OPERATION IN EUROPE

At the eleventh meeting of European Chiefs of Police, held in Oslo in June 1989, the Metropolitan Police Commissioner called for much greater police co-operation in advance of the removal of internal frontiers in 1993.

Sir Peter Imbert claimed that current police organisation and resources were not able to respond adequately. 'Unfortunately our strength is not as great as it should be because our organisation is fragmented, often unco-ordinated and at the official level often slow', he said. It could be claimed that the police forces of Europe have succeeded in spite of the formal structures rather than by virtue of them.

This part of the Report examines the structures and networks that currently exist to facilitate co-operation between law enforcement agencies in the European countries. It examines the extent to which Imbert's criticisms are valid and, if so, whether current developments seem likely to provide remedies.

Chapters 4 examines the major structures for facilitating police co-operation in Europe. The International Criminal Police Organisation remains at the heart of international co-operation in law enforcement and its role in Europe is of considerable importance. Alongside it new structures are rapidly developing, such as those of the Schengen Group and the Trevi Group. These are outlined and assessed in Chapter 4, which also looks at the importance of Title VI in the Maastricht Treaty and the work of the Council of Europe.

At the meso level of police co-operation there is a myriad of different groups, structures and networks which usually involve specialist police from different countries. This complex patchwork is examined in Chapter 5, which also explores some examples of police co-operation in different border regions.

At the heart of effective, practical, police co-operation are rapid and reliable communications and the exchange of information. There have been some remarkable developments in this field during the last few years and these are highlighted and evaluated in Chapter 6.

CHAPTER 4

MACRO-LEVEL STRUCTURES FOR POLICE CO-OPERATION

There are now three major structures for promoting police co-operation in Europe: Interpol; the Schengen Group; and the Trevi Group. This chapter examines the activities and *modus operandi* of these three, as well as considering two new structures emerging from the terms of the Maastricht Treaty, Title VI on Co-operation in the Fields of Justice and Home Affairs – the proposed K4 Committee and Europol. This discussion is somewhat speculative because there is still doubt about the organisation, structure and remit of both the K4 Committee and Europol. Finally, the chapter examines briefly the role of the Council of Europe.

4.1 Interpol: The International Criminal Police Organisation

4.1.1 Establishment of Interpol

The First International Police Congress was held in Monaco in 1914 and delegates, who included lawyers, judges, criminologists, academics and civil servants as well as police officers, came from 17 countries, 12 of them in Europe (Larnaude and Roux 1926). The Conference enthusiastically supported calls for greater trans-national police co-operation, and also endorsed proposals for centralised international criminal records and standardised extradition procedures – neither of which have yet been achieved.

Further progress was of necessity postponed until the end of the First World War. The next meeting was held in September 1923 when police officers from 20 countries met in Vienna (Sicot 1961). The result of their deliberations was the establishment of the International Criminal Police Commission (ICPC) with its headquarters in Vienna.

The activities of the ICPC grew slowly but in 1938, by which time police organisations in 34 countries had joined, the Commission was taken over by the Nazis. Claims were subsequently made of continuing Nazi influence within the organisation following its revival in 1946 (Meldal-Johnsen and Young 1979; Garrison 1976) although there is little evidence for this view.

4.1.2 Development of Interpol

a) **Postwar Re-Emergence of the Organisation**

After the Second World War European crime became a particular problem and necessitated international police co-operation (Anderson 1989, p.42). At the initiative of the Inspector General of the Belgian police a conference to revive the ICPC was held in Brussels in September 1946. At this meeting, attended by delegates from 19 countries, it was decided to establish a permanent headquarters in Paris. The organisation has subsequently been strongly influenced by the French police, and its first four Secretaries General were French police officers (Greilsamer 1986). In 1956 the governing body of ICPC, the General Assembly, approved new statutes which changed its name to the International Criminal Police Organisation (ICPO). It very soon became universally known as Interpol, a name first coined as a telegraphic address and popularised in the late 1950s by a television series entitled 'Interpol Calling' (Anderson 1989, p.53).

b)   Changes in the Character of Interpol

The number of countries participating in Interpol has increased greatly during the postwar years. In 1963 it had a membership of 78 countries and by 1990 this had reached 150 countries. With the development of new states in eastern Europe and the former USSR this has grown yet further, reaching a total of 174 countries by October 1993.

However, the increase has not been without difficulties. The character of Interpol has changed with the increase in member countries – most notably it has developed from being largely centred on Europe into a world-wide organisation.

4.1.3   Aims and Constitution

a)   The Aims of Interpol

These are set out in Article 2 of its Constitution:

> (i) To ensure and promote the widest possible mutual assistance between all criminal police authorities within the limits of the laws existing in different countries and in the spirit of the Universal Declaration of Human Rights.

> (ii) To establish and develop all institutions likely to contribute effectively to the prevention and suppression of ordinary law crimes.

To meet these aims, Interpol undertakes a number of activities discussed further below. Its central function, however, remains that of handling enquiries. It is perhaps worth stressing that, despite the popular view, Interpol is not an executive agency with international detectives who can be 'called in' to investigate some international *cause célèbre*, but rather it is an international communications system between different police forces.

b)   Constraints on Interpol's Activities

Divisions on various grounds, such as religion and politics, became evident within the organisation (see Fooner 1989 for a further description of what he calls a 'stormy history'). Article 3 of the Constitution forbids Interpol from undertaking any activities 'of a political, military, religious or racial character'. This led, for example, to the refusal of Interpol to aid the pursuit of Nazi war criminals until 1985 when the organisation issued a request for the arrest of Joseph Mengele.

Article 3 has also led many countries to refuse to co-operate in action against terrorists claiming such action to be politically motivated and therefore unconstitutional. In Luxembourg in 1984 the General Assembly sought to clarify the position by revising the 1976 guidelines on terrorism adopted by the Executive Committee. The General Assembly voted for revised guidelines which would apply to the interpretation of Article 3, and a new resolution was adopted on that point. The basic import of the resolution is that the motives invoked by terrorists are not sufficient to give a crime its legal nature; each case must be considered separately and its character is to be inferred from all the elements involved (Bossard 1988 p.179). This new procedure permits the distinction to be made between criminal terrorist offences and actions which are deemed politically legitimate and therefore not terrorist activities. Article 3 itself was not amended.

4.1.4   Structure and Operation

The general organisational structure of Interpol is shown in Figure 4.1.

a)   Policy-Making

The ultimate governing body is the General Assembly which meets once a year. Each member state has one vote in the Assembly although the delegations to the General Assembly are usually somewhat larger. The General Assembly takes all the major policy decisions and approves finances, working methods, instruments of co-operation and programmes of activities. It also approves applications for membership and elects office holders including 13 members to serve on the Executive Committee.

The Executive Committee, which normally meets three times a year, prepares the agenda for the General Assembly, approves the programme of activities and draft budget which are presented to the Assembly, monitors the implementation of the Assembly's decisions and supervises the work of the Secretary General.

b)   Central Administration

The day-to-day administration is the responsibility of the General Secretariat which is based at Lyon in France. It is staffed by some 283 personnel, including police officers representing 37 separate countries. Police officers constitute 93 of the total number, the remaining 190 are civilian support staff (Cameron Waller 1993, pers. comm.). The General Secretariat implements decisions taken by the policy-making bodies, maintains contact with other agencies and holds information on crime and criminals.

In overall charge at Lyon is the Secretary General, who is elected by the General Assembly for a five-year term. The present incumbent is Mr Raymond Kendall. He is responsible for the work of the three major sections of the Secretariat: general administration, police co-operation, and research and studies.

Figure 4.1 The Structure of Interpol

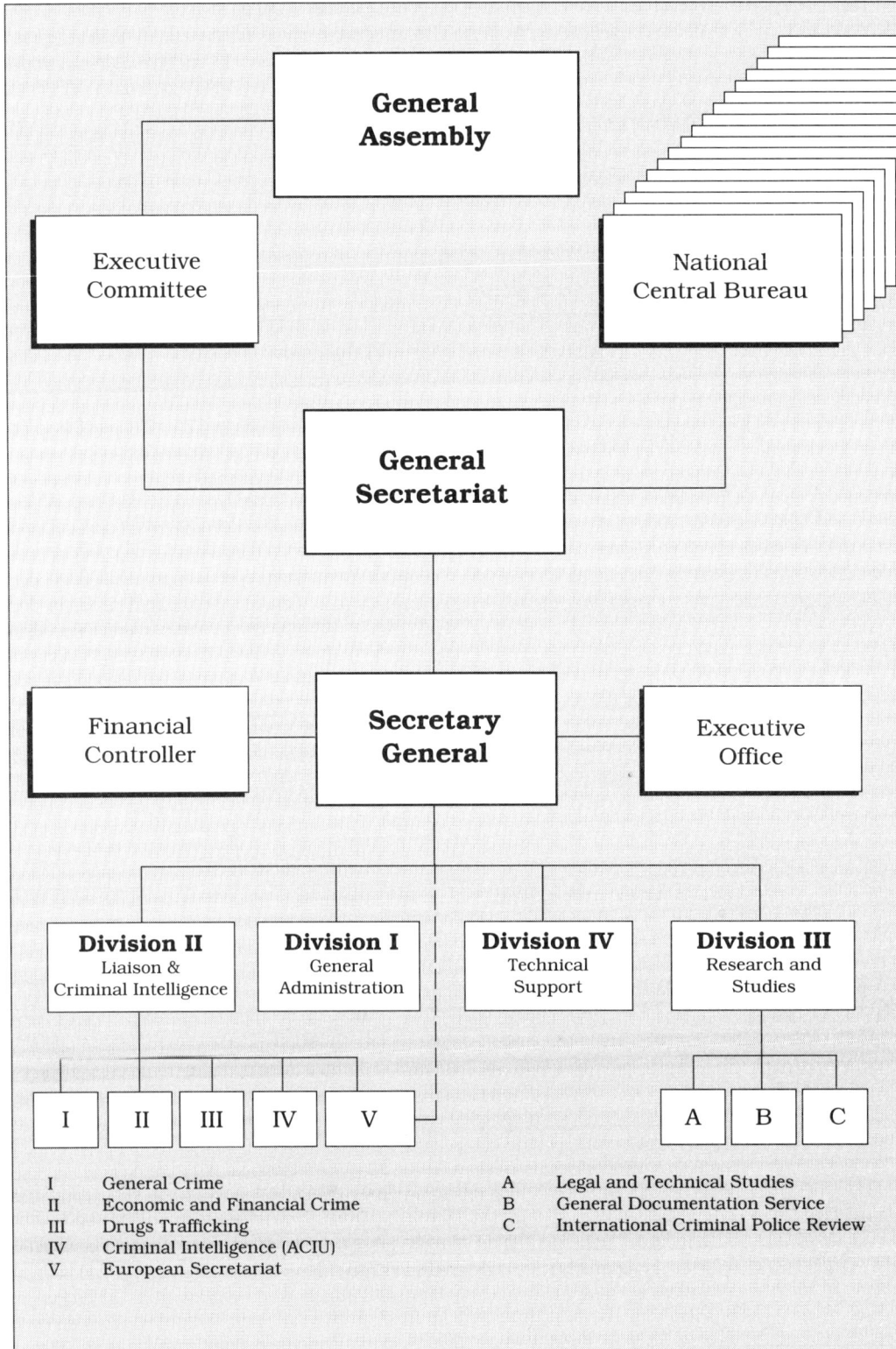

I	General Crime
II	Economic and Financial Crime
III	Drugs Trafficking
IV	Criminal Intelligence (ACIU)
V	European Secretariat

A	Legal and Technical Studies
B	General Documentation Service
C	International Criminal Police Review

c)   **The National Central Bureaux**

The National Central Bureaux (NCBs) are the vital cogs upon which the organisation turns. In each member state there is a NCB, usually located in a key policing organisation, and it is through these bureaux that Interpol's enquiries are channelled. It is the NCBs which ensure that requests received via Interpol from other countries are processed. Interpol is also dependent on the 174 NCBs (plus the 12 sub-bureaux) for information gathering and criminal statistics.

There are clear advantages and disadvantages with this system. One advantage is that each state has a central point through which contacts can be established. The build up of experience and knowledge by NCBs may help to facilitate international communication and co-operation in a way that lower-level contacts may not.

However, the effectiveness of Interpol is wholly dependent on the co-operation of the NCBs, and the willingness of all the agencies in the country to co-operate with it. Generally, the staff at the NCB do not go out and make their own enquiries. They must rely on other national police officers to fulfil this task, but in some countries the practice varies. For example, in Greece and Portugal NCB officers conduct their own enquiries. The willingness of the other agencies to answer requests speedily and effectively varies enormously from country to country, as do the resources available to police forces to deal with Interpol's requests.

4.1.5   *Interpol's Activities*

The primary purpose of Interpol is to promote mutual assistance between the police organisations of separate countries. It does this by passing on information and requests for action in the form of 'international notices' which give particulars of the people concerned, including where possible physical descriptions, photographs and fingerprints. Chapter 6 provides further details about communications to and from Interpol.

The police division of the General Secretariat analyses a great deal of information much of which is filed on computer by the criminal intelligence sub-division. Searches of the Interpol records are carried out on behalf of member states.

The areas of crime dealt with by Interpol are, in descending order of frequency: drugs; counterfeit currency; theft and other property crimes; fraud; and violent crime, including murder, wounding, and armed robbery (Schmidt-Nothen 1989, p.5). It has been suggested that up to 60 per cent of communications on the Interpol system relate to drugs offences (Bossard 1988, p.181).

Interpol co-operates with a number of other international organisations. For example, it works with the International Civil Aviation Organisation (ICAO) on security matters, with the International Association of Airport and Seaport Police on issues such as marine fraud, and the UN Education, Scientific and Cultural Organisation (UNESCO) on the protection of cultural property and prevention of theft of works of art. It also co-operates with many non-governmental organisations like the International Society of Criminology, and the International Centre for Sociological, Penal and Penitentiary Studies and Research.

Interpol organises a number of different conferences and symposia on various topics. It also holds a biannual meeting for heads of police colleges and it circulates lists of training resources, such as films and guides. It publishes the *International Criminal Police Review*, which outlines recent developments in police training, methods and technology, and also produces the more specialist *Counterfeits and Forgeries Review*.

4.1.6   The Central Role of European Countries

a)   Use of Interpol by European Countries

Interpol defines Europe rather more widely than the European Union, or indeed the Council of Europe. The European region includes 44 separate member states. The number may vary slightly from year to year as membership of Interpol is by subscription.

Historically, Interpol was primarily concerned with policing in Europe. Its scope has now expanded considerably although Europe continues to play a major role in its affairs. Eighty per cent of Interpol's messages are sent by European countries. In 1992, of a total of just over 1 million messages, some 800,000 were European, of which 400,000 were sent by European Union countries. The European region is represented by four members on the Executive Committee.

b)   Staff at Interpol's HQ

Among the 93 police officers working in the General Secretariat at Lyon are 25 from France, 6 from Germany and 4 British officers (two of whom are from Hong Kong). By comparison there are 13 from the United States. The present Secretary General, Mr Raymond Kendall, is a former Deputy Assistant Commissioner in the UK's Metropolitan Police. He was reappointed for another five year term in 1990. There are currently three other UK officers at HQ; the head of the European Secretariat, Mr Stuart Cameron-Waller, one Superintendent and a Detective Chief Inspector.

4.1.7   The European Secretariat and Liaison Bureau

a)   Co-ordination in Europe

As the result of a proposal in 1981 for a European Regional Bureau, a small group entitled the Technical Committee for Co-operation in Europe (TCCE) was set up. The large percentage of European communications led to a proposal for the establishment of a European Secretariat within the General Secretariat. This was set up in late 1986. Its purpose is to aid the co-ordination of criminal investigations in Europe. The European Secretariat deals with all criminal matters with a European dimension (except drugs matters which are dealt with by the separate drugs sub-division). The European Secretariat also acts as the permanent secretariat for the European Regional Conference, and in this role conducts research into identified crime problems, for example, international car crime and public order at major events.

b)   **European Regional Conferences**

In 1990 the House of Commons Home Affairs Committee welcomed the increased regional emphasis in the work of Interpol if it were to function more effectively in the future (House of Commons 1990a, p. xxviii). Given that Interpol had already instituted some degree of regionalisation prior to the 1990 report this is perhaps indicative of the lack of in-depth knowledge of the recent changes which have occurred at Interpol.

The membership of Interpol is divided into 9 regions, which each may hold its own conferences and make recommendations to the General Assembly. The regions are North America, Central America, South America, Scandinavia, Europe, North Africa and the Arab states, other African states, Asia, and the South Pacific countries.

The European Regional Conference is held every year, and over 30 countries attend. The number of countries attending the Conference is likely to be nearer 40 in future with the admission of the new members from eastern Europe in 1993. Additionally, conferences for national drugs units are held annually, and a European fraud symposium is held every two years. The annual meeting of the European Regional Conference reflects the fact that it is European message traffic which dominates the Interpol communications network. Each Regional Conference deals with particular problems relating to its region. For example, a special working group has been established to consider European crimes. One of the problems which this group is currently looking into is the difference in fingerprint identification methods used across Europe.

The European Regional Conference is not exclusively attended by European countries. Other countries may be invited to attend if their contribution to a particular problem is required. For example, Central and South American countries attend conferences on drugs-related problems.

c)   **European Liaison Network**

Another recent innovation has been the creation of a European Liaison Network based on identified European contact officers. Each NCB in Europe has nominated one officer whose task is to act as a 'trouble shooter' when problems arise. He or she is the person who is approached by other NCBs when difficulties occur. The job of the contact officer is basically to iron out problems, speed up answers to enquiries and facilitate co-operation. In the last six months of 1989, the UK European contact officer dealt with 448 enquiries.

d)   **Interpol and Eastern Europe**

Whilst, to some extent, law enforcement in Europe can be considered as 'inward looking' – EU-wide co-operation within the framework of Schengen, Trevi or the 'third pillar' of the Maastricht Treaty, all of which is orchestrated to some extent around the theme of securing the external borders – Interpol is keen to provide assistance particularly to the developing law enforcement agencies in eastern Europe. Interpol has invested in a modernisation programme to ensure that all of its NCBs can be linked by computer-to-computer communications and have direct access to a database of information on international crime and criminals (Cameron-Waller 1993b).

Moreover, those countries that cannot afford to pay will be provided with the equipment necessary to bring them up to a minimum standard free of charge. New NCBs in central and eastern Europe will receive personal attention, including visits, from the General Secretariat who will provide guidance on how the NCBs should be structured and operated. European Drugs Liaison Officers assigned to the General Secretariat will have an important role to play in these developments, as will the 16 officers from the European Liaison Bureau who come from the following 14 countries: Austria, Belgium, Finland, France, Germany; Greece, Italy, Netherlands, Norway, Poland, Russia, Spain, Sweden and the UK.

Given that 80 per cent of the 1 million messages transmitted through the Interpol central station annually involve a European country, and over 40 per cent relate to European Union member states, Interpol is not only committed to maintaining its European dimension, but more importantly, to investing in securing the development of police co-operation in the 44 European membership countries. The wider-European aspect of Interpol's work should not be underestimated, not least because of the crime threat to the European Union from emergent eastern European nations which are rapidly, and rightly, being drawn into Interpol's European Region sphere of influence.

e)   Interpol and Illegal Immigration

It is clear that illegal immigration is a growing law enforcement problem in Europe. Although it is frequently said that Interpol has no role to play in the control of illegal immigration, the sheer scale of the contemporary problem makes it difficult not to be involved in this area, not least because illegal immigration is closely tied to other forms of criminal activity. The recommendations of the ministerial meeting in Budapest in February 1993 called explicitly for criminal legislation to deal with those involved in trafficking illegal immigrants, as well as for the establishment of special units and the exchange of information on trafficking. If criminal legislation is accepted as part of the solution to the problem, then Interpol will have a clear role to play.

4.1.8   *Interpol and Bilateral Co-operation in Europe*

To some extent Interpol disapproves of direct bilateral contacts between investigating police officers which take place outside the Interpol system. Interpol argues that it possesses considerable expertise and experience in international enquiries and officers who 'go it alone' run the danger of duplicating other investigations, depriving other police of information and possibly jeopardising their inquiry by failing to understand other criminal justice systems, for example the key role of examining magistrates in some countries.

A number of countries expressly forbid direct contact and insist that all information is channelled through Interpol. For instance, in Germany it is an offence for an officer in a local force (that is, in a force other than the BKA) to make an inquiry abroad or to respond to such an inquiry from another country.

On the other hand, Interpol has taken some steps to promote bilateral contacts. There is, for example, a special agreement between Interpol, the German BKA and the British Metropolitan Police which was signed on 2nd May 1961.

While there may be good grounds for arguing in principle in favour of the 'official channels' of Interpol, it seems incontrovertible that the successful investigation of difficult cases, whether in one country or two, often depends upon the ability of detectives to develop personal contacts and work co-operatively outside formal structures.

4.1.9   *Research Findings About Interpol and European Co-operation*

a)   Criticisms in the Past of Inefficiency

There have in the past been various criticisms made of Interpol, not least by police officers themselves. One source reports that 'one finds no great enthusiasm' for the organisation's performance (Lewis 1976, p.232).

Some correspondents interviewed during this study made criticisms of the efficiency of Interpol, but to a large degree these views appear to be based on the past reputation of the organisation not on the present, greatly improved, set-up at Lyon.

Other commentators have offered encouraging statements about Interpol and its future. Fenton Bresler quotes 'Duke' Smith of the US Marshals' Service who blames Interpol's tarnished image on a lack of understanding by the public. Yet despite the public image of Interpol, he was very happy with its work and confident for the future (Bresler 1992, p.385).

b)   Security and Terrorism

There have also been criticisms of the security of Interpol, and these were made during the course of the present inquiry. It has been suggested, for instance, that information about serious crimes such as terrorism has 'leaked' from particular countries, in some cases to the terrorists themselves. However, it should be noted that if this were indeed the case then the criticism should be directed at individual NCBs and not at Interpol as a whole.

Bresler described one recent incident. He stated that in a letter to the Sub-Committee on Civil and Constitutional Rights of the US House of Representatives, written in March 1992, Interpol was described as 'a liability to effective law enforcement and a threat to the safety and privacy of citizens around the world'. The letter related to the Habash affair which caused some considerable controversy in France at the time. Habash, a known terrorist, was permitted to enter France to receive medical treatment. The sender of the letter claimed that Interpol had known of the planned arrival of this man but had failed to alert the French authorities. The charge was hotly denied.

It is difficult to gauge how much truth there is in such allegations, although it should be stressed that under the new regime at Lyon messages from one NCB to another via the Interpol network cannot be seen by a third party unless the sending country so authorises. General enquiries are of course seen by others, but presumably such messages do not contain sensitive or classified information.

c)   A Restricted Role in Europe

Interviews in Germany, Luxembourg and elsewhere generally revealed a high level of support for the work of Interpol. There were many compliments paid to changes at Interpol's Headquarters during recent years, under Secretary General Raymond Kendall.

However, the general impression, conveyed by respondents from several different European countries, is that Interpol's role in fostering police collaboration in European Union countries is constrained by the fact that it is the international police organisation of the world. Although it has developed its European role, correspondents reported, it must necessarily give primary attention to its world role. Although Europe is the single biggest user of Interpol it cannot be the sole user. Whilst Europe can afford to develop its own communications systems (Europol being the most recent example: see section 4.3.8), other countries without this option need the support of the larger organisation in order to be effective.

In addition, as noted in Chapter 2, the new-style international criminal is unlikely to respect either the internal or the external borders of the European Union. As Interpol's own statement put it:

> European crime does not have an identity of its own, however the boundaries are drawn. There are very few major international commercial frauds in Europe without equally important interests on the other side of the Atlantic. The European drugs problem cannot be viewed in isolation from the producer countries in South America and the Far East. This principle applies across the whole spectrum of criminal activity. There is no such thing as the European or the EEC criminal. (House of Commons 1990b, p.37).

A similar point was made by Sir John Dellow, Deputy Commissioner of the Metropolitan Police, who said:

> I think we would be foolish to concentrate totally on Europe when one is making decisions about policing Europe, one should have the backcloth of the globe to think about. (House of Commons 1990b, p.105).

Simply put, it would be foolish to jeopardise information exchange with countries outside Europe, especially those in Asia and the Americas, which are so closely linked to the source and trans-shipment of narcotics, and may also be centres for other serious international crime.

d)   Difficulties With European Regionalisation

The existence of the European Secretariat at Interpol Headquarters, the European Regional Conferences which are held annually, and the sheer volume of European messages, are undoubtedly part of the reason for the dissatisfaction expressed by some members of Interpol who resent what they perceive to be Interpol's increasing European emphasis. Given that non-European countries constitute over 80 per cent of the membership this could develop into a major problem. There is a lack of symmetry between Interpol's members and its users.

However, under the terms of the Maastricht Treaty, the recent establishment of the European Drugs Unit (EDU)/Europol may mean that many of the European states will prefer to use this new localised structure for communications. This in turn could mean a reduction in their use of Interpol thus lessening any resentment felt by non-European Interpol members. The development of Europol may help resolve conflicts about any perceived bias towards Europe. Europol could mean that Interpol is more free to serve its world-wide constituents.

Alternatively, the Europol proposal runs the danger of conjuring up an image of a group of European states reserving for themselves the right not to share information with 'undesirable' states. This is exacerbated if one of the reasons for the Europol initiative was continuing doubts about Interpol's security and efficiency. If Interpol is already subject to criticism because of its over-Europeanisation, the creation of Europol may merely reinforce other states' perceptions of European elitism.

It remains to be seen how the non-EU members of Interpol will view the development of Europol, and the proposed European Information System, assuming these become fully operational.

4.1.10   Assessment of Interpol and European Police Co-operation

In terms of the communication and exchange of information, Interpol remains a principal means for practical police co-operation in Europe. It is through the network of National Central Bureaux that messages are relayed. In recent years Interpol's efficiency has improved considerably, especially with the introduction of direct communications between the NCBs through the Automated Message Switch System (AMSS). Exchange of information on the Interpol network has become quite dynamic (see Chapter 6). Although criticisms continue to be made, this is a considerable achievement.

a)   Regionalisation

Further progress may be possible. The report from the UK Home Affairs Select Committee on Practical Police Co-operation in the European Community (House of Commons 1990a, p. xxviii) welcomed the movement towards regionalisation within Interpol and believed that this should be supported. This is, of course, a sensible recommendation and the European Secretariat and Liaison Bureau are undoubtedly performing a valuable role in expediting and facilitating European communications.

Impediments to further progress seem to centre on perceptions of an existing European bias in Interpol and the development of the EDU/Europol and the Schengen arrangements. The international community may resent and resist further 'Europeanisation' of exchanges in criminal intelligence.

b)   Micro-Level Activities

Against this there appear to be clear limits to the extent to which Interpol can develop as a regional centre for practical police co-operation.

First, substantial progress on European police co-operation may prove to be conditional on intergovernmental or macro-level agreements. It is clear that Interpol does not operate to any extent at the macro-level. It does promote some meso-level contact through its conferences and seminars, and each European NCB has appointed a contact officer. These middle-ranking officers meet and talk regularly to resolve case-specific problems (Kendall 1992, pers. comm.). Despite this level of co-operation it operates primarily at the micro level of individual cases.

Secondly, Interpol is constrained by its Constitution to remain primarily a 'clearing house' for enquiries. This is an important, but (by definition) a micro-level service. Significant developments would require a constitutional upheaval to permit macro-level activities. This does not seem likely.

Thirdly, Interpol does not have operational capabilities. Again this is a constitutional constraint and one which is unlikely to be changed. Even at the micro level Interpol's role is restricted. However, evidence received from Interpol itself suggests that it has made considerable efforts to efface its old image as purely a 'letter box', showing that it undertakes some valuable work over and above the communications function, and that 'it will continue to develop a concrete role of information analysis using its infrastructure and its technical and professional capabilities. It will analyse information supplied by the NCBs, thus facilitating police investigations' (Kendall 1992, pers. comm.). This is possibly as close as Interpol can get to operational policing.

c)   Interpol's Overriding World Role

Whatever its value as a channel for information, the relatively recent development of the European Secretariat and the European Regional Conference, as well as new bilateral arrangements for co-operation, all point in the direction of Interpol responding to a perceived need for a more prominent European emphasis in its activities. Meeting this need may not be possible. Quite apart from the dangers of alienating the non-European majority of members, Interpol is not capable of responding to a demand for increased European co-operation with operational significance. Indeed, the development of the Schengen Group, the Trevi Group and (through Trevi) Europol, may point to a new demand, namely co-operation at a level higher than that of information exchange, including meso-level operational arrangements and macro-level agreements. To this extent, the future role of Interpol in police co-operation in European Union countries is limited.

Interpol clearly performs a number of very valuable functions. It is, however, the police organisation with the responsibility to promote world co-operation in policing. As such, it seeks to encompass countries with very different cultures and traditions and different social, political, and economic problems. It has an important role to play in Europe but its primary focus must remain the wider international arena.

Although it is not possible to predict with accuracy what the future of European police co-operation holds, it is certain that in at least nine of the EU countries there will be at least three units charged with processing 'international' criminal information – the Schengen Information System, the EDU/Europol and Interpol. Multiple points of reference may cause degrees of confusion, especially in the 'early days' when the precise functions of each system are not fully understood.

In the immediate future Interpol would appear to have two important roles. First, Interpol may well continue to be the first and most obvious 'point of reference' for international criminal enquires, not least because of the efficiency of the AMS relay system. Secondly, however the new regional intelligence units may develop (SIS, EDU/Europol, EIS), it is likely that any regional intelligence unit will need to work in close co-operation with a central unit, such as Interpol's General Secretariat, so that each could, within the limits of national laws, take advantage of the information available to the others (Cameron-Waller 1993b).

The international dimension of some crimes (drugs trafficking, for example) suggests that Interpol may be the only information network of sufficient scale to cover the global aspects of offending – points of origin, trans-shipment routes and eventual points of distribution. One of the most important reasons for Interpol retaining its world-wide role is in relation to offences of drugs trafficking. These crimes are international in nature and are reported to account for some 60 per cent of all Interpol's communications. Whatever the future may be for European-wide police co-operation, Interpol will continue to provide a service for the 164 non-EU member countries, as well as affording the European Union member states an essential link with the remaining Interpol members.

d)   Accountability and Legitimacy of Interpol

There is another important aspect of Interpol's operations in Europe that needs to be considered. This concerns the accountability and legitimacy of the organisation.

While Interpol remains essentially a 'clearing house' for enquiries from individual countries there are few serious problems of accountability. In contrast, despite the 1984 guidelines on the interpretation of Article 3, there remains a lack of clarity about whether some terrorist offences are political (and therefore unconstitutional) or genuinely criminal. These uncertainties jeopardise Interpol's legitimacy.

Interpol quite fairly points out that its activities are subject to various forms of accountability. All NCBs are subject to the laws of the country in which they are located and the central station is bound by strict rules on access. There is also an independent supervisory board and this may be contacted by any individuals who wish to know what information is held on them. Furthermore, all delegates to the General Assembly may table motions for debate. These points are interesting and reassuring, but there is of course no political or parliamentary accountability of the organisation.

If Interpol were to assume a greater role at macro and meso levels of law enforcement in Europe it would surely require the introduction of more effective mechanisms to ensure political and public accountability. It would appear that some police officers, politicians and officials seriously underestimate the importance of well-developed and visible structures of accountability in order to command a high level of legitimacy, which is itself vital for effective policing in open, democratic societies.

4.2   The Schengen Group

4.2.1   *Schengen Agreement of 1985*

The original Schengen Agreement was signed in the small border village of Schengen in Luxembourg on 14th June 1985 by Belgium, France, Germany, Luxembourg and the Netherlands.

The 1985 Agreement acknowledged the need to abolish obstacles to the free movement of goods and persons, notably border controls. It authorised the detailed discussion of a number of issues concerned with police and criminal justice co-operation – including drugs, firearms, frontier controls, frontier surveillance, mutual judicial assistance, visas and asylum.

Italy joined the Schengen Group in 1990, and Spain and Portugal followed suit in July 1991. Greece had had observer status but at the beginning of November 1992 it was permitted to join the Schengen Group as a full member.

Denmark, Ireland and the UK have not joined the Schengen Group because they wish to maintain some controls at their internal European Union borders. In the case of Ireland and the UK this is primarily because of their island geography, and in the case of Denmark it appears to be because of difficulties with the other countries of the Nordic union.

4.2.2 Schengen Implementing Convention of 1990

The 1985 Agreement established the general goal of abolishing all frontier controls, and harmonising cross-border procedures for goods and persons. The measures required to implement this goal were set out in the Convention Applying the Schengen Agreement (the Implementing Convention).

The draft Implementing Convention was scheduled to be signed in December 1989 but was postponed until mid-June 1990, essentially at the request of Germany which was deeply involved at that time with reunification. The signing again took place in Schengen and the Implementing Convention largely reiterated the earlier commitments.

The Implementing Convention set out detailed measures necessary for the implementation of the aims contained in the 1985 Schengen Agreement. It is divided into eight titles, each of which treats a different area where co-operation is necessary. The areas detailed are as follows: definitions; abolition of checks at internal borders and movement of persons; police and security; the Schengen Information System; transport and movement of goods; protection of personal data; Executive Committee; and the final provisions.

4.2.3 Structure of Schengen

As the prime example of police co-operation at all levels it is important to understand the structure of the Schengen Group. In addition to the description below, this is shown diagrammatically in Figure 4.2.

a) Macro-Level Structure

Macro-level supervision of implementation of the Schengen Convention is provided by the Council of Ministers which meets biannually. This is the Executive Committee provided for in Title VII of the Convention. The presidency of this group is held in turn by each of the members of the Schengen Group. In July 1993 France assumed the presidency.

The practical work required by the terms of the Convention is directed by the Central Group (CG). This is a group of about 120 senior officials (civil servants and police) delegated from the member countries. The European Commission is also permitted to attend as an observer. The CG directs the working groups and presents decisions to the Council of Ministers. It is supported by a secretariat in Brussels.

The first official meeting of the Executive Committee took place on 18th October 1993. Unusually, three meetings of the Central Group were held in advance of the Executive Committee (on 22nd September and 6th and 14th of October) in order to agree the basic rules and regulations for governing Schengen operations to be put before the ministers.

Figure 4.2 The Structure of the Schengen Group

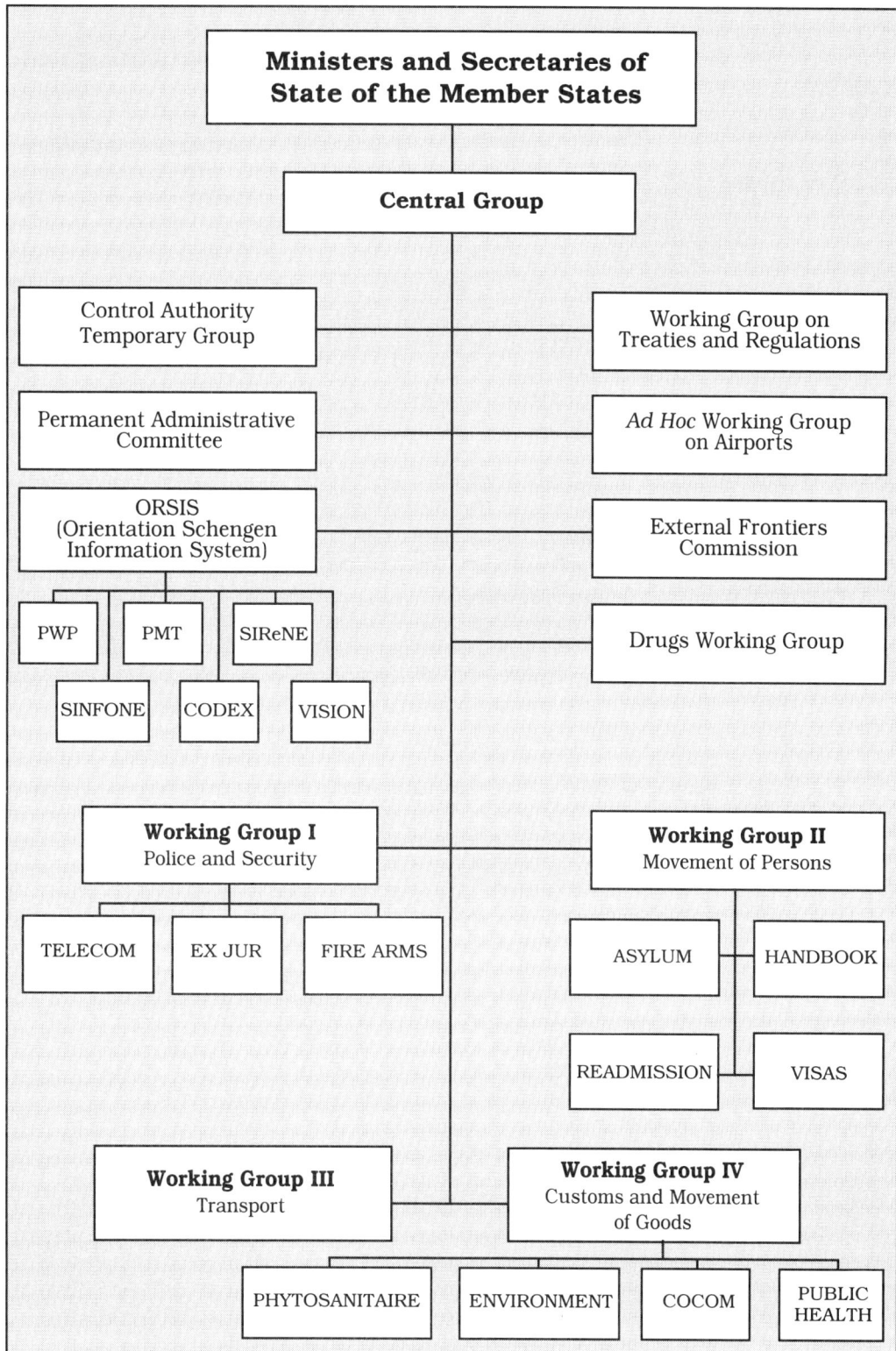

b)   **Working Parties**

The Schengen structure also incorporates a number of working groups. Some of these are sub-divided into subsidiary working groups.

i)   *Schengen I*

Schengen I, the working group on police and security, is probably the most active group and is sub-divided into further working groups.

- TELECOM (telecommunications) and FREQ (frequencies) may be considered together since they both deal primarily with police radio and telecommunications in border areas, and the problems in this field. The groups consist of radio and telecommunications specialists. The group faced various impediments to progress, including the number of authorities involved in such communications and the licences required for them. However, by September 1993 it was reported that significant progress had been made in two respects. First, agreement had been reached on the harmonisation of police telecommunications technology, for which an adaptation of the TETRA standard (mobile digital trunking under development by the European Telecommunications Standards Institute) is likely to be used.

  Secondly, agreement had been reached on the development of harmonised police radio frequencies, using the frequency range between 380 and 400 Mhz released by the military. This move has been agreed by the *Conférence Européene des Postes et Télécommunication* (CEPT) which is the body responsible for allocating frequencies.

- EX JUR (legal experts) is the third sub-group. Their work is largely complete since they were primarily involved in drafting the Convention, and there are no other legal problems requiring their attention at present.

- FIREARMS, the final subsidiary working group deals with controls on weapons. The initial provisions of the Schengen Convention have now been superseded by the 1991 EC Council Directive on Control of the Acquisition and Possession of Weapons, but the group has continued meeting to discuss ways in which the national laws can be harmonised.

ii)   *Schengen II*

Schengen II is concerned with the movement of persons and external border controls. There have been four subsidiary working groups. Three sub-groups deal with asylum, re-admission agreements and visas, respectively. The fourth sub-group developed a handbook on quality control for officials at the external frontiers of the Schengen area.

The asylum group is relatively inactive following the decision taken by the Schengen members to apply the provisions of the Dublin Convention on Asylum, when it has received the necessary ratification. The Dublin Convention supersedes the provisions for asylum contained in the Schengen Agreements. The re-admission group is currently involved in discussions with officials from Austria and Switzerland in preparation for signing re-admission agreements with these countries similar to the one which has already been signed with Poland. The visa group, in addition to drawing up a common list of countries the nationals of which will require a visa to enter Schengen territory, is also dealing with problems relating to documentation, forged documents and passports.

iii)   *Schengen III*

Schengen III deals with transport issues. As most of these are also dealt with by the EC, its work is considered to be of lesser importance than the other groups (van de Rijd 1993, pers. comm.).

iv)   *Schengen IV*

Schengen IV deals principally with customs, the movement of goods and agricultural products and the risks involved in their transportation. It too has several working sub-groups. PHYTOSAN deals with matters relating to agricultural products. ENVIRON considers problems and issues related to the environment. COCOM is the working group dealing with customs affairs. The accession of new members has created some problems in this area, requiring new rules to be drafted. Much of the work of Schengen IV has been completed.

v)   *Other Working Groups*

In addition to the officially titled Schengen Working Groups there are several other groups which also operate at this level and report back to the Central Group.

The first of these is STUP (stupefacients or drugs) which examines the work being carried out by other organisations and agencies active in this field. A particular concern of the group is an apparent policy difference between the Netherlands and other countries in the enforcement of drugs legislation. The group is also somewhat suspicious of duplication of effort in the drugs field generally. A recent European Parliament Civil Liberties and Internal Affairs Committee report also mentions problems because of differences in approach between Schengen members from northern member states and those of the south, but is not fully explicit on this (Van Outrive 1992a). These differences are noted as severely hindering the work of the group.

The second of these groups is ORSIS (Orientation Schengen Information System). Its membership includes police officers, administrative officials and experts in the protection of personal privacy. They deal with problems relating to the protection of personal data, including the development of practical measures to secure adequate safeguards. Under the ORSIS umbrella there are further sub-groups consisting of technical experts who deal with problems such as data processing and the SIReNE (Supplementary Information Request at the National Entry) system. This is discussed further in Chapter 6.

Three other groups operate at this level. These are the committee for the regulation of external frontiers, the airport group and the working group which deals with treaties and regulations.

Whilst some of the Schengen working groups and their subsidiary groups have made good progress and nearly completed their discussions, others are still negotiating over smaller points. The working parties have been criticised for not addressing or dealing with difficult problems, such as the interpretation of the terminology used in Articles 95–100 ('danger' to internal security and 'serious' criminal offences), as well as a lack of judicial and parliamentary oversight (Van Outrive 1992a).

4.2.4   Ratification of the Schengen Convention

The Schengen Implementing Convention specifies that it shall be subject to ratification, acceptance or approval, and that it shall not come into force until the first day of the second month following the deposit of the final instrument of ratification (Article 139).

Some informants interviewed in 1990 argued that it would take years to secure ratification, and these views proved correct. Whilst almost all the signatory states have now completed their domestic procedures for ratification, at the time of writing not all had deposited the necessary instruments of ratification with the Luxembourg government. Belgium and Luxembourg deposited their ratifications during March 1993, followed by France, Germany, Spain and the Netherlands on 31st July 1993.

There is a high degree of political determination that the Schengen Convention should be fully implemented as soon as possible. By late October 1993 the target date of 1st December 1993 for removing all internal border controls between the Benelux countries, France, Germany and Spain had slipped back to 1st February 1994, with Portugal joining these six soon afterwards. There appear to be continuing doubts about when Greece and Italy will be in a position to implement the Schengen provisions.

The particular problems of ratification for Schengen member states are discussed below.

a)   Belgium

The Belgian Council of State issued reservations concerning the democratic failings of the Agreements on the grounds that some articles of the Convention give the Executive Committee the power to take certain decisions which would not be subject to parliamentary ratification.

Until May 1993 there was some difficulty in the Belgian ratification of the Schengen Convention. Article 117 makes participation in the Schengen Information System subject to the establishement of a common data protection standard in participating countries. The minimum standard is that set out in the 1981 Council of Europe Convention for the Protection of Individuals with Regard to the Automatic Processing of Personal Data. Belgium finally ratified the 1981 Convention in May 1993 and will implement it in four stages by June 1995. As a result, there no longer appears to be any legal obstacles to Belgium implementing the Schengen provisions

b)   France

France was the first state to ratify the Convention on 3rd June 1991. However, despite the fact that they led the way with the ratification procedure, several problems subsequently emerged. These culminated in the announcement in April 1993 by the new French government that they were suspending implementation of the Schengen Convention in order to prevent illegal immigration. However, following much pressure from the other member states, it was announced on 30th June 1993 that France would implement the Schengen Convention as soon as legal and technical obstacles had been cleared. Subsequently, following the ministerial meeting on 18th October 1993, France agreed, with five other Schengen signatories, to implement the provisions from 1st February 1994.

The reason for the French hesitation was reported to have been misgivings over the provisions on asylum and controls on immigration. During August 1993 the French Constitutional Court ruled that the current government had to apply the provisions of the Schengen Convention, with the exception of the asylum provisions, even though the Schengen obligations were undertaken by a previous government. The Court cited a constitutional provision that international treaties take precedence over national laws and obliged the government to respect previously undertaken international obligations with regard to refugees and asylum seekers. Legally, an amendment to the French Constitution is required before France can implement all the Schengen provisions and this is not expected before the end of 1993. It is partly for this reason that the implementation of the Schengen Convention has been further postponed until February 1994.

One commentator has pointed to a 1993 cycle of old reservations and renewed commitments, possibly reflecting rivalries between French ministries as well as new conflict deriving from the 1993 change in government (Kerandren 1993).

c)   Germany

Until 1st July 1993 Germany guaranteed the right of asylum to all those who requested it. However, after amendments to the previously liberal asylum laws, German authorities can now automatically reject any person who enters Germany from a so-called 'safe country'. These include Poland and the Czech Republic, together with Austria, Switzerland and the Scandinavian countries, as well as all the European Union states. Obviously, this will severely reduce the numbers of persons who may seek asylum since many applicants had previously been from eastern European states.

The second part of the new asylum law also restricts the numbers of persons who are likely to be able successfully to request asylum in Germany. The authorities are now empowered to decide applications for asylum on the spot. If the application fails, appeals on the decision can only be made through a German consulate in the applicant's home state. Further measures include holding asylum seekers in secure accommodation until their applications have been decided. This has resulted in many persons being held at the airports or borders.

After the asylum law had been amended the way was then clear for ratification of the bill concerning the Schengen agreements. The *Bundesrat* gave its approval on 9th July 1993, it having already been approved by the *Bundestag* in June. On 31st July 1993, along with three other states, Germany was able to deposit instruments of ratification with the Luxembourg government. Following the inaugural meeting of the Schengen Executive Committee on the 18th October 1993, Germany declared its intention to implement the provisions in full by 1st February 1994.

d)   Greece

Although Greece was permitted to join the Schengen Group as a full member in 1992, by autumn 1993 it had yet to complete the domestic ratification procedure. No date had been set for Greece to introduce the provisions of the Treaty, but in October 1993 a senior Schengen source told the research team that Greece was unlikely to implement the key elements in the foreseeable future.

e)   Italy

Italy completed the domestic ratification procedure in March 1993 but by August 1993 had not yet deposited instruments of ratification with the Luxembourg government. There is concern in other Schengen countries about the Italians' preparedness to implement all aspects of the Schengen arrangements with the necessary rigour. By October 1993 it seemed most unlikely that Italy would not introduce the Convention's provisions before 1995 at the earliest.

f)   Luxembourg

Luxembourg seems to be the only member of the Schengen Group which has not experienced any problems in ratifying the Convention. The Convention was ratified by Luxembourg on 7th July 1992, and deposit of the instruments of ratification was made in March 1993.

g)   Netherlands

The Netherlands *Raad van Staat* or Council of State finally voted in favour of the Convention during February 1993, and complete ratification occurred in July 1993. The Council of State issued their opinion of the Convention which contained several reservations, including objections on the grounds that provisions in the Convention might clash with obligations under the 1951 UN Convention Relating to the Status of Refugees. The Lower House of the Dutch Parliament also criticised the lack of democratic accountability, although this objection was made at a later date (Den Boer 1993, pers. comm.). The Dutch Parliament has also been insisting that the European Court of Justice be given competence to deal with matters arising out of the Schengen Convention. Not all of the other member states agree with this, however, and it seems unlikely that this suggestion will find much support.

h)   Spain

Spain completed the internal ratification procedure in February and deposited its instruments of ratification in Luxembourg at the end of July 1993. It declared its intention to introduce the Convention's provisions on 1st December 1993, but this did not prove possible, partly as a result of delays in French ratification of Spain's inclusion and partly due to delays in developing the necessary computer infrastructure. As the date for implementation of the Schengen Convention has now slipped to 1st February 1994, France is expected to give the necessary approval to Spain's inclusion in the Schengen Group at the same time as amending the French Constitution. Spain is expected to join the other five states in implementing the Schengen Convention on 1st February 1994.

i)   Portugal

Portugal ratified the Schengen Convention in April 1992, but has not yet deposited its instruments of ratification. In October 1993 Portugal indicated that it was aiming to introduce the provisions of the Convention at the same date as the other six states. However, there remained doubts about Portugal's technical capabilities in implementing the Schengen Information System.

4.2.5   *Schengen Information System*

Work on the Schengen Information System (SIS) commenced in 1988 with the intention of developing a common computerised database containing information from each of the member countries. The system and its functions are discussed in detail in Chapter 6.

The Schengen Information System is intended to be used by all police and customs officers in the nine Schengen countries in order to access information on missing or wanted persons, people to be refused entry, and stolen or embezzled property. State security services will also have access to the SIS.

The Central Schengen Information System (CSIS) or main computer is based in Strasbourg and it is linked with the National Schengen Information System in each country (NSIS). Each NSIS holds national data, using Schengen-agreed information categories. The information is then passed to the CSIS which is responsible for relaying the data to the NSIS of all Schengen member states.

The Group has also developed an electronic mail infrastructure, known as the Supplementary Information Request at the National Entry (SIReNE), which is a complementary system to provide additional information for action to be taken – for example, to initiate extradition proceedings – and to facilitate the operation of the main Schengen Information System.

At the time of writing there are ongoing problems in operationalising the SIS particularly with respect to recording information on national databases. By late October 1993, the NSIS equipment of Belgium, France and Luxembourg had been tested and that of the Netherlands was reported to be ready. Germany's NSIS had not yet been tested.

The best estimate offered to the research team, by a very senior official involved in the Schengen Group, was that testing with 'dummy' data would probably be completed by mid-November. It would then take at least two months to enter real or 'live' data through the NSIS points so a realistic date for the Schengen Information System to begin operations was 1st February 1994.

4.2.6   *Visas and Asylum*

Under the Schengen Implementing Convention, asylum seekers arriving in the European Union will be subject to greater control. Each asylum seeker will only have one chance to apply for asylum. His or her request will be examined by one of the Schengen states, and the applicant will be prevented from filing parallel or successive applications in any of the other states. These provisions are controversial and proving problematic in their implementation as both the Netherlands and Belgium have expressed reservations about the asylum rules.

a)   **The Positions of Germany and France**

Germany had specific problems since the rules on asylum applications contained in the Schengen Convention were in direct conflict with Article 16 of the Basic Law which granted the right to seek asylum in Germany. The German government has removed the right to asylum from their law (see section 4.2.4 above) so there is now no obstacle with conflicting national legal provisions and the Schengen Convention.

The new German provisions have, however, run into difficulties as asylum seekers have been deported to so called 'safe countries' through which they had passed *en route* to their preferred destination. Two court decisions in late 1993 suggested that both Greece (in the case of an Iraqi asylum seeker passing through Turkey and Greece before reaching Germany) and the Czech Republic could not be considered as safe countries. To some extent these decisions throw the basis of the new German asylum legislation into question.

Following the decision by the *Conseil Constitutionnel* that all asylum seekers making an application in France have the right to have their claim examined because France has prior obligations (under the 1951 UN Convention Relating to the Status of Refugees), and notwithstanding the terms of the Schengen Convention, France is obliged to give precedence to the UN Convention. In effect, France appears to be a full party to the Schengen Convention with the exception of the provisions on asylum seekers and refugees, at least until the position is altered.

b)   Fairness and Judicial Review

The Schengen Information System will be used to provide mutual notification of data on asylum seekers and refugees (Groenendijk 1989; Stein undated). There will be mandatory refusal of entry to aliens who do not meet all the conditions for entry. Additionally, if third state nationals do not fulfil, or cease to meet, the conditions of residence they have to be deported from the entire territory of the Schengen Group, that is the nine participating countries.

Subjects, including refugees and asylum seekers, may not even know if they are registered on the Schengen Information System. This offers potential for arbitrariness in decision making, and could even stimulate bribery and corruption in order to subvert the 'outer ring' criteria (Groenendijk 1989).

In addition, no provision has been made for judicial review of any Schengen decisions, as no court has been given competence to consider disputes. The only body established to review the implementation of the Convention is the Executive Committee (provided for in Title VII), which consists of representatives of the member states. This could hardly be described as an independent review body. These reservations formed part of the reason for Dutch and Belgian parliamentary objections to ratification, although both countries have now fully ratified the Convention.

c)   Precedence of the Dublin Convention

In addition to the Schengen Convention, which is only operational between nine of the European Union countries, the 1990 Convention Determining the State Responsible for Examination of Applications for Asylum Lodged in One of the Member States of the European Community details provisions for the examination of asylum applications. The Dublin Convention, as this is known, is essentially a reflection of the Schengen provisions concerning asylum seekers.

The criteria to be applied to asylum applications are identical to those of the Schengen Convention. The Dublin Convention has been signed by all the members of the EC but by October 1993 it had only been ratified by six states. The Schengen signatories have agreed that once the Dublin Convention has been fully ratified it will take precedence over the Schengen provisions on asylum. Until it has been ratified the Schengen provisions will be applied.

In addition, attention should be drawn to the Declaration on Asylum which appears as one of the 33 declarations at the end of the Maastricht Treaty. These declarations do not have legal force (unlike the protocols) but do make important policy statements about the interpretation and implementation of Treaty provisions. The Declaration on Asylum states that the Council of Ministers 'will consider as a matter of priority questions concerning asylum policies with the aim of adopting, by the beginning of 1993, common action to harmonise aspects of them, in the light of the work programme and timetable contained in the report on asylum drawn up at the request of the European Council meeting in Luxembourg on 28th and 29th June 1991.'

Given the delay in ratifying the Maastricht Treaty, the target date at the beginning of 1993 has inevitably slipped by at least a year, but the overall commitment of the EU countries to introduce a common asylum policy appears undiminished.

d) Bilateral Agreements on Return of Persons

Bilateral agreements exist for co-operation in the return of those refused asylum in a member state. For example, Germany and Bulgaria have signed an agreement on co-operation aimed at reducing the number of asylum seekers from Bulgaria, and a similar agreement has been signed with Romania (*Platform Fortress Europe* 1992–93, p.3). The Schengen countries have recently jointly signed a re-admission agreement with Poland.

e) Visa Requirements

The Schengen Group has an elaborate mechanism for granting visas to non-Schengen nationals. This is seen as part of a compensatory device following the abolition of the internal frontiers in Schengen member states. Three lists have been drawn up by the Schengen working group responsible for visas. The first is a list of countries from which nationals do not require a visa to enter Schengen territory (approximately 20 countries). The second is a list of countries (123 countries by October 1993) the nationals of which require visas to enter Schengen states. The third is a list of countries where one Schengen state will require visas from visiting nationals who will only be allowed to enter that particular Schengen state. This last category is known as the 'grey list'. France, for example, is known to be particularly concerned about terrorist activities and is therefore more insistent than some other Schengen states on a strict visa policy. Notwithstanding these differences the nine Schengen countries are committed to the introduction of a common visa, although the details have not yet been finalised. It is expected that these will be arranged before the 1st December 1993 deadline date.

It should, however, be noted that the new Article 100c of the EC Treaty (the Treaty Establishing the European Community) affects the Schengen provisions on visas. This amendment to the treaty brings immigration policy into the EC decision-making structure. Article 100c states that the Council of Ministers 'acting unanimously on a proposal from the Commission and after consulting the European Parliament, shall determine the third countries whose nationals must be in possession of a visa when crossing the external borders of the member states.' The need for unanimity will be removed from 1st January 1996. Member states are permitted to exercise responsibilities in this field 'with regard to the maintenance of law and order and the safeguarding of internal security', which presumably means that any EC country could introduce more stringent visa requirements, although this would need justification. In effect, the various Schengen lists will almost certainly provide the basis for the EC-wide scheme of common visas to be implemented under the new Article 100c in the EC Treaty.

4.2.7 Pursuit Across Borders

The right of a police officer from one country to operate within another country's jurisdiction is a politically sensitive matter, raising issues of national sovereignty. The Benelux countries have long experience of police co-operation including 'hot pursuit'. Within a zone of 10 kilometres a pursuing police officer can arrest a suspect and can use firearms according to that country's laws.

The Schengen negotiations have encountered some difficulties in reaching agreements on 'hot pursuit'. Information given in 1990, from senior Dutch, Luxembourgeoise and German officers involved in the Schengen process, was that a 10 kilometre rule will apply for arrests in all countries except France, where all arrests must be made by a French police officer. The German authorities have stated that they would be prepared to set no limits on hot pursuit.

4.2.8 Firearms

A particular problem with the dismantling of border controls in the Schengen countries concerns the control of firearms. In France there is a long tradition of easy public access to firearms whereas in Germany controls are much stricter. In 1964 the Benelux Treaty was signed with the promise that laws on firearms would be harmonised but this has still not been achieved.

The 1990 Schengen Implementing Convention states that each country will inform the others of sales of firearms to one another's residents, and attempts will be made to harmonise, if only partially, laws on firearms. These provisions have since been superseded by the 1991 EC Directive on the Control of Acquisition and Possession of Firearms.

4.2.9 Drugs

The Schengen Convention also addresses the problem of drugs. Although the legislation of the nine countries is similar, there have been noticeable differences in enforcement. The Dutch are permissive about the use of soft drugs, such as cannabis, whereas the Germans adopt a much stricter policy. As a result of discussions, compensatory measures have seemingly been agreed in the Netherlands. For example, a senior Dutch police officer confirmed to the research team that there will be stricter enforcement against the illegal sale of soft drugs in 'coffee shops', although quite what this means is open to debate.

Another Dutch commentator points to continued friction between the Netherlands and all the other Schengen members concerning the former's so-called liberal policy towards the possession and use of 'soft' drugs – notably cannabis (Bal 1993). These are readily available and the authorities pay no attention to the purchase of small amounts for personal consumption. The Dutch law enforcement agencies hold that the successful prosecution of offenders is an impossible task and that a health-care model is preferable. This policy puts education and the provision of welfare services for drug users as a greater priority than strict law enforcement. Although the Dutch claim much success in the control of the distribution and consumption of soft drugs, other Schengen states see it as a dangerous first step in an uncritical acceptance of, and toleration towards, the use of heroin, cocaine and other synthetic psychotropic substances. They also perceive the lax Dutch policy as one of exporting the drugs problem to other countries, not least by affording a stamp of approval to the semi-licensed consumption of legally prohibited substances.

The Schengen Implementing Convention (Article 71) contains provisions for the harmonisation of drugs legislation and the regulation of narcotic substances, by means of criminal law, together with a commitment that the contracting partners shall undertake 'all measures necessary for the prevention and punishment of the illicit trafficking in narcotic drugs and psychotropic substances'. Although the Dutch authorities maintain the legal fiction of full law enforcement, the policy in practice is one of a 'pragmatic and rather tolerant drugs policy'. This amounts to the *de facto* legalisation of 'soft' drugs. It is justified by citing the expediency principle in Dutch law which counsels against prosecution whenever this is perceived not to be in the public interest. Whatever the merits of this policy, there is a clear difference between the Netherlands and the other Schengen partners on drugs law enforcement, and this is likely to remain a continuing source of friction.

4.2.10   *Research Findings About the Schengen Group*

During the course of the present study a great deal of information on the Schengen Implementing Convention, and its detailed implementation, has been provided by police officers and officials from the majority of the Schengen countries.

a)   Rapid Progress in 1993

It is clear that a number of stumbling blocks have been encountered, such as data protection requirements and the strong opposition to identity cards in the Netherlands. Interviews with J. Peek, from the Dutch Ministry of Justice, and Merle Hoefman of the *Centrale Recherche Informatiedienst* (CRI), confirmed the very strong opposition to compulsory identity cards. It was clear in the spring of 1993 that several major problems remained on issues such as visas and asylum and matters were brought to a head by the new French government's decision to suspend the implementation of the Schengen provisions. However, rapid progress occurred in June and July 1993 during which a number of the problems were overcome. By September 1993 it was clear that the renewed impetus behind the Schengen accord was being sustained, and the inaugural meeting of the Executive Committee was scheduled for 18th October.

b)   Political Commitment

The main finding of the study is that there is a high degree of political determination and commitment, at macro, meso and micro levels, that the Schengen Implementing Convention should be fully implemented as quickly as possible. By late October 1993 the target date of 1st December 1993, for removing all internal border controls between the Benelux countries, France, Germany and Spain was in danger of slipping back into early 1994, with Portugal joining these six during mid to late 1994 and Greece and Italy at some point thereafter. If Schengen does not have an unstoppable momentum it certainly has a considerable momentum – and enjoys

145

substantial support from politicians, government officials and different police organisations.

c)   Criticisms and Concerns

There are concerns and criticisms from some academics, human rights groups and from within the European Parliament, but their opposition has so far been generally muted. There have been a number of explicit criticisms of the Schengen Agreements from police officers themselves. The Commissioner of the *Police de l'Air et des Frontières* of the Alsace region was reported as saying that the removal of border checks poses real problems: 'Illegal immigration from the former eastern bloc countries and Turkey into Germany is on the increase' (*Police* June 1990). It remains to be seen whether any problems, particularly those relating to illegal immigration, which arise through dismantling the internal Schengen borders are resolved through the parallel increase of security at the external borders.

d)   UK Opposition to Schengen

Of the three non-Schengen EU-member states, the UK's opposition is spelled out most clearly. There are three major reservations. First, the UK's geographical status makes frontier controls at the point of entry sensible, not least because there is a natural frontier. Secondly, the continental tradition of some border countries together with other conditions to monitor internal movement (such as an aliens register, non-nationals reporting to the authorities, spot checks on 'status' and the carrying of identity cards) are anathema to the British tradition of freedom of movement within the country. They are seen to be intrusive. Thirdly, there is the British belief that its existing frontier controls are efficient and effective; and a view that the Schengen external borders, whatever the rhetoric of the ring of steel, are likely to be no more than a 'leaky sieve' or massively permeable (O'Keefe 1993a).

4.2.11   *Assessment of the Schengen Group*

The Schengen Agreement and the Schengen Implementing Convention are perhaps the most ambitious attempts to date to promote practical police co-operation on a large scale in Europe. The complexity of the arrangements makes assessment problematic but there are a number of interrelated issues.

a)   Levels of Operation

The Schengen Convention is certainly a large-scale project. Given its initial objective of removing border controls completely in at least five of the countries by a self-imposed deadline of 1st December 1993, with the others doing so during 1994 or as soon as possible, it necessarily entails some loss of sovereignty by each country in order to promote more effective law enforcement and crime prevention. Even if the majority of the Schengen member states only succeed in implementing the provisions of the Convention during the course of 1994, this will still be a prime example of extensive co-operation at the macro, meso and micro levels.

At the macro level it is concerned with constitutional and legal issues, including allowing police officers to operate in other countries and harmonisation of some laws and procedures. At the meso level it will allow information to be shared between forces and to dovetail various working arrangements. At the micro level it is designed to facilitate the prevention and investigation of specific offences.

b)   Implementation

There remain, however, some lingering doubts about whether the Schengen Implementing Convention will be implemented in its entirety, and when this will occur. Although the Convention was signed in June 1990, with ratification by a majority of the countries three years later, it is clear that a number of problems have yet to be completely resolved.

Germany was unhappy with the Netherlands' liberal drugs policy, but a compromise now appears to have been reached. The Dutch, however, remain unhappy with the agreed asylum provisions and are strongly opposed to personal identity cards, which appear to be implicit in the Schengen approach. France requires a constitutional amendment to implement the Convention in full, and at least initially appears to be unable to meet the full provisions on asylum.

All that can be said with certainty is that six of the nine signatories were committed to implementation by 1st February 1994 – Belgium, France, Germany, Luxembourg, Netherlands and Spain, probably to be joined by Portugal in early to mid 1994, Greece in mid to late 1994 and Italy at some more indeterminate point in the future.

The Schengen Information System (SIS) is not yet wholly operational and may still take some time to become fully functional, although police officers and officials interviewed for this study expressed a high level of support for the project. Recent information is that the target date for the system to be working successfully is the 1st February 1994. The Schengen Information System is discussed in more detail in Chapter 6.

c)   External Borders Policy

A fundamental question concerns the external borders policy – the so-called 'ring of steel' or 'hard outer shell'. Belgium has traditional ties with the Nordic countries and Germany has a reasonably open border with Austria, Poland, and the Czech Republic. The new situation in Germany means that many people who had previously been permitted to enter Germany will be returned to countries through which they passed on the way to Germany. Many refugees, economic and political, journey through Poland, and the Czech Republic, countries to which they will be returned in the future. Although Germany has agreed to help these countries, it is unlikely that they will be able to process properly the number of increased requests they are likely to receive.

There are likely to be problems in honouring existing bilateral arrangements. Similar difficulties may occur with existing visa arrangements, for example, those between Spain and some Latin American countries.

d)   Accountability and Legitimacy

The complexity of the Schengen Convention raises problems of accountability and legitimacy, primarily in relation to police powers, human rights and public approval.

i)   *Police Powers and Accountability*

Various groups have expressed concern about aspects of the Schengen Convention. Some have suggested that increased levels of police trans-border co-operation will entail an increase in police powers without, it seems, a corresponding increase in arrangements for ensuring police accountability.

Similar concerns have been expressed about the development of the computerised information system (SIS). The availability of this information, and the new rules on visas, refugees and aliens, raise human rights, privacy and data protection issues which have not, some argue, been properly addressed (Van Outrive 1992a, pp.19-20). These issues are considered further in Chapter 6.

ii)   *Human Rights Issues*

The provisions of the Schengen Agreements raise a number of questions relating to human rights. The Council of the Bars and Law Societies of the European Community (CCBE) supports the abolition of border controls and increased levels of co-operation, as long as civil liberties and human rights are protected. It has drawn up a Code of Conduct for lawyers dealing with cross-border cases in an attempt to maximise the protection of human rights in the face of the power of the state.

The provisions of the Schengen Implementing Convention give particular cause for concern in relation to asylum applications. Anxiety has been expressed about the provisions which specify that only one state will examine an application for asylum, this being the state which the asylum seeker first enters. The application of this 'first country' rule has already had questionable outcomes.

In two recent UK cases, asylum seekers were returned to a country through which they had passed for only a matter of hours whilst in transit to their final destination. In one of the cases the unintended entry to a 'first country' was a result of an emergency landing in the Azores although the passenger was on a direct flight to the UK. The asylum seeker was returned to Portugal. In the other case, eastern European refugees broke their journey to the UK in France, and on arrival in the UK they were returned to France. These cases were the result of the application of the 'first country' rule by the UK immigration authorities in accordance with the provisions of the Dublin Convention on Asylum, although there would have been an identical result under the Schengen Convention (Sage 1993). Germany has adopted similar policies but the courts have decided that both Greece and the Czech Republic may not be presumed to be 'safe countries'. These decisions throw the new German asylum laws into confusion.

The Schengen states have all ratified the 1951 UN Convention Relating to the Status of Refugees and such actions would seem to contravene the spirit if not the letter of the Geneva Convention.

Although the Schengen states seem determined to circumscribe the opportunities for asylum seekers to have their cases considered in more than one member state, the position is now different in France. The *Conseil Constitutionnel* has determined that all asylum applications have to be examined, at least for the time being.

iii)   *Public Support and Approval*

The Schengen Agreement was debated by the European Parliament in March 1990 and various criticisms were voiced. A number of MEPs complained about the degree of secrecy which had surrounded the negotiations, thereby preventing an input from interested parties and a fuller debate on Schengen's central features. Others were worried about the implications for civil liberties, notably the information which would be held on the Schengen Information System. Since 1990 many further questions relating to the civil liberties implications of the Schengen Agreements have been raised by various MEPs, but have received little or no response.

It seems essential that issues of accountability, which arise with the new structures and procedures as a result of the Schengen Agreements, should be properly addressed. In view of the different expectations and experiences in this field in the different member states, it may prove difficult to construct satisfactory mechanisms for accountability which command approval even within the member states (at an intergovernmental level), let alone support and approval from the general public. These should nevertheless be a matter of high priority.

vi)   *Parliamentary Oversight*

A major criticism of the Schengen agreements is that they derive from a 'flawed Convention', one with no parliamentary and very little judicial control (O'Keefe 1993b). Although there may be some 'creeping competence' for the Commission under the Maastricht Treaty, and a potential to attribute jurisdiction to the European Court of Justice under Article K.3, the cynical interpretation is that the Commission sees Schengen as a 'useful laboratory' for near EU-wide co-operation as well as something which maintains the political momentum towards pan-European law enforcement. In short, the long-term political benefits of the Schengen agreements outweigh any short-term disadvantages in terms of a democratic deficit.

e)   A Model for the Wider Europe?

When the Schengen Agreement and Convention were first drafted they were hailed as the model or 'laboratory' for wider European police co-operation. Some went as far as to suggest that a blueprint for policing Europe had been created. At the start of this research project, only a short time after the Schengen Implementing Convention had been signed, the research team found a high level of resolve to ensure that initial difficulties were overcome and that the detailed arrangements were put into effect.

The Schengen initiative has been seen as a model for a wider European Community initiative in the field of police co-operation without borders, an interpretation which is supported by the fact that the original five members have now been joined by four other states. However, as one writer pointed out, the dynamic of the original Schengen Agreement was gradually eroded, not least because the provisions were taking so long to implement (Den Boer 1991, p.33). Three particular points seem to support this view.

i)   *Delays in Implementation*

It was proposed originally that the Schengen Agreement and Convention would take effect before the EC's deadline at the end of 1992 for the abolition of internal borders. It was then proposed to take effect on 1st January 1993. Had either of these dates been met then the Schengen Group could have claimed that they had presented a blueprint for police co-operation on a European-wide scale – and done so in the most timely manner.

These deadline dates passed and the Schengen Group appeared little closer to achieving their objectives than the EC as a whole. The French government then dealt a further blow to the Schengen ideal in April 1993 by deciding to postpone the introduction of the Convention. The new French government stated it was concerned about increased illegal immigration following the removal of internal frontier controls and also considered the asylum provisions might be too liberal. The French were also reported to be concerned about increased opportunities for drugs trafficking.

In July 1993, however, six of the Schengen countries, including France, agreed that border controls would finally be removed on 1st December 1993, with Greece, Portugal and Italy reiterating their commitment to join as soon as practicable. To date six countries have deposited the necessary instruments of ratification with the Luxembourg government and are fully committed to implementation – Belgium, France, Germany, Luxembourg, Netherlands and Spain.

By late October 1993 the target date of 1st December 1993 for removing all internal border controls between the Benelux countries, France, Germany and Spain had slipped to 1st February 1994, with Portugal joining these six during early to mid 1994 and Greece and Italy at some point thereafter.

ii)   New Legislation

New legislation is beginning to supersede some of the provisions of the Schengen Convention. For example, the 1991 EC Directive on Money Laundering and the 1991 EC Directive on the Control of Acquisition and Possession of Firearms to a large extent supersede the provisions in these areas set out in the Schengen Convention.

In addition, the Schengen provisions for asylum applications have been replaced by the 1990 Dublin Convention on Asylum and agreed by the 12 member states of the European Union, although not yet subject to ratification by all the signatories. The Schengen states have agreed that the provisions of the Dublin Convention on asylum are to be applied above those of the Schengen Convention. At the most recent Trevi Group ministerial meeting, in Copenhagen in June 1993, the ministers discussed the progress to date in the ratification of the Dublin Convention. Six states have so far completed the ratification procedures – Denmark, Greece, Italy, Luxembourg, Portugal and the UK – and others are expected to follow shortly.

These developments suggest that although Schengen has been instrumental in promoting initiatives for up to nine of the European Union countries, there is evidence that the 12 member states are forging EU-wide agreements in some areas. This may well continue.

iii)   The Maastricht Treaty

The Treaty on European Union (the Maastricht Treaty), under Title VI on justice and home affairs, and particularly in the establishment of the EDU/Europol, provides a new impetus for many of the existing Schengen arrangements in respect of police co-operation. The critical point here is that the new initiative is being made on an European Union-wide basis.

The new Article 100c in the EC Treaty (the Treaty Establishing the European Community) gives the EC institutions competence in the field of visa control and states that the Council shall decide which countries' nationals must have visas to enter the external borders of the European Community. Although the Article includes the proviso that it is 'without prejudice' to action by individual countries to safeguard law and order and internal security, these Treaty provisions must presumably override those of the Schengen Convention. Article 100d states that the K4 Co-ordinating Committee, set up under Title VI of the Treaty on European Union, shall contribute to the preparation of Council of Ministers' proceedings on visa policy decisions.

Article 100c in the EC Treaty will also apply if the member states resolve at some point in the future to include certain other aspects of justice and home affairs. This would effectively mean bringing some other policy issues within the European Community institutions, rather than dealing with them on the existing intergovernmental basis. These issues are listed in Article K.1(1) – K.1(6) of the Treaty on European Union and include all aspects of immigration policy, international fraud and 'combating drug addiction'. Were the member states to decide to apply Article 100c in this way these matters, too, would presumably override the Schengen Convention.

The Declaration on Asylum, annexed to the Maastricht Treaty, commits the member states to the aim of harmonising asylum policy on the basis of the report drawn up at the request of the June 1991 European Council meeting in Luxembourg. It states that the possibility of applying Article K.9 to asylum matters will be considered by the end of 1993, which means that there is a likelihood of asylum policy being brought into the new Article 100c of the EC Treaty alongside visa policy. This, again, would presumably supersede the Schengen provisions.

In addition, through the EDU/Europol police officers will be able to exchange intelligence about drugs-related offences which, although narrow in scope initially, may well be extended in the future. There are some who hold that the Maastricht Treaty rather than the Schengen Convention offers the 'new' blueprint for police co-operation in Europe.

Finally, despite the fact that the EDU/Europol has yet to be properly established, the fact that it, at least initially, has a narrow and well-defined remit may mean that its implementation will be less problematic than operationalising the more complex Schengen Agreements. The Maastricht Treaty is discussed in more detail in section 4.4.

iv)   *Article 8A and the Convention on External Borders*

There is a view that the long-term future of the Schengen arrangements is problematic. There are two key considerations – Article 8A of the Treaty Establishing the European Community and the Convention on External Borders (O'Keefe 1993b). The former guarantees the free movement of persons which may be taken as having the same effect as the abolition of internal borders. If, as seems likely, the European Parliament seeks to have the meaning of Article 8A interpreted and resolved in the European Court of Justice, on the grounds that to date the Community has failed to abolish its internal borders, then the free movement of people would be guaranteed. Equally, if the Convention on External Borders were signed (on the assumption that the difficulties over Gibraltar had been resolved) then the strong external frontier of Europe would be achieved. In both cases, the new arrangements would take precedence over the Schengen arrangements because they would represent a higher legal authority. In effect, were these two developments to occur, the two 'pillars' of Schengen (free movement without internal barriers and a strong external frontier) would be realised, but for the European Union as a whole and not just for the Schengen contracting parties. There would then be a gentle irony that Schengen would become redundant at the point at which two of its principal features were realised.

4.3   The Trevi Group

4.3.1   *The Establishment of Trevi*

The Trevi Group is probably best described as a forum rather than an organisation. The decision to establish the Group was taken in December 1975 by the Council of Ministers and the first meeting was held in Luxembourg in June 1976.

The origins of the name are disputed. Some say its name is a pun on that of the Dutch initiator, the then Director General for Police and Alien Affairs at the Netherlands Ministry of Justice, Mr Fonteijn, and the Trevi fountains (*Fontana di Trevi*) which were close to the meeting in Rome in 1975 which decided to establish the Group. Other claim is an acronym for 'Terrorism, Radicalism, Extremism and Violence International' (TREVI). A representative of the UK Home Office stated categorically that the Trevi Group was named after the fountain and described the name as an 'abused acronym'. However, the majority of respondents to this study believed that Trevi was indeed such an acronym, and this is perhaps an indication of the lack of clear information about this group.

Trevi's initial objective was to provide a basis for greater European co-operation to combat terrorism, but its role has developed to include co-operation over policing drugs trafficking and other types of serious organised crime. Subsequently, consideration of the implications of the single European market and Europol were added to the Trevi Group's agenda.

The Trevi members are the twelve European Union member states. In addition, seven 'friends of Trevi' attend meetings as observers. These are Austria, Canada, Morocco, Norway, Sweden, Switzerland and the USA.

Although meetings at various levels are held regularly under the Trevi umbrella, Trevi has never had a permanent secretariat. The changes implied for Trevi under the Maastricht Treaty preclude Trevi having a permanent secretariat in the future. In fact, Trevi itself is likely to disappear with the full ratification of the Maastricht Treaty and the establishment of the Police Co-operation Group under Article K. It is essential, however, to discuss its work here as it has been an important forum for the establishment of European police co-operation for more than seventeen years.

4.3.2   *Three Levels of Trevi*

As shown in Figure 4.3, Trevi operates at three different levels. At the highest level are the meetings of the Trevi 'ministers', who are the ministers of the twelve member states with responsibility for policing and internal security matters. This level has overall political responsibility for Trevi. The Trevi group of 'senior officials' sits at the middle level, and consists of senior officials and civil servants from the member states, accompanied in some cases by senior police officers. This group has responsibility for policy advice to the ministers and for the co-ordination of reports from the working groups. The 'working groups' form the bottom tier of Trevi and consist of civil servants, police officers and occasionally representatives from relevant organisations. Their work is discussed in full below.

Figure 4.3 The Structure of the Trevi Group

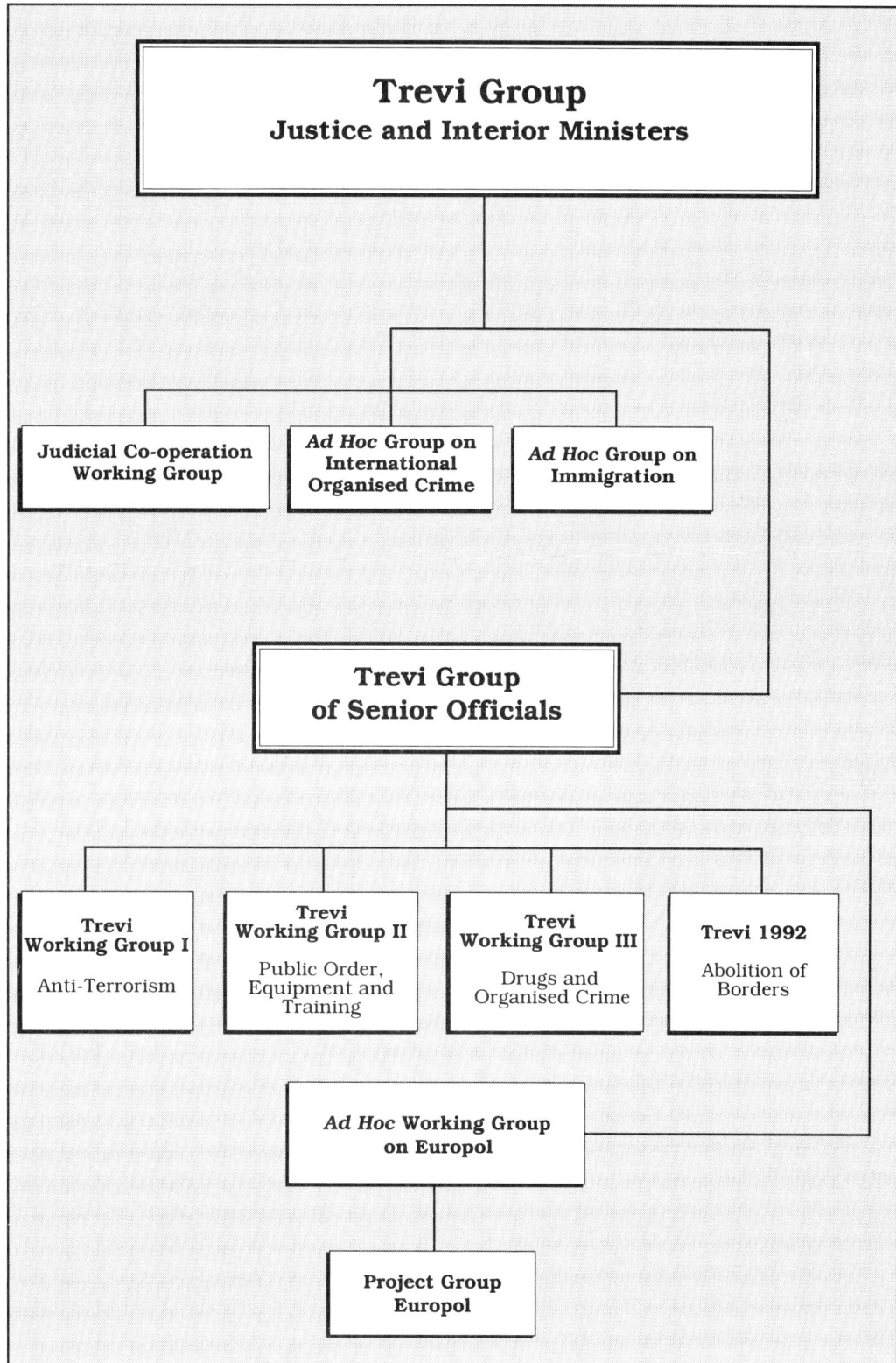

In addition to these three levels there are also *ad hoc* working groups. Only the *Ad Hoc* Working Group on Europol is actually part of the Trevi structure. The *Ad Hoc* Working Group on International Organised Crime and the *Ad Hoc* Group on Immigration are not, strictly speaking, Trevi groups – but because they report to the Trevi ministers they will be discussed in this section. For practical purposes the representatives of the *ad hoc* groups are identical to those on the Trevi working groups, meeting at the same times and at the same venues.

The Ministerial Group meets once every six months and meetings are hosted by the country which also holds the European Presidency. For example, in June 1992 the Trevi ministers met in Lisbon under the chairmanship of the Portuguese; in December 1992 they met in London under the chairmanship of the British; and in June 1993 the meeting was held in Copenhagen under the chairmanship of the Danish.

This formula produces yet another group – the *Troika*. Meetings involve representatives from the state which currently holds the presidency of the Trevi Group, representatives of the state which held the presidency immediately prior to the current presidency state and representatives from the state which is to hold the presidency next. The *Troika* is responsible for the administration of the Trevi Group rather than any substantive matters of policy.

The senior officials and working groups meet more frequently than the Ministerial Group. Conferences and seminars are also occasionally held. Before each six-monthly meeting of the ministers the working groups prepare a report which is channelled through the senior officials to the ministerial meeting.

4.3.3 Working Group I – Terrorism

Working Group I was established by the Trevi ministers on 31st May 1977, in order to facilitate concerted European action against terrorists. Information from informants suggests that it is in this field that Trevi has made a tangible impact, although for obvious reasons of security it is not easy to gauge how extensive this has been, nor is it possible to cite any concrete examples.

Working Group I regularly analyses information held on known and suspected terrorist groups, with particular attention paid to their strategies and tactics. Procedures have also been developed for the rapid communication of information using Trevi's own secure communications network. Action has also been promoted on terrorist funding and the security of ferries. This working group has also prepared a definition of terrorism which has been accepted by all European Union member states, this being 'the use or attempt to use violence by an organised group to achieve political goals'.

Recent initiatives include the compilation of a guide to the roles and responsibilities of organisations and agencies involved in investigating terrorist activities; information exchange about practical procedures for conducting security checks on vessels in ports; and information exchange about 'scenes-of-crime' procedures following terrorist incidents.

4.3.4 Working Group II – Technical Forum

Trevi Working Group II was also established at a meeting of Trevi ministers on 31st May 1977, and is concerned with promoting police co-operation and the exchange of information in a number of areas, notably: police training (including language training); public order; police equipment (including computers and communications); and forensic science and other scientific and technical matters. Meetings and seminars are held regularly to share information and promote greater understanding and collaboration. Recent seminars have dealt with policing road traffic and Automatic Fingerprint Recognition (AFR) systems.

In the wake of the Heysel stadium tragedy in 1985, the exchange of information and expertise on football hooliganism was added to the group's remit. The working group has tried to foster concerted action against football hooliganism by instituting a network of permanent correspondents in each country for the exchange of information. In addition, in advance of the 1990 World Cup, a conference was held in Rome to discuss football hooliganism, which was attended by police and others from all EC countries.

European police interviewed during the course of this study expressed satisfaction with some of the practical outcomes from Trevi Working Group II. For example, German police, including *Inspekteur der Bereitschaftspolizeien der Länder*, Gilbert Welter, and Herr Scheefeld, *Polizei Direktor*, pointed to practical steps such as agreement on a common reporting format to enable exchange of information on public security problems as being particularly useful.

4.3.5 *Working Group III – Serious Organised International Crime*

Working Group III was established in Rome in June 1985 to co-ordinate activities against serious crime, especially drugs trafficking, but also including armed robbery, stolen vehicles, environmental crime, money-laundering and illicit traffic in works of art. Further work has been undertaken on crime analysis, on developing a common police terminology and on the harmonisation of techniques of investigation. National contacts in each country have been identified and they meet under the Working Group III umbrella.

a)   Drugs Trafficking

An early initiative was the development of the system of Drug Liaison Officers (DLOs) posted in drug producer and transit countries. Through Trevi it was agreed that DLOs from different EC countries would work closely together and would pass on appropriate information to each other. A Dutch survey of the development of the liaison network was undertaken in 1992.

It was also agreed that each country would establish a national drugs intelligence unit and when this was achieved consideration would be given to the formation of a European Drugs Intelligence Unit to co-ordinate activities. This is now proceeding through the creation of the EDU/Europol. The UK established a National Drugs Intelligence Unit in November 1985, which since 1992 has been incorporated into the National Criminal Intelligence Service (NCIS). The developing European anti-drugs network is discussed further in the next chapter.

In addition, the 1990 Trevi Group *Programme of Action* provided for member states to attempt, by means of bilateral or multilateral agreements, to implement other forms of co-operation for combating drugs trafficking, as agreed in the 1988 United Nations Convention against Illicit Traffic in Narcotic Drugs and Psychotropic Substances.

In the course of this research many police informants, in several different EU countries, stressed the seriousness of the drugs threat to Europe. As discussed in Chapter 2, it is difficult to determine whether the extent of this threat is real or exaggerated, but there can be little doubt of the importance that senior European police officers attach to it.

Consequently, within Trevi, deliberations on increased co-operation to combat drugs trafficking have been accorded high priority. Indeed, along with terrorism, drugs trafficking has secured such high political visibility that it has almost become a testing ground for EU countries' commitment to greater law enforcement co-operation. The most recent example of this is the creation of the EDU/Europol.

b)   Money Laundering

Working Group III has sought to assist in harmonising police activities and to promote international initiatives against money laundering. For example, it has collaborated with the United Nations, the Council of Europe and the Financial Action Task Force. Work has been undertaken on the implementation of the Strasbourg Convention of 8th November 1990 on Laundering, Search, Seizure and Confiscation of the Proceeds from Crime and on the EC Directive of 10th June 1991 on the Prevention of the Use of the Financial System for the Purpose of Money Laundering. The Working Group is developing a training package on money laundering for senior detectives.

c)   Environmental Crime

The issue of environmental crime has become more important in the deliberations of Working Group III. On 11th – 12th September 1993 a meeting on the topic was held in the Netherlands involving representatives from Belgium, Denmark, France, Italy, the Netherlands and Spain. The meeting discussed the extent of the problem in Europe and how international environmental crime may be tackled. The results of the discussions were due to be reported to the autumn 1993 meeting of Trevi Working Group III.

d)   European Crime Analysis

Working Group III has also been considering the analysis of crime in the 12 European Union member states and how best to develop a comparative approach. The Working Group has been investigating operational crime analysis, which seeks to develop techniques to solve a particular crime or series of crimes, and strategic crime analysis, which is aimed at developing policies for the prevention of certain sorts of crime. In particular, Working Group III is trying to develop standardised definitions, categories and methods through the EU area. During 1993 the Working Group was concentrating on the development of a training package on crime analysis which it is hoped would help to promote a common approach amongst police officers in Europe.

4.3.6   *Working Group IV – Trevi 1992*

Between December 1988 and December 1992 Trevi had a fourth working group, Working Group IV or Trevi 1992. This dealt with a wide array of more political topics related to the policing and national security implications of the reduction of border controls, as well as measures which could be introduced to compensate for the relaxation of the internal frontiers. For example, this group was responsible for drafting the 1990 Trevi *Programme of Action*. During the UK presidency of Trevi in the second half of 1992 the work of this group was suspended on the grounds that it had reached the objectives set out in its original remit. There does remain a recall option, but as the remainder of the group's functions and responsibilities have been allocated to Working Group III, this option is unlikely to be exercised.

The majority of the European Union states have, of course, declared their commitment to abolish, or dramatically reduce, border controls and they have steered much of Trevi's work in the direction of considering how these changes may affect policing and other law enforcement activities. The three countries which decided to maintain border checks after 1st January 1993 – Denmark, Ireland and the UK – accepted this change of emphasis on the grounds that improvements in general police co-operation throughout Europe are greatly to be welcomed whatever differences remain about policing borders.

4.3.7   Statements of Intent

Trevi has played a critical role in developing the political commitment for closer police co-operation within the European Union. The clearest statements of intent are the Paris Declaration and the Dublin Programme of Action, both of which offer strategic objectives for the work of the Trevi Group as a whole.

a)   The Paris Declaration

On 15th December 1989 in Paris the Trevi ministers adopted a formal declaration (*The Paris Declaration*) which restated their determination to reinforce co-operation in the fields of law enforcement and security. The Preamble reiterated the Declaration of the European Council, in Rhodes on 4th December 1988, that the achievement of Community goals was dependent on progress in co-operation in combating terrorism, international crime and illegal trafficking in narcotics. *The Paris Declaration* rejected the notion that the European Community should be 'closed' to those outside, and stressed the importance of freedom of movement.

The Trevi Group noted with concern the development of crime across frontiers, the increasing adeptness of professional criminals to exploit the limits of national agencies and the gaps in police co-operation. Accordingly, the Declaration resolved to promote co-operation in meeting these threats within the of context of respect for individual and collective freedoms, human and civil rights and the rule of law.

The Trevi Group resolved to give priority to the fight against terrorism, drugs trafficking and other aspects of organised crime, including money laundering, and the Declaration outlined a number of particular measures considered necessary to do this. These included improved communication of information, the assignment of liaison officers, the exchange of intelligence particularly on drugs trafficking, and the investigation of a common information system designed to enable EC countries to pool their knowledge. Other measures included improvements in supervising frontiers and maritime borders and the examination of 'hot pursuit' across borders, the development of training activities, exchanges and language teaching, increased sharing of technical knowledge, and increased co-operation with non-EC countries.

b)   The Dublin 'Programme of Action'

The measures outlined in the 1989 Declaration in Paris were reiterated, and to some extent strengthened, by the *Programme of Action* agreed at the Trevi ministerial meeting in Dublin in June 1990.

The *Programme of Action* outlined a number of priorities for improved police co-operation. In order to combat terrorism, drugs trafficking and organised crime, exchanges of personnel and information would be increased and agencies involved in the policing of frontier points, such as ports, airports and railway stations, would meet regularly to pool information.

Among specific measures were the appointment of liaison officers, the display of 'wanted' posters, the further development of a rapid and protected communications system, the use of joint teams where appropriate, the promotion of suitable training and research, and sharing of information.

The *Programme* specifically mentioned increased co-operation at external borders and common frontiers and in communications. It set out Trevi's specific intention to investigate pursuit across borders and to research and establish a common information system.

4.3.8   *Europol*

a)   The Origins of Europol

Debates and discussions concerning the idea of Europol had been floated long before the Trevi ministers finally took the decision to establish a working group. Fijnaut (1987) traces the idea of 'Europol' or equivalent back to discussions in the early 1970s when police officers from a number of member states were dissatisfied with the then inefficiencies of Interpol.

i)   Police Enthusiasm

More recently, the concept of a single police force for Europe was beginning to receive enthusiastic support from police officers. One vision of Europol was offered by Rainer Schmidt-Nothen, former head of the Wiesbaden NCB:

> This concept presupposes there will be some form of unification along the lines of a confederation. A union of this type is the ultimate goal of the 12 European Community countries. If political unification of those 12 countries were to be achieved, there would be 11 fewer countries in Europe. For each member country of the Community, the 11 others would cease to be foreign states. If this were to happen it would be logical to establish a European Police Office which would operate as a central bureau for collecting information on offenders and crimes, tracing persons and stolen property, establishing computer and telecommunications links, identifying criminals, etc. In addition, an office of this type would be empowered to investigate important cases of serious crime over the entire territory of the European Community. Total harmonisation of the criminal law and procedure would therefore be necessary [...] EUROPOL would operate as the International Central Bureau for all the European Community countries while their own Interpol NCBs would disappear. (Schmidt-Nothen 1989).

ii)   *Chancellor Kohl and Trevi Working Group III*

In practice, the steps towards Europe-wide policing have been more modest. It was not until the European Council meeting in Luxembourg on 28th – 29th June 1991 that the notion of 'Euro policing' received official recognition. Chancellor Kohl tabled a motion for the creation of a single European Criminal Police Office which would combat international and European crime. The original proposal suggested that the unit should commence working from 1993, establishing competence in this area before 1994 and from then on it should have the competence and jurisdiction to investigate drugs-related and other organised crime. The proposal was accepted by the majority of other ministers despite their initial expression of surprise. The British minister was the only one to dissent from the proposal.

The agreement to establish this European police unit was to some extent also a result of work conducted by Trevi Working Group III and the confirmation of proposals for the establishment of national drugs intelligence units in every member state. These were to co-ordinate intelligence exchange relating to drugs trafficking. The guidelines for the Drugs Liaison Officers were agreed at the June meeting of ministers in 1991, the same meeting at which Chancellor Kohl presented his proposal for a European Criminal Police Office.

The two ideas were combined and the ministers established the *Ad Hoc* Working Group on Europol (AHWGE) from August 1991. Its remit was to work towards the creation of Europol. The concept of Europol had begun to take shape.

iii)   *The Maastricht Treaty*

The proposal was given added impetus in December 1991 by the inclusion in the Maastricht Treaty of Title VI and the annexed Declaration on Police Co-operation. Article K.1(9) of the Treaty on European Union states that EU countries will regard police co-operation as a 'matter of common interest' in connection with 'the organisation of a union-wide system for exchanging information within a European Police Office (Europol).' The Declaration on Police Co-operation reaffirmed the agreement of the member states on the objectives underlying Germany's proposals at the June 1991 Luxembourg meeting and agreed to examine various ideas for promoting practical police co-operation in Europe, especially the exchange of information.

b)   The Ad Hoc Working Group on Europol

The AHWGE was responsible for the establishment in the first instance of a European Drugs Unit (EDU), a name which first made an appearance during the UK presidency of the EC and Trevi. It should be noted that initially the unit was to be called the European Drugs Intelligence Unit (EDIU). The 'Intelligence' part of the title has since been dropped, perhaps implying that EDU/Europol will eventually deal in more than just intelligence (Den Boer 1992b).

i)   *Activity in 1993*

The EDU will be smaller than originally envisaged by Chancellor Kohl but with greater potential than that proposed by Trevi Working Group III. The EDU is the first stage of Europol. It will operate initially on a limited basis, and concern itself solely with intelligence related to illicit drugs trafficking and associated money laundering activities.

Of all the Trevi working groups the AHWGE has recently met most frequently (four times in the six months up to April 1993) and in this sense the title *ad hoc* is something of a misnomer. It is now reported to be meeting only once every 6 months. Until mid-1993 the working group had a permanent UK chair from the Police Department of the Home Office, which meant that the Home Office also provided a secretariat. Now, however, the chair of the working group changes with the presidency of the EC. At the time of writing, in November 1993, Belgium holds the chair of AHGWE. The working group reports to the Trevi Group of 'senior officials' who, in turn, pass any recommendations on to the Trevi ministers.

ii)   *Convention on Europol*

The AHWGE is concerned with preparing a convention which will provide the legal basis for the EDU. Some of the states were unwilling to see the EDU established without a convention to define the limits of its competence. However, it was decided that the establishment of the EDU and the drafting of the convention should be carried out simultaneously. The working title for the convention is the 'Convention for the Establishment of Europol'. It is not expected that the terms of the convention will be drafted until late 1994 and one informant predicted it would not be signed and sealed before 1995 or even 1996. The convention will not grant operational powers to the EDU/Europol, not least because this touches on issues of sovereignty. It is possible that an executive capacity for EDU/Europol will be developed in the future, but this is certainly not being planned for at this early stage.

A Ministerial Agreement was signed by Trevi ministers on 2nd June 1993. This established the parameters within which the EDU will work – its functions, arrangements for data protection, staffing, accountability and finance. The Agreement does not provide the legal foundation for the EDU, but does set out the basis of understanding between the ministers on the areas which the EDU will cover (Woodward 1993). The Agreement will come into effect as soon as a site has been agreed.

Progress on Europol had been hampered by a failure to agree where the unit should be sited. Bids were submitted by France, Germany, the Netherlands, Italy and Greece; but the only serious contenders were The Hague, Rome and Strasbourg. A decision was made on 29th October 1993 at the Brussels summit and EDU/Europol is to be located in The Hague.

c)   **Project Group Europol**

Recognising that it would be impossible for the AHWGE to develop the EDU alone, a project group was established to arrange the practical matters. This group is called Project Group Europol (PGE). The project group is accountable to the AHWGE. In theory each member state could nominate representatives to the group, but in practice numbers were limited because of insufficient work to justify all the member states sending a representative. Representatives are high-ranking police and customs officers with experience of drugs-trafficking intelligence (Peter Vowé 1993, personal interview).

During 1992–93 the project group was situated at a temporary location in Strasbourg, while political wrangling took place over a permanent site. This caused a delay in the development of EDU/Europol as plans which had been made could not go forward until the decision was taken. The issue was not resolved either at the December 1992 European Council meeting or, more surprisingly, at the meeting in Copenhagen in June 1993. The decision to locate EDU/Europol in The Hague was eventually made at the European Council meeting in Brussels on 29th October 1993.

It is arguably the case that the decision on where to site the project group will at least in part determine the scope and nature of its activities (King 1993). For example, there is some chance that the group's work will take on the 'flavour' of policing in the host country. More specifically, unless there are special provisions, the group will be subject to the national data protection laws of the host country.

The Ministerial Agreement signed by Trevi ministers on 2nd June 1993 details the role of Project Group Europol. Its remit is restricted to an investigation of the most efficient means for exchanging intelligence on drugs trafficking and associated money laundering activities. In September 1993 PGE was preparing regular reports on drugs trafficking and money laundering and was producing a report on trends in drugs trafficking.

4.3.9   *Ad Hoc Working Group on International Organised Crime*

The *Ad Hoc* Working Group on International Organised Crime (AHWGIOC) is not formally constituted as a Trevi group. However, for practical and financial reasons, meetings of the group follow the Trevi cycle. Additionally, members of the group are primarily Trevi personnel. The group reports directly to the ministers of the interior of the member states rather than to the Trevi ministerial group. The Commission of the EC and the Council Secretariat also attend meetings as observers, but have no formal role.

The group was established after the murders of the Italian anti-Mafia judges Giovanni Falcone and Paolo Borsellino in Italy during the summer of 1992. France and Italy wrote to the UK presidency to request an extraordinary meeting of all ministers of the interior and justice. When this was held in Brussels on 18th September 1992 the decision was taken to set up the *Ad Hoc* Working Group on International Organised Crime. The group was established to pursue action against international organised crime at an intergovernmental level.

The group reported to a meeting of ministers on 6th – 7th May 1993 in Denmark, tabling a paper documenting the nature and structure of the Mafia and other organised criminal groups operating across the European Union. It also offered an assessment of the wider threat to Europe and the international community posed by organised crime.

At this meeting four recommendations were adopted with the aim of extending and intensifying the co-operative efforts of member states to combat organised crime both within the European Union and internationally. First, it was agreed periodically to collect and analyse information on the spread of organised crime. Secondly, it was decided to establish a framework of contact points within existing co-operative structures (police, customs and judicial) in order to facilitate co-operation on specific cases. Thirdly, it was agreed to undertake a comparative analysis of differences in legislation in member states which may inhibit practical police co-operation. Finally, the meeting agreed to urge the Judicial Co-operation Working Group to intensify its work on reviewing extradition procedures. The mandate of the AHWGIOC was extended for a further six months, when final proposals will be placed before ministers for continuing the work through other mechanisms.

4.3.10   Ad Hoc Group on Immigration

Like the AHWGIOC, the *Ad Hoc* Group on Immigration (AHGI) is not strictly speaking part of the Trevi Group because it reports to the ministers of the interior of the member states not the Trevi ministerial group. The AHGI is an intergovernmental forum, established in London in 1986, operating under the co-ordination of the EC Commission. Its functional members are senior civil servants from immigration departments of member states, and it has a permanent secretariat at the Council of Ministers (Den Boer 1992b, p.4). The group is sub-divided into six further groups namely: Admission/Expulsion; Visas; False Documents; Asylum; External Borders; and Refugees (from the former Yugoslavia) (Cruz 1993).

The group has responsibility for the preparation of conventions on asylum and on external borders. It assisted in the drafting of the Dublin Convention (see above, section 4.2.2), and has been involved in drafting the Convention on External Borders. The passage of the latter has been delayed because of disputes between Spain and the UK over the status of the borders at Gibraltar.

A computerised list of so-called 'inadmissible aliens' who would not be granted entry rights to the European Union has been called for by the group. The idea was then incorporated into plans for the European Information System (EIS), the development of which is still under discussion within the Trevi structure.

At the most recent ministerial meeting, in Copenhagen in June 1993, the ministers discussed the progress to date in the ratification of the Dublin Convention. At the time of writing, in October 1993, six states have completed the ratification procedures – Denmark, Greece, Italy, Luxembourg, Portugal and the UK. The ministers also noted progress in an ongoing review of current asylum procedures in the 12 member states.

Ministers also expressed satisfaction with the development of the *Centre d'Information de Reflexion et Echange en matière d'Asile* (CIREA), or the Centre for Information, Discussion and Exchange on Asylum, and the progress in establishing CIREFI (Centre for Information, Reflection and Exchange on Frontiers and Immigration). This was approved at a meeting of immigration ministers on 30th November 1992 and is intended to monitor immigration flows, forged documents, illegal immgration and related issues.

4.3.11   Judicial Co-operation Working Group on Criminal Matters

The Judicial Co-operation Working Group on Criminal Matters (JCWG) is the main forum for senior officials to discuss judicial co-operation between the 12 member states. Its remit is to encourage judicial co-operation by preparing conventions and agreements which facilitate mutual legal assistance. It operates in a number of interrelated spheres: extradition, combating terrorist funding, fraud against the EC budget and mutual legal assistance.

a)   Extradition

Under the UK Presidency, the JCWG considered ways of simplifying and facilitating extradition procedures within the European Union. A seminar, attended by senior civil servants with responsibilities for extradition and police officers, produced recommendations to improve the way in which extradition cases could be handled within the existing legal framework. The JCWG was also invited to consider ways in which it might be possible to relax existing legal obstacles to extradition. If a draft ministerial agreement is agreed, this will lead to the drafting of a convention amending the operation of the European Convention on Extradition for member states.

b)   Terrorist Funding

Following a request from Trevi ministers, the JCWG is examining the legislative powers of member states to foreclose on the funding of terrorist organisations. In this respect the JCWG is working in parallel with Trevi Working Group I.

c)   EC Fraud

Similarly, the JCWG has discussed measures which might be taken by member states to use their national laws to deal with EC fraud. This work complements efforts being made by the EC's Unit for the Co-ordination of Fraud Prevention (*Unité pour la Co-ordination de la Lutte Anti-Fraude* or UCLAF).

d)   Mutual Legal Assistance

The JCWG has been considering ways to encourage more effective use of mutual legal assistance between the member states. A sub-group has been created to devise a scheme for the mutual recognition of driving disqualifications imposed in other member states.

4.3.12   Research Findings About the Trevi Group

a)   Criticisms of Trevi

The evidence of European police officers and others, including ministerial officials and academics, suggests that there are mixed feelings about the effectiveness and success of Trevi. While there is general agreement that the existence of Trevi has helped to create an impetus for improvements in co-operation, particularly with regard to anti-terrorist and anti-drugs measures, some informants claim that the fine words have not necessarily been translated into practice.

Tom O'Reilly, former Assistant Commissioner from Ireland's *Garda* who was interviewed in 1990, pointed to real achievements in terms of co-operation in policing World Cup football matches and controlling public disorder, as well as sharing information on matches with a potential for disorder.

i)   *Secrecy and Duplication*

However, criticisms of Trevi's methods of operation were also made by a number of respondents. It was suggested that it was too secretive; that it suffered by not being sufficiently connected to the EC's institutions; that there was insufficient input to the working groups from the police; and that there was lack of co-ordination within the structure – for example, working groups were often thought to be unaware of each others' activities, let alone aware of the views of the politicians themselves. The EC's response to such criticisms is to be found in the Treaty on European Union, Title VI, Article K.4 (discussed below at section 4.4).

ii)   Relationship to the European Community

The view that Trevi ought to be more closely tied in to the EC institutional structure is clearly widely shared. Some informants said that it did not particularly matter, but the majority considered that the Trevi Group ought to operate within the Community institutions. There were several reasons offered for this view.

If the Trevi Group's activities were to be formally and explicitly located within the EC's political process, this in itself would facilitate legal and political progress in police co-operation. In addition, Trevi would be seen to be more legitimate and accountable. In turn, Trevi's work could more readily be supported by the European Commission and the European Parliament. Finally, such steps might help Trevi to establish itself in a single location with a permanent secretariat. As discussed further below (sections 4.3.13 and 4.4) many of these points have been addressed in the 'third pillar' of the Treaty on European Union on justice and home affairs. The new structures likely to evolve during 1994 will at least involve the European Parliament and the Commission as specified in Article K of the Maastricht Treaty.

iii)   Lack of Consensus

German police and officials, for example, including Herr von Hutte of the *Bundesministerium des Innern*, Herr Kayser of the *Kriminaloberrat* and Herr Wolters, from the international co-operation department in the *Bundeskriminalamt* based in Wiesbaden, expressed the view that some valuable progress had resulted from Trevi deliberations, particularly in the working groups, but that there was a lack of consensus among the twelve states about how far to proceed on many key issues, and at what pace. Spanish police officers, while recognising some welcome developments, doubted whether Trevi could achieve real and sustained progress towards greater criminal justice and law enforcement co-operation until it had a permanent secretariat and headquarters, with the resources to monitor implementation of the Trevi Group's decisions. A senior Irish police officer described the 'travelling circus' of Trevi as cumbersome and inefficient.

iv)   Longer-Term Programme

Some respondents to this study argued that Trevi had tried to do too much too quickly and had consequently failed to do anything well, but a senior official in the British Home Office argued that Trevi had recently adopted a longer-term approach and developed a more coherent and disciplined programme, the progress of which can be regularly monitored. Other informants, including police officers, from Denmark, Belgium and Ireland, suggested that the principal level at which Trevi operates (the intergovernmental level) is not necessarily the most appropriate one for securing practical police co-operation between operational officers. However, despite these reservations, a number of other informants were optimistic that Trevi would evolve in such a way as to overcome these problems.

It is interesting to note that whilst Trevi has tended to be primarily a macro-level, intergovernmental forum many of the criticisms were made by police officers who could be expected to give greater priority to meso- and micro-level matters of operational significance.

b) **Obstacles to Progress**

Underlying many of the reservations about the Trevi Group are four points:

First, the Trevi Group operates primarily at the intergovernmental, political and senior official levels and may not be taking sufficient account of the meso- and micro-level responsibilities of law enforcement personnel 'on the ground'.

Secondly, the Trevi Group's structure is regarded as inefficient and incoherent, which may in part be a function of the lack of a permanent location and secretariat, with insufficient co-ordination between the working groups and also poor 'institutional memory'.

Thirdly, the Trevi Group is not seen as a fully accountable, legitimate structure for policy making or executive action, and as such is treated with some suspicion by those (including police officers) whose support is needed if practical progress in police co-operation is to be achieved.

Finally, sooner or later, if real progress is to be made, the differences between criminal justice and the legal systems of the European Union countries will need to be addressed more fully than is currently the case by the Judicial Co-operation Working Group on Criminal Matters.

4.3.13 Assessment of Trevi

a) **Political Commitment**

Undoubtedly, the Trevi Group has promoted the principle of increased police co-operation within the European Community. During the last decade it has helped to reduce national rivalries in the field of law enforcement and has promoted mutual respect and trust, the culmination of which has been the agreement for the establishment of Europol.

At the top levels, the forum which Trevi provides has assisted in reducing suspicions between governments that some states had taken insufficient steps to combat terrorism and other serious crime, and it has to some extent helped to overcome old antagonisms. In so doing Trevi has promoted European political commitment in this field. The level of activity in the Trevi working groups, which appears to have increased considerably in 1992 and 1993, has provided a considerable impetus for European police co-operation in a number of fields.

b) **Levels of Operation**

At the macro and meso levels Trevi has performed a useful function, but particularly at the micro level of police co-operation the group's effectiveness is in question. This may to some extent be a consequence of the relative difficulty of obtaining information about the operational consequences of Trevi agreements, but it is also probably a reflection of the widespread perception that the Trevi Group has been principally a 'talking shop'. Nonetheless, the increased working group activity in the last couple of years does seem to have provided a number of tangible developments at the meso level of co-operation.

It is difficult to determine whether the Trevi Group is driven from the top or whether bottom-up policy decisions are more often the norm. If it is the former this political will is surely to be welcomed, particularly if it creates sufficient momentum to resolve detailed constitutional and legal obstacles to police co-operation. If it is the latter, however, as is claimed by some informants, such as Heiner Busch, of the Free University of Berlin, then it is the working groups themselves which are making policy decisions, which cumulatively may affect major aspects of policing and criminal justice without any political agreement or accountability.

c)   Need for a Permanent Secretariat

Trevi has had no permanent secretariat, headquarters or budget in the past. According to the Home Office in the UK, 'Trevi values its informal character and has been at pains to avoid becoming over-bureaucratic'. Furthermore, the Home Office view is that Trevi's distinctive strength lies in the 'informal, spontaneous and practical character of its discussions' (House of Commons 1990b, p.5).

However, the lack of a permanent secretariat may have decreased the practical effectiveness of Trevi because the deliberations of ministers and senior officials may not have resulted in effective implementation. Explicit mechanisms for monitoring and evaluation are often a necessary condition for effective implementation in any organisation. Data collection, collation and analysis has been compromised by the peripatetic character of the Trevi Group. A permanent secretariat could offer such facilities.

Continued dependence on individual member states to put joint Trevi decisions into effect is to a large extent unavoidable, but the absence of effective lower-level structures guided by a central executive may adversely affect increased European co-operation in law enforcement. Without a central organisation there is a danger of lack of drive – the ministerial group may adopt positive proposals and their working groups may agree strongly, but in the absence of a permanent secretariat to push the proposals through to implementation momentum may be lost. It only needs one or two states to fall behind, or to fail to find the necessary funds, to jeopardise a European-wide initiative.

Under the provisions in the 'third pillar' of the European Union, in Article K of the Treaty, it appears that a permanent secretariat will be established to service the European Council of Ministers of Justice and the Interior. This will be drawn from the General Secretariat, as provided under Article 151 of the EC Treaty. In addition, Article K.4 of the Treaty on European Union establishes a Co-ordinating Committee of senior officials to prepare papers and reports for the Council and to co-ordinate activities in this field.

d)   The European Community and Policing Matters

There is substantial evidence that the separation of the Trevi Group from European Community political structures has not been widely supported. This is scarcely surprising given the way in which the EC has *de facto* involvement in police-related matters. As informants pointed out during the course of this research, there are already many ways in which EC activities impinge on policing – for example, EC directives on driving and vehicles, firearms and money laundering. In addition, although the Treaty of Rome does not give the EC competence in policing matters, the 'third pillar' of the Treaty on European Union does specifically locate justice and home affairs, including police and judicial co-operation, as matters coming within the 'common interest' of the member states (see section 4.4).

Following German ratification in October 1993, the Maastricht Treaty was implemented at the end of the month, and it now appears that Trevi will gradually be replaced by a new structure established under Article K of the Treaty on European Union. This is expected to occur during the second half of 1994. Under the 'third pillar' an intergovernmental Council of Ministers will be serviced by the Co-ordinating Committee set up under Article K.4. This same Co-ordinating Committee is charged under Article 100d of the EC Treaty with servicing the EC Council of Ministers which will determine visa policy. The new structure for promoting police and judicial co-operation will thus be intimately linked with the EC institutions and political processes, although technically remaining an intergovernmental rather than an EC structure.

e)   Questions of Secrecy

A recurrent criticism has been that the Trevi Group operates largely in secret without appropriate accountability.

The point was well made by Lord Bethell, MEP, who is European adviser to the Police Federation of England and Wales. He reported the view that 'it is no longer good enough to have decisions made by interior ministers of the EC meeting behind closed doors – there should at least be reports to the Legal Committee of the European Parliament' (Bethell 1990b). This problem may be resolved when the K4 Committee (see section 4.4) becomes operational, although in practice it remains to be seen whether there will be full accountability. At least Article K.6 explicitly states that the European Parliament shall be regularly informed of discussions and shall be consulted on proposals.

One British informant pointed to the irony that, at a time when Europe as a social system is determined to become more open, a major intergovernmental structure of the 'new' Europe remained firmly closed. There is certainly evidence to support the view that information on the Trevi Group (including its personnel, functions and working groups) has been differentially available across Europe. For example, colleagues and public servants in a number of European countries have been more informed – and more forthcoming with information – than their counterparts in some other countries. It is also interesting to note that certain information about Trevi working groups has been reported in countries which are not members of the European Union before such information has become available in the UK. For example, information about the *Ad Hoc* Group on International Organised Crime was reported in Swiss newspapers before it reached interested UK circles. The secretiveness surrounding the Trevi Group has given cause for concern.

One explanation, according to the UK Home Office, lies in different national laws restricting freedom of information in member states. Another more plausible explanation is that, although the 12 Trevi Group ministers may have made a collective decision about the information which would be publicly announced (a decision taken in effect by the *Troika*), some Trevi ministers have presented more information to the press and public than was previously agreed. In effect, some ministers adhered to the collective decision, whilst others felt that a more open approach was appropriate.

Alternatively, there may be good reasons for restricting information about the Trevi Group's activities. For example, it would be foolish to publicise agreements and decisions which have consequences for certain types of operational policing, particularly in the fight against terrorism and organised crime.

f)   Accountability

It is arguable that if the Trevi Group or its successor becomes less secret, demands for accountability will grow and prove increasingly difficult to resist. There are two major problems.

First, at a general level, the Trevi Group has had no mechanism for corporate accountability; individual ministers have been subject to political oversight at the national level, and this often appears to have meant very little oversight at all.

Secondly, at a more particular level, it is not clear whether Trevi Group decisions have been made at the ministerial level and then put into effect at the level of the working groups, or whether specific proposals forged in the working groups have been used to determine overall policy. It is clear that the Trevi Group has sometimes operated in a 'top down' manner – for example, in orchestrating the political will to promote police co-operation. It may also be the case that the Trevi Group has operated in a 'bottom up' manner – as one respondent put it 'are the ministers themselves even aware of all that goes on in the working groups?'.

g)   EDU/Europol

The creation of EDU/Europol is in part a product of the work conducted by Trevi Working Group III, including the establishment of national drugs intelligence units in every member state. Although it is too early to make an informed assessment of the Europol initiative, even in its infancy it offers a 'case study' in macro, meso and micro levels of co-operation. At the macro level, the initial impetus was given by the Trevi ministerial group, taken up by Chancellor Kohl and then consolidated in the Treaty on European Union. Overall control of Europol developments remains at the macro level. The *Ad Hoc* Working Group on Europol was subsequently created to provide a meso-level constitutional framework – to be worked out by senior officials. Finally, Project Group Europol is staffed by senior police officers who have the micro-level task of operationalising Chancellor Kohl's vision.

If Europol is ever to develop as an operational body rather than an organisation designed to facilitate co-operation between discrete national police forces, then it is possible to ask – but not yet answer – a number of questions about its role (Hadfield 1993). It may be sensible to pose some of these questions even whilst Europol is in its infancy:

• What crimes would such a force investigate?

• What forms of accountability would be exercised over it?

• Under what legal code would Europol pursue its investigations?

• Would its funding be determined on standard EC lines, or would its funding be linked to the investigations it undertook?

• What relationship would Europol have to existing national police forces, and what control would be exercised by chief officers?

4.4   The Maastricht Treaty and the K4 Committee

4.4.1   *The Maastricht Treaty on European Union*

The Treaty on European Union (the Maastricht Treaty), signed on 7th February 1992, answers some of the criticisms levelled at the Trevi Group. By October 1993 the Treaty had been ratified by all 12 of the EC member states with the Treaty coming into force on the 1st November 1993.

Title VI of the Treaty deals with provisions relating to justice and home affairs, including police and judicial co-operation. These are now deemed to be areas of 'common interest'. Previously they had been exclusively intergovernmental matters outside the competence of the European Commission and Parliament. Under Title VI co-operation in police and judicial matters will still be primarily intergovernmental concerns, but both the European Commission and Parliament will now have, for the first time, a formal role.

The relevant provisions of the Treaty on European Union are to be found under Title VI, Provisions on Co-operation in the Fields of Justice and Home Affairs, Articles K.1, K.2(2), K.4(2) and K.6.

a)   Matters of Common Interest: Article K.1

The Treaty, under Article K.1, provides that member states shall regard the following areas as matters of common interest:

1   asylum policy;

2   rules governing the crossing by persons of the external borders of the Member States and the exercise of controls thereon;.

3   immigration policy and policy regarding nationals of third countries;

(a) conditions of entry and movement by nationals of third countries on the territory of Member States;

(b) conditions of residence by nationals of third countries on the territory of Member States, including family reunion and access to employment;

(c) combatting unauthorized immigration, residence and work by nationals of third countries on the territory of Member States;

4   combatting drug addiction in so far as this is not covered by 7 to 9;

5   combatting fraud on an international scale in so far as this is not covered by 7 to 9;

6   judicial co-operation in civil matters;

7   judicial co-operation in criminal matters;

8   customs co-operation;

9   police co-operation for the purposes of preventing and combatting terrorism, unlawful drug trafficking and other serious forms of international crime, including if necessary certain aspects of customs co-operation, in connection with the organization of a Union-wide system for exchanging information within a European Police Office (Europol).

b)   Sovereignty: Article K.2(2)

Article K.2 (2) stipulates that Title VI 'shall not affect the exercise of the responsibilities incumbent upon Member States with regard to the maintenance of law and order and the safeguarding of internal security'.

c)   The European Commission: Article K.4(2) and K.6

The interests of the European Commission and the European Parliament in the provisions for co-operation in the fields of justice and home affairs are set out in Articles K.4(2) and K.6, respectively:

Article K.4(2)

The Commission shall be fully associated with the work in the areas referred to in this Title.

Article K.6

The Presidency and the Commission shall regularly inform the European Parliament of discussions in the areas covered by this Title.

The Presidency shall consult the European Parliament on the principal aspects of activities in the areas referred to in this Title and shall ensure that the views of the European Parliament are duly taken into consideration.

The European Parliament may ask questions of the Council or make recommendations to it. Each year, it shall hold a debate on the progress made in implementation of the areas referred to in this Title.

4.4.2   *The K4 Co-ordinating Committee*

Article K.4 of the Treaty provides for the establishment of a Co-ordinating Committee to organise police and judicial co-operation within the European Union. Members of the committee will be senior civil servants, although it is as yet unclear how they will be appointed. The Committee will apparently have a secretariat based in Brussels, drawn from the General Secretariat and under the direction of the Secretary General, in accordance with Article 151 of the EC Treaty.

Article K.4(1) makes it clear that the Co-ordinating Committee will have considerable influence over how matters develop in this field. Under this 'third pillar' of European Union, a European Council of Ministers of Justice and the Interior will meet regularly (presumably every six months). The Co-ordinating Committee of senior officials is empowered to give opinions for the attention of the Council, on its own initiative, and will contribute to the preparation of the Council's discussions. Clearly, the K.4 Committee and the various sub-groups will be important sources of momentum and ideas in the fields of justice and home affairs co-operation.

The actual functions and role of the Co-ordinating Committee, popularly referred to as the K4 Committee, will only be fully defined as the Maastricht Treaty is implemented. At present it seems likely that the K4 Committee will have three steering groups although some sources have suggested there may be four groups. One steering group will take over the work currently undertaken by the *Ad Hoc* Group on Immigration and will handle immigration and asylum issues, including visa policy, the control of external borders and the work of CIREA (Centre for Information, Reflection and Exchange on Asylum) and the activities of CIREFI (Centre for Information, Reflection and Exchange on Frontiers and Immigration).

Another steering group will deal with policing and security matters, including anti-terrorist work, combating serious crime, EDU/Europol, and training, scientific and technical matters, crime analysis and combating environmental crime and public disorder. This group will absorb the work currently undertaken by the Trevi Group. It is not yet clear whether it will also have responsibility for customs or whether a separate (fourth) group will handle these matters. It is also not clear which steering group will have responsibility for actions against international fraud.

The final steering group will have responsibility for co-operation on civil and criminal judicial matters, including extradition, mutual assistance, the recognition and execution of 'foreign' sentences and the transfer of proceedings. It may also handle the legal dimensions of attempts to combat terrorist funding and fraud. Each steering group will have an undetermined number of working groups to deal with the detailed, specialist business.

It is likely that practical pressures will in part define the functions and tasks of the K4 Committee and steering groups. It is in the nature of intergovernmental committees that an initial rather broad remit becomes more specific and focused as the work of the committee develops.

Under the terms of the Maastricht Treaty, the European Commission is to be 'fully associated' with the work of the K4 Committee and with developments in police and judicial co-operation. Similarly, the European Parliament will be regularly informed of the work of the K4 Committee. Article K.6 stipulates that the Presidency 'shall consult' the European Parliament on the principal aspects of activities under Title VI, and 'shall ensure' that the views of the European Parliament are taken into consideration. The Parliament may also ask questions and make recommendations, and each year will hold a debate on progress made in the implementation of the Title.

4.4.3   The Treaty Establishing the European Community

Article G (Title II) of the Treaty on European Union contains amendments to the old EEC Treaty renaming it the Treaty Establishing the European Community or EC Treaty. Most of the Maastricht provisions on police co-operation and related matters are dealt with in Article K (Title VI) and remain, at least for the foreseeable future, intergovernmental matters outside the new EC Treaty.

a)   Article 100c of the EC Treaty

However, this is not the case with co-operation on visas which is provided for in Article 100c of the new EC Treaty. This states that the European Council 'acting unanimously on a proposal from the Commission and after consulting the European Parliament, shall determine the third countries whose nationals must be in possession of a visa when crossing the external border of the member states.' After 1st January 1996 decisions will be made by a qualified majority. Visas throughout the European Community will also have a common format.

Article 100c does state that it is 'without prejudice to the exercise of the responsibilities incumbent on the member states with regard to the maintenance of law and order and the safeguarding of internal security.' This would enable individual countries to argue in favour of a tougher visa regime but presumably only in exceptional circumstances. Overall, this article gives the European Community institutions competence in this field and empowers the Commission to play a central role in initiating proposals and issuing directives and measures agreed by the Council. The European Parliament, too, is given a role in the procedure, albeit a rather more minor, consultative role.

b)   Link Between Article 100c in the Treaty Establishing the European Community and Article K in the Treaty on European Union

Significantly, Article 100c is linked to Article K in the Treaty on European Union. This occurs in two ways. The *passerelle* Article K.9 enables the Council to decide to apply Article 100c of the EC Treaty to areas such as asylum policy, wider immigration policy, action to combat drug addiction and policies to combat international fraud, which are listed as 'matters of common interest' in Article K.1(1) to K.1(6) (see above in section 4.4.1). This may be done by the Council acting unanimously on the initiative of the Commission or a member state. Article K.9 and Article 100c thus provide a ready means whereby European Community institutions may acquire further competence in the fields of justice, home affairs and crime prevention. Matters such as criminal judicial co-operation, customs co-operation and police co-operation, in Article K.1(7) to K.1(9), are excluded from this provision.

c)   The Two Roles for the K4 Co-ordinating Committee

In addition, the K4 Co-ordinating Committee is also specifically mentioned in Article 100d of the EC Treaty. This stipulates that the K4 Committee shall contribute to the proceedings of the Council under Article 100c, which at present is limited to visa policy. Thus, the same group of senior officials is charged with assisting the European Community institutions under Article 100, and with initiating and co-ordinating actions outside the European Community in the intergovernmental institutions established under Article K of the Treaty on European Union.

4.4.4   *The Declaration on Police Co-operation*

In addition to the Maastricht Treaty, the associated political Declaration on Police Co-operation was signed in February 1992. A declaration appended to an international agreement is a device whereby states can set out how they initially intend to implement the designated provisions. The political declaration commits the member states to co-operation in the exchange of information and experience in the following areas:

- support for national criminal investigations and security authorities, in particular in the co-ordination of investigations and search operations;

- creation of databases;

- central analysis and assessment of information in order to take stock of the situation and identify investigative approaches;

- collection and analysis of national prevention programmes for forwarding to member states and for drawing up Europe-wide prevention strategies;

- measures relating to further training, research, forensic matters and criminal records departments.

The member states are committed to consider on the basis of a report during 1994 whether the scope of this co-operation on police matters should be further extended.

The Declaration offers additional evidence of a commitment to promote police co-operation, as well as specific areas in which this will take place. It is at present unclear whether these developments will be subject to public scrutiny and debate, and whether procedures for ensuring accountability will be introduced.

4.4.5   Assessment of the Maastricht Treaty and Co-operation in Justice and Home Affairs

Title VI of the Treaty on European Union marks a watershed in the development of police co-operation in Europe. For the first time there is a formal agreement to pursue co-operation in justice and home affairs – and the matters of 'common interest' are spelled out in some detail. To some extent the new provisions place the existing work of the Trevi Group on a more formal footing, although Trevi seems likely to be superseded by a new structure during 1994. In particular, there is an explicit role for both the European Commission and the European Parliament.

In theory, the Treaty enables the development of a much clearer and more co-ordinated set of structures for enabling co-operation to take place. It brings under a single umbrella a range of activities which should facilitate greater horizontal co-ordination of police and law enforcement co-operation. There should also be continuity in progress towards greater police co-operation because it appears likely that those currently working at a senior level in the Trevi Group will continue to perform similar roles in the K4 Committee.

This positive interpretation is undermined by a number of self-evident problems.

a)   Lack of Clarity

Although the Treaty states explicitly that member states 'shall regard' co-operation in the fields of justice and home affairs as matters of 'common interest', it is not clear what this will mean in practice. At one extreme the provisions could stimulate European-wide co-operation in practical policing. At the other extreme the possible areas of co-operation could be 'considered' and 'regarded' with no outcomes of operational significance, or possibly even with no initial intention to promote practical co-operation. In addition, the letter and spirit of co-operation laid down in Article K.1 could be circumvented through the provisions of Article K.2 – where member states have a reserved right to exercise national responsibilities in maintaining law and order and internal security.

b)   Parliamentary Oversight

It is not clear how the K4 Committee will relate to the European Parliament. Although the Parliament is to be consulted and its views 'duly taken into consideration', the nature of the consultation and the extent to which the Parliament's views will be taken into account remain wholly undetermined. The requirement for an annual debate on progress in implementing co-operation in justice and home affairs is a modest step towards parliamentary oversight. If satisfactory parliamentary scrutiny is largely absent then the democratic deficit is a genuine cause for concern.

c)   Sensitive Issues of Sovereignty

The new Article 100c in the EC Treaty, and the possibility under Article K.9 that other policy areas may be incorporated in it, is also an important development. Visa policy will become, with the ratification and implementation of the Maastricht Treaty, a European Community field of competence to be followed soon, perhaps, by asylum policy and maybe other areas of immigration policy. The Commission thus has full powers of initiation and advice and responsibility for monitoring and evaluating implementation.

Why was it considered necessary to separate certain fields of co-operation, which will be within the competence of the European Community remit, from other fields of co-operation, which will remain outside it and be dealt with on an intergovernmental basis? The most obvious answer is that the political realities of the sensitive issues of sovereignty necessitated such a course. This argument is substantiated by the exclusion, as things stand, of judicial co-operation in criminal matters, customs co-operation and police co-operation (including Europol) from the K.9 provisions allowing policy fields such as asylum to be transferred in to EC competence under Article 100c. Certain issues, it seems, remain too politically contentious to be brought within the European Community structure. Hence the need for separate 'pillars' for the European Union.

d)   Retaining Control and Secrecy

However, it might also be argued that such an arrangement is convenient for all those involved in the process. By keeping police co-operation and associated issues outside the EC it will be possible to retain greater control and secrecy. The role of the European Parliament can be limited and – just as important – it will prove easier for some governments to prevent parliamentary scrutiny in their own countries. In the UK, for example, matters within the purview of the EC are liable to be scrutinised in either of the Houses of Parliament. Inter-governmental deliberations, on the other hand, can be kept secret and well away from awkward questions posed by parliamentarians.

Even the European Commission is likely to be fairly well pleased with the new arrangements. Certain matters, such as visas and probably asylum in the near future, will now be firmly within the EC structures. But the fields of judicial, home affairs and police co-operation which are intergovernmental in nature will also be susceptible to a high level of influence by the Commission and matters can proceed without undue 'interference' by representatives from the European or national parliaments.

e)　　　　　The Central Role of the Commission

Although it is still early days, it seems likely that the Commission will play a key role in the development of co-operation in the fields of justice and home affairs under Article K of the Maastricht Treaty. In early July 1993, Padraig Flynn, the Social Affairs Commissioner who has been given responsibility for these areas, announced that he intended to establish a team of about 20 people to work in this field. 'We intend to proceed prudently because this is an intergovernmental area which has always been handled with great sensitivity', Commissioner Flynn said, but he also stressed that he was hoping to produce a number of initiatives for consideration by the Council of Ministers by the end of 1993. These included proposals on strengthening the external borders – the so-called 'hard outer shell' – and initiatives on immigration and drug addiction. Mr Flynn also said he wished to bring forward ideas on the establishment of the European Information System (EIS).

It seems likely, therefore, that Commissioner Flynn and his team will exercise considerable influence over the deliberations of the intergovernmental Council of Ministers of Justice and Internal Affairs. The K4 Co-ordinating Committee will report to the Council and under this will be the as yet undetermined structure of subcommittees and working groups. The Commission will doubtless liaise closely with the K4 Committee and may be represented on it. The Co-ordinating Committee will apparently be serviced by a secretariat under the direction of the Council's Secretary General. Presumably this is what is meant by the Commission being 'fully associated', under Article K.4(2), with the work of the K4 Committee. Much of Trevi, it would appear, will be reconstituted within this structure. Article K.3 of the Treaty on European Union empowers the Council to draw up new intergovernmental conventions and to adopt joint measures.

f)　　　　　Effective Means for Creating Momentum

Although it may seem faintly ludicrous that the same ministers, advised by the same officials, at the same meetings may leap-frog between being in the European Community and being outside it, depending on the proposals they are considering, this may prove an effective device for creating the necessary momentum in the field of European police and criminal justice co-operation. The downside of this arrangement is again the lack of effective scrutiny and accountability and a possible loss of public legitimacy and consent.

This ambitious new framework for promoting co-operation on policing and related matters will take time to evolve. It will undoubtedly build on the work undertaken by the Trevi Group and seems certain to absorb some aspects of the Schengen Convention on visas and asylum. It is also possible that the proposed European Information System will be based on the Schengen Information System.

g)   Macro-Level and Meso-Level Initiatives

The new post-Maastricht structure and arrangements will operate at the macro level and predominantly at the meso level. At the macro level, the Treaty on European Union itself has established a framework within which meso-level developments may occur. It is also important to note that Article K.3 empowers the Council of Ministers to develop new macro-level initiatives in the form of conventions. It may also take meso-level steps in the form of joint actions and joint positions and may 'promote, using the appropriate form and procedures, any co-operation contributing to the pursuit of the objectives of the Union'. This form of words appears to embrace a wide range of possibilities for macro-level and meso-level initiatives. The subcommittees and working groups seem likely to concern themselves with an array of meso-level issues and practical steps to facilitate greater co-operation between operational police officers. However, little if any attention appears as yet to have been paid to the vital issues of accountability, legitimacy and public confidence.

h)   The Declaration on Police Co-operation

The Declaration on Police Co-operation, signed in February 1992, is strong post-Maastricht evidence for continuing political commitment in promoting police co-operation, and doing so in specific fields of police practice – such as support for criminal investigations and search operations, co-operation in forensic matters and the creation of information databases. Although it is not yet clear what the practical consequences of the Declaration will be, any more than it is clear how any developments will be subject to accountability, the Declaration itself can be seen as an unambiguous attempt to translate the general political momentum for police co-operation into more specific, and more focused, concerns which have operational significance.

4.5   The Council of Europe

4.5.1   *Background to the Council of Europe*

The Council of Europe was established on 5th May 1949 by 10 founding states: Belgium, Denmark, France, Ireland, Italy, Luxembourg, the Netherlands, Norway, Sweden and the UK. These have subsequently been joined by 22 others: Austria, Bulgaria, Cyprus, the Czech Republic, Estonia, Finland, Germany, Greece, Hungary, Iceland, Liechtenstein, Lithuania, Malta, Poland, Portugal, Romania, San Marino, Slovakia, Slovenia, Spain, Switzerland and Turkey. A further seven applications, by countries ranging from Albania to Russia, are under consideration.

The headquarters for the Council of Europe are in Strasbourg. It has a staff of only 1,000 and an annual budget for 1993 of ecu 150 million. Under the skilful leadership of Catherine Lalumière, who has been Secretary General since June 1989, the Council of Europe has undergone a process of revitalisation and is currently enjoying enhanced stature. It has played an important role in acting as a bridge between the EC countries and the former communist states and newly-emerged countries in central and eastern Europe. The Council's resurgence was reflected in the summit meeting of government leaders in mid-October 1993. At this meeting in Vienna, the EC's External Affairs Commissioner, Mr Hans van den Broek, suggested that it would now be appropriate for the European Community itself to join the Council of Europe and this may happen during 1994.

The Council's principal aims are to promote European unity, foster social and economic progress and protect human rights. It has established a number of committees and bodies including the European Commission on Human Rights, the European Court of Human Rights and the European Committee on Crime Problems. Its powers are limited to making recommendations, although the Court of Human Rights has had a significant impact on a number of member states through the 'political weight' of its decisions. Some cases have even prompted changes to national legislation. The UK has on several occasions been forced to amend legislation. For example, the decision in the *Malone v UK* case, which concerned telephone tapping, was instrumental in the introduction of the 1985 Telecommunications Act. At the Vienna summit meeting in October 1993 it was agreed to overhaul and simplify the system for enforcing human rights. It was also agree to launch an anti-racist campaign throughout Europe.

4.5.2 Migration, Refugees and Asylum Seekers

The Council of Europe has been active in the analysis and discussion of issues associated with migration within Europe and into European countries. As these matters have increased in importance during the last five years or so, the Council has taken the lead in collecting data and promoting discussion. For example, in 1991 the Secretary General helped to organise a conference of ministers on the movement of people from central and eastern European countries, which took place in Vienna on 24–25th January and was attended by representatives from 35 different countries. The Council of Europe also helped to organise the Fourth Conference of European Ministers Responsible for Migration Affairs which took place in Luxembourg in September 1991. The Council has also sponsored useful research into migration, refugees and asylum.

4.5.3 The Pompidou Group

In 1971 the Council of Europe set up the European Group to Combat Drug Abuse and Illicit Traffic in Drugs. This is usually called the Pompidou Group because it was created on the initiative of the French President of that name. Its purpose is to co-ordinate wide-ranging work on drugs, including drugs-related crime. The group has undertaken work in the following areas:

(i)   An examination of 'criminal justice' responses to the problems of drugs misusers.

(ii)   Exploration of ways to combat drugs traffickers by tracing and confiscating their financial assets.

(iii)   The collection and evaluation of data for policy formulation in the drugs field.

(iv)   The investigation of educational initiatives.

The Pompidou Group has promoted research into various aspects of drug addiction, including the treatment and rehabilitation of offenders.

It is a consultative group and tends to include officials and ministers rather than police officers, and it seeks to share ideas and promote best practice. At the time of its inception it appeared to offer the prospect of an international drugs commission for Europe but it has not developed in this way.

4.5.4   Other Activities

The European Committee on Crime Problems, established by the Council of Europe, has for many years undertaken research and discussions on different dimensions of crime and its prevention in European countries. Each year the Committee holds a conference and seminars at which papers are presented by experts from a variety of different states. Its work is perhaps not as well known as it should be. The Council of Europe has also been active in other fields associated with crime, police and human rights and has helped to mould the international framework within which police co-operation in Europe is developing. One example of this is the Council of Europe Convention for the Protection of Individuals with Regard to the Automatic Processing of Personal Data, approved in 1981, which is discussed further in Chapter 6 (section 6.1.2).

4.5.5   Assessment of the Council of Europe and Police Co-operation

a)   Migration, Refugees and Asylum

The data produced by the Council of Europe on migration, refugees and asylum are useful and supplement figures available from sources such as the United Nations High Commissioner for Refugees. Presumably, the new *Centre d'Information de Reflexion et Echange en matière d'Asile* (CIREA), and the associated Centre for Information, Reflection and Exchange on Frontiers and Immigration (CIREFI), will produce similar data for the European Union countries but the Council of Europe's work will continue to be most valuable as it covers 32 European countries.

The renewed emphasis on safeguarding the rights of minorities, and the anti-racist campaign, agreed at the October 1993 Vienna summit, may also prove significant in affecting developments in the European Union in the coming period. Similarly, the October 1993 decision to simplify the Council of Europe's system for enforcing the protection of human rights may lead to increased use of the European Court of Human Rights. Such cases may arise as a consequence of developments in police co-operation in the EU and the tighter external border controls.

b)   Pompidou Group

At present, the Pompidou Group does not appear to have significant impact in the field of police co-operation in Europe. No respondents mentioned the group at all, whereas Trevi, Interpol and Schengen were discussed by all informants.

It might be argued that the Pompidou Group has a potentially important contribution to make at the macro level, and perhaps at the meso level, of police co-operation against drugs trafficking. For example, in 1987 agreement was reached on a common approach to soft drugs in the Pompidou Group, and this was announced by the Dutch Minister of Justice. It is questionable whether this agreement has been operationalised given the recurring disputes between the Netherlands and other members of the European Union about the Dutch policy on to soft drugs.

The Council of Europe does have the advantage over the Trevi forum of embracing 32 countries rather than the 12 EU member states. However, perhaps because of its size and diversity, it does not appear to have had the political authority of the Trevi Group and so it has been less effective in providing the momentum to secure police co-operation.

At the minimum, effective linkages should be constructed between Trevi Working Group III and the Pompidou Group. The research commissioned by the latter may prove useful to Trevi and other networks, and indeed Trevi, Interpol and Schengen might each profitably follow the Council of Europe's lead and commission serious research on subjects with which they are concerned.

c)   Data Protection Convention

The impact of the European Committee on Crime Problems does not appear to have been very great and perhaps the detailed analysis of European crime is a field in which the Council of Europe could play a greatly enhanced role. In the area of data protection, however, the Council has had a significant impact and the 1981 Convention for the Protection of Individuals with regard to the Automatic Processing of Personal Data continues to provide the basic international framework in which the exchange of computerised information may occur. This was supplemented by the 1987 Recommendation (R(87)15) on the use of personal data in the police sector.

4.6   Summary of Findings

4.6.1   The general view is that Interpol will continue to serve as the major channel for operational enquiries, but its capacity to promote wider police co-operation is limited:

• Despite earlier criticisms of Interpol's efficiency and security, there is a high level of support for Interpol's current activities.

• Changes at Interpol's headquarters, including the introduction of new technology, are widely appreciated.

• Although Interpol appears to discourage direct bilateral European contacts, the introduction of direct communications between the NCBs through the Automated Message Switch System (AMSS) has led to the dynamic exchange of information.

• Interpol's role in fostering collaboration in Europe is constrained by its international world role.

• Interpol must remain primarily a channel for communications at the micro level of individual cases.

• There is some danger that Interpol may be increasingly bypassed by new macro-level, European-wide structures for the exchange of information (the SIS and the EDU/Europol).

- Although Europol may be perceived as an alternative to Interpol this is unlikely to be the case unless one or the other undergoes fundamental change. Europol, for the present, will deal purely with *intelligence* whereas Interpol deals in *information*, although it is developing some intelligence through its Liaison and Criminal Intelligence Division.

4.6.2 **The Schengen Agreement and Implementing Convention appear to offer a striking example of co-operation at macro, meso and micro levels of law enforcement. Schengen's role as a model or 'laboratory' for a wider European initiative is widely recognised amongst senior police officers and government officials throughout Europe, but central issues of accountability will need to be addressed:**

- The history of Schengen has been characterised by a high level of commitment and resolve, and although it ran into delays and difficulties in 1992–1993 rapid progress was made after June 1993.

- It appears that at least six Schengen member states will implement the Convention from 1st February 1994.

- The Schengen working groups have made major contributions to practical police co-operation – including steps to improve compatibility in radio and computing equipment and the exchange of officers.

- The Schengen Information System provides information for police in the six countries which are initially participating, followed by Portugal, Greece and Italy at a later date.

- The Schengen Agreements include macro-level policies on policing the external borders of the member states – including the development of a common visa policy.

- Doubts remain about the effectiveness of the 'hard outer shell' at the common external borders.

- There is some concern that the so called 'ring of steel' will disadvantage nationals from developing countries.

- The common system for dealing with requests for political asylum has provoked criticisms from human rights groups.

- The Schengen Information System raises human rights, privacy and data protection issues which it is alleged have not been satisfactorily addressed, although it would appear that the data protection measures are fairly comprehensive.

- The Schengen Agreements include macro-level policies on policing the internal borders of the member states – including 'hot pursuit'.

- The complexity of the Schengen Convention raises problems of accountability and legitimacy, primarily in relation to police powers, human rights and public approval. As yet, there is no overall judicial or parliamentary accountability.

- The EFTA countries which have applied to join the EC/EU have been strongly invited to join the Schengen Group, and Austria already has observer status.

4.6.3 There are mixed judgements on the effectiveness of the Trevi Group:

- It has promoted the principle of increased police co-operation and given it considerable political impetus.

- It has helped to reduce national rivalries in the field of law enforcement and has promoted mutual respect and trust.

- The working groups (of all types) appear to address a wide range of matters relating to police co-operation – terrorism; technical and forensic matters; serious, international and organised crime; immigration; judicial co-operation; and the development of the EDU/Europol.

- These are macro-level initiatives which resulted in a number of meso-level, tangible benefits in practical police co-operation.

- The Trevi Group is too secretive.

- It has suffered from not being connected to the European Community institutions and political process.

- The Trevi Group operates primarily at the intergovernmental, political and senior official levels and may not be taking sufficient account of the meso- and micro-level responsibilities of law enforcement personnel 'on the ground'.

- The Trevi Group is not seen as a fully accountable, legitimate structure for policy making or executive action, and as such is treated with some suspicion by those (including police officers) whose support is needed if practical progress in police co-operation is to be achieved

- The Trevi Group's structure is regarded as inefficient and incoherent, which may in part be a function of the lack of a permanent location and secretariat, with insufficient co-ordination between the working groups and also poor 'institutional memory'.

- The creation of the EDU/Europol was in part a product of the work conducted by Trevi Working Group III.

- Even in its infancy Europol offers a 'case study' in macro, meso and micro levels of co-operation. At the macro level, the initial impetus was given by the Trevi ministerial group and then consolidated in the Treaty on European Union. The *Ad Hoc* Working Group on Europol was subsequently created to provide a meso-level constitutional framework. Project Group Europol has the micro-level task of operationalising the initiative.

- Despite the work of the *Ad Hoc* Working Group on Europol, the full development of the EDU/Europol was hindered by the failure of the Trevi ministers to agree its location until the Brussels summit of 29th October 1993 where it was agreed that the EDU/Europol should be located in The Hague.

4.6.4   **Title VI of the Treaty on European Union marks a watershed in the development of police co-operation in Europe. For the first time there is a formal agreement to pursue co-operation in justice and home affairs:**

• Although the Treaty states that member states 'shall regard' co-operation in the fields of justice and home affairs as matters of 'common interest', it is not clear what this will mean in practice. In addition, co-operation could be circumvented through the provisions of Article K.2 – where member states have a reserved right to exercise national responsibilities in maintaining law and order.

• It is not clear how the K4 Committee will relate to the European Parliament. Although the Parliament is to be consulted and its views 'duly taken into consideration', the nature of the consultation and the extent to which the Parliament's views will be taken into account remain wholly undetermined.

• Political realities have dictated that only certain matters will fall within the competence of the European Community remit – visa policy (and perhaps asylum policy) under Article 100c in the EC Treaty and Article K.9 of the Maastricht Treaty is certainly within the EC's remit, whilst judicial co-operation in criminal matters, customs co-operation and police co-operation (including Europol) are excluded. This is probably because the latter are seen as issues which remain too politically contentious to be brought within the European Community structure.

• Such an arrangement may, however, prove to be convenient for all those involved. By keeping police co-operation and associated issues outside the EC it will be possible to retain greater control and secrecy. The role of the European Parliament can be limited and – just as important – it will prove easier for some governments to prevent parliamentary scrutiny in their own countries. In the fields of judicial, home affairs and police co-operation the Commission will exercise influence at the intergovernmental level, and matters can proceed without undue 'interference' by representatives from the European or national parliaments.

• It seems likely that the Commission will play a key role in the development of co-operation in the fields of justice and home affairs under Article K of the Maastricht Treaty. The K4 Co-ordinating Committee will report to the Council and under this will be the as yet undetermined structure of subcommittees and working groups. Much of Trevi, it would appear, will be reconstituted within this structure. Article K.3 of the Treaty on European Union empowers the Council to draw up new intergovernmental conventions and to adopt joint measures.

• Although it may seem faintly ludicrous that the same ministers, advised by the same officials, at the same meetings may leap-frog between being in the European Community and being outside it, depending on the proposals they are considering, this may prove an effective device for creating the necessary momentum in the field of European police and criminal justice co-operation. The downside of this arrangement is again the lack of effective scrutiny and accountability and a possible loss of public legitimacy and consent.

• The Declaration on Police Co-operation, signed in February 1992, is strong post-Maastricht evidence for continuing political commitment in promoting police co-operation, and doing so in specific fields of police practice – such as support for criminal investigations and search operations, co-operation in forensic matters and the creation of information databases. The Declaration itself can be seen as an unambiguous attempt to translate the general political momentum for police co-operation into more specific, and more focused, concerns which have operational significance.

4.6.5   The effect of the Council of Europe on police co-operation has been modest, although it has played an important role in the protection of human rights:

•   Under the leadership of Madame Lalumière, the Council of Europe is enjoying an enhanced reputation and with the recent accession of central European countries it now has a membership of 32 states. This number is likely to grow further in the near future.

•   The Council's work in the field of human rights, and the judgements of the European Court of Human Rights, has been influential and the October 1993 decision to simplify the system may lead to increased use of the Court as a consequence of developments in police co-operation in the European Union and the tighter external border controls.

•   The Council's activities in the analysis of migration, refugees and asylum have been most valuable. The renewed emphasis on safeguarding minority rights, and the agreement to launch an anti-racist campaign, is to be welcomed.

•   The Pompidou Group has promoted research into various aspects of drug addiction – including the treatment and rehabilitation of offenders and criminal justice.

•   The Council of Europe's 1981 Convention for the Protection of Individuals with regard to the Automatic Processing of Personal Data continues to provide the basic international framework in which the exchange of computerised information between the police forces of Europe must take place.

4.7   Proposals

4.7.1   Interpol, Schengen and the Trevi Group (or its successor) should follow the Council of Europe's lead and commission serious research.

It is remarkable that the intergovernmental agencies with the prime responsibility for promoting police co-operation do not undertake, or commission, more detailed research of the problems with which they are dealing. Proper research is a necessary condition for developing appropriate responses. This should certainly be an integral part of the development of 'Europol',

4.7.2   Suitable mechanisms to ensure the satisfactory accountability of the Schengen structures should be established.

Although experiences and expectations of levels of accountability for law enforcement bodies appear to vary considerably between European countries, it is essential that proper arrangements are made to ensure high levels of legitimacy and support throughout the Schengen sphere of influence – including macro-level policies on borders; data protection and safeguards for the SIS; and micro-level police practices, such as 'hot pursuit'.

4.7.3   Whilst the advent of the K4 Committee will address some of the criticisms levelled at the Trevi Group, a detailed appraisal should be undertaken to ensure that the failings of Trevi are avoided from the outset.

The historical separation of the Trevi Group and the EC has not been satisfactory. There is a clear democratic deficit. Although Title VI of the Treaty on European Union states explicitly that progress on co-operation in judicial and home affairs will be subject to oversight by the European Commission (Article K.4) and subject to scrutiny by the European Parliament (Article K.6), it is essential that the rather weak and vague provisions in the Treaty are met in full. Failure to secure proper accountability of the K4 Committee, and the work of sub-committees responsible to it, will only serve to perpetuate the development of police co-operation under a Trevi-type, intergovernmental veil of secrecy.

4.7.4   A European Union Police Forum should be established at which those involved in developing the structures for police co-operation would make an annual report on the progress achieved and future plans. This would enable police officers, those involved in human rights groups and others to engage in constructive criticism and comment.

The post-Maastricht momentum for greater police co-operation is most clear at the level of political commitment, but the evolving structures and mechanisms for securing co-operation (particularly the work of the K4 Committee under Article 100d of the EC Treaty and Article K of the Treaty on European Union) are less clear, as are the lines of accountability to both the European Commission and the European Parliament.

What is required is an ongoing review of developments rather than a post hoc historical assessment of what has been achieved. This is necessary to secure the proper degree of accountability which is required for legitimacy and consent in police co-operation. It is also necessary in order to avoid confusion and a wasteful duplication of effort. In the complex web of evolving structures for police co-operation the central point is at the macro level of government ministers and their senior officials.

It would be extremely useful if an annual report were to be made to a specially convened group of interested parties (including senior police officers from EU member states, representatives from police forces' trades unions, human rights groups, academics and others). This could take the form of a conference – a European Union Policing Forum.

The purpose would be both to report on progress made and to engage senior officials, senior police officers and others in a dialogue which would then inform the next stage in the process. This would certainly promote accountability and legitimacy. It would also offer a real mechanism for promoting co-operation through 'structured feedback' from police officers who would comment with the benefit of practical experience and operational responsibilities.

CHAPTER 5

MESO-LEVEL GROUPS, AGREEMENTS AND NETWORKS FOR POLICE CO-OPERATION

In addition to the major structures for European police co-operation outlined in the previous chapter, there is a number of other bilateral and multilateral agreements and less formal structures which exist to promote co-operation in particular areas.

This chapter examines co-operative arrangements in a number of policing and security fields. These include terrorism, drugs trafficking, football hooliganism, traffic, and technical and forensic matters. It also explores some of the mechanisms which exist for promoting co-operation in policing at ports and on railways, as well as customs co-operation.

Three illustrative examples of bilateral arrangements are discussed: co-operation between the UK and France and Belgium in policing the Channel Tunnel; co-operation between the UK and the Republic of Ireland at their mutual land border; and co-operation between French and Italian police at Bastia in Corsica.

Finally, the chapter briefly examines informal networks, associations and other arrangements for co-operation between police officers in the different European forces.

5.1 Terrorism

The Trevi Group, as explained in the previous chapter, has a responsibility for co-ordinating European police action against terrorists and their activities. In addition, other structures exist to promote co-operation and co-ordination between law enforcement agencies both within and beyond the European Union. This section discusses European liaison on terrorism through the Policing Working Group on Terrorism (PWGOT).

5.1.1 *Police Working Group on Terrorism (PWGOT)*

a) Origins and Functions of PWGOT

The Police Working Group on Terrorism (PWGOT) was established at a multilateral meeting held in 1979 in the Netherlands. Following the murder of the British Ambassador to The Hague, the Dutch *Centrale Recherche Informatiedienst* (CRI) *Bijzondere Zaken Centrale* held discussions with officers from the Metropolitan Police Special Branch (MPSB), the *Bundeskriminalamt* (BKA) *Ateilung Terrorismus* and the Belgian *Gendarmerie*. This meeting resolved to establish a working group on a more permanent basis.

The Police Working Group on Terrorism operates separately from the Trevi Group and focuses on practical, operational ways to counter terrorism. It meets regularly every six months with delegates from the various participating agencies. For example, in November 1988 the 20th PWGOT conference took place in London attended by 36 participants from 14 countries.

It aims to develop close links and trust between the specialist police forces in Europe involved in the prevention and investigation of terrorism. Information, particularly up-to-date intelligence, is shared throughout the network. Since 1980 there have been regular exchanges of officers between different forces for short periods in order to foster closer working relations. These exchanges also enable individual officers to learn more about different countries' laws, procedures and social structures and to develop their language proficiency.

A communications network has been established which permits contact to be made between member agencies at any time, including encoded facsimile facilities. The latter is used for most communications as there remains some reluctance to use Interpol for reasons of security. The communication system has proved very successful and the Trevi Group decided to install the same equipment.

b)   Membership of PWGOT

The group is a network of European police special branches, security services or other police organisations which have anti-terrorist responsibilities. It now includes the relevant agencies from all European Union countries and those from Finland, Norway and Sweden.

The full list of members is:

Belgium	*Groupe Interforces Anti-Terroriste* (GIA)
Denmark	*Politiets Efterentningstjeneste* (PET)
Finland	*Suojelpoliisi* (SUPO)
France	*Unité de la Coordination pour la Lutte Anti-Terroriste* (UCLAT)
Germany	*Bundeskriminalamt* (BKA) *Abteilung Terrorismus*
Greece	Anti-Terrorist Unit (EKAM) Ministry of Public Order
Ireland	*An Garda Siochana* Crime and Security Branch – International Liaison Office
Italy	*Direzione Centrale Della Polizia Di Prevenzione* (DCPP)
Luxembourg	*Gendarmerie, Sûreté Publique*
Netherlands	*Centrale Recherche Informatiedienst* (CRI) *Bijzondere Zaken Centrale*
Norway	*Politiets Overvakingstjeneste* (POT)
Portugal	*Direccao Central De Cambate Ao Banditisimo* (DCCB)
Spain	*Comisaria Generak De Informacion – Servicio De Informacion Exterior* (CGI-SIE)
Sweden	*Rikspolisstyreisen* (RPS)
UK	Metropolitan Police Special Branch (MPSB)

c)   European Liaison in Practice

In operational terms day-to-day liaison between security forces in Europe takes place through a network. For example, responsibility for European liaison on terrorism in the UK lay initially with the European Liaison Section (ELS) of the Metropolitan Police Special Branch. The UK unit was established at a time when there were no arrangements for police officers to share information and intelligence about terrorism in Europe. The Trevi Group had not been created. The UK unit was set up, and staffed by linguists, in order to facilitate quick communications with other police in the EC.

With the establishment of the Trevi Group, ELS was brought within the UK Trevi machinery (Home Office Circular 153/77). Since then ELS has become part of a network which includes the special branch or equivalent in all other EU countries and in addition Austria, Finland, Gibraltar, Iceland, Malta, Norway, Sweden and Switzerland. The membership of this network is rather wider than that of PWGOT, and its activities are the means by which the aims and objectives of PWGOT are operationalised.

There are staff at the European Liaison Section in Scotland Yard who speak each of the main European languages and who are familiar with different legal procedures. Regular contact throughout the network is maintained, although full details on how often meetings are held are not available.

The network has permitted police officers to be posted to work in other countries. For example, officers from UCLAT, the French Terrorism Liaison Bureau, have been posted to the Metropolitan Police Special Branch and British officers were in exchange posted to Paris.

The exchanges were judged to be a success and UK police report that relations with their French counterparts have never been better. The scheme has now been made long-term and there are permanent postings in France, Germany and the Netherlands. It is also intended to develop exchanges between the UK and Belgium.

d)   Scale of Activity

Some indication of the scale of activity on the PWGOT network can be provided by data from the British Metropolitan Police European Liaison Section.

The Section dealt with 935 communications on terrorism in 1987, rising to 1,193 in 1988 and reaching 1,969 in 1989. The total for 1990 was over 2,000 communications. The messages vary from straightforward checks on names to highly detailed enquiries which may take days to process.

The network also processes requests for visits by officers from one country to another. The visitors will usually be accompanied by an officer from the host country's member of PWGOT or equivalent.

e)   Special Conferences and Meetings

The Police Working Group on Terrorism also arranges various conferences and meetings. In January 1990, for example, a conference was held on 'The Preservation of Forensic/Fingerprint Evidence at the Scene of Terrorist Crime'. The conference, which was attended by 28 delegates from 14 PWGOT countries, critically reviewed

189

and assessed different forensic techniques in the collection of evidence at the scene of terrorist crimes in order to promote best practice.

Meetings have also been held to counter the Provisional Irish Republican Army (PIRA) threat and have included the Belgian GIA, the German BKA, the Dutch CRI, French agencies, the Royal Ulster Constabulary, the *Garda Siochana* and the British Metropolitan Police.

In addition, in February 1989 a seminar was organised, including representatives from Denmark, Iceland, Finland, Sweden and the United Kingdom, to discuss threats to the security of the Pope, and how to combat them, on his imminent visit to Scandinavian countries.

5.1.2 *Assessment of PWGOT*

According to police sources, the Police Working Group on Terrorism works well at both the meso and micro levels of co-operation. Within this network a good deal of personal goodwill and co-operation has been established between different national agencies involved in anti-terrorist work.

The effectiveness and success of the Police Working Group on Terrorism was summed up by a respondent from the Metropolitan Police Special Branch who was quoted by Fenton Bresler:

> I cannot stress too much the importance of the Police Working Group across the whole field of terrorism, including Northern Ireland. We know these people – they are our personal friends – they come here to the Yard when they happen to be in London. We make contact with them when we go abroad [...] It has become a very solid group of working colleagues. We trust each other implicitly and pass information to each other without question. (Bresler 1992, p.162).

Exchanges of personnel occur with positive results, and for specific instances of terrorist incidents the network operates to answer enquiries, provide intelligence and on occasions to enable liaison officers to be deployed quickly to the scene of incidents in other countries. This occurred, for example, in 1988 and 1989 with Provisional Irish Republican Army (PIRA) terrorist attacks in Belgium, Germany and the Netherlands.

The bomb attack on the Pan-Am aircraft, in late 1988 over Lockerbie in Scotland, offers another example. The incident revealed a good example of international police co-operation with the rapid installation of HOLMES (Home Office Large Major Enquiry System) equipment in Scotland, London, Washington DC and, in the former West Germany. The system was installed and operating within four days, using satellite and cable transmission, and was the first time that the BKA, the FBI and UK forces had been linked together in this way.

The activities of the Police Working Group on Terrorism, and associated liaison between security services, can be regarded as successful examples of police co-operation at the meso level, bringing together police officers with responsibilities for a particular specialist field and encouraging co-operative working practices and increased communications between forces. This successful meso-level collaboration has clearly led to good micro-level contacts and activities.

5.2   Drugs Trafficking

5.2.1   *The Drugs Intelligence Network*

a)   Background and Origins

As a result of discussions in Trevi Working Group III, it was decided that greater use should be made of Drugs Liaison Officers (DLOs), not only in postings between European states but also to non-EC countries. It was agreed that EC countries' DLOs elsewhere in the world would work closely together and would share information. It was subsequently decided that each Trevi Group member state should establish a National Drugs Intelligence Unit.

A further step is being taken with the establishment of the European Drugs Unit (EDU) as the first stage in the development of Europol. The EDU's major role will be to collect and analyse intelligence from member states in order to contribute to international efforts against drugs trafficking and drugs-related crime such as money laundering. The European Drugs Unit/Europol is discussed in greater detail in section 4.3.8 in the previous chapter.

b)   Activities of the Network

In the UK, the National Drugs Intelligence Unit (NDIU) has been reconstituted as part of the National Criminal Intelligence Service (NCIS) which was set up in 1992 as the national intelligence gathering and dissemination network. It is the focal point for the exchange of intelligence between European Drugs Liaison Officers. The Drugs Division is staffed by police and customs officers.

Interpol activities such as annual European meetings for heads of national drugs services have contributed to the success of this network. The customs services are also involved and a number of joint Interpol/Customs Co-operation Council (CCC) conferences for police and customs have added impetus to this work (see section 5.6.3).

c)   Findings

The information which this study has collected indicates that the network of Drugs Liaison Officers has increased co-operation in this field considerably. A number of instances of bilateral co-operation were cited by respondents. For example, in Spain it was reported that there is increased co-operation between the Spanish drugs squad and UK and Portuguese forces. Indeed, an example occurred while one of the research team was present in Madrid in July 1990. The *Nacional de Policia* was involved in a highly successful co-operative operation with the Portuguese police and customs police (*Guardia Fiscal*) which resulted in large seizures, a number of arrests and good intelligence about the source of the shipment and the people who were behind it.

5.2.2   *Comité Européen pour la Lutte Anti-Drogue (CELAD)*

The European Committee to Combat Drugs (ECCD), which is more commonly known by its French name and acronym *Comité Européen pour la Lutte Anti-Drogue* (CELAD), was established in 1990 following an initiative by President Mitterand of France. Its membership consists of government-nominated representatives from EU states. The European Commission is also represented.

Its initial task was to draw up a European-wide plan for the fight against drugs. The guidelines for the plan were submitted to and adopted by the Dublin meeting of the European Council in June 1990, and then endorsed by the Luxembourg meeting of the European Council in June 1991.

CELAD's programme of action is divided into five main areas: the co-ordination of anti-drug strategies in member states; the suppression of illicit trade in drugs; working towards the reduction in demand for drugs; EU participation at a multilateral level; and the creation of a European Observatory on Drugs (EOD) (Jamieson 1992, p.2).

5.2.3   *Assessment of the Drugs Intelligence Network*

There is no doubt that police efforts against drugs crime is one area where levels of co-operation are considerably developed. There are three possible reasons why this network has proved particularly successful.

First, drugs trafficking is a crime which has achieved a high level of political visibility. Government ministers in most, if not all, European Union countries have stressed their commitment to combat the problem. This political commitment seems likely to have galvanised the senior levels of the police organisations, which have in turn made this an area of priority for co-operation.

Secondly, the police involved in operations against drugs traffickers are mostly specialist officers who are able to work effectively with police drugs specialists from other countries.

Thirdly, a related point is that drugs squad officers have high status in their organisations, partly for the previous two reasons, and so they may feel comfortable co-operating with similar officers from other countries. This may be less true for officers involved in more general, lower status policing duties who feel less self-confident and secure in dealing with police from other countries.

If these points are valid, it seems likely that meso-level and micro-level co-operation will occur more readily and effectively between certain sorts of specialist police.

5.3   Football Hooliganism

5.3.1   *Networks and Structures*

Football hooliganism, although historically not a new feature of football matches, has taken on new and distinct dimensions in Britain and Europe over the last 30 years. It is a problem in many European countries other than England, particularly in Holland, Belgium, Italy and Germany. Violence at football matches has been a growing problem for football clubs wishing to participate in European and international tournaments.

a)   The European Convention on Spectator Violence

The European Convention on Spectator Violence, signed in 1985 by all Council of Europe members with the exception of Germany, marked an initial step towards an integrated European approach to this problem. The Convention undertakes to formulate and implement measures to prevent and control violence and misbehaviour by spectators. It emphasises the importance of 'close co-operation and exchange of information between police forces', as well as 'co-ordination of travel arrangements for away supporters and maintenance of stadia which facilitate fan segregation' (House of Commons 1991, p. xxxii). A standing committee, with a subsidiary research working party, was established under the terms of the Convention.

b)   Trevi Working Group II

Trevi Working Group II has a number of responsibilities which include public order and football hooliganism (see Chapter 4). In 1987 a Europe-wide network of permanent correspondents was created for the exchange of information about known football hooligans. In the UK the National Football Intelligence Unit (NFIU) was established and its head was the UK permanent correspondent. This unit is now part of the UK National Criminal Information Service (NCIS).

A set of guidelines for policing large-scale football matches, involving teams from different EC member states, was drafted by Trevi Working Group II following the 1988 European Championship competition and these were passed through the network to all European police. They were described as 'very valuable' (House of Commons 1991, p. xxxiii).

c)   Exchanges of Information and Personnel

International co-operation in this field has developed further during subsequent years. For example, in advance of the 1990 World Cup competition in Italy efforts were made by a number of EC interior ministries and police forces to liaise with the Italian authorities. As part of this process, Italian officials and police visited a number of other European countries to discuss methods and good practice. During the World Cup itself small teams of liaison officers visited Italy to assist the Italian police in handling groups of supporters from their respective countries.

More recently, there were examples of extensive co-operation during the 1992 European Championship competition and the 1993 World Cup qualifying matches. For example, Dutch and English police co-operated in the planning and conduct of operations to control fans who travelled to the Netherlands for the World Cup qualifying match on 13th October 1993. British police liaised with their Dutch counterparts in identifying people causing trouble, of which at least 250 were arrested. It should be noted that there were considerable criticisms of the way the operations were conducted in the Netherlands and of the scale of the arrests. The practice of responding to requests from the host country by sending a small team of liaison officers to handle groups of supporters from their respective countries continued. This is now established practice in European 'football crowd management', as is the routine exchange of information on supporters between police forces.

There is also evidence of co-operation between European police forces and the US authorities ahead of the 1994 World Cup competition. Exchanges of officers and information have taken place. For example, in 1993 US police officers visited the UK to attend a match between England and Holland in order to assess and learn from the co-operative efforts of Dutch and British police officers. Later in the year British police also collected information on offenders at the return match in Holland to add to the database held in the National Criminal Intelligence Service (NCIS) which, it was reported, would be passed on to the US authorities who could then refuse entry for the 1994 World Cup finals.

d)   Lack of Judicial Co-operation

Co-operation in policing 'international' football matches is reasonably well developed but a lack of judicial co-operation is a recurring source of frustration for police officers. When disorder and 'trouble' occur the host country will sometimes opt not to charge the violator (possibly because of the costs which would be incurred, especially if a successful prosecution led to a term of imprisonment), and simply prefer to deport the 'troublemaker'. This in itself is sufficient to frustrate police officers, but some have also commented that it makes a bad situation worse because hooligans feel that they can travel abroad and offend with impunity. Moreover, the offender's country of origin may find it impossible to exercise a legal restraint on future travel. For example, the British authorities cannot prevent known hooligans and persons who have already been the subject of deportation orders from leaving the UK unless they have been charged and convicted.

5.3.2   *Assessment of Co-operation on Combating Football Hooliganism*

Three important points have been made by respondents to this study concerning police co-operation over football hooliganism, and each was illustrated by experiences of policing the 1990 World Cup.

First, intelligence-gathering exercises have proved effective in predicting and halting violence. The Italian police were, for example, reported to be 'delighted' with the quality of the intelligence received through the work of undercover officers, and this in turn was understood to be instrumental in preventing serious incidents.

Secondly, the value of sending police officers from member states to escort their own nationals to matches in other countries has been recognised. For example, whereas the English police based controlling strategies on intelligence, the Dutch and Scottish police took an intermediary role between supporters and the local police. One commentator has noted how, in providing supporters with information, confrontations were prevented by the work of the Dutch police in Italy (Van der Brug and Meijs 1991, p.14, quoted in Williams 1992, p.58).

Thirdly, as the UK Home Affairs Committee pointed out, the Council of Europe's proceedings are primarily conducted at governmental level, while the Trevi Group operates on a rather more practical level. However, the limitation of Trevi to EU member states may make it impractical within the wider context of European football. The Committee recommended that membership of the football correspondent network of the Trevi Group should be extended to all member states of the Council of Europe. Additionally, it recommended that provisions which already existed for meetings of groups of experts should be used 'for regular police-to-police dialogue on the practicalities of co-operation against travelling hooligans' ((House of Commons 1991, pp. xxxii – xxxiii).

The European network for the policing of football matches and associated problems has developed considerably since the 1990 World Cup. Police respondents have pointed to a steady accumulation of knowledge and expertise during the 1992 European Cup and the 1992–93 World Cup qualifying matches. The network operates at the meso and micro levels and appears to have had significant and continuing success in pre-empting public disorder at international football matches.

5.4   Traffic Management and Control

5.4.1   *The Case for Co-operation*

The enforcement of road traffic legislation and regulations is an area where police in all EU countries can benefit from increased co-operation. Police officers and officials in any country may need to stop vehicles registered in another country to carry out checks on documentation, insurance, vehicle weights, driver hours, vehicle condition and tachograph records.

At present it is difficult to obtain information quickly on drivers and vehicles from other European Union countries, for example, on whether a driver is disqualified or a vehicle is stolen. Compatible computer-linked records, which can be accessed quickly on enquiry from an officer at the roadside, would be a great step forward.

Some mechanisms do exist for police co-operation in this field, but information from European police interviewed suggests that they are not well developed. At the micro-level of particular cases it may be possible to use bilateral contacts, or in a serious case an enquiry through Interpol.

At the meso-level, the European Traffic Policing Meeting provides a forum for discussion of matters of mutual concern. The meeting takes place each year and is attended by police officers from EU and Scandinavian countries. Recent topics which have been discussed include transport of hazardous chemicals, enforcement of speed restrictions, and policy and practice on drinking and driving.

The European Traffic Policing Meeting appears to provide an embryonic network for this important area of policing but at present it is little more than that. Much more could usefully be done to promote police co-operation and understanding in this field.

5.4.2   *Progress Towards Police Co-operation on Traffic*

a)   **EC-Level Action**

Until 1984 road safety was dealt with at EC level only if competition rules or the free movement of persons and goods were concerned. In 1984 the European Council adopted a Resolution to promote road safety, followed by measures from the Commission. Most of these legislative measures have been adopted.

In 1991 a working party was established to draw up a Community-wide road safety programme. Its brief was to define common objectives; establish the criteria needed to set priorities; determine the resource implications; and propose legislation needed to implement and extend the programme. The working group published a report in 1992 which forms the basis of a Commission communication to the European Council for an action programme on road safety. Most recently recognition of Community competence in this area has been confirmed in the terms of the Maastricht Treaty.

Having recognised the case for harmonisation of some aspects of traffic offences, specifically driver behaviour, two measures are currently being discussed by the Commission. A Directive has been proposed on fixing the maximum blood alcohol concentration for drivers, together with a suggestion for standardisation and type-approval of testing apparatus. The second proposed Directive concerns fixing speed limits for goods vehicles and buses throughout the EC, which are likely to come into effect in 1996 (Commission of the European Communities 1993b).

Trevi Working Group III is also examining issues relating to the policing of road traffic.

b)   Further Action

Mutual disqualification from driving would seem sensible where a driver has been banned as a result of a conviction in any of the European Union countries. As the UK Home Affairs Select Committee pointed out, 'It is absurd that a British driver banned for three years and sentenced to imprisonment on the Riviera for being seven times over the limit could drive as soon as his car was landed at Dover' (House of Commons 1990a, p. xxxiii).

Joint measures such as this could only be effective if police in different countries were able to call on a central bank of information. The Commission is already proposing the creation of a Community databank on road accident statistics and a documentary file on road safety. This would appear to be an excellent starting point for setting up a database containing information about drivers and motoring offences.

The whole field of traffic and driver regulation, and European police co-operation on such matters, is one that requires further detailed investigation. There is a difficulty in terms of the variety of offences, and how different laws and regulations, and court decisions, can be effectively enforced in different parts of the European Union. However, given that huge databases on motor vehicles are held nationally, notwithstanding the logistical difficulties, it is in principle straightforward to think in terms of pan-European information exchange in this area. There would, however, be some difficulties in reconciling different standards of data protection.

Limited co-operation along these lines is being tested in a pilot scheme between the UK, Spain, Portugal, Greece and Sweden. Germany and Denmark have also shown some interest in joining the project. From August 1993 officers from Kent in the UK have been able to check vehicle index numbers and drivers' licences of anyone committing traffic offences. The multi-million pound project, funded by the European Commission, will link police officers to the relevant agencies in other participating countries through the Driver Vehicle Licensing Agency (DVLA) in the UK. At this stage the project has a few practical problems which need to be resolved, for example, coping with the foreign languages, and more importantly, how to deal with violations under two or more criminal jurisdictions.

5.4.3   *Assessment of Co-operation on Traffic Matters*

Co-operation in traffic matters is developing in various ways and a number of imaginative and innovative projects are underway, some involving large-scale information exchange. There is a real possibility of extending these schemes to other European Union countries. Given the large number of motor vehicle offences (many of which jeopardise both personal and environmental safety), and the fact that about one-third of all known criminal offences are motor-vehicle related (and likely to increase – see Chapter 2), there are good grounds for urging the development of a European network in this area. Traffic policing may not have the cachet of policing terrorism or drugs trafficking, but offences in this area may impact more directly on European Union citizens than infrequent very serious offences.

5.5   Technical and Forensic Matters

5.5.1   *Police Technical and Forensic Contacts*

Among its other functions, Trevi Working Group II is responsible for promoting co-operation in technical fields and in 1991 it set certain objectives. The Declaration of Commitment was made with a view to implementing the relevant paragraphs of the 1990 Trevi Programme of Action (see section 4.3.7). The undertakings included:

- assistance by way of an agreed network of information exchange;

- communication of all progress in the field;

- sharing the results of research with a view to a more efficient fight against new forms of crime.

In addition, the Permanent Technical Committee for Co-operation, set up by the Interpol European Regional Conference in 1985, has promoted work in technical and forensic fields. As outlined in sections 4.1.5 and 4.1.7, these groups have organised specialist seminars on a number of relevant topics, including technological developments and fingerprint identification.

The existence of Trevi Working Group II has helped to promote a number of specialist technical networks which are fostering co-operation in relevant fields, such as computerised information systems and communications.

There are also many bilateral contacts which are helping to promote technical co-operation. For example, recent meetings have been held between the UK and German police to discuss secure speech and mobile data, and between Dutch and British officials and police to examine criminal records systems.

Forensic co-operation takes place between the European laboratories and a number of specialist seminars have been held on subjects such as DNA genetic 'fingerprinting' and on firearms and ballistics. Police forces have also been conducting a number of research projects in this area. The Forensic Information System for Handwriting, developed by the *Bundeskriminalamt* in Germany, has been shared with the US secret service and the Dutch police (Kube and Kuckuck 1992).

5.5.2   *Assessment of Co-operation on Technical and Forensic Matters*

Despite these contacts, there is a strong impression that more could be done to develop co-operation in these fields. This study has received little information on technical and forensic matters from the police and officials who have been interviewed. This appears to be regarded as a field in which only the specialists operate. Consequently, and despite Trevi Working Group II, there seems to be a lack of impetus in developing multilateral co-operative structures. This is another area in which more study is required to identify how much co-operation has been achieved, and ways in which further progress might most effectively be made. Particular attention could be paid to the ways in which greater co-operation could be promoted between civilian specialists (with their scientific knowledge) and serving police officers (with operational responsibilities).

5.6   Policing at the Borders: Ports

5.6.1   *Responsibilities for Policing at Ports*

As Chapter 3 indicates, responsibility for policing ports and airports varies between different European countries. In some it is the responsibility of the regular police, in others there are special police units. In a number of cases, policing organisations operate alongside private security personnel and immigration and customs officers. In the UK, for example, customs officers operate alongside the police at the National Criminal Intelligence Unit in collating and analysing information relating to organisations and individuals. HM Customs and Excise officers in the UK also act as Drugs Liaison Officers overseas operating alongside law enforcement agencies in other countries.

5.6.2   *Issues for Police Co-operation at Ports*

It is widely agreed that the abolition of checks at internal frontiers requires increased vigilance at the EU's external borders. In order to detect and deter drugs trafficking, terrorism, smuggling, illegal immigration and other trans-national crime, the policing of ports in the European Union will place a premium on continued and enhanced vigilance, and this in turn will depend on improved police co-operation. Obvious areas for attention are shared surveillance, common information databases, exchanges of personnel and improved standards of training.

One issue that has been raised by a number of police and other organisations is that of security at small ports and deserted stretches of coastline. It will clearly be difficult wholly to prevent the unauthorised entry of drugs, weapons and illegal immigrants. Around the European Union there are thousands of small ports and hundreds of thousands – perhaps an even greater number – of small boats and pleasure craft, many of which are capable of transporting illegal traffic into European Union countries. The British Ports Federation estimates at least 150,000 pleasure craft around the shores of the United Kingdom alone.

It is obviously not possible – and many would say it was not desirable – to keep a detailed watch on all the harbours and ports around the coasts of the external boundary of the EU, let alone the many thousands of miles of deserted coastline.

Nonetheless, the possibility of limiting illegal entry by such means is one that deserves detailed examination. One option is a system of compulsory registration for all small boats and pleasure craft in the European Union – France and Belgium already have such schemes – coupled with a central intelligence information system available for use by national border police. Such a network would at least in theory enable suspicious craft to be monitored across the EU, but whether such action is practicable is open to debate. Compulsory registration would, of course, facilitate the return of stolen boats to their rightful owners.

5.6.3   Assessment of Police Co-operation at European Ports

The existing European organisation for promoting co-operation in this field is the European Association of Airport and Seaport Police. It holds an annual conference at which issues such as security at ports and freight depots are considered, but the general impression is that it is not a very active organisation or network. In view of the obvious connection with drugs trafficking, and the potential connection with crimes such as terrorism and illegal immigration, there is a need for further research in this field, in conjunction with those responsible for policing ports, leading to the formulation of efficient co-operative procedures.

It is vital that co-operation occurs between the many different agencies that are involved in port and coastline security and policing. It is not clear that this occurs to any great extent at present, and further investigation of the possibilities for improvement is necessary.

5.7   Policing at the Borders: Railways

5.7.1   Background

Co-operation between police forces involved in policing railways has a long history in Europe. With the opening of the Channel Tunnel co-operation between transport police will be crucial. Initially this will involve police in Belgium, France and the UK as British Rail, the *Société National des Chemins de Fer Français* and the *Société National des Chemins de Fer Belge* will introduce direct freight and passenger services running through the Tunnel connecting London, Paris and Brussels. Services linking other countries will be introduced later.

These new services, together with massive investment in developing national rail infrastructures, will have a number of implications for trans-national crime. Some police believe that an expanded rail network will permit illegal goods and prohibited substances to be moved more readily within and between countries, will enable criminals to leave the scene of their crime more rapidly and will provide new locations for crimes such as robbery and theft.

5.7.2   Issues for Police Co-operation

Two of the most important issues in relation to co-operation between transport police in the European Union are the increase in crime on the railways, and questions concerning the powers of transport police across internal borders.

First, concern has increased over levels of crime on the European rail network. In March 1990, at a meeting in Paris of COLPOFER (the European railway police organisation), delegates were told that there had been a noticeable increase in criminals from eastern Europe, (the former) Yugoslavia and Africa, travelling and committing crime on the European rail system. The Austrian delegation reported eastern European nationals committing crimes on trains, and German representatives reported a 50 per cent increase in railway crime during 1989.

Secondly, there are unresolved issues over police powers and accountability on trains which enter another country's jurisdiction. Police from one country on a train which has entered another country may need to make arrests, collect evidence and transfer the detained person to the custody of another police force without formal extradition.

At present such matters are resolved by protocols between two or more countries, but there may be an increasing need for European-wide agreements if rail travel across Europe becomes more frequent. This is another area for further research.

5.7.3   *Mechanisms for Police Co-operation on Railways in Europe*

COLPOFER is the European organisation which represents railway police and security agencies and it has helped to establish a network for co-operation and understanding between the relevant EU police organisations. It has facilitated a number of international investigations into railway fraud and theft and has resulted in a pool of experience from which member agencies may draw.

Most co-operation is bilateral or trilateral. For example, the Belgian and French railways and British Transport Police maintain informal arrangements for liaison and they have undertaken exchanges on methods, procedures and training.

5.7.4   *Assessment of Railway Police Co-operation*

As with so many aspects of police co-operation, that which occurs between railway police in Europe has grown up in an *ad hoc* and incremental way. Although COLPOFER exists to promote meso-level contact it is not clear that the organisation yet works effectively to promote understanding and best practice. At the meso and micro levels bilateral and trilateral contacts may operate, but again with mixed results.

Different arrangements appear to exist in different locations and this is increasingly confusing for officers and citizens alike. As such forms of travel across Europe increase there is likely to be a growing need for a more coherent and standardised approach. There also appears to be a need for an active and well-founded European organisation to promote co-operation and common standards in this field.

5.8   Policing at the Borders: Customs and Excise

The roles and powers of customs organisations vary between European Union countries. In France, for example, the *Police de l'Air et des Frontières* (PAF) is responsible for immigration and policing duties at ports and frontiers (exercising authority over persons), but the *Services des Douanes* is responsible for customs (exercising authority over goods, vehicles and 'things' at the points of entry). In the UK, HM Customs and Excise is responsible for overseeing the movement of goods through ports, has powers of search and plays a crucial role in preventing smuggling of prohibited goods, whereas the Immigration Service is responsible for people entering the country. The police, especially the Special Branch, also exercise an important role at borders.

Several structures and organisations exist to promote international and European co-operation between customs and excise authorities. The completion of the Single European Market necessarily involved changes in the role of customs officials. International co-operation has been well established, and further initiatives at an EU level have also been developed.

5.8.1 The Customs Co-operation Council

International customs co-operation takes place through the Customs Co-operation Council (CCC) which has 131 member states. It was established in 1953 to promote co-operation between governments. Its remit is to work towards the harmonisation of customs procedures, to develop professional techniques and to exchange operational intelligence on the trafficking of illegal goods. Co-operation between different customs services of EU states occurs under the 1967 Naples Convention.

In 1988, at a regional meeting of the Customs Co-operation Council, the heads of all European customs organisations met in Brussels to discuss drugs trafficking in Europe. As a result of a series of workshops, joint plans have been put into effect on topics such as monitoring freight and road transport, confiscation of assets, and national co-ordination centres.

At the London G7 summit meeting in 1990, the CCC was invited to promote the strengthening of co-operation between customs and international traders and carriers, in order to improve the capacity of law enforcement agencies to target illicit drugs movements without hindering the legitimate circulation of people and goods. The Council seeks to achieve this through its Enforcement Committee and the development of a Central Information System.

Technical and financial assistance is provided to members in order to establish Regional Intelligence Liaison Offices (RILOs) in several regions including eastern Europe.

The Balkan Route Information System, operated by the German authorities in Cologne, involves the exchange of intelligence about drugs trafficking along the Balkan route. Intelligence gained through this system contributed to the seizure of 500 kgs of heroin at the UK's borders between 1990 and 1993 (Russell 1993).

The Customs Co-operation Council has worked to promote international collaboration and co-operation between transport associations. For example, the CCC's Carrier Co-operation Initiative was devised to improve co-operation between customs authorities, private carriers and international traders (Jamieson 1992, p.10).

5.8.2 Mutual Assistance Group 1992

In 1989 the Mutual Assistance Group 1992 (MAG 92) was established to address issues raised for EC customs authorities by the completion of the Single Market. It comprises customs representatives from each of the 12 member states. The group's remit is to deal with areas falling outside Community competence, though the Commission is closely involved with MAG 92 to ensure that parallel policy areas develop in a compatible fashion. The UK has been in the chair continuously since 1989.

The group has undertaken investigations of the customs-related implications of the removal of frontier checks and liaised with the Co-ordinators Group set up after the Rhodes European Council in December 1988 to co-ordinate action on the 1992 proposals.

Its discussions have focused on questions such as computerised information systems; mutual assistance arrangements; reinforcement of external frontier checks; drugs enforcement; training and exchange of personnel; technical and scientific aids; and joint customs exercises and operations. It is also examining national co-ordination centres, joint command centres at borders and joint surveillance.

The Mutual Assistance Group 1992 is working to update the 1967 Naples Convention on customs co-operation and to prepare a long-term, European-wide anti-fraud strategy.

In May 1992 the Directors General of the customs authorities represented in MAG 92 signed the Harrogate Declaration which provides a policy steer for future mutual assistance, including: the exchange of liaison officers and information, close co-operation on training, operational assistance and the development of anti-smuggling techniques (Russell 1993).

Within the terms of the Treaty on European Union, and under the framework established by Title VI, it now appears very likely that MAG 92 will continue to operate by being brought within an official and permanent structure. This will replace the *ad hoc* arrangements which have characterised its work to date. It is probable that the same personnel will continue to perform the same sorts of tasks, but with some measure of greater accountability and also a possible change of name for the group.

5.8.3 EC Matthaeus Initiative

The move towards improved customs co-operation has been assisted by the European Commission Matthaeus initiative (named after St. Matthew, patron saint of tax collectors). It enables the exchange of officers between EC customs services and organises joint training meetings.

Between 1989 and 1992, 1,875 customs officers participated in the scheme by spending several weeks in another EC country, doing the same work as they would 'back home'. In 1992, 394 officials participated in exchanges, with special emphasis on the exchange of instructors. A further 4,637 customs officers undertook language training as part of the Matthaeus programme

In 1992, 18 seminars were held under the programme on questions related to fraud prevention, including risk analysis for 'targeting' customs efforts, methods of checking the origin of fishery products, and audit systems and investigation methods in cases of fraud relating to anti-dumping duties (Commission of the European Communities 1993a, pp.39–40). In October 1992, around 200 customs officers and trades union representatives met in Brussels to discuss the implications of the removal of customs checks within the EC at the start of 1993 (*Target 92* 1992, p.2). Language courses and seminars are also run for customs officers who are unable to participate in exchanges.

5.8.4   Customs Information System

The EC-wide Customs Information System (CIS), otherwise known as *Système d'Information Douanière* (SID), was established in October 1992 by the European Commission and the twelve national customs authorities of the member states. It is seen as a vital component in the EU's external frontier strategy.

The Customs Information System is a computerised network which will eventually cover all areas of customs co-operation, including drugs. By late 1993 there were 33 CIS terminals in the UK and 160 terminals in total throughout the Community. The CIS will enable customs officers at external European Union borders and ports to exchange information on cases of fraud and on known or suspected cases of trafficking in prohibited goods. During its first year of operation around 15,000 messages were transmitted via CIS terminals.

The next phase in the system will involve the addition of a dedicated database. UK authorities report that a CIS Convention has been prepared, including full data protection provisions, to provide a legal basis for the database, with a view to ministers of finance signing the Convention before the end of 1993. The Convention will then be subject to parliamentary ratification in each member state.

The Customs Information System is the first European Union-wide initiative for law enforcement agencies to exchange intelligence information directly.

The CIS is an extension of the System Customs Enforcement Network (SCENT) set up in 1987. SCENT is an electronic mailing system for the exchange of information between member states and the European Commission about the import and export of goods. Thirty terminals have been set up in the member states along with two other terminals and a central computer at the Commission.

5.8.5   Changing Role of Customs

The abolition of all internal border controls in the nine Schengen countries, and changing methods of operation in the UK, Denmark and Ireland, mean quantitative and qualitative changes in the roles of the different customs authorities. Much of the work of customs officers will be redirected towards action at the external borders of the European Union.

In the UK, the government is committed to maintaining some customs checks at its internal borders. Anti-smuggling work will be confined to priority categories, namely drugs, pornography, firearms and a few other illicit goods, defined under Article 36 of the Treaty of Rome as harmful to public morality, public policy or public security.

Changes have also been made to the way in which controls are applied. Selective checks are now being made based on intelligence and profiles of high risk traffic, and customs officers will retain powers to ask any traveller questions in order to assist in customs work. There are now no systematic or random checks. All checks are now 'intelligent' checks based on specific intelligence or generic indicators which point to high risk traffic identified on the basis of previous results, trends over time or local factors. Increasingly, Memoranda of Understanding (MOUs) have been signed with individual businesses and associations, amounting to 7,000 traders including major airlines and other international carriers. These are agreements under which traders agree to supply information to the customs authorities to aid the detection of smuggling, particularly drugs trafficking. They are seen as providing valuable assistance to the customs authorities in the fight against drugs trafficking, but also as offering reduced risks to legitimate businesses.

A project called the Anti-Smuggling Project 93 (ASP 93) is being used to develop new policies and practice. Four areas of change have been identified each with a sub-project. First, there have been changes in procedures for intra-European Union passengers and freight transport – all intended to offer no visible sign of a regular or routine customs presence for internal travellers. Secondly, and partly as a compensatory device, Flexible Anti-Smuggling Teams (FASTs) are being deployed to create a flexible, mobile and more selective system of checks. Thirdly, greater emphasis has been placed on the use of information and intelligence, by increased co-operation with international trading partners, to enable spot checks to be targeted effectively in the short time available for interception. Finally, there will be changes to the legal powers exercised by officials. All existing powers will be retained, but in relation to intra-EU traffic at the frontier they can be used only for two purposes – the protection of the external frontier of the Union and for anti-smuggling purposes (HM Customs and Excise 1992).

5.8.6   *Assessment of Customs and Excise Co-operation in Europe*

Customs co-operation appears to have succeeded in a way which co-operation in other fields has not. There is one major international network co-ordinating global operations and liaison (the Customs Co-operation Council); and one computerised information network in Europe (the Customs Information System), supported by one initiative with a primary focus on the exchange of officers between EC customs services and the organisation of joint training (the Matthaeus initiative). The degree of co-operation between the members in each group appears to be high and this has led to successful individual and joint operations. The Customs Co-operation Council as a well-established network and the newly established Customs Information System appear to be in a position to continue and develop a longstanding tradition of co-operation.

5.9   Bilateral Co-operation: The Channel Tunnel

5.9.1   *Background*

The Channel Tunnel (also known as the Channel Fixed Link) is scheduled to come into use in 1994. Eurotunnel has a 55-year concession to operate the Tunnel. An estimated 30 million passengers and 15 million tons of freight will be carried through the Tunnel during the first year and this is expected to rise in subsequent years.

Two types of trains will run: Eurotunnel's own shuttles, between the two terminals, and through trains operated by Belgian, British and French railways. The Channel Tunnel offers exciting opportunities for police co-operation between the UK and France.

Certain arrangements for policing are included in the Anglo-French Channel Fixed Link Protocol, and there are other agreements (Memoranda of Understanding) between UK and French forces.

Responsibility for UK policing of the Tunnel lies with the Chief Constable of Kent, as set out in Section 14(1) of the Channel Tunnel Act 1987, while in France responsibility lies with the *Police de l'Air et des Frontières* (PAF) and the *Douane* (customs). Policing on the national trains will be the responsibility of the appropriate railway police (the British Transport Police and PAF).

5.9.2   *Policing Issues*

Successful policing of the Channel Tunnel will rely on workable procedures for co-operation between the police forces involved. These include the exchange of information and the exchange of expertise and also, importantly, the establishment of good working relationships on the basis of the trust and understanding established through regular face-to-face contact and meetings.

The UK police force responsible for the Tunnel area, Kent Constabulary, has developed a good working relationship with other law enforcement agencies in Belgium, France and the Netherlands. In 1968 the Cross Channel Intelligence Conference was established and this has met regularly ever since. The conference hosts seminars and meetings on various types of cross-border crime and their prevention and detection. Sources in both France and England have reported that it is a most valuable means of promoting co-operation.

a)   Kent Constabulary's European Liaison Unit

In 1991 Kent Constabulary established a European Liaison Unit, consisting of five officers with support staff, based at Dover East Port. The Unit co-ordinates European activity by Kent police and acts as the central point through which all European enquiries are channelled. Although it works principally with the various French police organisations, the Unit also co-operates closely with the Belgium police, especially with the *Gendarmerie Nationale* in Western Flanders, and with the Dutch police, particularly the CRI and police in Zeeland, Rijnmond and Haaglanden. The Unit receives and analyses information, documentation and intelligence and passes this on to the appropriate divisions within the force. It also produces a regular *Euro Brief* which is widely circulated.

Each year the Unit handles at least 2,000 separate enquiries. It arranges visits and exchanges of officers with French police divisions such as the *Renseignements Generaux* and the *Police de l'Air et des Frontières*. The European Liaison Unit has been provided with its own office in Calais and reciprocal arrangements exists for the PAF in Dover. As a result of the foresight of the Kent Constabulary, and the energy, commitment and ability of the officers involved the Liaison Unit has made, and continues to make, an important contribution to practical police co-operation.

b)   Memoranda of Understanding

Kent police has been working closely with officials from the *Préfet de Police* of the *Pas de Calais Département* and with officers from the *Police Nationale* and *Gendarmerie*. Memoranda of Understanding exist between the UK and French forces for Kent and the *Pas de Calais*. The Chief Constable of Kent has been working particularly closely with the *Chef du Service* of the *Police de l'Air et des Frontières*.

The Memoranda of Understanding are important means of facilitating practical co-operation between police officers in the cross Channel area. The Memoranda have been exchanged between the Kent police and the relevant police bodies in Belgium as well as France. For at least 25 or 30 years good informal contacts, developed through meetings of bodies such as the Cross Channel Intelligence Conference, helped to resolve problems and promote co-operation. With the advent of the Channel Tunnel, all the police organisations involved felt it was necessary to formalise these contacts and the Memoranda of Understanding have proved an excellent mechanism.

This appears to be an ideal case of micro-level contacts, facilitated by the meso-level Cross Channel Intelligence Conference, giving rise to more developed meso-level agreements. The meso-level Memoranda of Understanding provide a framework for, and also give encouragement to, operational officers to develop further their micro-level co-operation. A number of measures to facilitate co-operation were included in the UK Criminal Justice (International Co-operation) Act 1990. Bi-national plans have also been developed in the field of public safety to prepare for any emergencies in the Tunnel and to draw up 'disaster plans'.

c)   Language Training and 'PoliceSpeak'

Kent Constabulary is also implementing an intensive language training programme so that key officers have basic grounding in the French language. Links have been established between the Kent Police Training School and similar training schools in France. (For a detailed account of the Kent Constabulary's preparations for policing the Channel Tunnel, see Gallagher 1992.)

Another initiative is the so-called 'PoliceSpeak' project. This aims to 'standardize and refine the language of police operations, thereby improving communications efficiency and speeding the flow of information, with the ultimate objective of increasing inter-agency co-operation across national and linguistic frontiers' (*PoliceSpeak* 1993). The 'language' they have arrived at is not strictly speaking a language, rather it is recommended usage for natural language in such a way as to maximise efficiency in the context the language is required. It is not, in other words, some kind of pigeon English, or its French equivalent.

The PoliceSpeak team has attempted to identify terms and phrases which may be ambiguous in cross-Channel communications, and to replace them by straightforward terminology which is consistent and unambiguous. The lexicon they have produced is intended to be for the use of police, interpreters and translators on both sides of the Channel and of course those in the Channel Fixed Link itself. Interest has been expressed by others who are not directly involved in the Channel Tunnel, and the PoliceSpeak team themselves suggest that the 'language' might well become a prototype for other bi-lingual and multi-lingual lexicons of policing and emergency services (*PoliceSpeak* 1993, p.3).

5.9.3   Assessment of Channel Tunnel Police Co-operation

The research has revealed a great deal of preparatory planning which has been undertaken in advance of the opening of the Channel Tunnel. There appears to be full co-operation from both police forces. It is worth noting that co-operation has been based upon both formal and legal agreements, and on informal contact between those who will have the task of policing the tunnel.

Respondents to this study, who will ultimately have that task, have expressed satisfaction with the co-operation that has been achieved, and have indicated their belief that wider European police co-operation should be based on mechanisms they have developed. It remains to be seen how this co-operation will proceed across the Channel in practice, and this case study merits continued investigation.

Co-operation is taking place at the meso level to ensure that micro-level co-operation can occur when the Tunnel is in use. It is only then that this will be tested. Co-operation has also taken place at the macro-level with the drafting of protocols which will facilitate the meso-level and micro-level arrangements.

5.10   Bilateral Co-operation: The *Garda Siochana* and the Royal Ulster Constabulary

5.10.1   Background

The United Kingdom and the Republic of Ireland share a 300-mile common land frontier. For some years the border had only minimal customs controls and there is no immigration control. In 1993 the customs controls were removed. Because of different rates of duty in Northern Ireland and the Republic of Ireland, smuggling has been a problem since the border was established in 1922.

There are 226 vehicular crossing points, which are roads or tracks, but of course it is possible to find innumerable other routes across the border on foot or in certain types of vehicle. On main routes traffic crossing the border is monitored but on minor roads there are only occasional spot checks. There are 18 Permanent Vehicle Check Points on the UK side of the border, all of which are operated by military personnel with occasional RUC presence.

Terrorist activities led the British Parliament to pass the Prevention of Terrorism (Temporary Provisions) Act 1989, renewing earlier legislation. Schedule 5 of the 1989 Act gives powers to police, customs and immigration officers to examine and detain passengers who are entering or leaving Northern Ireland or Britain in order to determine whether they are involved in terrorist activities.

5.10.2   Co-operation Between the Two Police Forces

The *Garda Siochana* and the Royal Ulster Constabulary have joint responsibility for policing the common land frontier. During the last decade or more a high level of co-operation and liaison has been developed at each level of policing.

Some of this liaison is formal, at Commissioner/Chief Constable level for example, while much of it is informal day-to-day contact to share information, to co-ordinate action and to deal with requests for assistance. This co-operation occurs at regional and district levels. For obvious reasons it has been difficult to obtain details of the forms of information exchange between the two forces, but the evidence that is available suggests it is extensive and frequent.

One important means of border control are mobile patrols by the UK army, sometimes accompanied by police, on the UK side, and by the *Garda* on the Irish side. The patrols are co-ordinated by Border Superintendents and by Operational Planning Inspectors. This co-operation occurs daily.

Much of this activity has developed over many years, but it was formalised by the Anglo-Irish Agreement which was signed in 1985. Article 9 provides for a programme of action to increase co-operation between the *Garda* and the RUC. This includes joint threat assessments, exchange of information, liaison structures, technical co-operation, joint training and operational planning.

5.10.3 *Assessment of Co-operation Between the Garda Siochana and the Royal Ulster Constabulary*

There is a high level of co-operation between the two police forces, and this has been enhanced by the Anglo-Irish Agreement. Unlike the Schengen Agreements, the right of either force to engage in pursuit across the border into the other country has not been agreed. This is a sensitive issue, in both Northern Ireland and the Republic of Ireland. The formal and informal forms of co-operation reflect the political commitment of the two sovereign governments to combat terrorism and other cross-border crime. Yet again, this example illustrates the vital importance of a macro-level political agreement in order to facilitate and encourage effective meso-level and micro-level practical police co-operation.

5.11 Bilateral Co-operation: The French – Italian Border

5.11.1 *French Border Policing*

As discussed in Chapter 3, there is a great array of different law enforcement agencies operating in European countries. The legal systems are also distinctive. In France, the *Police Nationale* come under the Minister of the Interior. The same minister is responsible for frontiers. In addition, the *Préfet* can declare a border control zone extending inland from a border.

Goods are the responsibility of the *Service des Douanes* (Customs), who also have duties relating to the detection of explosive devices at entry points. Movements of people are controlled by the *Police de l'Air et des Frontières* (PAF). The *Gendarmerie Nationale* (GN) is part of the Ministry of Defence and has special anti-terrorist and anti-drugs units. The *Gendarmerie* operate throughout France and have some responsibilities at frontiers.

5.11.2   Italian Border Policing

There are four separate police organisations in Italy: *L'Arma dei Carabinieri*, the *Polizia di Stato* (the public security police), the *Guardia di Finanza* (the treasury police) and the *Vigili Urbani* (the local community police).

The *Polizia di Stato* (PS) is responsible to the Minister of the Interior and has responsibilities which include maintenance of public order, protection of life and property, and investigation of offences. The *Polizia di Stato* is divided into three sections of which one, the Special Police, is responsible for highway and railway policing and policing the frontiers.

The prevention and investigation of smuggling, illegal immigration and tax evasion are the functions of the *Guardia di Finanza*, which are under the control of the Minister of Finance. They perform customs and excise, and also coastguard tasks. The *Carabinieri* may also operate at frontiers.

5.11.3   Cross-Border Co-operation at Bastia

Bastia in Corsica is the point of entry for travellers from Italy. An examination of police co-operation between the French and Italian authorities illustrates the sorts of arrangements which exist.

Since 1988 there has been a system of exchanges of serving officers at various levels, encouraged by the authorities in Paris. Italian officers are exchanged with their French counterparts for a month as part of their training and in-service career development. This is reasonably straightforward at a place such as Bastia, where language differences are not a major problem, but in other places this is an obstacle. A recent memorandum from Paris has called for increased language training to facilitate such exchanges but it is not clear how this will be achieved.

Where the exchanges have taken place, French and Italian informants report immediate benefits. An Italian officer, serving for a month with the French police in Bastia, is able to contact his or her Italian colleagues directly to ask for further details or documents, or to pass on information. However, the French courts would not recognise evidence that rested on such contacts nor would they necessarily accept documentary material, however legal and correct in Italy, that was passed across the border.

5.11.4   Findings on Police Co-operation at Bastia

Interviews were held with officers from the *Service des Douanes, the Police de l'Air et des Frontières* (PAF) and the *Gendarmerie Nationale*.

Any unusual cross-frontier co-operation usually takes place through the special co-operation commissions in Paris, and French informants indicated that there is considerable deference to Paris.

Periodic visits by relevant officers take place between Bastia and Italy and these help to foster personal contacts. An individual local officer of senior rank might make use of these personal contacts and the ease of local communications to make special requests for information or documentation from the Italian authorities.

However, the organisations in France and Italy do not wholly mirror each other, so the personal ties are important in facilitating this communication and exchange of information. This is particularly the case with the *Police de l'Air et des Frontières* which has no exact Italian (or British, Spanish or Greek) equivalent.

5.11.5   *Assessment of Co-operation at French – Italian Frontier*

With regard to different national views and legislation, there appear to be few serious problems in this particular case. A more general point that was made is that the different national views and legislation may cause complications. For example, the relatively more permissive attitudes and legislation on drugs, in the Netherlands and Spain, may affect action by the French authorities.

Nonetheless, the surveillance and tracking of ships and aircraft, suspected of carrying drugs or other contraband, is effectively carried out with information passed from one force to another, although for the French this is controlled from Paris.

Where legislative incompatibility and organisational differences may inhibit co-operation, the respondents interviewed by the research team confirmed the view that officers on the ground will often find ways around obstacles in order to collaborate if necessary.

However, these *ad hoc* arrangements may not be the most efficient or effective means of developing closer law enforcement co-operation, particularly if such co-operation needs to expand to include other EC countries' personnel.

Co-operation appears to occur at many different levels. The case of Bastia tends to confirm information from other sources that in many cross-border locations informal arrangements for co-operation have evolved, which may or may not be backed up by more official policies and structures.

At the micro-level of co-operation day-to-day operations necessitate some means of collaboration, based essentially on personal contacts. At the meso level there is less direct contact, although it may still occur, and normally such co-operation as there is will be routed through headquarters, in Paris in the case of the French. It seems reasonable to suggest that more agreement at the macro level would help to facilitate lower-level co-operation. This is gradually occurring through mechanisms such as the Schengen Agreements.

5.12   Other Networks

Two other associations merit examination. Both the European Network for Policewomen (ENP) and the *Union Internationale des Syndicats de Police* (UISP) are associations for co-operation which are oriented to the police themselves, rather than towards co-operation over crime-fighting. There are also secret networks, which exist for the international exchange of intelligence, and widespread informal contacts.

210

5.12.1   The European Network for Policewomen

The European Network for Policewomen (ENP) was established in 1989 at the International Conference for Policewomen, held in the Netherlands. Its aim is to optimise the position of policewomen in European police forces, and it works to achieve this through the establishment of a network for the exchange of support, ideas, experience and research relating to the work of policewomen. Its principal goal is to encourage equality of opportunity in police work.

The network is based in the Netherlands and is funded by the Ministry for Home Affairs at present. The co-ordinator works closely with Dutch organisations dealing with equal opportunities within the police service. The European Network for Policewomen publishes a regular newsletter, and has also published surveys of the conditions of service for policewomen throughout Europe (ENP 1992a, 1992b, 1992c).

This is a young organisation, and evaluation of its role is possibly a little premature. That it should receive government funding is, however, recognition of a perceived need for a network and service of this kind.

5.12.2   The Union Internationale des Syndicats de Police

The *Union Internationale des Syndicats de Police* (UISP) was established in the early 1950s, and its objectives include working for co-operation between national police services and working for freedom of association and civil status for all police officers. In particular, it is committed to the establishment of professional organisations for police officers where none exist (UISP 1987).

It is based in Hilden, Germany. Around 500,000 police officers are represented through this organisation, drawn from a number of police professional organisations.

The UISP's *Report of Activity for 1992* details its work in a number of areas, such as consideration of the political developments in Europe and their repercussions on the work of the UISP, action to secure trades union rights for police employees, action towards securing civilian status for all police, and collaborative work with regard to EC bodies (UISP 1992).

It is apparent that the UISP has played an important role with regard to securing civil and trades union rights for police officers, particularly in Greece and Portugal. It has, however, been sharply criticised by the Police Federation of England and Wales, which has accused the organisation of being 'an ineffective talking shop, much given to posturing about civil rights, and occasionally meddling in the internal affairs of separate countries' (Alan Eastwood, quoted in *Police* 1992b, p.18). Evaluation of the usefulness of the UISP on the basis of present information is difficult.

It is worth noting that further comparative research on the various police professional organisations needs to be undertaken in order to complement existing knowledge of police organisations in Europe.

5.12.3   Secret Networks

Secret networks exist for the exchange of intelligence on an international and European level. The activities of such groups and networks are often hidden from public view. For example, a UK television documentary in 1992 listed a number of European police co-operation organisations about which little or no information was publicly available ('Bordering on Big Brother', broadcast 28th October 1992 as part of the *Dispatches* series.)   One such network, 'Kilowatt', is apparently an information alliance between the security services of around eighteen countries. Some information on this group became available after the siege of the US Embassy in Tehran in 1982 (*Statewatch* 1991, p.2), but it is a shadowy organisation about which little is known other than the prominent role reportedly played by the Israeli *Mossad*. Recent reports suggest that it has changed its name.

Other secret groups which aim to promote co-operation on policing and security activities include the Vienna Group and the Berne Group. The former, also called the Vienna Club, was formed in 1978 as the result of proposals from the ministers of the interior of Austria, France, Germany, Italy and Switzerland. It is a shadowy meso-level network which enables information to be exchanged and meetings to be held with the aim of fighting terrorism in the participating countries. It is sometimes confused with the Vienna Immigration Group which was established as the result of a conference sponsored by the Council of Europe in January 1991. This group includes European Union, Scandinavian and eastern European countries and seeks monitor and control migration.

The Berne Group, or Berne Club, appears to perform a similar role to the Vienna Club but with a larger membership, which includes all 12 European Union member states with the addition of Austria and Switzerland.

Information on secret organisations is obviously very difficult or impossible to obtain. There is no doubt that largely secret police organisations (national and international) may be essential, especially in the fight against terrorism and international organised crime. Secrecy may be a necessary condition for effective police action. Even so, it is arguable that there should be some formal mechanism to ensure accountability and public confidence.

Where there are non-secret structures and organisations for police co-operation, as reviewed in this and the preceding chapter, the argument for fully visible and transparent mechanisms to ensure accountability become all the stronger. Paradoxically, the existence of secret networks may make the non-secret structures more susceptible to demands for democratic oversight. There is some evidence from the provisions in the Treaty on European Union, specifically in the way the European Commission is to be 'fully associated' with the work of the K4 Committee, and the way the Presidency 'shall consult' the European Parliament on the activities taken under Title VI, that the democratic deficit in police co-operation is slowly beginning to be formally addressed at the highest level.

5.12.4   The Value of Informal Support

Finally, there is a number of issues surrounding the use (or abuse) of informal support and contact networks between police officers. Most serving police officers interviewed as part of this study recognised the value of completely informal contacts with colleagues in different forces and in different countries. This is a recurring theme – where shared professional interests and a common 'cop culture' prove to be stronger than differences in language, procedures and judicial systems. As J. Wilzing, Director of the Netherlands Detective Training College, noted in 1987 when addressing an international symposium on surveillance:

> You will undoubtedly agree, that it is during the informal get-togethers at a conference that sound agreements are made with far-reaching impacts in terms of improved co-operation and intensification of contacts. In this respect [...] the *Rechercheschool* is happy to be able to make its facilities available to the international company gathered here. The *Rechercheschool* has a reputation to live up to, which is not only restricted to the claim of being the Dutch police training institution with the largest lounge and the longest bar! Although this cannot be denied, it has to be said at the same time, that within this very climate, many excellent agreements on co-operation were made, and often they were even more effective than the ones made through the official channels of The Hague! (Wilzing 1987, p.12).

Micro-level, informal contacts between police officers are a key component in structures for police co-operation. This area certainly merits further study and investigation not least because 'informality' is so pervasive – and, many officers have claimed, so useful. Conversely, informal networks contain the potential for abuse, for example, the improper use and exchange of intelligence (Robertson 1992, unpaginated), which affords a second argument for further investigation and research.

5.13   Summary of Findings

5.13.1   There are several well-developed specialist police networks in Europe operating primarily at the meso and micro levels of co-operation:

Terrorism

• The Police Working Group on Terrorism (PWGOT) works well at both the meso and micro levels of co-operation, with a good deal of personal goodwill. Exchanges of personnel occur with positive results. It is generally regarded as effective in promoting collaboration and co-operation on general threats, as well as intelligence on specific incidents.

• The activities of the Police Working Group on Terrorism, and associated liaison between security services, can be regarded as successful examples of police co-operation at the meso level, bringing together police officers with responsibilities for a particular area and encouraging co-operative working practices and increased communications between forces. It is also arguable that successful meso-level co-operation will offer operational dividends at the micro level.

Drugs

• Trevi Working Group III resolved that greater use should be made of Drugs Liaison Officers (DLOs), not only in postings between European Community states but also to non-EC countries. It was subsequently decided that

213

each Trevi Group member state should establish a National Drugs Intelligence Unit and these are now being incorporated in the member states' National Criminal Intelligence Systems.

• A further step is being taken with the establishment of the European Drugs Unit (EDU) as the first stage in the development of Europol. The EDU's major role will be to collect and analyse intelligence from member states in order to contribute to international efforts against drugs trafficking and drugs-related crime such as money laundering.

• The European Committee to Combat Drugs (ECCD), which is more commonly known by its French name and acronym *Comité Européen pour la Lutte Anti-Drogue* (CELAD), is in the process of drawing up a European-wide plan for the fight against drugs.

• There is no doubt that police efforts against drugs crime is one area where levels of co-operation are quite highly developed: drugs trafficking is a type of crime which has achieved a high level of political visibility; and the police involved in operations against drugs traffickers are mostly specialist officers who are able to deal effectively with police drugs specialists from other countries.

Football Hooliganism

• Trevi Working Group II has created a Europe-wide network of permanent correspondents for the exchange of information about known football hooligans.

• The European network for the policing of football matches and associated problems has developed considerably. The network operates at the meso and micro levels and appears to have had significant and continuing success in pre-empting public disorder at international football matches.

Traffic

• Co-operation in traffic matters is developing and a number of imaginative and innovative projects are underway, some involving large-scale information exchange. These include attempts to achieve harmonisation on the maximum blood alcohol concentration for drivers, mutual disqualification from driving, and cross-national checks on vehicle index numbers and drivers' licences.

Technical Matters

• Trevi Working Group II has helped to promote a number of specialist technical networks which are fostering co-operation in relevant fields, such as computerised information systems and communications. Forensic co-operation takes place between the European laboratories and a number of specialist seminars have been held on subjects such as DNA genetic 'fingerprinting' and on firearms and ballistics.

Ports

- It is vital that co-operation occurs between the many different agencies that are involved in port and coastline security and policing. It is not clear that this occurs to any great extent at present, and further investigation of the possibilities for improvement is necessary.

Railways

- Two of the most important issues in relation to co-operation between transport police in the European Union are the increase in crime on the railways, and questions concerning the powers of transport police across internal borders. At present such matters are resolved by protocols between two or more countries, but there may be an increasing need for European-wide agreements as rail travel across Europe becomes more frequent.

Customs

- Customs co-operation appears to have succeeded in a way which co-operation in other fields has not. There is one major international network co-ordinating global operations and liaison – the Customs Co-operation Council (CCC); and one computerised information network in Europe – the Customs Information System (CIS), supported by one initiative with a primary focus on the exchange of officers between EC customs services and the organisation of joint training (the Matthaeus initiative). The degree of co-operation between the members in each group appears to be high and this has led to successful individual and joint operations.

Bilateral Co-operation: The Channel Tunnel

- Co-operation is taking place at the meso level to ensure that micro-level co-operation can occur when the Tunnel is in use. It is only then that this will be tested. Co-operation has also taken place at the macro-level with the drafting of protocols which will facilitate the meso-level and micro-level arrangements. Meso-level Memoranda of Understanding, involving Belgian, English and French police, have also proved effective.

Bilateral Co-operation: The Garda Siochana and Royal Ulster Constabulary

- There is a high level of co-operation between the two police forces, and this has been enhanced by the Anglo-Irish Agreement. The considerable political commitment at the macro level has proved an important impetus for meso-level arrangements and for the daily micro-level co-operation between operational police officers.

Bilateral Co-operation: The French – Italian Border

- Co-operation appears to occur at many different levels. The case of Bastia tends to confirm information from other sources that in many cross-border locations informal arrangements for co-operation have evolved, which may or may not be backed up by more official policies and structures. It seems reasonable to suggest that more agreement at the macro level and the meso level would help to facilitate lower-level co-operation.

Professional Organisations

- Further comparative research on the various police professional organisations, the European Network for Policewomen (ENP) and the *Union Internationale des Syndicats de Police* (UISP), needs to be undertaken in order to complement existing knowledge of police organisations in Europe.

Secret Networks

- There is no doubt that largely secret police organisations (national and international) may be essential, especially in the fight against terrorism and international organised crime. Secrecy may be a necessary condition for effective police action. Even so, it is arguable that there should be some formal mechanism to ensure accountability and public trust.

5.13.2 **In some respects, there is a danger of an over-proliferation of unconnected European police associations and networks where similar activities are being undertaken simultaneously by different organisations:**

- As policing functions become more highly differentiated the impetus to establish new international associations becomes greater.

- The most effective networks have been set up in criminal policing fields with high political visibility, such as drugs and terrorism.

- The establishment of associations and international groupings generally appears to be *ad hoc* and haphazard.

- There seems to be more than one network or association existing in some fields of specialist policing.

- There is no clear picture of existing co-operative associations and networks.

- It would appear that no single agency or institution is aware of all the existing European arrangements in specialist police fields.

- There is a danger of duplication and lack of co-ordination of co-operative arrangements.

- The proliferation of databases and mechanisms for information exchange raises questions about data protection and human rights, and also about accuracy and efficiency.

- The level of political, public and legal accountability of many of these networks appears to be woefully low.

5.14   Proposals

5.14.1   There is a distinct need for a clear and comprehensive account of existing networks and associations.

The present *ad hoc* and haphazard growth of associations and groupings is clearly not the best way to proceed. However, without a detailed account of which networks function well and which areas of specialist policing require further developments, it will not prove possible to promote efficient and effective means of European police co-operation, or proper accountability.

5.14.2   Areas of specialist and technical police activity which would benefit from increased European co-operation should be identified.

The most effective police networks are in fields such as terrorism and drugs: those with high status and visibility. There would appear to be other areas of criminal police work, such as stolen vehicles, fraud and technical activities, including forensic work, which would benefit from more effective European police networks.

5.14.3.   The changing nature of informal intelligence exchanges requires further study.

In the light of rapidly changing technology and substantial expansion in the number of specialist networks, the status of informal information exchange needs consideration. Such an investigation should be placed within the context of current debates about the role of the police in economically developed democratic societies, and informed by contemporary theories of social control.

CHAPTER 6

COMMUNICATIONS AND INFORMATION EXCHANGE

Good communications are at the heart of effective practical police co-operation. As the demands grow for closer European police co-operation, the need for rapid and reliable communications systems becomes more pressing. This, in turn, requires compatible equipment and, where necessary, the development of new, shared, systems for information exchange.

The creation of 'Europe Without Frontiers' has significant implications for communications and information technology. The demand for sophisticated information systems (in policing as elsewhere) is undergoing far-reaching changes brought about by the pace of technological development, and the way in which potential 'users' can see large-scale storage, retrieval and exchange of information as being to their advantage. On the other hand, there are increasing demands for proper data protection and for adequate safeguards that information held on individuals is accurate and not misused.

This chapter examines issues relating to police communications and information exchange. The first section discusses general questions of the regulation and accountability of police communications. This is followed by a detailed review of the systems of communication developed for the three major structures for police co-operation in Europe – Interpol, the Schengen Group and the Trevi Group, including Europol. The final section briefly examines possible future developments in the structures and mechanisms for the collection and exchange of police information and intelligence within the European Union.

6.1   Police Communications: Control and Accountability

6.1.1   *Different Forms of Police Communications*

There are various forms of modern police communications. Police agencies of different countries can communicate bilaterally through modern electronic systems, such as telex, telefax, or special radio networks. In this case the exchange is legally no different from making or responding to a request for information by mail or morse code in earlier days. Special branches of police organisations as well as some secret services have installed protected communication networks between themselves for special purposes. The Trevi Secure Fax Network (TSFN) is one example.

Another form of communication is by means of direct on-line computerised access to foreign police databases. This is possible for various European countries for police files on stolen goods, in particular for motor vehicles. Direct access is still not possible in the case of data relating to persons. This is due to data protection issues, opposing mutual assistance laws and differing national legislation on criminal law procedure (discussed in detail below).

The facility for access to foreign police files (bilateral or on-line) should be distinguished from the nature of the files themselves, particularly in respect of the establishment of new common files and information pools, like the Schengen Information System (SIS). Common information systems may differ in content and function. They may either merely contain files which list persons and things to be searched for, similar to the SIS, or contain databases which work as an information pool, including all kinds of information gathered through police inquiries. The former tend to store basic 'information' where the latter deal in 'intelligence'. In addition, the latter systems usually work at a more sophisticated level because they have analytical capabilities.

6.1.2   Legal Issues of Control and Accountability

With respect to legal problems the distinction should be made between the general exchange of professional experience between police forces, such as investigation methods, technical know-how and developments in criminal strategy, and the exchange of information on actual suspects, crimes and circumstances. Only the latter are legally relevant.

Two important questions can be asked in this respect. Do the new forms of information exchange fulfil the conditions set by existing laws and conventions on mutual assistance in criminal matters? If they do not, how can such differences be reconciled?

a)   Hard Facts and Soft Information

A distinction also needs to be made between information and intelligence. Information may be defined as 'hard facts', that is facts which are empirically verifiable. Modern police intelligence systems used for operational purposes contain so-called 'soft information' or intelligence. A good definition of what this includes was given by the Lindop Committee on Data Protection in 1978. The committee stated that criminal intellignce 'may be speculative, suppositional, hearsay and unverified, such as notes about places frequented, known associates, suspected activities, or even just that a certain car was believed to have been involved in a certain robbery' (Lindop 1978, p.80, para.8.05). This raises questions about the purposes for which such information may be used, and how it is controlled.

There is also a problem of language and interpretation. The fact that 'soft information' is a mixture of facts and evaluations and opinions, means that the margin for misinterpretation is wide. If the person who files the information and the one who reads it use a different language, and have different cultural, legal and police backgrounds, the potential for 'inadvertent abuse' becomes all the greater. Direct on-line access also deprives a state of the opportunity to place restrictions on the availability of information.

b) **The Council of Europe 1981 Data Protection Convention**

The major international agreement on data protection is the Council of Europe Convention for the Protection of Individuals with Regard to Automatic Processing of Personal Data which was signed in 1981. The Convention, which has the force of law between the contracting parties, stipulates that signatory countries should enact laws which safeguard data on individuals that are held on computers and should set up national regulatory bodies. While encouraging the free flow of data where proper safeguards exist, the Convention allows for the prohibition of the transfer of data where the receiving country does not have adequate protection, or where the data may be passed on to another country which does not conform to the provisions in the Convention.

The European Commission strongly backed the 1981 Council of Europe Convention and recommended that all EC member states should ratify it. By November 1993, the 1981 Council of Europe Convention had been ratified by the following EC countries: Belgium, Denmark, France, Germany, Ireland, Luxembourg, Netherlands, Portugal, Spain and the United Kingdom, leaving only Greece and Italy yet to do so. In addition, Austria, Finland, Iceland, Norway and Sweden have also ratified the Convention. It should be noted that several countries have opted out of at least some of the provisions in the Council of Europe's 1987 Recommendation (R(87)15) on the use of personal data in the police sector.

The 1981 Convention sets out the international framework within which automated data on individuals, held on computers, may be transferred from one European Union state to another and, as such, governs the legal basis for EU-wide computerised communications and information exchange about individuals by police officers. There may, however, be some derogation for intelligence affecting national security and public safety.

c) **Rights and Responsibilities**

The data protection field thus poses a number of problems. To what extent is the exchange of information possible between states, insofar as different data protection standards are applicable? This is generally a problem for countries with a relatively high standard of data protection. This issue in turn raises the question of who should be responsible for the accuracy of information and liable for damages if the information contained therein is incorrect.

It is also necessary to consider the rights of the person on whom the data is held (the data subject) to access and, where appropriate, rectification and erasure of data. For which purposes may the stored information be used (the purpose limitation principle)? The use of common databases raises more general legal questions relating to the type of data stored in the system. Who assumes the role of the data protection agency (in the UK, for example, the data protection registrar fills this role) and what powers should such a controlling body have?

Where one state requests another to carry out a particular act, the legality of the requested measure should also be questioned. If one assumes, for example, that the circumstances require the arrest of a person, that person can only be arrested if the legal requirements of the requested country are met. Who should decide whether these requirements are met – the requesting state, which has stored information concerning the person, or the requested state which carries out the arrest? This matter is addressed by the Schengen Implementing Convention, which is discussed below in section 6.3.

221

6.2 Exchange of Information and Interpol

6.2.1 Background

International criminal investigations are not conducted by Interpol, rather they are conducted *through* Interpol. The history, aims and organisation of Interpol are detailed in Chapter 4. Interpol provides the principal channel for practical police co-operation throughout the world. By October 1993 there were 174 member countries, which was a growth of 24 on the 1990 membership, largely as a result of the accession of new states from eastern Europe and the former USSR.

In 1976 some 246,000 messages were transmitted through the Interpol network; by 1992 the number had risen to more than one million messages. Currently, about 80 per cent of the telecommunications traffic is sent by or to the 44 countries in Interpol's European region and around 47 per cent of all Interpol's work relates to Europe (PRSU 1992). Some 400,000 communications in 1992 involved European Union member states.

The number of files opened at the General Secretariat on international offenders or on criminal cases with international ramifications has risen from 27,585 in 1976 to 140,000 in 1992 – a five-fold increase. Of these, the vast majority relate to Europe.

Of the six countries paying the highest annual budget contributions, four are European – France, Germany, Italy and the United Kingdom – the other two being Japan and the USA. In 1990 these six countries contributed 34 per cent of Interpol's budget. Contributions are based on budgetary units. In 1990 France, Germany, Italy and the UK each paid 72 budgetary units (Bresler 1992, p.200); in 1992 it was suggested to the research team that the figure had risen to 100 units per country (Harrison 1992).

In 1986 a European Secretariat was established at Interpol headquarters to deal specifically with crime which has a European dimension, excluding drugs trafficking which is dealt with by a special division. The European Secretariat acts as the permanent secretariat for the European Regional Conference, and in this role carries out research into identified crime problems, for example, international car crime and public order at major sporting events.

6.2.2 Exchange of Information Through Interpol

a) Interpol's Communication Network

The communications network of Interpol has a three-tier structure, based on the central station, regional stations and national stations. Interpol headquarters in Lyon houses the central station, and is also the regional station for the European/ Mediterranean/North American network. The six other regional stations are centred in Abidjan, Buenos Aires, Canberra, Nairobi, Puerto Rico and Tokyo. National stations are sub-divided into two types: the national stations in Europe, North Africa and Northern America, which communicate directly with the central station, and others which rely on their regional station to relay messages to the central station in Lyon.

b)   International Notices

Interpol's central communications function is to pass on information and requests for action in the form of 'international notices', of which there are five types:

(i)   *Wanted* (red) notices represent a request for the provisional arrest of a person for extradition.

(ii)   *Enquiry* (blue) notices seek information about a named person, such as the address, previous convictions or merely any movements or activities.

(iii)   *Warning* (green) notices alert other forces about individuals.

(iv)   *Missing person* (yellow) notices give details of a missing person.

(v)   *Unidentified body* (black) notices contain descriptions and any other details.

The notices contain identification data as well as information on crimes the person is suspected of having committed, criminal records, photographs and fingerprints. Other types of notices may also be sent, for example, *modus operandi* sheets and art/antique sheets and Interpol also circulates information about other stolen property.

Interpol not only transmits information but also keeps its own files on persons, stolen objects and cases, as outlined further in section 6.2.4.

6.2.3   *Criticisms and Responses*

a)   Complaints About Delays and Insecurity

Various criticisms have in the past been levelled at Interpol, and many of these were heard during the course of this research study. One particular criticism is that the arrangements for international exchange of information are 'bureaucratic and laborious' (House of Commons 1990a, p.25). Another complaint is that Interpol's communications are insecure, particularly in relation to terrorism. There are some member countries which have strong links with terrorist activities, for example, Libya.

The latter point was made by the Metropolitan Police Special Branch which argued that Interpol staff were not experienced in dealing with classified material, did not possess the required levels of security clearance and that the 'politics and motives' of some of its member agencies were 'questionable'.

Long delays and widespread insecurity add up to a fierce indictment. Some serving police officers have made major criticisms of an organisation which continues to be one of the principal mechanisms for fighting crime on an international front. The UK Home Affairs Committee elegantly summarised these doubts about Interpol by stating that they centred on 'the speed of responses, the formality of its procedures and its poor level of security' (House of Commons 1990a, p. xxv). These are not minor quibbles.

In some comments made to the research team there was also an undercurrent of opinion that much of Interpol information is 'cold intelligence' or old facts and figures, possibly useful but not necessarily crucial or of immediate operational significance. Exponents of this opinion apparently consider specialist network contacts to be more useful than the hi-tech facsimile transmission of wanted posters. However, this view may also result from the perception that Interpol is basically a global conduit for communications of a general kind.

A more scholarly assessment is provided by the Edinburgh University academic Malcolm Anderson (1989), although the major misgivings are re-stated.

b)   Metamorphosis into a Responsive and Efficient Organisation

In Interpol's defence, Sir Roger Birch, former Chief Constable of Sussex and chairman of ACPO's International Committee, claimed that Interpol's image problem of bureaucracy and inefficiency, symbolised by mountains of paperwork and a morse code system, was a grossly unfair picture (Birch 1992b, p.121).

Raymond Kendall, Secretary General of Interpol, has made a number of specific responses to these criticisms. Since moving to their new Lyon headquarters in 1989 the response to inquiries has improved dramatically due to the use of new computer technology, and the average time taken to respond to enquiries had fallen from 14 days in 1986 to two hours in 1989 (Mason, 1991). By 1992 it was claimed that a further half hour had been shaved from this time (Kendall 1992, pers. comm.). Communication techniques have improved enormously since 1986, and in 1993 the technology is even more advanced.

The tarnished image of Interpol is slowly diminishing, but the fact that it has not enjoyed a high reputation over previous years has meant that the old image has proved hard to dispel. However, Interpol has also received more favourable verdicts:

> Mistrust of Interpol should not be perpetuated on the basis of past failings.
> (House of Commons 1990a, p. xxix).

A visit to Lyon would allow the sceptic to understand the 'metamorphosis' which has taken place in recent years. The UK Home Affairs Committee went on to welcome Interpol's transformation from a monolith to a responsive, efficient organisation and recommended that the role of Interpol should be 'enhanced'. Interpol should become 'regionalised' and the new computer and communications systems could be used by EC member states to the exclusion of other countries. In effect, there could be a European Union Interpol.

6.2.4   *Technological Improvements*

a)   New Systems

Several new computer systems have been installed by Interpol as part of its modernisation drive. First, a Criminal Information System (CIS) was installed to improve methods of storing and retrieving information and to speed up responses. Secondly, an Electronic Archive System (EAS) has been developed to keep criminal record files on computer rather than on paper cards. The EAS stores data on optical discs and is able to keep in the archive existing criminal files and new information sent in by the NCBs.

The CIS contains six files: the nominal file, and others on drug seizures; counterfeit currency; stolen, lost or recovered property; stolen art; and current cases. The latter file contains information about criminal cases, classified by type, date, place and *modus operandi,* and these are usually linked to the nominal file, which includes names, aliases, description and any other information on wanted or missing persons, suspects and criminal gangs. The nominal file also includes information on all international notices. Together the CIS and the EAS provide a formidable means for the storage, classification and rapid retrieval of a huge amount of data.

The third dimension of Interpol's new approach is the development of the Message Research and Response Branch (MRRB), which manages the files held in the Criminal Information System. Fourthly, an automated office and electronic mail system has been introduced. Finally, an Automated Search Facility (ASF) was introduced in June 1992 to facilitate the access of the NCBs to the information held at the General Secretariat.

b)   Telecommunications

The central station, situated at the Interpol General Secretariat in Lyon, is equipped with an Automated Message Switch System (AMSS) which has been in operation since 1987. The system utilises ciphering radio modem (cryptographic ARQ), telex, teletex via Transpac (packet switching network) and teletex via telephone or messages from the NCBs of the network and sub-bureaux that have a telex link with the central station. Phototelegraphy permits the transmission and reception of images (photographs and fingerprints). The Automated Message Switch System processes about one million messages a year – 350,000 messages received and 650,000 messages transmitted – and is principally responsible for the dramatic improvement in the message response time.

At the time of the installation of the AMSS the General Assembly adopted a strategy which was to take Interpol through the next few years. Modernisation of message transmission was the key element of the strategy using the new international protocol X400. The plan involved changing the means of communication at many of the NCBs. Once the modernisation of the NCBs attached to the central station has been completed, the existing AMSS will be phased out and X400 equipment will be used. Interpol anticipates that this will occur during 1993–94. The current five-year plan for the modernisation of Interpol communications was approved by both the Executive Committee and the General Assembly in 1992. The modernisation of regional stations is the next phase of the plan. Mini AMSS is being installed at the regional stations beginning in 1993 with the South American zone. These will then be able to communicate with the X400 AMSS which was installed at headquarters in 1991.

The use of radio communication and morse code are gradually being phased out, and the use of telex is being reduced. Unfortunately, there are still some 10 countries with whom communication is only possible by post, and morse code is still used by some countries, none of which are European offices.

The second phase of the five-year plan will be put in motion after the communications networks are suitably operational. It is intended that the NCBs will be able to search on the Automated Search Facility (ASF) which was brought into operation in 1992. This will be carried out by the same computers used for the X400 AMSS. It is intended that by the end of 1993 twenty five countries will have access to ASF.

The Automated Search Facility will allow NCBs to control the information which is entered in the computer database and control who has access to it, granting or denying access to any other member country. In an extreme case, it would be possible for information to be available to a single individual in the receiving country if he or she alone possessed the decrypting device. The system can send images of photographs and fingerprints, using encryption if necessary, although the majority of NCBs do not yet have suitable equipment.

6.2.5 *Assessment of Interpol's Role in European Information Exchange*

a)   New Systems

Whatever the validity of past criticisms, in recent years Interpol has invested and is continuing to invest heavily in sophisticated telecommunications and computer systems. The Automated Message Switch System and the Automated Search Facility are prime examples of a substantial 'technology upgrade'. If Interpol is to maintain and enhance its world-wide role in criminal information it will need to be at the cutting edge of communications technology. The recent evidence suggests that this is in fact the case.

The ASF and the X400 AMSS provides Interpol with one of the most sophisticated automated search and image transmission systems in the world. It enables rapid, reliable and secure exchange of information. NCBs will have access to an enormous store of data on crimes and those suspected of committing them, enabling them to co-operate with other NCBs and the General Secretariat. The idea that Interpol is merely a 'letterbox' is clearly out-of-date.

b)   Legal Limitations

Paradoxically, as the old misgivings are replaced by a new-found technological confidence, a fresh set of information-exchange problems are beginning to emerge – legal issues in relation to data protection. There are four interrelated problems.

i)   Data Protection

First, the Interpol statutes, agreed in 1983, contain data protection regulations. They include most of the provisions called for by the 1981 European Council Convention on Data Protection. However, critics have stressed the fact that Interpol has never been subject to any national data protection regulation (a special exemption was made in respect of the French law of January 1978). This means that the French data protection agency has no regulatory power over Interpol files. Instead, an internal supervisory board was established, comprising five persons of different nationalities with expertise in electronic data processing, data protection or senior judicial experience. Some commentators criticise the perceived lack of external control, but data subjects do have a right of representation to an independent supervisory board (created under Interpol's internal regulations) to seek to rectify or erase inaccurate information. The extent to which data subjects can exercise this right, however, is open to question.

ii)   National Legislation

Secondly, the membership of Interpol reflects social and political differences, wide variations in police structures and judicial systems between the member states, and disparities in national data protection legislation. Notwithstanding these differences Interpol is constitutionally constrained to act only in accordance with the national laws of member states. This causes a particular problem with the transmission of data between NCBs, using the AMSS, when one country has a high standard of data protection and another country has a lower standard or no protection at all, and vice versa.

For example, in the case of the transmission of information from a high data protection standard country to a low data protection standard country, the member state receiving information may regard the data as disappointingly incomplete. Conversely, in the case of the transmission of information from a low data protection standard country to a high data protection standard country, the member state receiving information can only accept the material by being in breach of its national data protection regulations; it will therefore have to refuse the information,

iii)   *Criteria Governing Stored Information*

Thirdly, Interpol has explicit criteria governing information stored and processed by the General Secretariat. It requires that information submitted leads to the conclusion that:

(a)   a person is liable to engage in international criminal activity, or

(b)   the person's criminal activity is liable to evolve at the international level. (Cameron-Waller 1993a, p.5).

Many would regard the latter criterion as reasonable – established criminal activity being used as the basis for predicting future international criminal activity. It is more questionable whether the former criterion is reasonable. There is certainly a degree of 'interpretational latitude' over precisely what would count as evidence of being 'liable' to engage in international crime. The difficulty here is not so much with who could be included in the General Secretariat's information database, but who would be excluded.

iv)   *Development of Criminal Intelligence*

Fourthly, following an independent study carried out by at the General Secretariat by the National Intelligence Service of the Netherlands (CRI), Interpol is committed to developing analytical techniques which may usefully be applied to the information available. These techniques in crime analysis have led to the establishment of a dedicated unit – the Analytical Criminal Intelligence Unit (ACIU). As Cameron-Waller put it:

> By standardising the use of crime analysis techniques at the General Secretariat, Interpol intends to increase its contribution in the area of crime intelligence as opposed to simply operating as a clearing house for information. (Cameron-Waller 1993b, p.12).

From October 1993 the new unit has been supplementing the activities of the Organised Crime Group, set up following a decision of the General Assembly in 1988 to co-ordinate information submitted by member countries concerning specific organised criminal groups. The Analytical Criminal Intelligence Unit has four main projects: Project OCSA on organised criminal gangs of South American origin which are active in Europe; Project MACANDRA on the Mafia, Camorra and N'Drangheta; Project ROCKERS on motorcycle gangs; and Project EASTWIND on organised crime of Asian origin (Cameron-Waller 1993a, p.10).

These initiatives, under the umbrella of crime analysis, indicate a significant shift towards using 'soft' data (criminal intelligence) rather than 'hard' data (criminal information). For example, with respect to the motorcycle gang project, information will be available on criminal activities (hard data), their *modus operandi* (softer data) and their membership and hierarchy (much softer data). To the extent that ACIU uses suppositional and unverifiable information this raises questions about the purposes for which such information may be used, and how it is controlled. It is certainly a long way from the traditional Interpol role of acting as a conduit for 'hard facts' to aid the identification of a person or an object. It is interesting to note that the activities of the Organised Crime Group and the Analytical Criminal Intelligence Unit, together with other groups, take place in what is now called the Liaison and Criminal *Intelligence* Division (emphasis added).

6.3   The Schengen Group and Information Exchange

6.3.1   *Direct Communication Between Police Forces and the Schengen Information System*

The nine signatories to the Schengen Convention have made the most concerted effort to establish a European cross-border police communications system. In 1989 proposals emerged for a common information system – the Schengen Information System (SIS). Although this common police information system is the primary focus of this section, as the major innovation of the Schengen Implementing Convention, two other provisions of the Convention regarding the exchange of information between police forces should be mentioned.

a)   Article 39

Article 39 contains an obligation on the Schengen states for their police authorities to render mutual assistance in providing information upon request for the purpose of preventing or detecting criminal offences. Police officers can, however, only respond to such a request in compliance with national legislation; and provided the request does not involve the application of coercive measures by the requested party.

b)   Article 46

Article 46 permits the exchange of information which may help to prevent future crime or threats to public order and security without the need for the information to be requested. In general, information shall be exchanged through a central body to be designated. In particularly urgent cases, the exchange of information may take place directly between the police authorities concerned, in which case the central body shall be informed as soon as possible.

c)   The Regulation of Mutual Assistance

The significance of these provisions is that for the first time in a large multilateral convention direct mutual assistance between the police forces has been regulated. All information exchange is subject to national laws; and unrequested information has to pass through a central body or, in exceptional cases where it takes place police-to-police, the central body has to be notified. Previously, mutual assistance in information exchange between police forces has taken place in a largely unstructured fashion through micro-level, informal contacts on a case-by-case basis. It is, of course, possible – perhaps even likely – that this will continue in the future on an unofficial basis.

6.3.2   Technical Features of the Schengen Information System

A lack of compatibility between national police computer systems, as well as variations in data protection standards, led the nine Schengen states to recognise that a new computer system had to be developed, rather than using an existing police computer system or linking different national systems.

a)   The System and its Components

There is one new main computer in Strasbourg which is linked with the individual information systems in the participating countries (Alfred Kayser, *Bundeskriminalamt*, Germany 1990, personal interview; Lieutenant-Colonel Georges Rauches, *Directeur adjoint de la Police*, Luxembourg 1990, personal interview). The new system has two components.

First, each member state has its own databank holding national data, the National Schengen Information System (NSIS), each one using Schengen-agreed information categories (see section 6.3.3).

Secondly, there is the central unit based in Strasbourg, the Central Schengen Information System (CSIS), to which all NSISs are connected. The Central Schengen Information System is responsible for copying the national databanks and thus providing a central resource for all Schengen member states. Any changes in information held on a national databank are downloaded to the central system which then updates all the other national systems within five minutes.

Collectively, the two parts of the system are known as the Schengen Information System (SIS).

b)   Using the System

The national units of the SIS may not be linked to other national police computer systems. This means that no country has access to the general national computer systems of other states by way of the SIS, but only to the data which other states have included in their own NSIS which is then made available through CSIS. The Schengen Information System forms a separate common system, distinct from national police files.

It has two important features. The Central Schengen Information System acts only as an updating mechanism and a conduit – it receives information from the member states independently and then downloads data collectively to all parties. It is not possible to amend CSIS data other than at the NSIS point-of-entry to the system. This has the effect of giving individual members complete control over their data inputs. In addition, only certain categories of information can be entered into the system (see section 6.3.3).

229

The Schengen Information System provides information necessary to identify a wanted person or object and indicates the action asked for by the requesting state. A code can also warn that the person concerned is likely to be armed and dangerous.

The Schengen Information System was scheduled to become operational between the five founder states of the Schengen Group and Spain by December 1993, although it now seems that this date has been postponed again until 1st February 1994. Testing of the SIS was scheduled for November 1993. Following a ministerial meeting of the signatory countries on 18th October 1993 a decision was reached that six of the Schengen member states (Belgium, France, Germany, Luxembourg, Netherlands and Spain) would bring the various agreements into operation on 1st February 1994, with Portugal to follow a short while later in the year. Greece and Italy, although signatories to the agreements, will operationalise the SIS at some point in the future. The delay is due to judicial and technical reasons.

c)　　　　　　**Supplementary Information Request at the National Entry**

i)　　　　*Background*

As long ago as 1988, when the development of the SIS was in its infancy, it was already clear that the operation of the SIS would require a broader information exchange infrastructure, perhaps not as swift as the SIS, but certainly capable of exchanging an important number of more diverse data (Verraes 1993). An additional network was required to exchange supplementary information between the member states, specifically in relation to requests for arrests with a view to extradition. A national magistrate requires additional information to extend extradition detention over and above the simple identity of a person and a request for him or her to be arrested. The magistrate needs information on the warrant for arrest, a description of the criminal offence and information on the maximum imposable prison sentence.

Given that the maximum period for which a person arrested following an initial SIS request is limited (most commonly 24 or 48 hours), it is essential that supplementary information is forwarded rapidly. The infrastructure which permits this exchange of information is called the Supplementary Information Request at the National Entry (SIReNE). The system was scheduled to become operational between the five founder states of the Schengen Group and Spain by 1st February 1994.

ii)　　　*Using the System*

Each member state has a national SIReNE (N-SIReNE) which is an information exchange network between central agencies of each member state providing additional information on persons registered on the SIS, over and above the categories of information specified in Article 94 of the Implementing Convention. The additional facility (SIReNE) enables police officers to request supplementary information from a colleague elsewhere.

A SIReNE office has been, or will be, established in each of the nine Schengen countries. In many respects the N-SIReNE office is similar to the NCB of Interpol: round the clock staffing, including translation facilities, as a directly accessible national contact and information point for the exchange of information between competent national authorities. A N-SIReNE office is usually staffed by representatives of national police forces, customs services and legal experts. The purpose is to achieve rapid communication between police forces in different countries with the benefit of legal advice on national legal procedures. In addition, national security forces will use this channel for their international contacts.

230

iii)   *Technical Details*

The network uses a relatively simple X25/X400 electronic mail system on which standardised forms are exchanged in form of X400 messages. In the near future it will be possible to exchange fingerprints and pictures via the network in order positively and accurately to identify a wanted person. In its first stage the SIReNE network shares the 9.6 KBaud communication line with the SIS, but it will have its own 64 KBaud lines at some date during 1994.

iv)   *Principal Functions*

Although each member state may decide on the information which flows through the SIReNE network the system has 10 principal functions. These are detailed below including, where appropriate, reference to the relevant Article of the Schengen Implementing Convention:

- The certification of whether a report could or should be made on the network prior to making a report.

- The exchange of information at the time a report is made.

- The exchange of information in the case where two countries have made a report about the same person but where different action is required ('double signalling'). The SIReNE network establishes which action takes precedence (Article 107).

- The exchange of information in the interval between a SIS report being made and any subsequent action in order to give that action the required legal status in the requested country; or for one country to signal or 'flag' that the action will not be taken in their country (Articles 94(4), 95(3), 97 and 99).

- The sending of information to the central authority (CSIS) when a required action had been executed – known in Schengen circles as a 'hit'.

- The exchange of information in the case of non-admissible aliens. The central authority must be told when an inadmissible alien has been found in Schengen territory after being subject to a SIS report, or when an inadmissible alien not subject to a SIS report has been stopped at a Schengen border. (It is understood that there are some difficulties in applying this provision because of the large numbers of inadmissible persons.)

- The requesting state must be informed in all cases where it proves impossible to execute the action required in a report.

- The requesting state must notify other Schengen partners where the purpose of a report changes.

- The exchange of information in order to amend or remove an erroneous report.

- The exchange of information on national data protection rules and requirements.

d)   **Visa Inquiry System in an Open-Border Network**

The SIReNE network is to be extended to permit the exchange of information on visas. Excluding other EC and EFTA citizens, most non-Schengen nationals need a visa to enter Schengen territory. Once a visa has been issued to a non-Schengen national there is an increasing demand for this to be recorded for the benefit of the other member states. The Visa Inquiry System in an Open-Border Network (VISION) will enable central authorities entrusted with the delivery of visas to consult each other in accordance with Article 17(2) of the Schengen Implementing Convention. The system is expected to be operational in 1994 although political wrangling could continue to delay the implementation of VISION (Jaap Verraes 1993, pers. comm.).

This new network could prove to be a substantial project. One estimate suggests that the Schengen member states will be dealing with 2.5 million visa requests a year. In addition, France has requested information on all visas issued to persons from the former USSR as a matter of course. To the extent that other Schengen member states adopt similar policies VISION will be exchanging visa information on a very large scale. It has been suggested that the costs of VISION should be borne by those member states which make requests for additional visa information.

6.3.3　*Information Held on the Schengen Information System*

The Schengen Information System has a maximum capacity of 8 million personal records and 7 million records on objects.

Although the original intention was to create a comprehensive interstate police information system, the SIS has developed as a more limited mechanism for exchanging specific information provided at the national level; and there is some indication that the nine countries also intend to limit inputs to information relevant to exercising controls at the *external* frontiers of the Schengen states.

In general, the Schengen Information System will be used to store data and to permit the exchange of information between the authorities of the nine countries on: asylum applications and refused applications; identification papers; travel routes; aliens qualified as undesirable by one of the countries; persons to be expelled or extradited; persons under surveillance by one of the national services; and persons wanted for criminal prosecution.

a)　**Categories of Person**

More specifically, the Schengen Implementing Convention provides that information shall be entered on the SIS for certain specified categories of person and objects, if:

(i)　The person is wanted for arrest for extradition purposes (Article 95).

(ii)　The person is an alien, subject to non-admission or subject to a deportation, removal or expulsion order; or an alien perceived to be a threat to public order or national security and safety (Article 96).

(iii)　The person is reported as missing (Article 97).

(iv)　The person is a witness or suspect summoned to appear before a court in criminal proceedings, or a convicted person (Article 98).

(v)　The person intends to commit or is committing or gives reason to suppose that he or she will commit extremely serious offences, in order for that person to be placed under covert surveillance or made subject to a specific check (Article 99).

(vi)   Objects subject to seizure or wanted as evidence in criminal proceedings (motor vehicles, trailers and caravans, firearms, blank documents, identification documents, registered bank notes) (Article 100).

b)   Categories of Information

In respect of persons, the categories of data entered on the SIS shall be no more than: real and assumed names; distinguishing physical marks; date and place of birth; sex; nationality; whether the person is armed or violent; reason for the entry (for example, serving of sentence, criminal prosecution, perceived threat to public safety or national security); and action to be taken (Schengen Implementing Convention, Article 94).

6.3.4   Data Protection

a)   General Safeguards

Implementation of the Schengen Convention is examined in Chapter 4. In addition to the ratification required under Article 139 of the Convention, there is a requirement for the Schengen states to make national arrangements necessary to achieve a level of protection of personal data at least equal to that resulting from the 1981 Council of Europe Convention on Data Protection and Recommendation R(87)15 of the Committee of Ministers regulating the use of personal data in the police sector.

b)   Safeguards in the Schengen Implementing Convention

The Schengen Implementing Convention contains two sets of data protection regulations: one applies to the exchange of information in general (Article 39); and the other, a more detailed one, applies specifically to the SIS (Articles 102 – 118). With respect to the latter there are six interrelated protections.

i)   Council of Europe

Automatic processing of personal data is to be subject to the Council of Europe Convention of 1981, and in compliance with Recommendation R(87)15 of the Committee of Ministers made in 1987 (Article 117).

ii)   National Data Protection Legislation

Reports shall be subject to national data protection legislation, and only the reporting party shall be authorised to amend, supplement, correct or delete data which it has introduced (Articles 104 – 106).

iii)   A Three-Tier Structure

There is a three-tier structure for ensuring accountability and oversight: each party shall designate an authority to take responsibility for its national unit (Article 104); each party shall designate a supervisory authority, in compliance with national law, to carry out independent supervision (Article 114); and a joint supervisory authority, consisting of two representatives of each national supervisory authority, shall be established (Article 115).

iv)   *Data Subject Access*

Any person may have access to the SIS in order to have factually inaccurate data corrected or to have legally inaccurate data deleted (Articles 109 – 111). However, communication of information to the person concerned shall be refused if it would undermine the performance of the legal task specified in the report, or if the purpose of the report includes discreet surveillance (Article 109).

v)   *Purpose Limitation*

Data may only be used for the purposes set out in each type of report. If any change from one type of report to another is proposed this must be justified on the grounds of the need to prevent an imminent serious threat to public order and safety, serious reasons of state safety or to prevent a serious offence. The permission of the state which reported the information initially must be requested (Article 102).

vi)   *Time Limits*

Data included in the SIS shall be kept only for the time required to achieve the purpose of the report. A review must be held after three years and information cannot be held for longer than 10 years (Articles 112 – 113).

c)   **Lacunae in the Regulations**

The regulations appear extensive, and the attempt to harmonise data protection practices certainly merits acknowledgement, but they still contain several *lacunae*. Despite the requirement that all countries adhere to the minimum standards set out in the Council of Europe Convention on Data Protection, there is considerable variation in national legislation, In addition, the Council of Europe standards are rather vague and somewhat imprecise. Differences in interpretation could also have a substantial impact. For example, the definition of purpose in the purpose limitation provision has not yet been detailed. Finally, there is a range of attitudes towards data protection regulation among the Schengen countries.

6.3.5   *Differences Between the SIS and Interpol: Problems of Legal Control*

The Schengen Information System has a limited and well-defined function. It is a information databank which serves to trace and identify persons and things but it does not hold criminal intelligence. In this respect the SIS is similar to Interpol. The principal difference between Interpol and the SIS is that requests for a search will not be transmitted to the National Central Bureau of each country by telex or other methods, but will be directed through a common computer system of identical databanks. This leads to differences in assessing the legality of the requested measure.

Under Interpol procedures the requested state, upon receiving a request, examines the case on the basis of the information given; and only if the national legal conditions are fulfilled is the person then included in the national 'wanted persons' file.

Under the Schengen Information System the requested state cannot check the legal requirements because the data entered on the system may not provide sufficient information. This places the requesting country under an obligation to examine whether the measure – covert surveillance, for example – is legally permitted under the law of the requested member state prior to making the request.

No agreement has been reached on how the requesting state, that is, the state which wishes to perform a legal check, is to receive the information necessary to reach a decision. In the case of a report for arrest and extradition, Article 95(2) provides that further information on the case is to be submitted to the other parties. There is no similar provision for other search categories. It can only be assumed that information will be offered or given on request through SIReNE. In either case information is being 'traded' in a non-transparent manner without accountability.

6.3.6   Assessment of the Schengen Information System

a)   A Major Achievement

The Schengen Information System is a very ambitious attempt to create a European-wide common information network. Most of its major structures are in place and with nine participating members the SIS appears to have an unstoppable (political) momentum.

The system offers a highly sophisticated solution to the technical problems of incompatibility between police forces' national computers and to the legal problems of variation in national data protection regulations. It does so by establishing autonomous national units (NSISs) which feed a central core (CSIS) as a Schengen-wide resource, which in turn updates each NSIS. All data in the individual components of the SIS are thus the same.

The Schengen Implementing Convention affords explicit data protection safeguards: the Council of Europe Convention on Data Protection; national data protection regulations at the point-of-entry to the system; a three-tier structure for ensuring accountability; rights of access for data subjects; purpose limitation; and restrictions on the retention of data. In addition, the Schengen Information System only contains 'hard' data (that is, information subject to verification) rather than 'soft' criminal intelligence.

b)   Minor Difficulties

Most of the work on the SIS had been completed by October 1993 and members of the Schengen Group described the system as being operational, although tests were still being conducted. Other sources suggested that some of the problems are more serious (*Migration News Sheet* No.125/93-08, p.3). Harmonisation of the transcription of data stored in each NSIS had not been achieved and there were particular problems in storing the proper names of subjects. For example, where Chinese names are involved it had not been decided whether to use Latin characters or a numerical system.

Spanish and Portuguese names were also causing problems. Both include two surnames – one from the father and one from the mother – but in Portugal the mother's name is written first whereas in Spain the father's name is written first. There were other difficulties with names still to be resolved. Should the name Mr van den Brink be entered under 'V' (as in Belgium) or under 'B' (as in the Netherlands)?

Conflicting reports were offered to the research team about the date by which the SIS would become operational. Some respondents suggested that the problems were resolved and predicted the system coming 'on stream' by mid-November 1993. Other sources suggested, following a meeting of national Schengen officials, that because the SIS was not legally required to be operational until 1st February 1994, there was more time available for testing and proving the systems.

c)   The European Information System

One of the consequences of the SIS initiative has been to stimulate a Trevi Group interest in a common information system. The *Programme of Action* (Trevi Group 1990, para.15) required member states to study the development of a common information system paying due attention to data protection. The non-Schengen countries, under the Trevi Group umbrella, appear to be keen to see a purpose-built EU-wide common information system. This is being developed under the External Borders Convention. The European Information System (EIS) will hold a computerised list of people who are not to be permitted to enter the European Union. This single information system will apparently be based on the SIS.

If there is to be a European-wide information system, whether it is a Trevi Group (or its successor) initiative or an expanded version of the Schengen Information System, given that such a system is operational between six states already, there seems no reason to believe that the problems of scale, operating language, and data protection cannot be overcome across the twelve states. The Schengen Implementing Convention offers a 'blueprint' for the way in which European police co-operation can be promoted at a practical level (Article 39) and the way in which large-scale information may be exchanged (Article 46).

If there is a problem it is likely to be political rather than technical. A stand-alone EIS would have the political cachet of incorporating all European Union member states, but it would mean an enormous duplication of effort alongside the SIS. An expanded SIS would be the most cost-effective solution, but it may cause political resentment from current non-Schengen states who would see themselves as having been carried away by what has been called Schengen's 'unstoppable momentum'.

One view is that the SIS already offers an operational organisation and the technical capabilities for orchestrating police co-operation in Europe (Verraes 1993). It reflects very close, direct and intensive co-operation between the Schengen member states and stands as a symbol for, and pointer towards, the 'inevitable evolution' of the SIS into a European-wide system. If Europol is ever destined to have operational capabilities, then the SIS could provide a proven infrastructure.

d)   UK Opposition to the Schengen Information System

The available evidence shows that there are long-standing misgivings about the SIS in Britain, which is not party to the Schengen Agreements. The UK opposition stems primarily from the dispute over border controls and immigration checks. A senior civil servant commented:

> The United Kingdom has been very keen to ensure things do not stampede away [...] We are very anxious to stop the bandwagon of the Schengen system. (House of Commons 1990b, p.93).

David Waddington MP, then Secretary of State at the Home Office, took the same view. He argued that an all-European information system could be achieved through

Interpol and said that UK investment in Interpol 'backs up my caution which I expressed some time ago about going down the road which the Schengen countries would like to go down' (House of Commons 1990b, p.186).

By 1993 it was clear that the Schengen countries had travelled a long way down the road leaving the United Kingdom far behind. Unfortunately, if predictably, the Home Office ministers and advisers had yet again failed to perceive how matters would develop and had completely misjudged the Schengen countries' resolve. In mid-1993 there was evidence that British police chiefs hoped to be able to pool criminal information through the SIS, and that this was favourably received by senior Schengen officials as offering 'real progress'. The 'sticking point' appeared to be political – whether the UK could join the SIS without abolishing its internal border controls.

e)   Lack of Clarity

The Schengen Information System as it is currently conceived will hold data on up to 8 million persons and 7 million objects. Although there are those who would object to the SIS simply in terms of the sheer scale of the enterprise, there is a more fundamental reservation. It concerns the categories of persons on whom information may be held (Articles 95 – 100) rather than the nature of the information itself (Article 94).

Few would disagree that information should properly be held on persons wanted for arrest and extradition, aliens subject to deportation orders, missing persons and persons required for criminal proceedings. It is much less clear, however, that it is legitimate to hold information on aliens perceived to 'pose' a threat to public order or national security (Article 96); and it is even less clear why data should be collected on a person who 'intends' to commit, or 'gives reason to suppose' that he will commit, exceptionally serious offences (Article 99). Although these categories do have the virtue of being formally stated in the Implementing Convention, it is far from clear who would be included – and even more importantly who would be excluded – under these headings. There is little point in pernickety attention to detail about the nature of the information stored on data subjects if there is scant regard for who might be included in the first place.

In addition, parts of the SIS are far from clear. The relationship between the national units (NSISs) and the central system (CSIS) is clear and well worked out. The relationship between these and the Supplementary Information Request at the National Entries (SIReNE), and more particularly with national SIReNE (N-SIReNE), is more problematic. A charitable interpretation is that the N-SIReNEs offer additional information within the framework of the Convention. A less charitable interpretation would see the N-SIReNEs as being capable of subverting the data limitation regulations of Article 94 of the Implementing Convention.

6.4   The Trevi Group and the Exchange of Information

The Trevi Group's initial objective was to provide a basis for greater European co-operation to combat terrorism, but its role developed to include co-operation over policing drugs trafficking and other types of serious organised crime. Subsequently, consideration of the implications of the single market and Europol were added to the Trevi Group's agenda. In each of these areas the Trevi Group has an interest in information exchange and police communications.

6.4.1   *Trevi Working Group I*

Trevi Working Group I analyses information held on known and suspected terrorist groups, with particular attention paid to their strategies and tactics. Procedures have also been developed for the rapid communication of information using Trevi's own secure facsimile network (TSFN). This is particularly important in the immediate aftermath of a terrorist incident. Concrete information on cases can be exchanged rapidly in order to secure a co-ordinated investigation. At a more general level the Group is instrumental in promoting information exchange on practical procedures – for example, conducting security checks on vessels in ports and 'scenes-of-crime' procedures following terrorist incidents.

6.4.2   *Trevi Working Group II*

Trevi Working Group II is concerned with promoting police co-operation and the exchange of information in a number of areas, notably: police training (including language training); the policing of road traffic; public order; police equipment (including computers and communications); and forensic science and other scientific and technical matters. The Group has had some success in information exchange relating to football hooliganism and public order.

The Trevi-inspired network of permanent correspondents to monitor and exchange information on football supporters is well established, as is the exchange of officers in this area. These are examples of meso-level and micro-level, face-to-face, co-operation.

The Group has also developed a standardised telegram report format for exchanging information on marches and demonstrations, as well as noting disorder at major sporting events. The common reporting format includes: information on events; dates; organisations; duration; patrol points and police numbers; incident descriptions; victim descriptions; and other information including, for example, special police methods deployed, or the routes followed.

In December 1992 it was reported that Trevi Working Group II was working on the production of a directory of police training in Europe and on a communications system for all member states.

6.4.3   *Trevi Working Group III*

Trevi Working Group III was established to improve co-operation against serious organised international crime, particularly drugs trafficking. In this context, the principal means of information exchange is the close working relationship between European Drugs Liaison Officers. This initiative was the precursor of the UK National Drugs Intelligence Unit, which has since been subsumed into the National Criminal Intelligence Service (NCIS) established in April 1992. The unit has five regional offices (Birmingham, Bristol, London, Manchester and Wakefield). To date 80 per cent of its work has been drugs-related, presumably reflecting its origins, although this may change in the future.

It is intended that there will be a link between European criminal intelligence agencies, under the EDU/Europol initiative. Information available at present suggests that only the UK and the Netherlands have such services established, although it is possible that the German *Bundeskriminalamt* considers itself to function as the NCIS for Germany. Other countries have one year in which to establish their own versions of the National Criminal Intelligence Units. The Group has also examined topics such as the protection of witnesses in cases against organised crime, stolen vehicles and works of art, and armed robbery. Working Group III has been recently examining money laundering and exploring crime analysis and environmental crime.

These activities may be seen as a precursor of the EDU/Europol initiative with a continuing Trevi interest through the *Ad Hoc* Working Group on Europol.

6.4.4   Trevi 1992

Between December 1988 and December 1992, when the Working Group was disbanded, Trevi 1992 had the job of examining the police and security aspects of the free movement of people, paying particular attention to compensatory measures to counteract the relaxation of controls at intra-Community borders. The *Dublin Programme of Action* was at the centre of its remit.

One aspect of this included intensifying the exchange of information. Trevi 1992 worked with MAG 1992 and the *Ad Hoc* Group on Immigration to explore the possibility of a European-wide computerised information system for law enforcement purposes.

6.4.5   EDU/Europol

Community ministers established the *Ad Hoc* Working Group on Europol (AHWGE) in August 1991. Its remit was to work towards the creation of Europol, with an initial responsibility for establishing a European Drugs Unit (EDU).

The European Drugs Unit/Europol was to have become active in spring 1993, a date which was delayed as a result of indecision on the location of the headquarters. As outlined in Chapter 4, the expected decision on the location of the EDU/Europol was not taken at the ministerial meeting at the end of June 1993. However, after pressure by Germany, the UK and others, it was decided at the European Council on 29th October 1993 that it would be based at the The Hague.

The EDU in its first phase will be built up gradually. Its task will be to facilitate the exchange of information about drugs trafficking and associated money laundering. When it becomes operational, it will deal initially only with the exchange of information on drugs trafficking and associated crime. The intelligence system of the drugs unit, however, is likely to be a sophisticated one and it will contain intelligence information in addition to 'hard' data.

The *Ad Hoc* Working Group on Europol has begun to work on drafting the Convention which will form the legal basis of the EDU/Europol. This is expected to take a number of years. It will be some time before it is possible to compare the terms of the Europol and Schengen Conventions. The Schengen Convention provides explicit data protection safeguards for individuals (see section 6.3.4).

The embryonic EDU data protection safeguards are based purely on agreements between member states. A Ministerial Agreement was signed by Trevi ministers on 2nd June 1993 which sets out the parameters within which the Unit will function.

239

Liaison officers will only be able to access information on databases held in their own countries. This will be governed by national data protection legislation. Information received by a member state must be afforded the same degree of data protection as applicable in the state from which it originated. Finally, national data protection authorities are to be invited to ensure that information systems, and the data contained in them, comply with national data protection laws. Further data protection agreements will presumably evolve as Europol develops.

6.4.6   *Assessment of the Trevi Group and Police Communications*

a)   Macro-Level Impetus for Meso-Level and Micro-Level Information Exchange

The major contribution of the Trevi Group to international police communications has been in providing the macro-level political impetus to facilitate meso-level and micro-level information exchange. Much of the practical progress has been made at the operational level of face-to-face dialogue between police officers with a common interest in a particular type of crime.

Trevi Working Group I has undoubtedly been successful in promoting co-operation against terrorism through its liaison network of specialist officers, but it is not possible to offer an informed assessment of its dedicated secure information network. It was reported, however, at the December 1992 Trevi Group Meeting that the growing volume of communications between Trevi officials in the 12 EC countries was causing serious congestion on the Trevi Secure Fax Network (TSFN)! Working Group II has facilitated information exchange between officers on public order offences, including football hooliganism. Working Group III has instituted a European-wide network for the exchange of drugs trafficking information, and this was instrumental in providing the impetus for the EDU/Europol.

These initiatives have clear operational significance, and they relate to highly-focused police activities in restricted, discrete, specialist areas, such as drugs, terrorism or disorder. They are also relatively low-tech enterprises. A good deal of the contact is face-to-face liaison.

b)   EDU/Europol

The creation of the EDU/Europol is the most recent example of developments in European police communications and it is undoubtedly of considerable importance. Even in its infancy the EDU/Europol poses three difficult questions in relation to information exchange.

i)   Data Protection Safeguards

Although right from the beginning there has been an attempt to provide data protection safeguards, these are to date only at the level of working 'agreements'. The *Ad Hoc* Working Group on Europol will seek to incorporate data protection regulations in the draft 'Convention for the Establishment of Europol' which will place data protection on a legal footing. At this stage there is a world of difference between the safeguards offered by the Schengen Implementing Convention and the Europol 'agreements'.

The European Court of Justice (ECJ) does not have competence to deal with data protection issues unless it is specifically granted competence in a convention. Article K(2)(c) of the Treaty on European Union (the Maastricht Treaty), specifies that conventions drawn up for adoption by member states:

> [...] may stipulate that the Court of Justice shall have to interpret their provisions and to rule on any disputes regarding their application in accordance with such arrangements as they may lay down.

It is possible that when the K4 Committee structure assumes the work of the Trevi Group this may become subject to the jurisdiction of the European Court of Justice, although this would have to be on the initiative of one of the member states. The Commission itself is not able to take the initiative (Article K. 3(2)). Co-operative action in matters relating to the police remain solely the prerogative of the member states. What is more likely, given that a Europol convention is already being discussed and drafted, is that the actions of the EDU/Europol will be subject to some controlling body, possibly the European Court of Justice.

ii)   Information and Intelligence

In contrast to the Schengen Information System, the EDU/Europol databases will contain intelligence or 'soft', unverifiable information. The Ministerial Agreement signed by Trevi ministers on 2nd June 1993 details the role of Project Group Europol. Its remit is restricted to an investigation of the most efficient means for exchanging intelligence on drugs trafficking and associated money laundering activities. To the extent that the EDU/Europol deals in criminal intelligence it will face the same data protection difficulties as Interpol under its Liaison and Criminal Intelligence Division. Where criminal intelligence uses suppositional and unverifiable information this raises questions about the purposes for which such information may be used and how it is controlled.

iii)   Unresolved Relationships

Another issue concerns the as-yet unresolved relationships between Europol and Interpol and between Europol and the Schengen Information System.

With respect to the former, the current Secretary General of Interpol, Raymond Kendall, highlighted two difficulties. On the one hand, there is the risk of duplication of effort between Europol and Interpol. This would be wasteful of resources, and care should be taken to prevent it. Given the way in which Interpol is already dominated by European 'traffic' it is debatable whether a second, parallel network is necessary. On the other hand, and more fundamentally, Kendall questioned the ability of Europol to function across countries with very different legal jurisdictions and languages. He suggests that 'only when an appropriate legal infrastructure has been established would it be wise to go forward and create a supranational police force for the European Community' (Bresler 1992, p.395).

Interestingly, information made available to this study has indicated that there is communication at a senior level between Interpol and Europol personnel, and the likelihood of duplication of effort and communications difficulties has been well appreciated by those involved in the development of the new organisation (Woodward 1993).

With respect to the latter, to the extent that the EDU/Europol moves beyond its remit in the field of drugs trafficking, it could duplicate the work of the Schengen Information System. This would be wasteful and it would not be cost effective.

241

Anything other than a parallel existence raises intriguing possibilities: that the EDU/Europol replaces the SIS; or that the SIS displaces the EDU/Europol. In the long term it is likely that there will be only one European-wide criminal information system. It is more likely to be based on the SIS national databanks and central unit. In the short term there will probably be uncertainty (and even conflict) over what the common information system is to be called. Avoiding an unnecessary duplication of effort in information exchange is technically straightforward; but this may prove politically sensitive and problematic.

Finally, it should be noted that various police officers and officials in Europe confidently expect Europol to develop a capacity for operational policing. For example, on 14th October 1993 Colonel Fernand Dietrich, Commandant of the Luxembourg *Gendarmerie*, publicly foresaw an operational role in the future for Europol. This view was greeted with some consternation by UK Home Office officials who were present. However, despite UK reservations, this perception seems widespread in some policing and official circles in Europe.

6.5 The Future of Communications and Information Exchange

6.5.1 Recurring Themes

The structures and mechanisms for the exchange of police information and intelligence on a European Union-wide scale have two common features.

a) Macro-Level Agreements

The new mechanisms for information exchange are underwritten at the macro level by intergovernmental or equivalent agreements. Interpol has a world-wide membership of 174 countries and a single Constitution. The Schengen Group has orchestrated its efforts through the Schengen Agreement of 1985 and the Implementing Convention of 1990. The Trevi Group is co-ordinated at ministerial level. To a large extent the actual exchange of information is premised on macro-level political agreements.

b) Sophisticated Information Technology

Information exchange itself is increasingly characterised by a heavy investment in sophisticated information systems. Interpol is at the cutting edge of communications technology. The Automated Message Switch System and the Automated Search Facility are prime examples of a substantial 'technology upgrade'. The Schengen Information System is a very ambitious attempt to create a European-wide common information network. The system offers a highly sophisticated solution to the technical problems of incompatibility between different police forces' national computers and to the legal problems of data protection. It does so by establishing autonomous national units (NSISs) which feed a central core (CSIS) as a Schengen-wide resource. The creation of the EDU/Europol is the most recent example of developments in European police communications and in the long term it is arguably the most important, even though initially it will deal in information and intelligence relating solely to drugs trafficking and associated crimes.

242

6.5.2   *Technological Developments*

These examples all reflect a new-found commitment to computer-based information exchange, even to the point of there being a distinct prospect for duplication of effort between Interpol, the SIS and Europol. It seems likely, however, that the use of computers in policing will continue to expand. There are a number of reasons for this expectation.

First, the new information systems are underwritten with considerable political authority and a general commitment to pan-European policing is a prominent part of the 'third pillar' of the Treaty on European Union. Secondly, police work itself is firmly grounded in the collection, collation and analysis of 'crime' data. It would be inconceivable for police officers not to take advantage of new technologies which make old tasks more straightforward.

Thirdly, the power of modern processors allows for data collection on an unprecedented scale and, more importantly, offers unparalleled analytic capabilities. Fourthly, with networking facilities it is relatively straightforward to link databases irrespective of national boundaries. Finally, most major computer systems are now capable of reading data inputs from alternative software packages thus reducing problems of compatibility.

6.5.3   *The Impact of the Schengen Information System*

The Schengen Information System is the most highly developed European system of information exchange for practical police co-operation. As such it stands as a role model for future developments or, perhaps, as the model for the future. There are four reasons for taking the latter view.

First, the SIS has successfully bypassed the problems of incompatibility between national police computer systems by creating a series of stand-alone national databases (NSISs) feeding a central unit (CSIS) which then acts as a resource for all member states. Information received suggests that the SIS can handle an entry every second and provide NSIS updates within five minutes. In technical terms these are considerable achievements.

Secondly, the Schengen Information System through the Schengen Implementing Convention offers a mechanism for information exchange with formal instruments of governance. For example, for the first time in a large multilateral convention direct mutual assistance between police forces has been regulated (Articles 39 and 46). Previously, mutual assistance in information exchange between police forces has taken place in a largely unstructured fashion through micro-level, informal contacts on a case-by-case basis.

Thirdly, the Schengen Information System has well worked out data protection regulations. Information exchange is subject to national laws, and to oversight by three supervisory bodies; and data subjects have rights of access, including those of rectification and erasure.

Finally, there appears to be strong political will and commitment which underpins the Schengen Information System. With nine participating members and a target date of 1st February 1994 for operationalising most of the provisions of the Schengen Implementing Convention, for at least six of the countries, a European system for police co-operation on the exchange of information is substantially in place.

When these points are taken in aggregate it is likely that the SIS has an unstoppable political momentum and that it could force its standards (technical and otherwise) on the three EU states which have not yet joined (Denmark, Ireland the UK) and also on European countries further afield. It has, for example, been reported that the EFTA countries which are currently negotiating membership of the European Union have been vigorously 'invited' to join the Schengen Group and, indeed, Austria already has observer status.

6.6　　Summary of Findings

6.6.1　Good communications are a necessary condition for efficient and effective police co-operation. However, a number of different legal issues must be considered:

- Data protection and the rights of data subjects.

- The distinction between 'hard' criminal information and 'soft' criminal intelligence.

- The legality of some sorts of information exchange.

- Compatibility with the 1981 Council of Europe Convention for the Protection of Individuals with regard to Automatic Processing of Personal Data and with the Council of Europe 1987 Recommendation (R(87)15) on the use of personal data in the police sector.

6.6.2　Paradoxically, as Interpol is showing a new-found technological confidence, a fresh set of information-exchange problems are beginning to emerge – legal issues in relation to data protection:

- Whatever the validity of past criticisms, in recent years Interpol has invested and is continuing to invest heavily in sophisticated telecommunications and computer systems (AMSS and ASF). If Interpol is to maintain and enhance its world-wide role in criminal information it will need to be at the cutting edge of communications technology. The recent evidence suggests that this is in fact the case.

- Although Interpol data subjects have a right of representation to the independent supervisory board to seek to rectify or erase inaccurate information, the extent to which they can exercise this right is open to question.

- Interpol is constitutionally constrained to act only in accordance with the national laws of member states. This causes a particular problem with the transmission of data between NCBs, using the AMSS, when one country has a high standard of data protection and another country has a lower standard or no protection at all, and vice versa.

- Interpol is constrained to use information submitted only if it leads to the conclusion that a person is 'liable' to engage in international criminal activity, but there is a degree of 'interpretational latitude' over how this criterion could be used.

- Interpol is committed to developing analytical techniques on criminal intelligence through the Analytical Criminal Intelligence Unit (ACIU) in its Liaison and Criminal Intelligence Division. This represents a significant change of emphasis. It is certainly a long way from the traditional Interpol role of acting as a conduit for 'hard facts'.

6.6.3   **Despite new initiatives and the continuing importance of specialist networks, Interpol continues to be by far the most important structure for the transmission of basic criminal investigative information between European Union countries, and between EU countries and further afield:**

- In 1992 some 400,000 communications through Interpol involved European Union states, representing some 40 per cent of the total. The wider European region of 44 countries was responsible for some 80 per cent of all Interpol communications.

- Most information exchange between European police forces concerns local 'ordinary' crime and the revamped Interpol service appears to handle this function efficiently and effectively.

6.6.4   **The Schengen Information System is the most highly developed European system of information exchange for practical police co-operation. As such it stands as a role model for future developments or, perhaps, as the model for the future. It is likely that the SIS has an unstoppable political momentum and that it could force its standards (technical and otherwise) on those European Union countries which have not joined:**

- The Schengen Information System has successfully bypassed the problems of incompatibility between national police computer systems by creating a series of stand-alone national databases (NSISs) feeding a central unit (CSIS) which then acts as a resource for all member states.

- The Schengen Information System through the Schengen Implementing Convention offers a mechanism for information exchange with formal instruments of governance. Previously, mutual assistance in information exchange between police forces has taken place in a largely unstructured fashion through micro-level, informal contacts on a case-by-case basis.

- The Schengen Information System has well worked out data protection regulations. Information exchange is subject to national laws, and to oversight by three supervisory bodies; and data subjects have rights of access, including those of rectification and erasure.

- There appears to be considerable political will and commitment behind the Schengen Information System. With nine participating members and a target date of 1st February 1994 for operationalising the provisions of the Schengen Implementing Convention, for six of the countries, a European system for police co-operation on the exchange of information is substantially in place.

- There is evidence that EFTA countries which are negotiating entry to the European Union have been strongly invited to join the Schengen Group and Austria already has observer status.

6.6.5 **The Supplementary Information Request at the National Entry system (SIReNE) is an innovative infrastructure which enables the participating Schengen states to exchange information on particular entries in the main Schengen Information System:**

- The SIReNE is a rapid information exchange structure based on an electronic mail system on which standardised messages are sent from one participating country to another.

- A national SIReNE (N-SIReNE) office is being established in each country which will have round-the-clock staffing, translation services, and access to competent authorities, in order to respond quickly to requests which are sent.

- The supplementary requests which will be handled by the SIReNE include further information about extradition and ten categories of information about entries on, and the functioning of, the main Schengen Information System (SIS).

- Although technically separate from the SIS, the SIReNE is closely attached to it. It will have its own dedicated communication lines and is scheduled to be fully operational between the initial six participating countries by 1st February 1994.

- The proposed Visa Inquiry Open-Border Network (VISION) will probably operate through the SIReNE network. This will enable the relevant authorities in the Schengen countries to consult each other about the issue of visas to individuals (in accordance with Article 17 of the Schengen Implementing Convention). VISION is expected to become operational during 1994.

6.6.6 **The major contribution of the Trevi Group to international police communications has been in providing the macro-level political impetus to facilitate meso-level and micro-level information exchange. Much of the practical progress has been made at the operational level of face-to-face dialogue between police officers with a common interest in a particular type of crime:**

- Working Group I has undoubtedly been successful in promoting co-operation against terrorism through its liaison network of specialist officers, but it is not possible to offer an informed assessment of its activities or of its dedicated secure facsimile information network (TSFN).

- Working Group II has facilitated information exchange between officers on public order offences, including football hooliganism. The Group has also been working on a directory of police training in Europe and on the exchange of information about technical and scientific advances. It has apparently been examining the development of a communications system for all European Union member states.

- Working Group III has instituted a European-wide network for the exchange of drugs trafficking information, and this was instrumental in providing the impetus for the EDU/Europol. Trevi Working Group III has also promoted the exchange of information on money-laundering, armed robbery, stolen vehicles and stolen works of art, and is currently exploring environmental crime and the development of comparative crime analysis in the EU.

- These initiatives have clear operational significance, and they relate to highly-focused police activities in restricted, discrete, specialist areas, such as drugs, terrorism and disorder. A good deal of the contact is face-to-face liaison.

6.6.7 **The creation of the European Drugs Unit/Europol is the most recent example of developments in European police communications and information exchange, and is arguably of long-term importance, but there are difficulties:**

- At present data protection safeguards exist only at the level of working 'agreements', although the *Ad Hoc* Working Group on Europol will seek to incorporate data protection regulations in the draft Convention for the Establishment of Europol. This is not expected to be approved until 1994 or 1995 at the earliest.

- The EDU/Europol databases will contain intelligence or 'soft', unverifiable information. This raises questions about the purposes for which such information may be used and how it is controlled.

- The relationships between Europol and Interpol and between Europol and the Schengen Information System have yet to be resolved. There is potential for duplication of effort; and attempts to rationalise activities may prove to be politically contentious.

- Some police officers and officials in Europe expect Europol to develop specialist operational policing capabilities and tasks, but this view is not shared by UK officials.

6.7   Proposals

6.7.1 **A study should be mounted to explore officers' perceptions of pan-European police communications and exchanges of information, drawing a sample from officers with specialist policing responsibilities (such as terrorism, drugs or fraud).**

There are clear differences in the types of police communication: for example, face-to-face contacts, specialist networks or Interpol-type communication. It would prove most useful to undertake a study to ascertain which forms of information exchange and communication are seen to be the most effective in different fields of police work.

6.7.2   An information systems compatibility audit should be commissioned in order to identify the points of similarity and difference throughout Europe.

There is an unacceptable lack of information about the compatibility of police information systems throughout Europe. Only a painstaking investigation will reveal the current position and suggest how progress might be made.

6.7.3   A major initiative is required to bring together police officers, academics and information technology specialists in order to examine the range of practical and legal problems concerning the use of information technology for international police co-operation.

The practical problems include: secure networks (for voice, data, image and video); communications standards, including open systems; command and control systems; co-operation in major international investigations; and contingency planning (security and disaster planning). The legal problems include the governance of systems for information exchange with a particular emphasis on data protection regulations.

At present the three major organisations (Interpol, the Schengen Group and the EDU/Europol) are addressing these difficulties in different ways and at different levels.

PART IV

EUROPEAN POLICE CO-OPERATION:
PROSPECTS AND PROPOSALS

The human, social, economic and political costs of crime are enormous. The vision of a prosperous European Union will be defeated if crime continues to grow unchecked. In an open Europe fit for the twenty-first century, there will need to be major adjustments in thinking about police work. Narrow, national and provincial attitudes will have to be replaced by ones which cater for the new, broad Europe. Just as criminal opportunities will increase, so the forces of law and order will need to change accordingly.

Part IV draws together the principal themes of the Report and makes proposals for action and further research to improve police co-operation in Europe which is the key to successful policing on a European-wide basis. This is not a luxury which can come in the wake of the removal of internal borders, it is essential for its realisation. Without efficient and effective policing throughout the member states, the social and economic benefits of European Union will be compromised.

However, there is a balance to be struck between practical structures for law enforcement and the protection of the rights of individuals and minority groups. The new Europe will be judged by its treatment of disadvantaged people, such as those seeking asylum in order to escape adversity. Just as minority rights must be protected so, too, must proper forms of accountability be established. Arrangements to foster police co-operation within the European Union should be subject to parliamentary and judicial accountability and, where appropriate, new bodies should be established to scrutinise and review the operation of the mechanisms and procedures.

The new European Union, which came into existence on 1st November 1993, provides the framework within which a more coherent approach to co-operation in justice and home affairs may develop. There is, however, the possibility of a three-speed process with the more active Schengen Group members on the fast track, followed by Greece and Italy, with Ireland and the UK in the slow lane. This would be unfortunate and inefficient. Developments need to take place in a structured evolutionary way, across the whole of the European Union, with clear goals in view.

The principal conclusion of this research study is that much more knowledge and understanding is required in order to establish effective and appropriate structures and procedures for police co-operation within the European Union. Unless and until there is a firmer knowledge base and greater appreciation of the problems there is a real danger of proliferation, duplication and confusion as the countries of Europe continue to muddle through.

CHAPTER 7

POLICE CO-OPERATION IN EUROPE:
TOWARDS THE FUTURE

This concluding chapter outlines the principal findings of the study and seeks to examine what needs to be done to promote effective and publicly-supported police co-operation in Europe. It includes further proposals for additional research based on the findings and assessments included in the body of the Report.

The chapter first undertakes a review of the investigation as a research exercise, highlighting the innovative features and the difficulties experienced. The scope of the inquiry is discussed, and the principal findings and conclusions are then listed and explained. Where there is a particular information deficit this is noted. The Chapter also considers further proposals which are generated by the findings of the study and includes options for further research. Finally, conclusions are drawn about the prospects for future police co-operation in Europe.

7.1   The Scope of the Inquiry

7.1.1   *Macro-Level Inquiry*

a)   Multiplicity of Issues

The scope of this inquiry into police co-operation in Europe has been broad. The investigation has concentrated on two large themes – policing and crime in the European Union, with immigration and external border controls as important subsidiary themes. The intention has been to provide a solid overview of the issues in these fields. However, such a broad area of research presents considerable problems, notably how to delineate and manage the field of inquiry. There are many separate but interconnected issues related to policing, crime and immigration in Europe, such as policies on refugees and asylum, clandestine immigration, the treatment of minority groups, the growth of nationalism and associated racism, the accountability of law enforcement bodies and the operation of different criminal justice systems. Inevitably, it has proved necessary to exclude some important and interesting law and order and human rights questions from the central focus of the research.

b)   First Step

More positively, an increased knowledge and understanding of some of the basic features of policing in Europe, such as policing arrangements and structures for co-operation, can be seen as a necessary condition for, or even as a first step towards, addressing the wider issues. It is, for example, impossible to analyse the Trevi Group initiatives without raising issues of political accountability and control. It is not possible to review the Schengen arrangements, particularly the Schengen Information System, without examining the concept of the external 'ring of steel' and the implications for entry to the European Union for nationals from developing countries. Similarly, it is not possible to discuss the implications of the Maastricht Treaty and its provisions for the EDU/Europol without reference to the important question of the possible future role of the European Parliament in scrutinising and holding to account police co-operation in Europe.

c)   Interconnections and Interdependency

The field of police, crime and justice in the new Europe includes a myriad of different issues, problems, institutions and procedures, all of which interconnect and affect each other. It is possible to examine these issue-by-issue and institution-by-institution – the micro-level approach – but by so doing the interrelationships are not seen and appreciated. A meso-level analysis of each area helps to reveal these interconnections but the overall picture is obtained only by a macro-level investigation. Inevitably, such an inquiry cannot examine everything in detail but it does enable an overview of the interdependence and common threads – and perhaps also raises questions about duplication.

To this extent the current Report raises as many questions as it answers. This is not a matter for apology. Without the current research these matters may not have been raised at all; or, if they had surfaced, they would be addressed in something other than their proper context.

7.1.2   *Broad Overview*

The phrase 'police co-operation in Europe' has a deceptive simplicity, seemingly offering the researcher a straightforward invitation to catalogue examples of collaboration, harmonisation and co-operative activities. However, this perception is mistaken. As the evidence contained in this Report indicates, an examination of the subject of police co-operation in Europe means addressing some highly complex and interconnected issues.

Given the breadth of the topics and the complexities of the subject matter, the research team considered that a preliminary and introductory account of the major issues was required. The principal themes surrounding police co-operation in Europe have been documented in order to provide a broad overview, and the Report should be seen in this context. It is intended that more detailed work should develop from this macro-level inquiry, as the suggestions for further research in each chapter indicate.

7.1.3   *Lack of Information*

The study began without the benefit of an accumulated body of knowledge derived from previous research. There was a paucity of even basic data. In those cases where information did exist it was often difficult to uncover and, once uncovered, it was frequently inaccurate, incomplete or misleading. Sometimes, even 'official' sources offered out-of-date published material and much official police literature tended to be something of a public relations exercise. There are several reasons for the relative absence of basic published information.

First, much of the material produced by individual police forces throughout the European Union has been prepared and presented for domestic or internal consumption, with no view at all to forming part of a European-wide 'jigsaw' of policing. The individual pieces were not seen as part of a wider, coherent whole. This has made assessing these contributions difficult and militates against comparative analysis.

Secondly, the complex arrangements for police co-operation forged at the macro and meso levels, such as the Trevi Group or the Schengen Convention, are major developments, but frequently they have taken place at ministerial and intergovernmental levels – without being readily accessible to public scrutiny and, by definition, to informed debate. Other major developments, such as Europol, are so new (and changing so rapidly) as not to be fully amenable to informed analysis.

Thirdly, and possibly most importantly, there are underlying sensitivities about law enforcement and political sovereignty which have inhibited pan-European dialogue. It has suited many of the participants to obscure developments, and not to publish material about them, as this has minimised discussion on politically-contentious issues.

7.1.4   Changing Climate

During the course of this study there have been significant changes – all pointing in the direction of an increased willingness to participate in the new debate on policing in Europe. There have been developments at different levels.

a)   Macro-Level Developments

At the macro level, one of the most significant changes was the signing of the Treaty on European Union (the Maastricht Treaty), the final ratification of which took place in October 1993. For the first time, albeit in embryonic form, the notion of formally agreed pan-European policing has (through Europol) received intergovernmental recognition. Whatever the eventual outcomes may be in terms of operational significance, the Europol 'stamp of approval' will undoubtedly add a new, explicit dimension to the impetus for police co-operation in Europe. The Maastricht Treaty came into effect on 1st November 1993.

Also at the macro level, during the second half of 1993 there have been significant developments with the implementation of the Schengen Convention. After some apparently serious problems in April–May 1993, progress with the new Schengen arrangements forged ahead and the inaugural meeting of the Executive Committee was held in Paris on 18th October. It was announced that Belgium, France, Germany, Luxembourg, the Netherlands and Spain will implement the provisions of the Convention on 1st February 1994, with some measures phased in before this date. As soon as outstanding technical difficulties are resolved Portugal will join them, although it seems likely that there will be further delay before Greece and Italy are in a position to do likewise.

b) Meso-Level Activities

At the meso level, during the last few years, there has been a burgeoning interest in European police co-operation. This has been reflected, for example, in police exchanges, police conferences and new networks for police liaison (some of which are discussed further in Chapter 5). There has also been the development of formally established research and conference programmes at major universities (Leicester, England and Edinburgh, Scotland) and at police and research training centres (for example, *Fachhochschule für Polizei*, Villingen-Schwenning in Germany, and the *Nederlandse Politie Academie*, Apeldoorn in the Netherlands).

c) Micro-Level Co-operation

At the micro level, the generous support and co-operation secured from police officers and academics throughout Europe, who have willingly contributed information to the present study and who have also requested to remain part of the now established network of interested parties, is strong evidence of a decisive shift. It is worth observing that significant changes may take place at the macro level, and new opportunities may be promoted at the meso level, but real progress of a detailed nature often occurs at the micro level where specialists work together to develop practical arrangements. It is here that utilitarian flesh is put on the intergovernmental bones as efforts are made to turn macro-level potential into micro-level operability. However, these micro-level negotiations and activities are often hidden from view and the research team is deeply grateful to those participants, from various parts of Europe, who have provided data about, and insights into, recent developments.

7.1.5 Size, Scale and Complexity

This Report is a modest attempt to contribute to the increasing openness about policing in Europe. It reflects the rising interest in this field which is placing police co-operation in Europe higher on political and research agendas. It also bears witness to the increasing appreciation that European political and economic integration entails social changes which need to be addressed and managed. The opportunities presented by a more open economic and social system also include the potential menace of greater crime against individuals and organisations, increased violence against racial and ethnic groups, and threats against member states and EC institutions themselves.

The awakening interest in the possible social costs of European Union, and the perceived need to understand and manage them, is being accompanied – at least in some quarters – by a growing realisation that if the new policing and law enforcement structures, and concomitant rules and procedures, are inappropriate and insufficiently transparent and accountable, they will fail to command the necessary public trust and support and will consequently not function in a fully effective way.

Within the framework provided by this changing climate, the research team has endeavoured to produce the most comprehensive description and analysis to date of the contours and context of police co-operation in the new Europe.

However, the size of Europe, the scale of crime, the diversity of the police forces, and the complexity of the structures for securing police co-operation across frontiers, together mean that the present study can only be seen properly as a preliminary investigation. It would be disingenuous to pretend otherwise. Although the study offers the first broad account of the structures of policing in the European Union, and the principal mechanisms for co-operation, there are inevitably many unanswered questions and various aspects of the field which are only touched upon. Indeed, one of the purposes of the research has been to uncover issues, problems, institutions and procedures which require further, detailed investigation. It is clear from the study's findings that there are many such issues, institutions and procedures in need of more thorough examination.

7.2   Principal Research Findings

7.2.1   *Crime and the Abolition of Internal Frontiers*

A number of assessments and predictions has been made about the possible increase in crime levels in Europe following the removal or relaxation of internal border controls within the European Union. As the evidence presented in Chapter 2 indicates, many of these fears have been articulated without reference to empirical data. Indeed, there is some evidence that the rhetoric of 'crime concern' is inversely related to the threat posed. Data which are available on the rising crime levels in the separate member states of the European Union should certainly give cause for concern but strategies for crime prevention and the policing of crime need to be founded on more concrete information than is currently available. Speculation and rhetoric need to be replaced by firmer knowledge of the extent of different sorts of crime and a better appreciation of the trends and the reasons for them.

a)   Unnecessary Fears

The removal of internal border controls within the EU, and the consequent establishment of more rigid border controls at the external boundaries, is a necessary corollary of the establishment of the Single Market and the development of the European Union.

It must be stressed that the effects on crime levels within the EU of these developments cannot be predicted accurately on the basis of existing knowledge. Nonetheless, evidence available to the research team has indicated that, despite fears of a 'crime wave' voiced by prominent public figures, there will be no sudden or fundamental changes in the nature of serious crime, particularly in the fields of drugs trafficking and terrorist activities. Whilst it is possible that this type of criminal activity will increase as a result of other factors, it is unlikely to be affected to any great extent by the removal of internal border controls.

It is, however, possible that some other forms of crime will increase as a result of the abolition of frontier checks within the European Union. These include less serious offences committed by criminals who take advantage of the greater freedom to travel, various types of fraud of a cross-border nature and different forms of environmental crime. The theft and transportation of valuable vehicles and works of art and antiques, while a growing problem, seem unlikely to increase to any marked extent because of the reduction in frontier checks, although non-criminal victimisation, including motor vehicle safety, may be adversely affected to some extent.

An overall assessment suggests that there is insufficient evidence upon which to form a sound judgement of the effects on cross-national crime of the removal of internal frontiers. Unnecessary and unsubstantiated fears of a 'crime wave' have been voiced in the absence of firm knowledge and understanding. Some increase in certain sorts of crime within the European Union seems likely, with or without the abolition of border controls, and increased information, based on sound, long-term research, and police co-operation of an appropriate kind, should be encouraged as a matter of priority.

b)   Terrorism and Drugs Trafficking

The general point that there will be no sudden or fundamental changes in the nature of serious crime must not be misunderstood in relation to offences of terrorism and drugs trafficking. These very serious crimes pose a real and genuine threat to the well-being of the people of the European Union, and every effort is required to combat them. The threats are real and the consequences could be most harmful. What is at issue, however, is the extent to which 'frontier-free Europe' will lead to an increase in these threats. The evidence from this inquiry is that the removal of borders is likely to have little impact on the overall levels of these types of serious crime.

Committed international terrorists were operating throughout Europe prior to the abolition of the internal borders. There is no reason to suppose that they will operate with greater impunity in a Europe without internal frontiers. This, of course, does not remove the obligation on member states to co-operate in the fight against terrorism and to afford it the highest priority.

If there is an increase in the drugs problem in the member states of the European Union in the coming period it is more likely to occur as a result of the increased freedom of movement in eastern Europe, and a breakdown in law and order and a growth in organised crime in the former communist countries, rather than from the abolition of European Union internal frontiers. Of course, fundamentally any increase in drugs trafficking will be the result of increased *demand* in EU countries and ultimately any solution to the problem needs to address the reasons for this demand.

c)   Mobile Offenders

Although perceptions of increased crime as a result of the dismantling of frontiers within the European Union have been subject to exaggeration, the study has found some evidence to suggest that the removal of internal border controls may lead to a rise in levels of acquisitive crime. 'Mobile offenders' within the Community may be better able to exploit criminal opportunities for travelling with relative impunity. Such criminals may be able to avoid arrest and conviction by crossing from one criminal jurisdiction to another, and may find it easier to fence or 'market' stolen goods well away from the scene of the crime.

Although less serious than high-visibility crimes, such as terrorism and drugs trafficking, these much more numerous lower-level offences impinge to a greater extent on the lives of ordinary people. This is the level of 'normal' crime. If the removal of internal frontiers were to lead to an increase in the incidence of offenders committing such crimes in other EU states, and a reduction in their chances of being caught, this would be a significant development. This possibility needs to be monitored over the next few years to determine whether further action to combat the problem is required.

d)   Stolen Property

The research project has also received evidence of concern that the abolition of internal borders will lead to a rise in crime involving high-value property. This concern particularly relates to valuable motor vehicles and construction plant and precious works of art and antiques.

There is, indeed, growing evidence of motor-vehicle theft and the theft of valuable construction plant taking place on an international scale. Organised criminal gangs are allegedly supplying an increasing demand in eastern Europe, the Middle East, Africa and Asia, which includes a lucrative market for heavy construction vehicles, lorries and luxury cars. For example, the *Lietender Polizeidirektor im Bundesgrenzschutz* from Koblenz reported that in 1992 more than 60,000 vehicles stolen in Germany were never recovered and were presumed to have been smuggled out through the Czech Republic by criminal gangs. Evidence that this is occurring is provided by the number of stolen vehicles which are discovered at the external borders. In 1992 the German police found 614 stolen cars and 552 commercial vehicles, worth tens of millions of pounds, which criminals were trying to take across the eastern border.

Thefts of works of art and antiques are also a growing cause of concern and they are often linked to other types of organised international crime, such as drugs trafficking and money laundering. As with the 'export' of stolen motor vehicles and construction plant, this is an under-researched field, but the evidence which exists suggests that many paintings and antiques which are stolen in European countries are transported to other EU states or to countries outside the European Union.

Some high-value property is recovered at internal EU frontier checkpoints each year. For example, in 1991 Kent police impounded stolen vehicles worth £1.25 million which were passing through Dover. This is, however, certainly only the tip of the iceberg and in general European Union internal border controls appear to be easily circumvented by criminals transporting both valuable vehicles and precious paintings and antiques. Spot-checks on containers, lorries and other possible means of transporting stolen vehicles and other property should continue throughout Europe, but the most effective way to tackle these crimes would appear to be increased information and intelligence and improved co-operation between different police forces and other agencies.

e)   Fraud

A broad field of crime in Europe which has not received the attention it merits is that of fraud. Of course, fraud and 'white collar' crime are characterised by relative invisibility, complexity and a lack of publicity, but the data on fraud within Europe which do exist reveal its enormous extent, amounting to tens of billions of pounds sterling each year in the twelve EU member states.

The great majority of cases of fraud occur within individual EU countries. However, cross-border fraud of various kinds appears to be a growing problem and so, too, does the problem of credit-card and cheque-book fraud. Fraud against the European Community itself is also a serious problem, as the European Court of Auditors regularly points out. A report in November in 1993 estimated that fraud against the EC amounts to almost 10 per cent of the annual budget of ecu 66 billion. Finally, the problem of smuggling of contraband and the consequent evasion of taxation should be noted. This form of fraud appears to be an extensive problem within and between the countries of the European Union.

It is worth reiterating the point that these offences are far from transparent not least because institutional victims are often reluctant to acknowledge they have occurred for fear of damaging commercial operations, or because the offence is deemed to be no more than accepted business practice or part of 'commercial risk'. Cases of large-scale fraud are also notoriously difficult to solve and even more difficult to prosecute.

Evidence received by this study suggests that fraud is an extensive and growing problem within the European Union and the completion of the Single Market and the removal of internal controls appears likely to stimulate fraud and business-related crime yet further. Greater mobility, for example, is likely to boost credit-card fraud or deception associated with commodity investment or 'long firm' fraudulent ordering of goods. As outlined in Chapter 2, there are various opportunities for increased fraud in the new 'frontier-free Europe'. This is one field where real threats appear to exist and consequently where further research and European-wide law enforcement initiatives are required.

f)   Environmental Crime

Another area of increasing concern, where police co-operation in Europe is required, is environmental crime. Very little data on this topic exist at present, but there is growing public and political pressure to tackle crimes such as illegal trafficking and transportation of hazardous and toxic waste, illegal dumping and air, water and land pollution.

This is clearly a subject on which much more research needs to be conducted. Preliminary evidence received by this study suggests that the relaxation of border controls may lead to easier illegal transportation and an overall increase in environmental crime.

g)   Non-Criminal Victimisation

A final aspect of the removal of frontiers within Europe in the field of law and order concerns what might to be termed 'non-criminal victimisation'. This includes fear of rabies entering the UK, which seems generally exaggerated, and concern that checks on motor vehicles at borders will be reduced leading to lower levels of road safety. There is, perhaps, some basis for this concern but it seems a poor argument to support the continued retention of border controls. Instead, it would seem sensible to conduct spot checks in individual countries and to continue EC initiatives to harmonise road safety standards across the whole Community.

h)   Extradition

The abolition of internal border controls focuses attention on police co-operation in the exchange of information, the powers of arrest and detention of offenders and also on how they may successfully be prosecuted and punished. A particular issue, given added impetus by the development of the Single Market, is the question of extradition.

The principal mechanism for dealing with wanted people who have crossed European borders to escape national jurisdiction is the 1957 European Convention on Extradition. Extradition is allowed on the basis of a formal request, an arrest warrant, a statement of facts, and evidence of law and identity. This is supplemented by the Council of Europe 1959 Convention of Mutual Assistance in Criminal Matters.

Respondents to this study suggest that generally extradition between European Union member states works reasonably well, but there remain three loopholes which need consideration. First, the 'political offence' exception in the Convention still enables some terrorists to avoid extradition. Secondly, the principle of double incrimination and the requirement that extraditable offences must carry a minimum of one year's imprisonment, inhibit the extradition of relatively minor offenders. Thirdly, states may refuse to extradite their own nationals on the basis that they will try them under their own law and Belgium, Germany and Greece routinely do this.

7.2.2 *Immigration and the 'Hard Outer Shell'*

Predictions about the effects on crime of removing internal frontier controls within the European Union have frequently been alarmist and the prognostications have been based on little, if any, information and analysis. Such fears are, though, understandable given the lack of data and, indeed, given the history of nation states and the apprehension of 'loss of control' over the influx and movement of 'foreigners'. It has been accepted since the Single European Act of 1986 that a necessary corollary of the abolition of internal controls is a strengthening of the external borders. Political consensus is that greater freedom of mobility within the new Europe requires a 'hard outer shell' at the external borders.

a)   Threat to Social Stability

The central issue continues to be fear of an influx of immigrants, and this concern has been closely tied by some commentators to fears of growing crime. During the past two or three years concern about illegal immigration has become a significant political factor and some perceive it to be potentially a fundamental threat to social stability within the European Union. Issues such as refugees and political asylum have become bound up with the question of 'illegal immigrants', despite the clear differences between them. As with the fears of growing cross-border crime in the EU, there appear to be widespread misperceptions.

b)   Illegal Immigration

For some years many commentators have been warning of an imminent 'flood' of illegal immigrants from the east and the south and there is evidence of growing numbers of illegal entrants. No one knows how many illegal immigrants there are in European Union countries. According to the Council of Europe *Report on the New Countries of Immigration* (Document 6211, 1990) the largest numbers of illegal immigrants are in the Mediterranean countries of Greece, Italy, Portugal and Spain, amounting to perhaps 1.5 million in 1990. More recent estimates from the International Labour Organisation in June 1993 suggest that at least 2.5 million illegal immigrants are living within the European Union.

i)   *Widespread Fears*

There have been suggestions that the numbers of clandestine migrants are growing for a variety of reasons but at least partly because it has become more difficult to gain legal entry. The demand has increased but the supply of legal ways in to the EU has diminished and people are prepared to pay others who offer to circumvent the controls. It does seem that the planned removal of internal border controls has fuelled the widespread fears and perceptions of increased illegal immigration.

ii)   *Six Dimensions*

During the research project six dimensions of the issue of illegal immigration have been raised. First, respondents have drawn attention to the perceived permeability of the long land and sea borders around the European Union. Secondly, some have highlighted the bilateral and multilateral agreements between European Union and non-Union states, which makes the idea of the 'hard outer shell' look rather less convincing than its proponents have portrayed it. Thirdly, the disintegration of the former communist countries in central and eastern Europe is seen as likely to lead to a steady exodus of people seeking greater security, stability and prosperity.

Fourthly, it has been argued that some illegal immigrants are forced to turn to crime to pay off the exorbitant 'fees' charged by those who helped them gain entry to the European Union. Fifthly, data on the extent of illegal immigration are largely absent. Finally, it remains unclear how and to what extent the EU states will adopt a common position on illegal immigration under Title VI of the Treaty on European Union.

iii)   *Lack of Knowledge*

As discussed in Chapter 2, the misperceptions about, and conflation of, illegal immigration and visas and asylum policies must give cause for concern. The confusions are at least partly based on lack of data on which to build a clear and coherent approach. Lack of knowledge is resulting in lack of understanding. It is also worrying that much of the current discussion is conducted with implicit – and sometimes explicit – nationalist, xenophobic and racist sentiments.

c)   Visas

A central feature of the proposed 'ring of steel' is the development of a common visa policy through the European Community. This is being introduced under the 1990 Schengen Implementing Convention and the meeting of the Executive Committee on 23rd November 1993 in Paris was expected to approve a harmonised visa for the nine countries involved. This will be extended to all EC states under Article 100c of the Treaty Establishing the European Community, with the gradual implementation of the Maastricht Treaty which came into force on 1st November 1993.

The common visa seems likely to apply eventually to nationals of well over one hundred countries, almost all of which will be developing countries in Africa, Asia, south and central America and eastern Europe. These provisions conjure up the prospect of even longer lines of black and brown people held up for hours at the major airports and seaports of European Union countries. Mistakes by pressurised immigration officers, and no doubt resultant discourtesies and confrontations, seem likely. There is also the prospect of growing injustice in the allocation of visas, the continued separation of families and also, perhaps, increased bribery and corruption as visas to gain entry to the EC become increasingly difficult to obtain. As the supply of visas falls so their value will increase.

d)   Refugees and Asylum Seekers

The evidence received by the research project confirms that entry at the perimeter of the European Union is set to become considerably more difficult as the internal barriers come down. This is an inevitable result of the implementation of the 'hard outer shell'. Unfortunately, it is leading to the perception of 'fortress Europe' where apparently the principal people to be kept out are those from the developing world. It is not clear that suitable differentiation will be made between those in genuine need and those who wish to move to Europe for economic reasons. It is alleged that the doors are closing on all of them.

i)   Increasingly Stringent Approach

The position of people seeking asylum in European Union countries is of particular concern. Throughout the world certain groups of people are threatened as the result of political and social upheaval. This is evident in some countries in central and eastern Europe, in states such as Iraq and Iran, and in some countries in Africa, Asia and southern America. Data from the United Nations High Commissioner for Refugees (UNHCR) showed that the number of people seeking asylum in EU countries rose from 420,000 in 1991 to 560,000 in 1992, with an estimated 400,000 in the first half of 1993. In addition, many asylum seekers arrived in the EFTA countries: Austria (16,000 applications in 1992), Finland (3,625), Norway (5,238), Sweden (83,200) and Switzerland (18,000).

There is evidence that some European Union countries have, during the last few years, been adopting an increasingly stringent approach. According to the UNHCR, while France granted some 28 per cent of asylum requests in 1992 followed by the Netherlands (14%), the success rate was much lower in Belgium (8%), Germany (4%), Ireland (3%), Italy (5%), Spain (4%) and the United Kingdom (3%). It appears that some 506,000 applications out of a total of 556,947 requests made to EU countries were refused in 1992 – a 'refusal rate' of 91 per cent.

ii)   Xenophobia and Racism

The findings of the research project are that the language of politicians and commentators has become more uncompromising in the last few years, conveying increasing hostility towards refugees and sometimes marked by racist undertones. This doubtless reflects the increased nationalism and xenophobia evident in some parts of Europe, and politicians' concern about political extremism, racial attacks and social instability. There is, however, the possibility that the approach being adopted will exacerbate such problems, for by pandering to racism and xenophobia politicians may in fact encourage extremism and racial hatred, giving their proponents a spurious legitimacy.

There are, of course, strong and compelling reasons for limiting both legal and illegal immigration to the European Union. The Schengen Convention and the Dublin Convention of 1990 both set out to achieve this in what appears to be an even-handed way. However, people in genuine need should surely be given the assistance they require and no asylum seekers or visa applicants should be discriminated against on the grounds of their race, colour or creed merely to pander to extremism, xenophobia, and racism. Strong and courageous political leadership is instead required to confront and defeat such views.

e)   The Role of Customs

The customs authorities of the member states have an important role to play in the development of the 'ring of steel'. Evidence presented to the research project shows that international criminal activities, such as drugs smuggling and other forms of organised crime, encounter their greatest hurdle at the point of crossing the EU's external boundaries.

The Mutual Assistance Group 1992 (MAG 92), set up in 1989, has prepared a customs strategy for the external frontier to tackle the illegal importation of drugs, weapons, serious pornography and other contraband. Risk analysis was undertaken to identify the ways in which smuggling is conducted and MAG 92 has also made recommendations on the development of intelligence, training and technical aids and equipment. The Group is currently working on updating the 1967 Naples Convention on Customs Co-operation.

Among the results of the work of MAG 92 have been the Harrogate Declaration, signed by all twelve EC countries in May 1992, and the Customs Information System which was launched on 1st October 1992.

The customs organisations of the member states of the European Union are responsible for enforcing prohibitions on a wide range of items and their importance is set to grow further with the abolition of internal borders and increased emphasis on the external frontier. The customs services, therefore, seem to be at the forefront of attempts to create the European Union's 'hard outer shell'.

7.2.3　　Police Forces in the European Union

The law enforcement agencies of the twelve EU member states lie at the heart of co-operative efforts to police the European Union. Chapter 3 documents the organisation of these law enforcement agencies and briefly outlines the judicial systems in each state. Two particular features emerge from the study – the difficulty in defining 'police' and the problems of counting the number of police forces and officers in the EU.

a)　　　Definitions of Police

The definition of 'police' is not as might be expected merely a matter of fitting the forces to a definition. The term itself has wide-ranging connotations throughout Europe and officers from the various forces perform different tasks, with different structures and organisations. For example, the image of a police officer in the UK might well be that of the 'bobby on the beat', but this would be quite different to that of the military-style *Gendarmerie Nationale* in France.

The *Bundeskriminalamt* in Germany with the emphasis on handling serious criminal investigations, as well as being the centre for co-operation between federal and state law enforcement agencies, presents a different image. In Portugal the *Guarda Fiscal* is essentially a customs and tax police service, whereas in the UK these functions are exercised by separate bodies. Moreover, apart from the differences in image and function, the nature of policing is not constant. The demilitarisation of *Polizia di Stato* in Italy and, more recently, the *Gendarmerie* in Belgium, fundamentally altered those frameworks for policing.

b)　　　Numbers of Police Forces and Police Officers

Notwithstanding the definitional difficulties, a broad overview of the basic structures in the European Union is presented in Chapter 3 as a first step towards conducting a wider and more detailed comparative investigation. The differences are obvious (for example, some states operate a national force, others use national and local forces and others deploy a large number of quasi-autonomous police forces), but it is possible to present some European-wide findings as outlined in Chapter 3 (Table 3.1 and Figure 3.1). For convenience, these data are also presented in Table 7.1 and Figure 7.1.

Throughout the EU there are 105 separate police forces (and more if port and forestry police are included), which gives approximately eight forces per member state. Even on the assumption that the large number of forces in the Netherlands and the UK were deemed to be one national force in each country, there would still be an average of two police forces per European Union member state.

For the EU as a whole there are some 1.3 million police officers. This finding surprised nearly all contributors to the inquiry. With few and isolated exceptions 'informed guesstimates', mostly from European police officers, suggested a significantly lower figure. With a total population of some 344 million people there is approximately one police officer for every 257 people in the European Union.

It is also possible to calculate the number of police officers per head of population in each of the twelve member states of the Community. There is significant variation between member states. At one extreme, there are relatively more police officers per head of population in Italy (191 head of population for a single police officer) while, at the other extreme, there are considerably fewer police officers per head of population in Denmark, with just one police officer for every 499 people.

c) Variety and Differentiation

These data suggest that whatever the inclination might be to perceive 'policing' in Europe in terms of homogeneity and uniformity, the reality is different. Policing in Europe is best characterised by differentiation – differences in image, differences in structure and organisation, variations in roles, responsibilities and powers and significant differences in the number of police officers per head of population.

The variety and extent of these differences is perhaps one of the single most important findings from this inquiry, and the start made in charting this differentiation has been an important research task. Both may be seen as a necessary condition for a more detailed comparative investigation.

Basic knowledge of different policing structures is clearly an important prerequisite for the effective promotion of co-operation between different law enforcement agencies. Whatever the current levels of police co-operation, as outlined in Chapters 4, 5 and 6, the majority of police respondents involved in this study expressed the view that co-operative efforts should be grounded in a better understanding of the operational structures of the different forces in Europe. It is hoped that the preliminary comparative study in Chapter 3 will be useful in its own right, and will serve to facilitate and stimulate police co-operation throughout Europe.

d) Training Preparations for the Single Market

The diversity amongst law enforcement agencies within the European Union is reflected in the different approaches towards training and education about the Single Market and its consequences for policing. Trevi Working Group II has apparently sponsored a European Police Studies course in France, although it has not proved possible to obtain further details. A number of specialised courses has also taken place, on topics such as the detection of forged documents. Annual courses are held at the national police academies in France, Germany, the

Figure 7.1 Number of Population Per Police Officer by European Union State, 1993

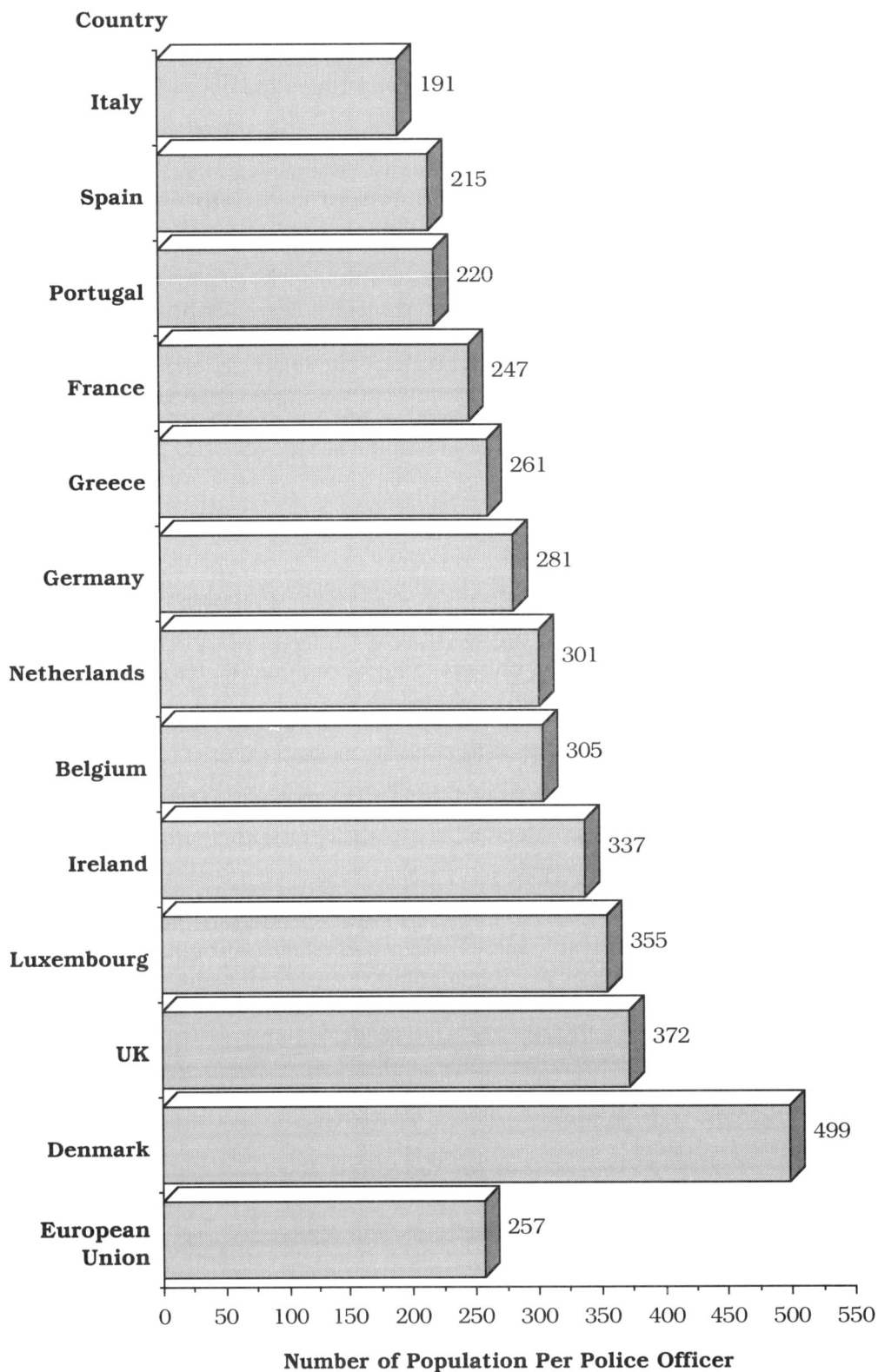

Country

Italy — 191

Spain — 215

Portugal — 220

France — 247

Greece — 261

Germany — 281

Netherlands — 301

Belgium — 305

Ireland — 337

Luxembourg — 355

UK — 372

Denmark — 499

European Union — 257

0   50   100   150   200   250   300   350   400   450   500   550

Number of Population Per Police Officer

Table 7.1 Principal Police Forces
in the European Union

Country	Police Force		Number of Police	Population (millions)	Number of Population Per Police Officer
Belgium	Gendarmerie		15,647		
	Police Communale		15,704		
	Police Judiciare		1,340		
		Sub total	**32,691**	9.97	305
Denmark	Rigspolititiet				
		Sub total	**10,300**	5.14	499
France	Police Nationale		116,300		
	Gendarmerie Nationale		96,313		
	Police Municipale		15,000		
		Sub total	**227,613**	56.18	247
Germany	Landespolizeien		255,047		
	Bundpolizei		27,700		
		Sub total	**282,747**	79.50	281
Greece	Hellenic Police				
		Sub total	**38,783**	10.14	261
Ireland	Garda Siochana				
		Sub total	**10,500**	3.54	337
Italy	Arma dei Carabinieri		104,211		
	Polizei de Stato		96,178		
	Guardia di Financia		57,181		
	Vigili Urbani		25,922		
	Others		18,000		
		Sub total	**301,492**	57.60	191
Luxembourg	National Police		500		
	Gendarmerie		600		
		Sub total	**1,100**	0.39	355
Netherlands	25 Regional Forces and 1 Central Force				
		Sub total	**49,500**	14.89	301
Portugal	Policia de Seguranca Publica		18,641		
	Guarda Nacional Republicana		17,212		
	Guarda Fiscal		7,795		
	Policia Judiciara		1,921		
	Policia Maritima		500		
	Aliens Police		700		
		Sub total	**46,769**	10.30	220
Spain	Cuerpo Nacional de Policia		51,109		
	Guarda Civil		75,346		
	Policia Autonomica		15,000		
	Municipal Police Corps		40,000		
		Sub total	**181,455**	38.96	215
United Kingdom	52 Semi-Autonomous Forces				
		Sub total	**154,738**	57.60	372
European Union			**1,337,688**	**344.21**	**257**

Netherlands, Spain and the UK. At present, such joint training initiatives appear to be few and far between although all police respondents to this study who had been involved in them were unequivocal in their support.

Proficiency in languages varies considerably amongst the police officers of the European Union. In north Europe a high proportion of the population, including police officers, is able to speak a number of European languages but in southern Europe and France, Ireland and the UK the position is rather different. Senior officers in such countries appear to have been hesitant and unwilling to devote resources to language training for their more junior colleagues. There are exceptions, however, such as Kent police in the UK where day-release and residential courses in French have been provided.

Kent Constabulary has also been in the forefront of interesting developments such as the 'PoliceSpeak' project, the aim of which is to ensure accurate communication, using a common lexicon of terminology, between French and English police officers when the Channel Tunnel opens in 1994. More generally, some other European police organisations have invested in training and education for senior officers.

The evidence available to the research team suggests that there is much more that could – and should – be done to educate police officers about the European Union, about policing in other EU member states and, indeed, about the means and procedures for police co-operation.

There appears to be considerable enthusiasm amongst police officers for information and training on policing and police co-operation in the European Union. As yet, however, there is no systematic approach and little evidence of commitment or leadership. Unfortunately, it is not clear which organisations should take the initiative.

7.2.4 *Macro-Level Structures for Police Co-operation*

Three levels for understanding police co-operation are suggested in the introduction to this Report, and indeed they provide a theme running through subsequent chapters. Chapter 4 deals with co-operation at the macro and meso levels, examining the institutions and formal agreements which seek to promote and facilitate working arrangements between different EU police forces. Interpol, the Schengen Group and the Trevi Group are each considered to provide an overview of their organisation, spheres of influence and methods of operation. In addition, the implications of the Maastricht Treaty and the nascent K4 Committee are explored and the activities of the Council of Europe are briefly examined.

a) **Interpol**

The future role of the International Criminal Police Organisation as a mechanism for promoting police co-operation in Europe is far from clear. On the one hand, Interpol has a proven capability to transmit messages rapidly between European police forces and has also developed other specialist European services and activities. On the other hand, Interpol is constrained by its Constitution and its wider world role and may, in any case, be overtaken by other developments in European police co-operation.

i)   *Activities in the European Region*

There are currently 174 different countries in membership of Interpol, which is a significant rise over the number three years ago as the result of the admission of new states from eastern Europe and the former USSR. The European region now includes 44 separate states and some 80 per cent of all messages passing through Interpol involve these countries. The twelve European Union states alone account for 40 per cent of the messages.

The European Secretariat was set up in 1986 to aid the co-ordination of criminal investigations in Europe and it also acts as the permanent secretariat for the annual European Regional Conference. In addition, a conference for national drugs units is held each year and a European fraud symposium is organised biennially. Another innovation has been the establishment of a European Liaison Network, based on identified contact officers whose task is to act as 'trouble shooters' to iron out problems, speed up answers and facilitate co-operation.

ii)   *World-Wide Role*

Interpol, thus, remains a principal means for practical police co-operation in Europe and has developed its capacity further during recent years. The research team has heard a number of complimentary assessments of Interpol's activity and, indeed, has been most impressed by information received from Interpol itself. However, the study has also received adverse comments about Interpol's efficiency and security. Such views, which seem considerably outdated given the enormous strides made since the relocation of Interpol to Lyon, continue to undermine the organisation's reputation, at least in some quarters.

More seriously, one must note that Interpol's activities are constrained by its Constitution, notably Article 3 which excludes activities 'of a political, military, religious or racial character', and by its world-wide role. The constitutional constraints seem largely to have been overcome, but the potential conflict between Interpol's European role and its position as the international police organisation of the world remains. It has been suggested to this inquiry that there is a degree of resentment among some member countries about Interpol's emphasis on European activities, although it should be reiterated that Interpol's European region includes 44 countries not just the 12 European Union member states.

iii)   *Competing Developments within the European Union*

It would obviously be foolish to do anything which might jeopardise information exchange and co-operation with countries outside Europe. Interpol performs the valuable micro-level service of channelling communications between different forces and countries and also promotes some meso-level contacts through its conferences and seminars. Recent developments through the Schengen Group and the Trevi Group, and likely progress under the provisions of the Maastricht Treaty, suggest that other mechanisms are evolving to facilitate certain forms of police co-operation within the European Union. Interpol is also developing an intelligence role and this is discussed further in Chapter 6 and below in section 7.2.6.

To the extent that Interpol remains primarily a 'clearing house' for enquiries (information exchange at the micro level) the developing structures for police co-operation (such as the EDU/Europol), perhaps eventually with operational capabilities, may compromise its role in the European sphere. Alternatively, such developments may indeed be in the interests of Interpol, leaving it to concentrate on its world-wide role. International criminals operate within and without the

European Union and Interpol remains the cornerstone of international police co-operation.

b) The Schengen Group

The forms of law enforcement and co-operation which are being developed as a result of the Schengen Implementing Convention of June 1990 have been seen by some as a 'pilot model' or 'laboratory' for the 12 countries of the European Union – and perhaps even for beyond. The original Schengen Agreement was signed on 14th June 1985 by Belgium, France Germany, Luxembourg and the Netherlands, and they have subsequently been joined by Italy (1990), Spain and Portugal (1991) and Greece (1992). Amongst the EU member states only Denmark, Ireland and the UK remain outside the Schengen agreements.

i) Macro-Level and Meso-Level Structures

The provisions of the Schengen agreements constitute the most ambitious attempt to date to promote large-scale practical law enforcement co-operation in Europe. At the macro level the Schengen Convention is concerned with legal and constitutional issues, while at the meso level it is establishing operational police structures, practices and procedures which are intended to facilitate micro-level co-operation on the prevention and investigation of specific offences.

The structure of the Schengen Group reflects these levels, with macro-level supervision conducted by the Executive Committee of ministers, the first meeting of which took place on 18th October 1993. The second meeting, scheduled for 23rd November in Paris, was expected to agree further progress. At the meso level the Central Group of about 120 senior civil servants and police undertake preparation of the agenda for the Executive Committee and co-ordinate the work of the micro-level working parties.

In October 1993 there were working parties on police and security, the free movement of people, transport and goods and customs, and sub-working groups on telecommunications, visas, asylum and other related matters. A number of sub-groups appear to have finished their work on subjects such as firearms and legal matters and so the structure of the Schengen Group has changed somewhat over the last few years. It is likely to change further as the Executive Committee makes decisions on its preferred permanent organisational structure to operate the new arrangements.

ii) Micro-Level Structures

Also reporting to the Central Group is the Steering Committee for the Schengen Information System (SIS). It also has various sub-working groups on different aspects of the project and liaises closely with a separate working party concerned with the development of the Visa Inquiry System in an Open-Border Network (VISION) which is expected to become operational during 1994.

The Schengen Information System, which is discussed further below and is outlined in detail in Chapter 6, will enable all Schengen countries to have access to identical data on wanted persons, aliens classified as undesirable, asylum seekers, persons to be expelled or extradited, persons under surveillance, stolen goods and related information. In addition, an electronic mail system attached to the SIS will enable rapid transfer of additional information – for example, more details in order to extradite an arrested person. This infrastructure is known as Supplementary Information Request at the National Entry, or SIReNE.

The Schengen arrangements also provide a meso-level framework for other aspects of micro-level co-operation on law enforcement, including judicial co-operation, cross-border observations and 'hot pursuit' and the control of firearms and drugs.

iii)   *Asylum and Visa Applications*

Under the Schengen Implementing Convention, common arrangements for handling asylum and visa applications are being introduced. Critics see this as part of an 'outer ring of steel' around Europe – a compensatory device for enhanced mobility within Europe for nationals of Schengen states.

Asylum seekers will be subject to greater control and will only have one opportunity to apply for asylum within the Schengen area. There is mandatory refusal of entry to aliens who do not meet all the conditions for entry, including deportation from the entire Schengen states.

The nine Schengen countries have agreed that they will subscribe to the 1990 Dublin Convention on Asylum once it is ratified by all 12 EU states and so these provisions will eventually take precedence. The commitment of the 12 European Union countries to introduce a common asylum policy was underlined in the Maastricht Treaty, both in the Declaration on Asylum and under Title VI, Article K.1(1) which affirms that asylum policy is a matter of 'common interest'. The *passerelle* Article K.9 enables the member states to bring asylum policy within the European Community framework at some point in the future.

The Schengen countries have also agreed to introduce a common visa system to regulate entry into their territories. A list of some 123 countries, the nationals of which will require visas, had been drawn up by October 1993 and this was expected to grow further. The provisions of the Maastricht Treaty, as it moves beyond ratification to implementation, will also supersede this aspect of the Schengen Implementing Convention. Article 100c of the EC Treaty commits the whole of the European Community to introduce a common visa.

iv)   *Political Determination and Commitment*

In terms of practical police co-operation the Schengen Group has forged impressive macro-level agreements, created meso-level structures and facilitated micro-level mechanisms for operational police co-operation, including sophisticated information exchange and 'hot pursuit'.

Achievements at these three levels reflect a high degree of political determination and commitment that the Schengen Convention should be fully implemented as soon as possible. On 18th October 1993 it was announced that the target date of 1st December 1993, for removing all internal border controls between the Benelux countries, France, Germany and Spain, had slipped back to 1st February 1994, with Portugal joining these six as soon as possible during 1994. There appear to be continuing doubts about when Greece and Italy will be in a position to implement the Schengen provisions.

v)   *Accountability and Scrutiny*

There continue to be serious concerns and criticisms voiced by some parliamentarians and human rights activists. These include the view that the mechanisms for accountability and scrutiny of the new arrangements are woefully inadequate. In particular, it has been argued that the development of the SIS and the SIReNE, together with the new rules on visas, refugees and asylum, raise data protection, privacy and human rights issues which have not been satisfactorily addressed. The degree of secrecy which has surrounded the Schengen developments has also been criticised, notably by MEPs.

In many respects, the developments by the Schengen Group have been remarkable. This is the first attempt to embed European police co-operation in a fully-fledged legal and organisational framework. Although there is no overall supervisory court structure, the provisions of the treaty are subject to each country's own legal and judicial arrangements and so concerned citizens could, presumably, use their own country's courts to bring cases about the way the procedures operate and to ensure proper judicial review. The absence of any effective parliamentary scrutiny is a continuing matter of concern.

vi)   *Blueprint for the European Union*

Developments as a result of the Maastricht Treaty seem likely gradually to supersede some of the Schengen provisions. However, it seems possible that at least some of the Schengen structures and procedures will be adopted as the basis of European Union-wide developments. This may occur, for example, in terms of asylum and visa harmonisation and with the Schengen Information System and the SIReNE, which could be expanded into a system serving the police forces in all 12 EU member states. The notion of Schengen as a 'pilot model' or 'laboratory' for European Union-wide developments is thus of some substance.

The Schengen experience shows that individual EU states are prepared to sacrifice some sovereignty over policing and law enforcement when they are persuaded that their overall interests are served by so doing. It is also evident that rapid progress can be accomplished if there is the necessary political will and leadership. The development of the Schengen arrangements also reveals that human rights issues, and those around accountability and scrutiny, will tend to be downplayed unless sufficient external pressure is brought to bear.

c)   **The Trevi Group**

The Trevi Group, established in 1975, has a record of promoting police co-operation in Europe. It operates at three different levels – ministerial, senior official and working group.

i)   *Working Groups*

Working Group I (Terrorism) is claimed by respondents to have made a tangible impact in the fight against international terrorism, although no concrete examples have been given.

Working Group II (Technical Forum) has produced agreements on standardised reporting formats to enable the exchange of information on public security problems, including football hooliganism.

Working Group III (Serious Organised International Crime) was established to co-ordinate activities against serious crime, including drugs trafficking – and was instrumental in setting up Drugs Liaison Officers (DLOs) throughout Europe, as well as establishing a national drugs intelligence unit in each EU country. It has also sought to promote co-operation and international initiatives against money laundering and recently has begun to examine the problem of environmental crime within the European Union. Most recently, the working group has been considering the analysis of crime in the 12 EU member states and how best to develop a comparative approach.

Working Group IV, or Trevi 1992, had the task of preparing ground for the reduction of border controls on 1st January 1993. It was wound up in late 1992, on the basis that it had achieved the objectives in its remit, although the formal abolition of border checks was delayed and is now expected to occur on 1st February 1994 in six of the EU states and at some undetermined date for the other six countries.

ii)   *Statements of Intent*

The Trevi Group has played an important role in developing the political commitment for greater police co-operation in the EU. This is exemplified in statements of intent, such as the 1989 Paris *Declaration* and the 1990 Dublin *Programme of Action*. These are discussed further in section 4.3.7 in Chapter 4. Both these statements committed the EC states to collaborative efforts to combat crime and they outlined priorities, such as improved communication of information, the exchange of intelligence, exchange of personnel, promotion of research and training, and the use of joint teams where appropriate. The Dublin *Programme of Action* also specifically mentioned increased co-operation at external borders and the need to establish a common information system.

iii)   *European Drugs Unit/Europol*

The ideas outlined in the Dublin *Programme of Action* were given further impetus a year later at the Luxembourg summit in June 1991 when Chancellor Kohl proposed the creation of a European Criminal Police Office. As a result, the *Ad Hoc* Working Group on Europol was set up in August 1991 to work towards the establishment of a European police unit to co-ordinate criminal intelligence, in the field of drugs trafficking in the first instance. The Maastricht Treaty reaffirmed the European Union states' commitment to the proposal.

The work of the *Ad Hoc* Working Group on Europol led to further progress during 1992–93. The first stage of Europol will be known as the European Drugs Unit (EDU) and this is being established at the same time as the Convention for the Establishment of Europol is being drafted. This is not expected to be signed and ratified before 1995 at the earliest.

Trevi ministers signed an agreement on 2nd June 1993 which established the functions, arrangements for data protection, staffing, accountability and finance of the EDU/Europol. Disagreement on where to locate the unit delayed progress during mid-1993 and it was temporarily based in Strasbourg. At the European Council meeting on 29th October 1993 it was agreed to site the EDU/Europol permanently in The Hague.

iv)   *The Ad Hoc Working Groups*

There are also two *ad hoc* working groups which are closely associated with the Trevi Group, although not formally part of the Trevi structure. The *Ad Hoc* Working Group on International Organised Crime (AHWGIOC) was set up in the Autumn of 1992 after the murders in Italy of judges Falcone and Borsellino. The group reported to a meeting of EC ministers in Denmark in May 1993 and as a result four recommendations were adopted with the aim of intensifying EU and international co-operation against organised crime. A further report from the AHWGIOC is expected before the end of 1993.

The *Ad Hoc* Group on Immigration (AHGI) was established in 1986 and it operates under the co-ordination of the EC Commission. It has six sub-groups on admissions and expulsions, visas, false documents, asylum, external borders, and refugees. The AHGI helped to draft the Dublin Convention on Asylum and has been involved with the drafting of the Convention on External Borders.

v)   Judicial Co-operation

Another body, the Judicial Co-operation Working Group on Criminal Matters (JCWG), is charged with investigating how best to facilitate European Union-wide mutual legal assistance and with preparing the necessary conventions and agreements. Its efforts have concentrated on ways of overcoming legal obstacles to extradition, action to prevent funding for terrorist organisations, measures to deal with EC fraud and the means to encourage legal assistance and mutual recognition of court decisions, such as driving disqualifications.

vi)   Criticisms of Trevi

The research has found mixed feelings about the success and effectiveness of Trevi. At the macro (ministerial) level Trevi has undoubtedly promoted political commitment to police co-operation and there is clear evidence of meso-level initiatives against drugs trafficking and terrorism. Most recently, Trevi was instrumental in giving momentum to the Europol initiative.

Against this, there are counter claims that the rhetoric of Trevi has not always been translated into practice, and that it has, at least until recently, been little more than a ministerial 'talking shop'. To the extent that Trevi operates at the political and senior official level it is seen by some as ignoring the operational needs of practising police officers deployed at the micro level of law enforcement.

In addition, Trevi is seen as lacking in democratic accountability and legitimacy – a largely secret organisation which suffers from being insufficiently connected to European Community institutions. Many of the respondents to the research project considered that the Trevi Group ought to operate within the EC. One reason was the lack of accountability to institutions such as the Parliament and the Court, another was the lack of a permanent base and secretariat. The implementation of the 'third pillar' of the Treaty on European Union should overcome the criticisms in respect of the secretariat – one will be provided from the General Secretariat and the K4 Committee will perform the overall co-ordinating role – but Trevi's (or its successor's) activities will remain intergovernmental and thus beyond the scope of EC institutions, although Article K.6 does involve the Parliament to some extent.

vii)   Macro-Level and Meso-Level Activities

There can be little doubt that the Trevi Group has helped to promote increased law enforcement co-operation between EU member states. It has assisted in the reduction of national rivalries and has promoted the respect and trust which is of fundamental importance if real progress is to occur. The activities of Trevi have been characterised by a high degree of political commitment at the macro level of ministerial meetings and as a consequence there has been progress on agreements, conventions and statements of intent.

Trevi has performed useful functions at the meso level. There has been increased working group activity during recent years and, despite some views to the contrary, progress has in many respects been rapid. Each of the working groups can point to achievements, in fields such as tackling drugs trafficking, combating football hooliganism, and sharing scientific and technical advances. Further progress may be anticipated in areas such as money laundering, environmental crime and European crime analysis.

Also at the meso level, the *ad hoc* working groups appear to be making an impact. The EDU/Europol is clearly a mid-term project, but progress appears to be occurring. The group looking at organised crime is expected to make its final report by the end of 1993 with a number of practical recommendations, while the more established *Ad Hoc* Group on Immigration has undertaken important work in areas such as visas, asylum and external borders. Practical measures to improve co-ordination between different states' legal institutions are being pursued by the Judicial Co-operation Working Group.

viii)   Specialist Concerns

Criticisms of the effectiveness of the Trevi Group have tended to focus on its impact at the micro level of operational policing. It is not readily apparent how Trevi's deliberations have affected practical police co-operation 'on the ground', and this helps to explain the disparaging comments that it is essentially 'a talking shop'.

Such criticisms are, however, somewhat misplaced for almost inevitably much of the Trevi Group's work is directed towards specialist fields of policing, such as terrorism, drugs trafficking and organised crime, which are not the everyday concerns of most European police officers – rather they tend to be the preserve of specialist groups which need to collaborate with similar units elsewhere in the European Union. Furthermore, it can be argued that the Trevi working groups' activities are engaged in a mid to long-term enterprise to establish EU-wide, meso-level structures and procedures which, given time, will facilitate micro-level police co-operation.

The criticism about the unnecessary secrecy of the Trevi Group, and the lack of political and public accountability, appear to have more validity. There may be good reasons for secrecy in respect of operations against terrorists and serious criminals, but in general there would appear to be good reasons *for* publicising the action being taken at an intergovernmental level to combat crime. It is surely in the interests of the public – and indeed in the interests of ordinary police officers themselves – to be apprised of the activities of the Trevi working groups.

ix)   Metamorphosis of the Trevi Group

Similarly, there are strong arguments for proper levels of accountability and scrutiny. Institutions and procedures which are transparent and open are generally more likely to command public trust, legitimacy and confidence. At present, the Trevi Group has no mechanism for corporate accountability, although this may change with the implementation of the Maastricht Treaty and the provisions in Article K (Title VI) which came into force on 1st November 1993.

The implementation of the Maastricht Treaty is also likely to bring about the gradual demise of the Trevi Group and its replacement by a new structure established under Article K of the Treaty of European Union. The intergovernmental Council of Ministers will be serviced by the Co-ordinating Committee set up under Article K.4. As discussed in Chapter 4 (and below in section d), the same Co-ordinating Committee is charged under Article 100d of the EC Treaty with servicing the EC Council of Ministers which will oversee visa policy. The new structure for promoting police and judicial co-operation will thus be intimately linked to the EC institutions while formally remaining an intergovernmental rather than an EC structure.

d)   The Maastricht Treaty and the K4 Committee

The 'third pillar' of the Treaty on European Union (the Maastricht Treaty), signed on 7th February 1992, deals with provisions in the fields of justice and home affairs, including police co-operation. These are now deemed to be 'matters of common interest' and although they will continue to be dealt with on an intergovernmental basis both the European Commission and Parliament will have a formal role.

i)   Matters of Common Concern

The Treaty identifies the following areas as matters of common concern: asylum; controls at external borders; immigration policy, including ways of stopping illegal immigration; combating drug addiction; combating fraud; judicial co-operation in civil and criminal matters; customs co-operation; and police co-operation in combating terrorism, drugs trafficking and other international crime, and in establishing an European Union-wide information system within a European Police Office (Europol). Article K.2 enters the caveat that member states may continue to exercise their responsibilities with regard to the maintenance of law and order and the safeguarding of internal security.

ii)   The K4 Co-ordinating Committee

Article K.4 of the Maastricht Treaty states that the Commission 'shall be fully associated' with these activities. Under this Article a Co-ordinating Committee is being set up to advise on and supervise the development of police and judicial co-operation and other policy fields listed in Article K.1. This Committee will replace the Co-ordinators' Group (sometimes known as the Co-ordinators of Free Movement Group) which was set up in 1988 to implement the Palma Document.

The K4 Committee will apparently have a secretariat based in Brussels under the direction of the Secretary General and it appears that it will exercise considerable influence over how matters develop in this field. At present it seems likely that the K4 Committee will have three steering groups although some sources have suggested there may be four such groups. One steering group will take over the work currently undertaken by the *Ad Hoc* Group on Immigration and will handle immigration and asylum issues, including visa policy, the control of external borders and the work of CIREA (Centre for Information, Reflection and Exchange on Asylum) and the activities of CIREFI (Centre for Information, Reflection and Exchange on Frontiers and Immigration).

Another steering group will deal with policing and security matters, including anti-terrorist work, combating serious crime, the EDU/Europol, and training, scientific and technical matters, crime analysis and combating environmental crime and public disorder. This group will absorb the work currently undertaken by the Trevi Group. It is not yet clear whether it will also have responsibility for customs or whether a separate (fourth) group will handle these matters. It is also not clear which steering group will have responsibility for actions against international fraud.

The final steering group will have responsibility for co-operation on civil and criminal judicial matters, including extradition, mutual assistance, the recognition and execution of 'foreign' sentences and the transfer of proceedings. It may also handle the legal dimensions of attempts to combat terrorist funding and fraud. Each steering group will have an as yet undetermined number of working groups to deal with the detailed, specialist business.

iii)   *Common Visa Policy*

Although most of the provisions in the Maastricht Treaty on home affairs and police co-operation are dealt with in Article K (Title VI), and are thus intergovernmental matters outside the new EC Treaty, there is one important exception. This is co-operation on visas, which is provided for in Article 100c of the Treaty Establishing the European Community and which will be an EC rather than an intergovernmental matter. The Commission is empowered to play a central role in initiating proposals and issuing directives and measures and the European Parliament must be consulted.

iv)   *Role of the European Parliament*

Interestingly, Article K (Title VI) of the Treaty on European Union also provides a role for the European Parliament in the home affairs matters which remain intergovernmental in nature. Article K.6 stipulates that the Parliament shall be regularly informed of the discussions, shall be consulted on 'the principal aspects of activities' in the field and the Presidency of the EC 'shall ensure that the views of the European Parliament are duly taken into consideration'. Furthermore, the Parliament may ask questions and make recommendations in this field and each year will hold a debate on the progress which has been made with implementation.

v)   *Linkage Between Article 100c and Article K*

Article 100c of the EC Treaty is linked to Article K in the Treaty on European Union in two ways. First, the *passerelle* Article K.9 enables the EC member states to bring certain areas, such as asylum policy, other aspects of immigration policy, and action to combat drug addiction and international fraud, within the ambit of the EC Treaty. In this way, these intergovernmental matters may be brought within the EC structure under Article 100c.

Secondly, the K4 Co-ordinating Committee is charged with contributing to the preparation of proceedings under Article 100c – that is on visa policy. Thus, the same group of officials will assist the European Community institutions under Article 100 and will advise on and oversee the intergovernmental activities under Title VI.

vi)   *Declaration on Police Co-operation*

The commitment of the 12 European Union states to develop police co-operation is reiterated in the Declaration on Police Co-operation, which is one of 33 declarations annexed to the Maastricht Treaty. The Declaration confirms that the EU states 'are willing to envisage the adoption of practical measures' in the exchange of information and experience, including support for national criminal investigations and security authorities (in particular in the co-ordination of investigations and search operations), creation of databases, central analysis and assessment of information, collection and analysis of national prevention programmes for forwarding to member states and for drawing up European-wide prevention strategies, and measures relating to further training, research, forensic matters and criminal records departments. The Declaration also commits the 12 states to consider during 1994 whether the scope of police co-operation should be extended further.

vii)   *A Watershed in EU Co-operation in Policing and Home Affairs*

The Maastricht Treaty marks a watershed in the development of co-operation on policing and related matters in the European Community. Article 100c in the

Treaty Establishing the European Community brings visa policy within the ambit of the EC institutions. Although other 'matters of common interest' in the fields of home affairs, justice and police co-operation remain outside the EC, Article K (Title VI) of the Treaty on European Union establishes a formal framework within which the member states will work together. Both the European Commission and the Parliament are given an explicit role and under the *passerelle* Article K.9 it will be possible for certain policy areas, such as asylum, immigration and co-operation against fraud and drug addiction, to be brought within the EC Treaty under Article 100c.

Once the implementation of the Maastricht Treaty begins to gather pace it seems certain that the Trevi Group will be superseded by the new structure, established under the Article K provisions. The *Ad Hoc* Group on Immigration and MAG 92 also seem destined to be brought within this structure. The K4 Co-ordinating Committee, with its three or four steering groups, will thus play a central role in the new arrangements.

It remains to be seen how matters develop as a result of the Maastricht accord. Taken together, Article 100c, Title VI and the Declaration on Police Co-operation make it clear that the 12 European Union states are committed to increasing levels of co-operation in this field. In theory, the Treaty enables the development of a more co-ordinated set of structures and activities, building on the work of the Trevi Group, MAG 92 and the *Ad Hoc* Group on Immigration and adopting some of the Schengen measures, for example those on visas and asylum.

viii)   *Scrutiny and Accountability*

In practice, however, it is far from clear what the new arrangements will mean or how they will work. The Commission seems likely to play a key role and in July 1993 it was announced that Social Affairs Commissioner Padraig Flynn had been given responsibility for these areas. The K4 Co-ordinating Committee and its associated structure will apparently work closely with the General Secretariat which (under Article 151 of the EC Treaty) will service the Council of Ministers. Administrative expenditure under Article K will be charged to the EC budget, but operational expenditure seems likely to be charged to the member states.

The European Parliament must be consulted and its views must be 'duly taken into consideration'. Title VI stipulates that it shall be regularly informed about discussions and may ask questions of the Council and make recommendations to it. Each year, the Parliament will debate progress in the fields of home affairs and judicial and police co-operation. At face value, this introduces a welcome and much-needed element of parliamentary oversight and scrutiny and it is to be hoped that the Parliament will use its newly-established role to the full.

However, some believe that the Parliament will continue to be excluded from some areas covered by Article K. Political realities and sensitive issues of sovereignty appear to have been the reasons why the 'matters of common interest' in Article K have been kept outside the EC institutions as intergovernmental matters. This arrangement will enable the European Union member states to retain greater control and secrecy and to limit scrutiny by the European Parliament and by the national parliaments.

ix)   *Macro-Level and Meso-Level Initiatives*

At the macro level, the Maastricht Treaty establishes a new framework for police co-operation, and collaboration on associated issues, in Europe. At the meso level, the K4 Committee and related structures are likely to initiate various practical measures to facilitate greater co-operation between operational police officers and others involved in law enforcement. The provisions in Article K.3, which enable the Council of Ministers to draw up new conventions and adopt joint positions and actions, mean that further macro-level and meso-level initiatives may be taken.

This ambitious new framework will take time to evolve. It seems likely to absorb some aspects of the Schengen Group's activities as well as those of the other groups and institutions. It will probably prove an effective means for sustaining momentum on co-operation in the fields of home affairs and judicial and police matters, but there are continuing doubts and anxieties about whether there will be effective parliamentary, judicial and public scrutiny and accountability.

e)   The Council of Europe

The principal aims of the Council of Europe are to promote European unity and social and economic progress and to protect human rights. In November 1993 there were 32 member countries with a further seven applications under consideration. Amongst the Council's institutions, the European Commission on Human Rights and the European Court of Human Rights are particularly important. The Council has also established a European Committee on Crime Problems.

Under the leadership of Catherine Lalumière, who has been Secretary General since June 1989, the Council of Europe has undergone a process of revitalisation. This was reflected in the first-ever summit meeting of member states in mid-October 1993, at which the EC's External Affairs Commissioner suggested that the EC itself should consider joining the Council. At the summit it was agreed to overhaul and simplify the system for enforcing human rights.

i)   Migration, Refugees and Asylum Seekers

The Council of Europe has paid particular attention to issues such as refugees, asylum and immigration. In 1991, for example, the Secretary General helped to organise a conference of ministers on the movement of persons from central and eastern European countries. This was held on 24–25th January in Vienna and was attended by representatives from 35 countries. In September 1991 the Council of Europe was involved in another conference on the topic. This was the Fourth Conference of European Ministers Responsible for Migration Affairs which took place in Luxembourg. The Council has also sponsored useful research into migration, refugees and asylum.

ii)   The Pompidou Group

In 1971 the Council of Europe established the European Group to combat Drug Abuse and Illicit Traffic in Drugs, which is more usually known as the Pompidou Group. It has undertaken various work in this field, including exploration of ways to combat drugs trafficking by confiscating financial assets, investigation of educational initiatives and research into other aspects of drug addiction.

iii)   Limited Impact on Policing Issues

The Council of Europe embraces almost three times as many European countries as the European Union and so is an ideal forum for wider pan-European initiatives. It has been active in promoting research and debate in the fields of migration, refugees and asylum and in drugs trafficking and abuse. The European Convention on Human Rights, and the related Commission and Court, are important means for protecting human rights within the EU and beyond.

However, overall the impact of the Council of Europe in the field of police co-operation appears rather disappointing. For example, no respondents to the present study even mentioned the Pompidou Group although all discussed Interpol, Trevi, and Schengen. These bodies might, however, profitably follow the Council of Europe's lead and commission detailed research on appropriate topics.

In the field of data protection, the Council has had a significant impact and the 1981 Convention for the Protection of Individuals with regard to Automatic Processing of Personal Data continues to provide the basic international framework. This was supplemented by the 1987 Recommendation on the use of personal data in the police sector. The Council of Europe's renewed emphasis on safeguarding the rights of minorities, and its anti-racist campaign agreed at the October 1993 Vienna summit, may also prove significant in affecting developments in the European Union.

7.2.5   *Meso-Level Groups, Agreements and Networks for Police Co-operation*

In addition to the major formal structures for promoting police co-operation in Europe, there is a large number of other bilateral and multilateral agreements and less formal structures which exist to foster collaboration in particular fields. It would appear that no-one is certain how many such agreements, associations and networks are actually functioning within the European Union area. Chapter 5 outlines a number of them.

a)   Police Working Group on Terrorism

The Police Working Group on Terrorism (PWGOT) is the principal mechanism for facilitating European police action against terrorists. It was established in 1979 following the assassination in The Hague of Sir Richard Dykes, the UK Ambassador to the Netherlands. It grew out of discussions involving the anti-terrorist specialist units in Belgium, Germany, the Netherlands and the United Kingdom and now embraces all the European Union countries plus the Scandinavian countries and Finland.

The PWGOT meets regularly every six months but it also functions on an informal basis. It aims to develop close links and trust between anti-terrorist specialists in Europe and as such operates at both the meso level and the micro level. Information, particularly intelligence, is shared throughout the network and the group has established a secure communications system which has been in operation since 1988. The PWGOT has also promoted the exchange of officers between different countries. Specialist conferences and seminars are held on particular threats and organisations, and on preventative and investigative techniques.

From the available evidence, the Police Working Group on Terrorism appears to be a successful quasi-formal network which operates at the meso level and the micro level. Although the PWGOT appears to be associated with the work of Trevi Working Group I it is a separate group. A Metropolitan police anti-terrorist officer spelled out its value and effectiveness in promoting cross-national co-operation: 'We know these people – they are our personal friends [...] It has become a very solid group of working colleagues. We trust each other implicitly and pass information to each other without question' (Bresler 1992, p.162).

There are various other groups which facilitate co-operation against terrorists. These include Kilowatt, and the Vienna and Berne Groups which are outlined briefly in section 5.12.3 and mentioned in section 7.2.5 (m) below.

b)   Drugs Intelligence Network

In the field of action to combat drugs trafficking there has been the development of the drugs intelligence network. Trevi Working Group III has been instrumental in boosting this network, first by the decision in 1987 to make greater use of Drugs Liaison Officers (DLOs) and, secondly, by the agreement to establish national drugs intelligence units in all EU countries. The more recent decision to establish the European Drugs Unit/Europol, discussed in Chapter 4, will give a further boost to the exchange of information and intelligence in this field.

This area of police, customs and other law enforcement agencies' activities is one where levels of co-operation are considerably developed. Various international groups and organisations are involved in combating drugs trafficking. In Europe, these include Trevi Working Group III, the Pompidou Group, Interpol, and the *Comité Européen pour la Lutte Anti Drogue* (CELAD). In addition the Schengen Group undertakes collaborative work in this field, customs agencies have developed their own co-operative arrangements (discussed in Chapter 5 and mentioned below), and bilateral and multilateral structures, such as the Cross-Channel Intelligence Conference, also play a role.

This broad drugs intelligence network operates at the meso level and the micro level of activities within a developing macro-level framework. This, of course, is a field with high public and political visibility and concern, and those involved tend to be specialists with relatively high status in their own organisations.

c)   Tackling Football Hooliganism

There is evidence of some successful European police co-operation in respect of tackling football hooliganism. Informal links between the police in a number of countries were formally encouraged in the 1985 European Convention on Spectator Violence which recognised the importance of 'close co-operation and exchange of information between police forces'. Two years later, Trevi Working Group II instituted a European-wide network of permanent correspondents to assist in sharing information about football hooligans.

Subsequently, co-operation occurred during the 1990 World Cup finals in Italy and during the 1992 European Championships. This has been continued during World Cup qualifying matches in 1992 and 1993. For example, Dutch and English police co-operated in the planning and conduct of operations to control fans who travelled to the Netherlands for the World Cup qualifying match on 13th October 1993. British police liaised with their Dutch counterparts in identifying people causing trouble, of which at least 250 were arrested. The British police also collected information on offenders to add to the database held in the National Criminal Intelligence Service (NCIS) which, it was reported, would be passed on to the US authorities who could then refuse entry for the 1994 World Cup finals. It should be noted that there were considerable criticisms of the way the operations were conducted in the Netherlands and of the scale of the arrests.

Evidence given to the research project indicates that the sharing of information and intelligence has been useful and there has been considerable value in sending small numbers of police officers to escort their own nationals who are attending matches in other European Union countries. In summary, some effective co-operation has occurred at meso and micro levels in the field of policing football matches although there would appear to be scope for further initiatives. The concern about 'heavy-handed' and arbitrary policing should also be noted.

d)   Traffic Management and Control

The European Traffic Policing Meeting provides a meso-level forum for discussions in this field and appears to be an embryonic network, but at present little more than that. Some mechanisms do exist for police co-operation on traffic management and control, but information from European police suggests that they are not well developed. Trevi Working Group III has also undertaken some work in this field, but it would appear that there is much more that could be done both in terms of harmonisation of standards and recognition of courts' decisions in other European Union countries – for example, disqualification from driving – and in terms of practical police co-operation, especially the sharing of information.

e)   Technical and Forensic Developments

There is also some meso-level co-operation in technical and forensic matters. Some of this has been promoted by Trevi Working Group II and other activities have been undertaken by the Permanent Technical Committee for Co-operation, set up by the European Regional Conference of Interpol in 1985. Examples of activities include specialist seminars on technological developments, fingerprint identification, criminal records systems, DNA genetic 'fingerprinting' and firearms and ballistics. There is, however, a strong impression that considerably more could be done to foster co-operation in technical and forensic matters.

f)   Policing at Ports

A great deal of informal micro-level co-operation occurs between different European Union police organisations at borders and there are some macro-level agreements and meso-level structures to facilitate it. One such meso-level organisation is the European Association of Airport and Seaport Police, which holds an annual conference, but which does not otherwise appear to be particularly active.

One issue raised during the research project is the question of security at small ports and deserted stretches of coastline, particularly in view of the large number of small boats in EU countries. Some have suggested that such boats should be registered throughout the European Union.

Responsibility for policing seaports and airports varies between European Union states and involves a large number of different agencies. At present, the extent of the co-operation between these different bodies appears to vary greatly and further investigation of the possibilities for improvement seems desirable.

g)   Railway Policing

There is a long history of co-operation between different bodies involved in policing railways. The imminent expansion of rail travel, as a result of the Channel Tunnel and other developments, means that such co-operation will assume even greater significance. Some police officers believe that a growth in the European Union rail network will permit illegal goods to be moved more readily and will provide new possibilities for crimes such as robbery and theft. There continue to be some unresolved issues about the extent to which police from one country may operate on a train which may technically be within another's jurisdiction.

COLPOFER is the European body which represents railway police and it has helped to establish a meso-level network for co-operation in this field. However, it is not clear that COLPOFER has the resources or indeed the strategy necessary to promote a coherent approach in terms of training, information exchange and research.

h) Customs Co-operation

i) *Customs Co-operation Council*

By way of contrast, co-operation between different customs organisations appears to have developed rapidly and seems generally to be effective. International customs liaison takes place through the Customs Co-operation Council (CCC) which has 131 member states. It appears to be an active and effective body which organises workshops, co-ordination of plans and operations and the exchange of information.

ii) *Mutual Assistance Group 1992*

In 1989 the Mutual Assistance Group (MAG 92) was set up to address customs issues which arose as a result of the EC's Single Market. It has liaised with the Co-ordinators' Group set up at the Rhodes European Council in December 1988 and has been working to update the 1967 Naples Convention which provides the basis of customs co-operation between European Union states. MAG 92 has promoted initiatives on training and exchange of personnel, technical aids, joint exercises and operations, drugs enforcement, anti-fraud and anti-smuggling strategies and the development of computerised information systems. The Harrogate Declaration of May 1992, formulated as a result of MAG 92's work, commits EU customs agencies to further close co-operation.

It seems likely that during 1994 MAG 92 will be brought within the ambit of the K4 Co-ordinating Committee, established as a result of the Treaty on European Union.

iii) *Matthaeus Initiative*

Co-operation between customs bodies has been furthered by the EC's Matthaeus initiative which was introduced in 1989. It has enabled the exchange of customs officers between EC countries and has led to a comprehensive series of seminars on a range of different specialist topics. In 1992, 394 officers participated in exchanges and a further 4,637 customs officers undertook language training under the Matthaeus programme.

iv) *Customs Information System*

An European Union-wide Customs Information System has also been established which will eventually cover all areas of customs co-operation. It is an extension of the Systems Customs Enforcement Network (SCENT) which enables the rapid exchange of information about imports and exports.

v)   *Macro-Level, Meso-Level and Micro-Level Co-operation*

As a result of the Single Market, and the reduction or removal of internal frontier controls, much of the work of customs officers is being redirected towards the external borders of the European Union.   Greater reliance is being placed on intelligence and profiles of high-risk traffic and on increased collaboration, including information exchange.

Customs co-operation seems to be developing in an effective and organised way and contrasts favourably with co-operation in some other fields. The Customs Co-operation Council is the single major international organisation. In Europe, MAG 92 has taken the lead in developing various meso-level initiatives and a single computerised information system is being developed. This is supported by the Matthaeus initiative on exchange of staff and expertise.

Effective and coherent co-operation is occurring at the meso level and this is enabling real micro-level collaboration on investigations and operations. The overall macro-level framework is encouraging the meso-level developments and is itself gradually being adapted to the new circumstances.

Two further points are worth noting. First, it is not clear how the developments as a result of the implementation of Title VI of the Treaty on European Union will affect co-operation between customs organisations in Europe. It is possible that by bringing MAG 92 under the K4 structure the successful customs co-operation may be adversely affected, particularly if it subsumed under police and security co-operation. Secondly, in common with so many other aspects of co-operation in law enforcement, there appears to be virtually no public or parliamentary scrutiny or accountability of these developments.

i)   Co-operation in Policing the Channel Tunnel

There are many examples of bilateral and multilateral arrangements for fostering police co-operation between neighbouring European Union states. The research project has examined three examples, details of which are reported in Chapter 5.

In the case of the Channel Tunnel, some arrangements are set out in the Anglo-French Channel Fixed Link Protocol and others are in separate Memoranda of Understanding. The relevant police and other law enforcement agencies in England, France, Belgium and the Netherlands have developed good working relations which go back many years and have been fostered in part by the Cross-Channel Intelligence Conference which has met regularly since 1969.

Kent Constabulary and officers from the *Police Nationale*, especially from the *Police de l'Air et des Frontières*, have been working closely together and have exchanged Memoranda of Understanding (MOU).   These meso-level agreements provide a framework within which operational officers can develop their micro-level co-operation.

The research has revealed a great deal of preparatory planning which is being undertaken in advance of the opening of the Channel Tunnel in May 1994. Co-operation is based on formal macro-level legal agreements, on formal written meso-level MOUs and on micro-level informal contacts and meetings. It is worth noting that under former Chief Constable Paul Condon (who has been Commissioner of the Metropolitan Police since early 1993) Kent Constabulary developed a particularly proactive approach towards co-operation with the police elsewhere in Europe. Kent is the only UK force with its own European Liaison Unit and this has achieved a great deal as a result of committed and dynamic leadership.

j)   Co-operation on Policing the Northern Ireland Border

Co-operation between the *Garda Siochana* and the Royal Ulster Constabulary (RUC) is also well developed. The forces have responsibility for policing the 300 mile common land frontier between the Republic of Ireland and the United Kingdom. Although there is a history of co-operation extending back many years, the Anglo-Irish Agreement of 1985 formulated a programme to increase it.

This macro-level framework has encouraged meso-level initiatives such as joint threat assessments, exchange of information, liaison structures, technical co-operation, joint training and operational planning. Much micro-level co-operation occurs in the form of informal day-to-day contacts, sharing of information and co-ordination of activities.

k)   Co-operation on Policing Bastia in Corsica

Bastia in Corsica is the point of entry for travellers from Italy and co-operation takes place between French and Italian police officers. Since 1988 there have been exchanges of officers at various levels and both French and Italian respondents to this study reported benefits, particularly in terms of increased understanding of the other country's procedures and in terms of improved liaison and exchange of information. The resulting personal contacts are used when information or documentation is required, although unusual requests for cross-border operations and co-operation are handled at a higher level. One example of the latter is the joint surveillance and tracking of ships and aircraft, suspected of carrying drugs, contraband or illegal immigrants.

Co-operation occurs at various levels. At the micro level personal contacts facilitate day-to-day mundane tasks while meso-level co-operation occurs at a higher level through specialist networks and, in the case of special operations, through Paris and Rome. At the macro level, the frameworks provided by the Schengen accord, and to some extent through the Trevi Group, are facilitating meso-level and micro-level activity. It is worth noting that operational officers appear often to find a way round obstacles, in order to co-operate with their colleagues from the other countries, when they consider circumstances so require.

l)   Professional Networks

i)   European Network for Policewomen

The research project has identified various other associations and networks which help to promote different forms of police co-operation in Europe. One example is the European Network for Policewomen (ENP) which was established in 1989 with the principal aim of encouraging equality of opportunity in police work. It is currently based in the Netherlands and receives funding from the Ministry for Home Affairs. The ENP publishes a regular newsletter and undertakes other activities.

ii)   Union Internationale des Syndicats de Police

The *Union Internationale des Syndicats de Police* (UISP) is some 40 years old and its objectives include working for co-operation between national police services. It is based in Germany and around half a million police officers are represented through the UISP. The Union lists among its activities action to secure trades union rights for police officers, collaborative work with EC bodies and analysis of the potential impact on police work of political developments in Europe. The organisation has been criticised by the Police Federation of England and Wales for being 'an ineffective talking shop' which is both 'posturing' and 'meddling'. Further research is needed on the work of such organisations, and also on the influence and activities of professional police organisations in different European Union countries.

m)   Secret Networks

i)   Kilowatt

There also appear to be various secret networks involving police officers and security agencies in European Union countries and further afield. Some of these have received occasional mention in television programmes or written reports. One such group was until recently apparently called 'Kilowatt', although it is now reported to have been renamed. Formed in the late 1970s to combat terrorism associated with conflicts in the Middle East, this network is believed to include the security agencies of all EU countries plus Canada, Israel, Norway, Sweden, Switzerland and the United States.

ii)   Vienna Group

The Vienna Group, sometimes known as the Vienna Club, is another shadowy organisation with the aim of combating terrorism. Formed in 1978 on the basis of a macro-level initiative by the Interior Ministers of Austria, France, Germany, Italy and Switzerland, it appears to function as a macro-level and meso-level network within which information is shared and discussions held.

The Vienna Club usually has annual meetings at which ministers are briefed on terrorist organisations and threats and other related issues, such as attacks on minority groups. The divisional heads of the security agencies also have an annual meeting at which they discuss co-operation against terrorism and related matters.

iii)   Club of Berne

This appears to perform a similar role to the Vienna Group but with a larger membership. It was formed in 1971 and apparently now includes Belgium, Denmark, France, Germany, Italy, Luxembourg, the Netherlands, Switzerland, the United Kingdom and the United States. It holds conferences of the heads of various services and ministers to discuss the suppression of terrorism and espionage.

iv)   Star Group

Another secret network is the Star Group which was founded in 1972 at the initiative of the heads of the BKA and *Länder* judicial police of Germany. Its purpose is to evaluate, harmonise and develop effective measures to combat drugs trafficking and to co-ordinate activities. It meets twice a year and its membership has grown to include Austria, Belgium, the Czech Republic, Denmark, France, Luxembourg, the Netherlands, Poland, Slovakia, Switzerland and the US Drugs Enforcement Agency as well as German federal, regional and border police and customs.

n)   Complex Patchwork of Structures and Networks

This preliminary study has revealed a surprisingly complex patchwork of institutions, agencies and structures which aim to promote different forms of police co-operation in Europe. Bilateral and multilateral agreements and groups exist alongside associations and less formal networks. Together they form a complicated, interconnecting, mesh of relatively invisible – and sometimes highly secret – channels, through which collaboration and liaison occurs between law enforcement agencies in the European Union, and sometimes with those elsewhere in Europe and beyond.

Some of the groups have been established for 20 years or more, whereas other are relatively recent. There seems to have been an increase in their number since the late 1980s, reflecting increased interest and concern about cross-border movements and international crime and also resulting from the activities and encouragement of the Trevi Group. The macro-level political commitment, and the meso-level discussions, of the Trevi Group have spawned a variety of meso-level structures to facilitate micro-level contacts between operational officers.

o)   Meso-Level and Micro-Level Collaboration Between Specialists

The most successful networks involve high-status specialist police who are engaged in combating crimes such as terrorism and drugs trafficking, which are matters of high visibility and public and political concern. The least developed structures appear to be in more general fields of policing, such as traffic management and control.

The majority of police respondents to this study stated that real, practical co-operation takes place through these more specialist and less formal arrangements. They enable officers to develop personal contacts with their colleagues from other European Union countries, to discuss matters of common professional interest and to develop greater understanding of different countries' approaches to the same problems. On the basis of the trust and confidence which these informal contacts develop, when the occasion arises officers can use a telephone or other means of communication to consult their counterpart in another country. In this way, the meso-level networks foster micro-level collaboration.

p)   Lack of Accountability and Control

These networks are, however, subject to criticism. First, many if not all of these groups and networks appear to have virtually no accountability whatsoever. They are rarely held answerable for their activities and few parliamentarians, or others such as journalists, seem even to be aware of their existence. And yet, through these structures information about individuals is being exchanged and operations against individuals may indeed be discussed and planned.

Serious human rights issues are raised if these informal networks lead to action against European citizens. The lack of accountability means that there may be no possibility of redress. Furthermore, data on individuals may be of commercial value and these groups have the potential to leak information held by the police and security agencies. It is not clear what mechanisms, if any, exist to prevent the improper use of information and intelligence. In general, there appear to be disturbingly low levels of legal, political and managerial accountability and control.

q)   **Dangers of Duplication and Confusion**

Secondly, although these less formal structures appear to be highly-differentiated there also seems to be considerable overlap between them. There is a danger of over-proliferation of meso-level initiatives which may lead to duplication and confusion.

r)   **An Unclear Picture**

A third, and related point, is that no-one seems to be aware of how many such structures exist, at what level and in which spheres. The findings reported in Chapter 5 are the result of a preliminary study of these networks and there is surely a great need for a more detailed and comprehensive investigation to map out and delineate the structures, groups, associations and agreements which appear to operate at the specialist meso-level of EU police co-operation. This needs to be done to further efficiency and effectiveness and to ensure proper scrutiny and accountability.

7.2.6   *Communications and Information Exchange*

The major structures to facilitate European police co-operation in the field of communications and the exchange of information are reviewed in Chapter 6.

The collection and application of information lies at the heart of the investigation and prosecution of criminals. The prevention of crime also depends to a large extent on the effective analysis of information. Information is knowledge whereas intelligence is understanding and effective police work depends on both. Practical police co-operation in Europe necessitates the sharing of useful information and, where appropriate, exchange of intelligence. If the perpetrators of crime in the European Union are to be thwarted information about them must be available to the police wherever the criminals try to operate or hide.

The exchange of information must also be rapid and this requires fast and reliable communications systems with compatible equipment and, where necessary, the development of new, shared, systems. Far-reaching technological advances in recent years have realised the means for large-scale storage, rapid retrieval and analysis, and reliable exchange of information. This capability has also resulted in increasing demands for proper data protection and for adequate safeguards that information held on individuals is accurate and not subject to abuse.

a)   *Control, Accountability and Protection*

i)   *Council of Europe Convention of 1981*

The major international agreement on data protection is the Council of Europe Convention for the Protection of Individuals with Regard to Automatic Processing of Personal Data which was approved in 1981. This was supplemented in 1987 by the Council's Recommendation (R(87)15) on the use of personal data in the police sector. This sets the legal framework within which automated data may be transferred between different police organisations in Europe. There is a particular problem for countries with a relatively high standard of data protection which are asked to exchange information with countries which do not have such a high standard. The rights of the data subject must also be considered: can an individual gain access to the data and, if necessary, ensure rectification of inaccuracies and erasure of unlawfully-held information? The Council of Europe Convention had been ratified by a total of 15 countries by November 1993 – that is nearly 13 years after it was approved in January 1981. European Union member states which have ratified the Convention are Belgium, Denmark, France, Germany, Ireland, Luxembourg, Netherlands, Portugal, Spain, and the United Kingdom, leaving Greece and Italy yet to do so.

ii)   *Issues of Legality*

Another issue raised by data protection is the purpose for which information may be used. This arises in the case of new common databases about which there may also be questions of accuracy and verification and supervision. For such computerised systems, which are shared by several countries, there may be issues of legality around actions requested by one or more members.

iii)   *Information and Intelligence*

A central issue is the distinction between information and intelligence. As mentioned earlier, information consists of verifiable knowledge or 'hard facts', such as the name, address, age and criminal record of a person. Intelligence, which contributes to understanding, consists of 'soft information' such as evaluations, opinions and speculation, which is much less amenable to verification. As the UK Lindop Committee on Data Protection pointed out in 1978, criminal intelligence 'may be speculative, suppositional, hearsay and unverified'.

One problem with intelligence held on computers is that were subjects to be given access to it they might be able to identify the source. Equally significantly, were suspected criminals able to see the intelligence held on them they may well be able to evade capture or conviction. Conversely, poor quality intelligence held on international (or indeed national) police databases, perhaps given to the police by someone with a grudge, could seriously jeopardise the rights and interests of a completely innocent citizen.

b)   *Exchange of Information and Interpol*

As outlined in Chapter 4, Interpol currently has 174 member countries throughout the world, of which 44 are in the European region. Over one million messages are transmitted each year through the Interpol network, of which around 80 per cent are sent by or to countries in the European region. Some 400,000 messages each year involve EU member states.

i)   *Central Function*

Interpol's communications network is based on national stations, in the NCB in each country, which are grouped into six regional stations, and the central station in Lyon, which also serves as the regional station for Europe, the Mediterranean and North America. The central function of Interpol is to pass on information and requests for action in the form of international notices, of which there are five types. Interpol also circulates information about stolen property and it keeps its own files on wanted persons, criminal cases and stolen property. In 1992 it opened some 140,000 such files.

ii)   *Unfounded Criticisms*

In the past various criticisms have been levelled at the efficiency, reliability and security of Interpol and many of these have been heard during the present inquiry. However, as previously mentioned in section 7.2.4(a) and detailed in section 6.2.3, these criticisms seem quite wrong in view of the 'metamorphosis' which has occurred under the leadership of Secretary General Raymond Kendall.

iii)   *New Technology*

Over recent years, Interpol has installed an impressive array of new computer hardware and other technology, and has developed the necessary software and overall approach to create a rapid, reliable and secure means of transmitting messages and storing and analysing data. Among these innovations are the Electronic Archive System and the Criminal Information System which is managed by the Message Research and Response Branch. The introduction of an automated office and electronic mail system and the Automated Search Facility are also contributing to the greater efficiency of Interpol.

The Automated Message Switch System (AMSS), introduced in 1987, is a principal reason for the dramatic increase in the speed at which messages are transmitted. This was superseded in 1991 by the X400 AMSS at the centre of the Interpol X400 network with a large number of different methods of communication, of which computer-to-computer transmission is the most rapid and reliable. The new five-year plan was approved by the General Assembly in 1992 and this entails modernisation of each of the regional stations and provision for the NCBs to utilise the Automated Search Facility.

iv)   *Data Protection*

Interpol's heavy investment in the most up-to-date and sophisticated telecommunications and computer technology is paying handsome dividends in terms of fast, accurate and secure exchange of information between different police forces. The organisation has also faced up to data protection issues and has established an independent supervisory board which may require Interpol to modify or delete data held on its computers. Any individual may ask the board to verify data held on the subject, but may not have direct access to the data, which is the position in France and many other countries.

A more problematic issue is the extent to which information may be transmitted from a country with high data protection standards to another with much lower standards. Presumably, in such a case the sending NCB should withhold data which may not be protected adequately, and conversely a high standard country should not receive information which comes from a state without adequate protection for data. The extent to which this occurs is doubtful.

v)   *Intelligence Capacity*

There is also a problem over Interpol's criterion that it may hold and process information which leads to the conclusion that a person 'is liable to engage in international criminal activity'. This would appear to be a category embracing a very large number of people and would often fit the Lindop Committee's definition of intelligence as 'speculative, suppositional, hearsay and unverified' data.

Interpol is, indeed, committed to the development of an intelligence capacity and has established the Analytical Criminal Intelligence Unit within its Liaison and

Criminal Intelligence Division. This Division includes other specialist groups on subjects such as organised crime, anti-terrorism, fraud and counterfeiting and drugs trafficking. The Drugs Sub-Division, for example, operates an effective intelligence reporting system. A weekly intelligence message is sent to all NCBs, highlighting major drugs seizures, drawing attention to new trends, types of drugs, routes used and *modi operandi.* Such intelligence may be very valuable to police forces, but the questions remain about how such data are controlled and whether innocent people may be wrongly implicated.

vi)   *Meso-Level Infrastructure*

The evidence presented to this study suggests that Interpol is at the forefront of inter-state communication and information exchange in Europe as it is elsewhere in the world. It provides an effective meso-level infrastructure for micro-level enquiries about particular cases, which is rapid, reliable and secure. If a police officer in Italy wished to trace a suspect in Germany, to take a hypothetical example, it would appear that the first course would be to send a message from the Italian NCB through Interpol. However, with the advent of the Schengen Information System, and its associated SIReNE infrastructure, it may be that the first course for a police officer in the Schengen countries will increasingly be to use the SIS rather than Interpol.

Interpol also appears to be developing a meso-level intelligence function, circulating data and suggestions about trends and *modi operandi.* In this it would seem to be doing more than is permitted in the Schengen Information System. Adequate safeguards will, however, be needed if this function is set to develop further. A major finding in this study is that Interpol has a proven capacity to facilitate international police communication and information exchange.

c)   ***The Schengen Group and Information Exchange***

The most ambitious attempt to establish cross-border information exchange in Europe is the Schengen Information System (SIS) and its accompanying Supplementary Information Request at the National Entry system (SIReNE). Of the nine signatories to the Schengen Convention, it appears that only Belgium, France, Germany, Luxembourg, Netherlands, and Spain will be participants in the SIS at the outset on 1st February 1994, with Portugal joining as soon as practicable in 1994. It is not clear when Greece and Italy will be in a position to join others.

i)   *Common Database*

The Schengen Information System (SIS) consists of a central computer (CSIS) in Strasbourg which is linked to a national computer (NSIS) in each country. As soon as entries are put into the national databanks the CSIS copies them into each of the other countries' NSIS information stores. The Schengen Information System is thus a unique common database shared by the participating countries, each of which may add its own new entries. The CSIS can handle one new entry every second and will update all the NSIS databanks within a maximum of five minutes. The maximum capacity of the system at present is 8 million personal records and 7 million records on objects.

ii)   *Data to be Included*

The Schengen Information System is a critical compensatory measure for the removal of internal frontier checks and as such is intended to facilitate external border controls and increase police co-operation in apprehending wanted people. The SIS will store data on: persons wanted for arrest for extradition; people to be expelled or deported; missing persons; witnesses or suspects summoned before a court; suspects who should be placed under covert surveillance or checked; and objects subject to seizure or wanted as evidence.

The categories of data which may be entered are limited by Article 94 of the Schengen Convention. They are: real and assumed names; distinguishing marks; date and place of birth; sex; nationality; whether the person is armed or violent; reason for the entry; and action to be taken. This appears to be basic information and so the SIS will not apparently include intelligence.

iii)   *Supplementary Information Request at the National Entry (SIReNE)*

In view of the limited factual information on the SIS it became clear that the participating countries' police forces would require another common communication system in order to exchange further information in answer to specific queries. For this reason the Supplementary Information Request at the National Entry (SIReNE) infrastructures has been set up. It is a sophisticated electronic mail system on which X400 messages are exchanged on standardised forms. It is intended that fingerprints and photographs will also be sent on the network.

The original purpose of the SIReNE was to enable further information to be sent from one Schengen country to another about extradition. Once a suspect has been detained, as the result of an entry on the SIS, in a number of European countries he or she can only be held for a relatively short period before extradition proceedings must be started or the suspect must be released. The SIReNE was thus needed so that the police in the country in which the person has been detained can notify the police in the country in which he or she is wanted and they can then send the necessary details for extradition proceedings to begin.

Subsequently, the purpose of the SIReNE has been extended to embrace ten functions which will enable the SIS to operate more smoothly. The communications system will also probably provide the infrastructure for the Visa Inquiry System in an Open-Border Network (VISION) which is expected to become operational during 1994.

A SIReNE office has been set up in each of the six countries which are the initial participants and it is similar to the National Central Bureau (NCB) of Interpol in each country. It is staffed at all times, with translation facilities and with access to the relevant authorities.

iv)   *Data Protection*

The details of the Schengen Convention are discussed in Chapter 4 and Chapter 6. The Convention sets out relatively high data protection standards in accordance with the Council of Europe Convention of 1981 and the September 1987 Council of Europe Recommendation on data held by the police. 'Sensitive data', such as that on race, political opinions, religious beliefs, health and sexual orientation, must not be recorded and every tenth transmission must be monitored to ensure the rules are being observed.

Any person has the right to see their entry to have it corrected or erased, although this may be refused if it would jeopardise the task specified in the entry (for example, surveillance). There is a purpose limitation placed on the use of the information and there are time limits set on retaining the data. Perhaps most importantly, an element of independent control has been established to monitor compliance.

v)   *Macro-Level and Meso-Level Structures*

The Schengen Information System and the SIReNE together constitute the most ambitious attempt yet to create a common European police information network. At the inaugural meeting of the Schengen Executive Committee on 18th October 1993 in Paris it was announced that the system would be phased in during December 1993 and January 1994, to be fully operational on 1st February 1994 for the six countries which are involved in the first phase. Portugal is expected to join quite soon after February. There are, of course, bound to be some initial teething problems but Schengen officials appear confident that the system will soon settle down and become an indispensable tool for the police in a frontier-free Europe.

As pointed out previously in section 7.2.4(b), the Schengen Group has established an effective macro-level legal and constitutional framework within which practical meso-level structures are being constructed. For the first time, police co-operation between different European countries is being embedded in a well-formulated legal and constitutional framework. The political commitment and drive is most clearly represented in the Schengen Information System and the SIReNE which is enabling the complete removal of frontier checks between Belgium, France, Germany, Luxembourg, the Netherlands and Spain, soon to include Portugal. Micro-level communications and exchange of information between these countries' police organisations seem set to become a daily – perhaps an hourly – occurrence within the meso-level infrastructure.

vi)   *Lack of Judicial and Parliamentary Oversight*

There are, however, continuing criticisms and anxieties about the forms of accountability and control of this impressive new structure. The central feature of these concerns is that there is no independent judicial or parliamentary review of the Schengen Information System or the SIReNE, or indeed of other aspects of the implementation of the Schengen Convention. It is, of course, possible for parliamentary scrutiny to take place through the national parliaments and for court cases to be brought in individual countries. However, there are lingering doubts whether this would prove effective. One possibility, which may be pursued, is to give the European Court of Justice, or some newly-established court, powers to hear cases and conduct judicial review. This, however, would require agreement to the necessary protocols by the contracting states.

vii)   *Future Growth of the Schengen Group*

Finally, it must be noted that only six countries are likely to be initially involved in the full implementation of the Schengen Convention. Although this is set to become seven by early to mid-1994, it is not clear when Greece and Italy will be ready to join the others. Denmark, Ireland and the United Kingdom are obstinately refusing to become involved, although agreement on the Convention on External Borders, and action in the European Court of Justice under Article 8A of the EC Treaty, could propel these countries into the Schengen Group. This, however, is unlikely to happen for some time and a more likely development is that some of the EFTA countries will overtake them by joining the Schengen Group during the next few years, after their accession to the European Union.

d)   Exchange of Information and the Trevi Group

Since its inception in 1975, the remit of the Trevi Group has gradually widened so that by 1993 it included an array of different dimensions of law enforcement co-operation between European Union countries. At least partly at its instigation, several specialist communications networks have grown up, in fields such as anti-terrorism, anti-drugs trafficking and police control of football hooliganism. These are mentioned above in section 7.2.5 and outlined in Chapter 5.

i)   *Trevi Working Groups*

Each of the Trevi working groups has promoted the exchange of information between specialist police in Europe. Trevi Working Group I, for example, remains one of the lead agencies in the fight against terrorism. Trevi Working Group II has organised seminars and circulated information on scientific and technical matters and on road traffic policing, as well as on public disorder and football crowds. It is currently promoting the exchange of information on police training. In addition to its work on drugs trafficking, Trevi Working Group III has encouraged information exchange in specialist fields such as armed robbery, thefts of works of art, stolen vehicles and the protection of witnesses.

ii)   *European Drugs Unit/Europol*

The recent work of the *Ad Hoc* Group on Europol is of particular importance. The decision to establish the European Drugs Unit/Europol can be traced back to the European Council meeting in Luxembourg on 28–29th June 1991. The proposal was given the seal of approval by its mention in Title VI of the Treaty on European Union and in the annexed Declaration on Police Co-operation. It was intended that the EDU would be functioning by the spring of 1993 but indecision over a permanent site for the Unit caused delay throughout the summer. A decision was finally taken at the European Council meeting in Brussels on 29th October 1993 when it was agreed to locate the EDU/Europol in The Hague.

The task of the EDU will be to facilitate the exchange of information, including intelligence, about drugs trafficking and money laundering. The second phase is intended to be the establishment of Europol on which progress is reported to be slow. The *Ad Hoc* Group is meeting regularly but is understood to be having some difficulties in drafting the necessary Convention, which will set out the parameters within which Europol will function, including data protection regulations.

iii)   *Difficulties in Agreeing Data Protection*

Given that the Schengen Group has agreed a comprehensive set of data protection stipulations for the SIS it is not readily clear why the EDU/Europol Group should be making such relatively slow progress. Of course, this group includes all twelve European Union countries and apparently has a regular membership of around 60 which may be too large to function effectively.

More importantly, the EDU/Europol will include intelligence as well as information and it is undoubtedly more difficult to agree watertight regulations for soft data than for relatively simple hard facts, such as those which are held on the Schengen Information System. Taking the Lindop Committee definition that criminal intelligence 'may be speculative, suppositional, hearsay and unverified' it is clear that such data (if indeed they are data) are difficult to categorise within firm guidelines. The accuracy of intelligence must inevitably be open to question and it may not be possible to allow data subjects access to it to demand correction. The interests of individuals may well be jeopardised in such circumstances. That said, national police and security agencies hold intelligence on computers and so, it seems, does Interpol.

iv)   *European Information System*

Another dimension of the field of communications and information exchange is the proposed European Information System (EIS). The *Programme of Action*, agreed at the Trevi ministerial meeting in Dublin in June 1990, stated that the countries would study the development of a common information system, paying due regard to data protection. The purposes of the proposed European Information System seem in some respects similar to those of the Schengen Information System, that is to hold data on people who should not be admitted to the European Union area, or who should be arrested if they are found in a member country.

The project is closely linked to the as yet unsigned Convention on External Borders as the creation of the European Information System has been seen as an important compensatory measure to enable the removal of the internal frontiers and the strengthening of the 'hard, outer shell' at the external borders. The *Ad Hoc* Group on Immigration has been particularly involved in the discussions about the EIS, as has the Co-ordinators' Group of senior officials, which is set to become the K4 Co-ordinating Committee under Title VI of the Maastricht Treaty.

By November 1993 it appeared that the proposed functions of the European Information System were growing to embrace the various matters of common interest set out in Title VI of the Treaty on European Union. Negotiations were understood to be taking place over a convention to establish the EIS which is expected to be ready for approval during 1994. The extent to which the proposed EIS will link to the even more vague European Nervous System (ENS) is unclear. The ENS, first mentioned in 1989 by Commissioner Pandolfi, is apparently intended to cover customs, insurance, tax and medical records but what, if any, progress has occurred recently is not known. In any event, as reported in Chapter 5 (section 5.8) a European-wide customs information system, known as SID, came into operation in October 1992.

v)   *Meso-Level Activities*

At the top of the Trevi structure, the meetings of ministers have provided macro-level political impetus which has led to meso-level activity. Much of this has been of a specialist nature in quite highly-focused and discrete areas of policing. The two major infrastructure projects at the meso-level which are associated with the Trevi Group – the EDU/Europol and the European Information System – have made some progress but compared to the rapid developments of the Schengen Group the overall pace seems rather tardy. By comparison with Schengen and Interpol, Trevi appears to have made the least impact on police communications and information exchange in Europe.

vi)   *K4 Co-ordinating Committee*

This may be set to change with the implementation of the Maastricht Treaty from 1st November 1993. The significance of Title VI of the Treaty on European Union is discussed in section 4.4 of Chapter 4 and above in section 7.2.5(d). The K4 Co-ordinating Committee and its associated structure will clearly play a key role in how matters develop. If the Co-ordinators' Group, the Trevi structure, and related bodies such as MAG 92, in their new embodiment are galvanised into action there could be rapid developments during 1994.

vii)   *Possible Future Developments*

It seems evident that the Schengen Information System and the SIReNE provide a model for the wider European Information System. There would appear to be no sensible reasons why the SIS should not grow to become the EIS – although this does not necessarily mean it will happen.

The development of the EDU/Europol is more problematic because of the difficulties of devising satisfactory data protection safeguards for intelligence data. However, were there to be sufficient political drive the problems would doubtless be overcome, although almost certainly not to the satisfaction of those concerned with the protection of individual human rights and civil liberties.

7.3   Major Proposals

At the end of each chapter the main findings, and proposals arising from them, are summarised. For ease of reference these are shown in Appendices I and II.

Some of the proposals are aimed at particular organisations while others make more general suggestions, for example about further studies which need to be conducted. Indeed, one of the main overall findings is the worrying lack of knowledge about central issues in crime, migration, and policing in the European Union. Many of the proposals are for more research to establish a firmer basis upon which to build.

7.3.1   *European Centre for Research into Crime*

a)   Widespread Ignorance

The proposals at the end of Chapter 2 reflect the concern that much of the contemporary discussion, about the effects of abolishing internal border controls, the potential for large-scale immigration and the need for improved police co-operation, is founded on the shifting sands of ignorance, half-truth and prejudice. In such circumstances, the scaremongers and fear-merchants can practise their rhetoric, uninhibited by facts. It is no wonder that moral panics arise about 'foreigners', 'terrorists' and other threatening foes.

b)   Greater Knowledge and Understanding

Discussion needs to be grounded on a firmer foundation as a result of detailed research into different sorts of crime in Europe. Crime *is* a growing problem for the people of Europe, and much of it could profitably be tackled at a pan-European level, but first greater knowledge and understanding is needed. New crimes, such as environmental offences, also need investigation. For these reasons, a major proposal of this study is that a European Centre for Research into Crime should be established. This could be federal in nature, with different parts of the Centre located in different European Union states. Such a Centre would enable the governments and police of Europe to draw on a great array of knowledge and understanding amongst experts in various institutions.

7.3.2   *Comparative Study of Police Forces in the European Union*

a)   Lack of Clarity and Knowledge

This investigation has found a widespread lack of comparative knowledge of the policing structures and organisations in different European Union countries. Without a clear outline and account of the existing police forces, and their responsibilities and ways of operating, attempts to promote increased cross-national co-operation are likely to be haphazard and ill-conceived. There would appear to be a very strong case for a detailed comparative study of policing in the different countries of the European Union.

b)   Diversity and Variation

The key word to characterise policing in Europe is diversity. There are variations in responsibilities and powers, and in structures and methods of operation. There are differences in recruitment and training, and in conditions of service. The legal and judicial systems are different and so, too, are the traditions and cultures within which policing takes place. The arrangements for accountability, and supervision and monitoring, vary and so do relations with local government and community structures. There are also noticeable differences in the use of civilians in police forces and in the development of specialist units and groups.

There is thus a need for a comprehensive comparative study of the police and other law enforcement organisations with responsibilities in the countries of the European Union. Such a study would provide the basis for a more coherent and efficient approach to cross-national police co-operation structures and procedures.

7.3.3   *Investigation into Police Networks and Associations in Europe*

a)   Complex and Varied Patchwork

There is also a distinct lack of knowledge and understanding about the various specialist groups and networks and associations which exist to promote different kinds of co-operation. Chapter 5 examines some of these, but it is clear that there are others in different specialist fields of policing which have yet to be identified.

There is a complex patchwork of these networks and groups, with some overlapping activities and membership. Some have a narrow remit, others take a broader approach; some are relatively inactive, whereas others appear to have a range of activities; the membership of some is drawn from only a few EU countries, while others are genuinely pan-European. In some specialist fields there seem to be only a few groups, in others there appear to be more. Some networks involve quite high-ranking police, while others draw their membership from a lower level.

b)   Uncharted Territory

At present this is uncharted territory. No one seems to know how many such groups there are or what they achieve. This study has formed the view that there is considerable duplication and confusion. A detailed investigation to provide an account of these European police networks and groups would clear the way for a more efficient and coherent approach.

7.3.4 *European Fraud Squad*

a) Extent of Fraud

One of the major crime problems highlighted in Chapter 2 is fraud, and yet it does not seem to have received the attention it merits. The removal of internal frontier checks and the development of the Single Market and the European Union may lead to an increase in certain types of fraud. The evidence that is available shows that the extent of fraud is already enormous but much of it is relatively invisible, publicly unacknowledged and often highly complex.

For a number of reasons, fraud is notoriously difficult to police. The technological developments that have made business fraud so much simpler have also made its investigation much harder. Attempts have been made to deal with some dimensions of the problem under the 1990 Council of Europe Convention on Laundering, Search, Seizure and Confiscation of the Proceeds from Crime.

There is also evidence of a growing problem with credit-card and cheque-book fraud, which seems to be increasingly organised by criminal gangs. Defrauding the EC itself is also a major problem.

b) Bringing Expertise Together

There are now strong arguments in favour of creating a European Fraud Squad (EFS). Member states already have local or regional fraud squads and, increasingly, more centralised units, in addition to the support provided by the EC's own anti-fraud unit UCLAF. It would be a logical progression to use these developments as the basis for a European-wide agency.

A European Fraud Squad would have to meet three criteria. First, it would require staffing by police and customs officers, accountants, lawyers and information technology (IT) specialists. They would need to act in partnership. No single group could succeed on its own. The EFS would need to operate from a central office. The EC's own fraud unit might serve as a starting point.

Secondly, the EFS would need an operational arm. This is contentious. It is a qualitative leap from an 'intelligence' unit to an 'operational' unit. Without genuine powers of investigation, however, it would be an empty vessel. As one police officer put it bluntly: 'It is no good chasing villains if you can't nick them'.

Thirdly, a proper career structure would need to be built-in for both officers and non-police personnel, in order to attract high-quality staff.

c) Successful International Co-operation

The European Fraud Squad proposal merits serious and overdue consideration. The proposal for a European Fraud Squad may succeed because it is in each individual country's interests and it is non-threatening. Commercial crime is a specialist field where successful international co-operation between separate police forces may be more forthcoming than in other areas.

The European Fraud Squad would have to be accountable to a committee of officials drawn from each European Union country and should make annual reports to the European Parliament. How such a force could be established with executive, operational functions should be investigated. Protocols or indeed a treaty would be necessary, because although such action could be taken within the European Community's existing remit in the field of financial services, the EC has no criminal jurisdiction. There are many such speculative questions which cannot be answered at this stage, and further research and consultation would be necessary. The research team do however emphasise this proposal as a central conclusion to this Report.

7.3.5   *European Police University*

a)   Teaching, Training and Research

The final proposal as a result of this research is for the establishment of a European Police University. There are two major reasons for this suggestion. One is the need to undertake teaching and training for police, customs and other law enforcement officers who are charged with preventing crime, protecting safety and security and catching offenders in the new Europe. The other reason is to conduct appropriate research into detailed areas, some of which are identified in this Report.

b)   History of Similar Recommendations

The idea of a research institute, or network of such institutes, devoted to the study of European policing issues has been advocated by various authorities.

For example, Piet van Reenen, former Director of the Netherlands Police Academy, pointed to gaps in the research field (van Reenen, undated). He noted that there was no centre where the problems and possibilities of policing Europe could be studied. Although some individual police training centres do offer training on European and international policing issues, this is usually undertaken in addition to their primary training responsibilities, which are domestically-oriented.

Similarly, Sir Roger Birch, former Chief Constable of Sussex, England, called for a European Centre for Police Studies or a 'Police Council for Europe'. He noted that this would provide a venue where expertise could be shared and ideas developed by practitioners and researchers in Europe. Four years later the need for such an institution has increased, especially in the light of the provisions for police co-operation in the Treaty on European Union and the developments within the Schengen Group, and yet no progress has been made.

This research project has received various evidence and comments in favour of the idea of a European Police University.

c)   Roles and Functions

Realistically, one single institute would not be capable of co-ordinating all the training, research and information needed on police co-operation in Europe. A number of designated centres throughout Europe would be needed, and together they would constitute the federal European Police University.

However, it would be important for each college in the University to be principally devoted to teaching and research in *European* policing matters. The work could also embrace wider international policing questions, but it would not be satisfactory to graft the European Police University (EPU) on to existing national bodies, for almost certainly the national issues would take priority at the expense of the European dimension.

Teaching and training would be a central function of the EPU. The topics to be covered might include general overviews and analyses for police managers and more detailed work in particular fields for specialists. The courses could include reasonably short periods of a few weeks on defined topics, such as drugs trafficking, stolen vehicles and counterfeiting, and longer courses, perhaps leading to an appropriate qualification, for policy makers and managers who need to know about the broader field of policing issues.

The institution would also need to have a strong research orientation. The research team has been critical at times of the lack of available research findings, or lack of research at all, into certain aspects of policing in Europe. The European Police University would need to have the resources available to conduct detailed research.

The University would also need to have an active input from police officers themselves. Knowledge needs to be shared, and a major role of the institution would be the dissemination of practical police information. This would be by means such as personal contact, conferences and seminars and publications.

d)　　Resources and Funding

The proposed European Police University would obviously need adequate funding to enable it to undertake the necessary teaching, training and research. One arrangement could be the mechanism which will be used to finance the European Drugs Unit/Europol or the sliding scale of contributions by which Interpol is funded. Funding could also come from the budget of the European Community, as provided for in Article K.8(2) of Title VI of the Treaty on European Union. The costs of training courses, conferences and seminars would be met by payments from individual countries and organisations, although it would be essential that potential participants were not deterred because of cost.

The EPU would draw on a range of teaching and research resources. Police and customs officers themselves would be involved as would experts from specialist organisations and groups and other universities and research centres. The proposed European Police University would work closely with the European Centre for Research into Crime proposed in section 7.3(a) above.

7.4　　Towards The Future

7.4.1　　*European Union*

The countries of the European Union are becoming more closely bound together by economic, social and political ties. The Single European Act, which was signed in

February 1986, explicitly provided for greater economic cohesion and for the implementation of the Cockfield Single Market provisions. The goal of European Union was reaffirmed in the Treaty on European Union, which was signed by all the member states on 7th February 1992. After overcoming various hurdles, the Treaty was at last ratified by all the countries and the European Union was finally born on 1st November 1993.

The opening words of the Preamble to the new Treaty Establishing the European Community reiterate that the 12 states are 'determined to lay the foundations of an ever closer union among the peoples of Europe'. Different political leaders of European countries appear to have rather different conceptions of what European Union entails, but all of them seem to accept that at least it includes greater economic union and consequent economic progress and developments. Indeed, the projected potential scale of such progress is enormous. In its publication *Europe Without Frontiers* (1989, p.13), the Commission estimated that the creation of an open market in Europe would save annual costs of some ecu 24 billion and produce up to 5 million new jobs. Furthermore, the economies of scale in manufacturing and marketing would add at least 2 per cent to the total gross product of the EC.

The Treaty on European Union states at the outset that the 12 member states are 'resolved to mark a new stage in the process of European integration undertaken with the establishment of the European Communities'. This new stage is the creation of a European Union founded on the European Communities. Its objectives are to promote economic and social progress and cohesion, to implement a common foreign and security policy, to introduce citizenship of the Union, and to develop close co-operation on justice and home affairs.

7.4.2   *Proliferation of Arrangements for Police Co-operation*

a)   Process of Adaptation

Economic change inevitably leads to social and political change. Some of these developments may be planned and so, for example, the Maastricht Treaty includes provisions on citizenship, social policy, education, health, consumer protection and the environment. The Treaty Establishing the European Community also amends the powers and responsibilities of institutions such as the European Parliament and establishes new bodies such as the Committee of the Regions.

Often, however, political and institutional developments as a consequence of economic change tend to be piecemeal and incremental. Organisations, structures and procedures evolve gradually step-by-step to cope with the new circumstances. There is to some extent an inevitability about such a process of adaptation but it is, by its very nature, *ad hoc* and may on occasions be too slow or incoherent to deal satisfactorily with undesirable or unforeseen social or political problems which arise as a consequence of economic change.

b)   Diversity and Complexity

One field in which there is just such a danger of incoherent and haphazard developments in the new European Union is that of law enforcement and justice. This study has revealed some of the extent of the diversity and complexity of policing arrangements within and between the countries of Europe. There is a perplexing array of different police and other law enforcement organisations; a complex, interconnected, lattice of groups, associations and networks which exist to promote cross-national co-operation; and a small number of major structures to facilitate various forms of collaboration between police organisations in Europe.

c)   Incremental and Incoherent Developments

The overall picture is hazy and confusing – and it would appear that the great majority of European police officers, let alone the public, are unclear and confused. There is also evidence of incremental and unplanned developments, inconsistency in approaches and yet duplication of some functions.   Government and police initiatives in this field have in some respects been haphazard and disjointed, often characterised by short-term expediency rather than by longer-term strategy and planning. The exceptions would appear to be the Schengen initiative and, of course, Interpol, and some of the specialist police and customs networks.

The development of the Trevi Group's structure and activities seems to illustrate the piecemeal, rather haphazard, approach. From its inception, as a forum for co-operation between states on anti-terrorism, it has grown to embrace a wide range of law enforcement concerns, but this growth appears to have been disjointed with new responsibilities being grafted on as short-term reactions to pressing problems. The number of *ad hoc* working parties is testimony to this approach. More recently, however, there has been evidence that the Trevi Group is adopting a more proactive and coherent mode and the new arrangements under Title VI of the Treaty on European Union, with the establishment of the K4 Co-ordinating Committee and its subsidiary structure, are likely to lead to a more effective and clear division of responsibilities.

d)   Duplication of Activities and Information Systems

However, there will continue to be duplication in some respects between the Trevi/ K4 Group's activities and those of the Schengen Group and Interpol. This is most apparent in the field of communications and information exchange. For example, the proposals for a European Information System (EIS) would appear largely to replicate the Schengen Information System (SIS), while the proposed European Drugs Unit would seem to some extent to duplicate the work of the Drugs Sub-Division of Interpol's Liaison and Criminal Intelligence Division. It is worth noting that Interpol holds the most complete database on international drugs traffickers in the world.

There is also apparent duplication between the activities of these information and intelligence systems and those of other specialist groups and networks. For example, in the field of drugs trafficking as well as Interpol's work and that of Trevi and Schengen there are the specialist Drugs Intelligence Network, the *Comité Européen pour la Lutte Anti Drogue* (CELAD) set up in 1990, the older Pompidou Group, and the secretive Star Group, and the Dublin Group which co-ordinates policing assistance to drug-producing countries.

The customs service is also active in this field with co-operation through the Customs Co-operation Council and the Mutual Assistance Group 1992. Of particular importance is the SID (*Système d'Information Douanière*) which is the EC's customs information system. This came into operation in October 1992 and provides a European Union-wide exchange of intelligence information on all areas of customs co-operation, including drugs. There must be the prospect of duplication in some respects between the proposed European Drugs Unit and the SID.

7.4.3   *Effects of Professionalisation of Policing*

a)   Common Interests

The field of police and customs activity against drugs trafficking illustrates the extent of the proliferation of meso-level groups and structures. One reason is that this is a high-profile specialist area of law enforcement activity and the findings from this research project show that it is the specialist, elite, branches of police operations which are the most likely to establish effective co-operative networks. Officers and civil servants involved in such work tend to have the resources to invest in practical arrangements for liaison and collaboration and share a common interest, and often a common discourse, with their counterparts in other European countries. They are also likely to receive support for their work from politicians and opinion leaders in the media.

b)   Specialisation in Law Enforcement

An important dimension of the impetus behind meso-level and macro-level initiatives is the increasing emphasis on expertise in certain branches of European law enforcement. This is linked with the process of professionalisation of policing which has been evident in a number of European countries. Characteristics of a profession include autonomy and self-regulation and the development of specialised, technical knowledge. Each vocation has its own skills, behavioural codes and ethics and usually controls entry and training. A key characteristic of professionalisation is specialisation. All these aspects are evident in contemporary European policing, notably the increased number of specialised squads and units devoted to particular areas of law enforcement. These experts tend to liaise closely with their counterparts in other countries and together promote their own interests through specialist groups and networks.

c)   Centralisation of Specialist Functions

The professionalism of policing, and the concomitant growth in specialist units, thus helps to explain the proliferation of networks and groups. A counterbalancing tendency is the centralisation of policing functions in organisations such as the *Bundeskriminalamt* (BKA) in Germany, the *Centrale Recherche Informatiedienst* (CRI) in the Netherlands, and the UK's National Criminal Intelligence Service (NCIS). These are also specialist branches, usually made up of several even more specialist groups, but they tend to operate on a wider front and hence are more likely to promote macro-level international co-operation, such as that through Interpol or Trevi, than highly-specialist meso-level networks. These expert groups also tend to have good contacts at a senior level in their country's ministry of the interior, or equivalent, and so are able to promote their interests through political and administrative channels.

7.4.4   *Need for Increased Police Co-operation in the EU*

The power and influence of elite, specialist, police units could arguably mean that the development of certain macro-level and particularly meso-level structures was in their interests but not necessarily in the interests of the public or indeed of the state. This prompts the question why, and in what respects, co-operation between different law enforcement agencies is really required as a result of the reduction or abolition of internal border controls within the European Union.

a)   State Security and Public Order

The principal concerns of the governments of Europe are with threats to national security and social and political stability. These are problems which most worry the political, social and economic elites. More 'ordinary' crimes against property are problems to be dealt with, but state security and public order are the principal objectives to be achieved. Terrorism is the most obvious threat and it is no surprise that there is a long history of co-operation to combat terrorists between security and police agencies in different European countries. Indeed, the Trevi Group was founded for this reason. Drugs trafficking, too, is seen as a major threat, principally against social stability and also because of the organised crime and violence associated with it.

However, such evidence as there is suggests that the removal of internal borders in Europe is unlikely to lead to any great increase in either terrorism or drugs trafficking. The critical factor in the case of the latter will be the level of demand for drugs. And yet, the rhetoric from politicians and some police officers has tended to concentrate on these threats as the reason either for retaining border controls or for increasing police co-operation and capabilities. The obvious point that, unfortunately, both terrorism and drugs trafficking were occurring long before the Single European Act or European Union were agreed goes largely unremarked.

b)   Property Crimes

This study has concluded that the free movement of people and goods within the European Union may result in some increase in crimes such as thefts, burglaries and robberies committed by 'mobile offenders', who travel from one area to another, and this possibility should be monitored. There may also be a rise in crime involving the theft of high-value property, such as motor vehicles and construction plant and precious works of art and antiques, and its transportation to other EU countries or out of the European Union territory altogether.

If such predictions are correct, there would seem to be good arguments for the development of appropriate pan-European police liaison arrangements. Some moves have been made in this direction but there is much more that could be done, and it is noticeable that rather less progress seems to have been made in these areas than in those which are seen as threats to state security or social stability.

c)   The Growing Problem of Fraud

The same point seems to be true in the case of police co-operation against fraud. There is, apparently, some Trevi Group interest in this field and there is evidence of some European customs co-operation against fraud, but the absence of well-developed networks and structures seems remarkable. Many police officers interviewed for this study have suggested that cross-national fraud of various kinds is likely to be a growing problem in a frontier-free Europe. The estimated scale of fraud is enormous, dwarfing other crimes, and there is potential for it to increase further.

In addition to international business crime, deception associated with commodity investment and 'long-firm' fraudulent ordering of materials, there is also the growing problem of organised credit-card and cheque-book fraud. A recent estimate of world-wide credit-card fraud put its value at £1.25 billion per year. Consumer fraud is also reported to be a growing problem. This varies from goods sold by mail-order catalogues to time-share properties purchased from companies in another EU state. In September 1993, the Director of the EC's Consumer Policy Service, Peter Prendergast, drew attention to this growing area of fraud and called for concerted action to tackle it.

Fraud against the European Community itself is also a serious problem which UCLAF (*Unite pour la Co-ordination de la Lutte Anti-Fraud*) tackles with some limited success. Smuggling of contraband and the evasion of tax is also a serious problem for the countries of the European Union.

d)   Lack of Action Against Fraud

Much of the fraud in Europe is relatively invisible, publicly unacknowledged and often difficult to understand. Unlike terrorism and drugs trafficking, this is not a subject on which many politicians make impassioned speeches and yet the problems of fraud within Europe seem extensive and likely to grow. As outlined earlier in section 7.3.4, this study has come to the view that there are strong arguments in favour of the creation of a European Fraud Squad, staffed by experts from law and accountancy as well as the police, and with operational powers of investigation and surveillance.

Fraud is a field of crime where enhanced means of cross-national police co-operation are required but, at present, it does not seem to be a matter of great concern to the national governments, as it is not perceived to be a major threat to national security or social stability. Instead, political attention has increasingly focused in immigration as a major problem for the new Europe.

7.4.5   *Fears About Immigration*

Immigration appears to have displaced terrorism and drugs trafficking as the perceived principal threat faced by the countries of the European Union, although it is often linked to terrorism, drugs importation and other crimes in political and media discussion. During the last few years, member states have devoted considerable – some might say – disproportionate attention and energy to how to limit immigration from developing countries. The Trevi Group, and associated bodies such as the *Ad Hoc* Group on Immigration and the Schengen Group, have considered various dimensions of immigration, such as visas, asylum, refugees and clandestine immigration. Much of the debate about increased police co-operation now seems implicitly, and sometimes explicitly, concerned with immigration control rather than action to combat crime within the European Union.

a)   Spectre of Right-Wing Extremism

The reasons appear to be a perception that immigration poses a threat to social stability and an associated fear of the political consequences of immigration. The issue is often linked to rises in crime, and in some cases to urban disorder, and around it lurks the spectre of right-wing political extremism. Unfortunately, there is also evidence of growing numbers of racially-motivated attacks in European countries, such as those by neo-Nazis on refugee hostels and Turkish people in

Germany, in 1992 and 1993, and on north Africans in France in the same period. In August 1993 there were reports of attacks on Sikhs in Belgium and on African people in Italy. In total, in the EU member states there were reportedly 54 racist murders in 1992.

b)   **The 'Ring of Steel'**

The response of European governments has been to tighten laws on asylum and refugees, to make visas more difficult to obtain and to try to identify and expel clandestine immigrants. Key compensatory measures for the removal of internal frontiers checks have been the introduction of the Schengen Information System and a commitment to strengthen the 'ring of steel' at the external borders. However, speaking in July 1993, Stefan Teloeken, of the United Nations High Commissioner for Refugees office in Bonn, said: 'From now on the issues will be illegal immigration. Our experience is that if people want to get in badly enough, very little can stop them from doing so.'

c)   **Rights of Refugees**

Refugees are seeking to escape from social turmoil and political threats. Often their very lives, and those of their families, are in danger. It is surely essential that such people are not turned away by the European Union countries and that their rights to protection from persecution in the 1948 Universal Declaration of Human Rights are honoured. The 1951 Geneva Convention relating to the Status of Refugees, and its 1967 Protocol, lays down that refugees should not be penalised for arriving in another country if their lives or freedom are at risk. Both the Schengen Convention and the 1990 Dublin Convention acknowledge these rights.

d)   **Illegal Immigrants**

Illegal immigrants are usually seeking to gain entry to European Union countries for economic reasons. Attempts to stop them at the external borders can only ever be partially successful as the so-called 'hard outer shell', with thousands of miles of coastline and a long land border, is inevitably permeable. The only mid-term answer would appear to be to tackle the reasons why people wish to migrate to the EU. This would necessitate aid to, and investment in, the economies of those countries from which the migration is taking place. The International Labour Organisation is seeking to persuade EU countries to invest in Algeria, Morocco and Tunisia. It is estimated that annual remittances from migrants to their home countries amount to ecu 56 billion, which is more than all foreign aid added together.

e)   **Confronting Xenophobia and Racism**

During the last few years, the language of many politicians has become more uncompromising towards asylum seekers and immigrants, doubtless reflecting the increased political salience of the issues and the rise of political extremism. However, such an approach and the portrayal of immigrants as the cause of various social problems may, in fact, encourage the proponents of extremism and racial hatred by giving them a spurious legitimacy. Strong and courageous leadership is required to confront xenophobia and racism.

7.4.6   *Legitimacy and Police Co-operation*

a)   Policing and Minority Groups

The increased emphasis on immigration, as a principal reason for co-operation between European Union states in the field of policing and home affairs, raises worrying questions about the protection of minority rights and about the role which the police may be expected to adopt. It is not clear that there are adequate procedures or institutions to ensure that the rights of refugees, asylum seekers or clandestine immigrants will be properly safeguarded. It also seems probable that the police, and other law enforcement agencies which are involved, will be expected to identify illegal entrants and detain them for possible deportation. How will this be carried out? Will police officers be instructed to conduct 'passport raids' on people's homes or at their place of work; will there be an increase in random identity checks of people 'who look foreign'?

b)   Proper Conduct and Effective Performance

A fundamental issue which lies behind such questions is that of police legitimacy – and, indeed, the legitimacy of the wider system. Legitimacy is essentially the quality of being lawful and right. A claim that something is legitimate rests upon the assertion that it is proper according to accepted rules and principles. Dahrendorf (1980, p.397) has suggested that behaviour by the state or its agents is legitimate 'if what it does is right both in the sense of complying with certain fundamental principles, and in that of being in line with prevailing cultural values'. The behaviour and actions of the police are important sources of legitimacy in two senses: in terms of proper conduct and in terms of effective performance, according to prevailing values and expectations.

Some people in important governmental positions in European Union states appear to underestimate the importance of legitimacy for political stability and effective governance. It is from perceptions of legitimacy that much voluntary compliance arises, and from it comes public consent, identity and allegiance. Lowenthal (1984) pointed out its significance in managing social and political change and suggested that key bases for legitimacy are effectiveness of the procedures, a value consensus and the confidence of the governed. Police legitimacy thus requires proper behaviour, not only according to the law but also in line with principles and values of justice.

c)   Consensus and Legitimacy

The legitimacy of co-operative efforts within the European Union to combat terrorism and drugs-trafficking is unlikely to be seriously questioned: these are widely perceived to be criminal activities against which different police forces should co-operate. The same will be true of collaboration against fraud and crime involving stolen property. However, there is likely to be much less value consensus about police co-operation against refugees, asylum seekers and clandestine immigrants. A majority of people may support such activity, but a significant and often articulate minority are likely to be critical. If police action is viewed as arbitrary, unjust and directed towards particular racial or minority groups, the extent of the criticism will be all the greater.

7.4.7   *Importance of Accountability*

a)   Parliamentary and Judicial Scrutiny

Another dimension of legitimacy is accountability. The hallmark of a democratic society is a high level of accountability by the state's agents. The accountability may be through the courts, parliamentary committees, the media or other bodies, but institutions should be answerable in acceptable ways for their policies and activities. Unfortunately, it is not clear that the new arrangements for police co-operation in the European Union are sufficiently accountable in any of these respects. Indeed, the lack of adequate accountability is a theme running throughout this Report. Ministerial decisions are made at the macro-level, without publicity let alone parliamentary or judicial scrutiny. A myriad of networks and groups exists at the meso level, about which most politicians appear to be largely ignorant. Micro-level contacts occur on a daily basis, often without any records or checks.

b)   Unnecessary Secrecy

The absence of openness, transparency and proper accountability is endangering the legitimacy of the arrangements and structures, in some cases before they are even fully functioning. It is, of course, widely accepted that some police operations would be jeopardised if they were publicised, but in such cases there are various forms of accountability which could be instituted, such as an annual review by a parliamentary committee. Most co-operative police activity could be openly accountable in various ways. There is, at present, too much unnecessary secrecy about developments and this is threatening the legitimacy of the new structures.

7.4.8   *Political Sovereignty and Police Co-operation*

Underlying the secrecy which shrouds many of the macro-level and meso-level structures is the central issue of political sovereignty. Policing is closely bound up with notions of sovereignty of individual nation states, for the police are the principal means, short of calling on the armed forces, whereby a state imposes its authority and rule within its own territory. As such, states jealously guard their control over their own police.

a)   Opposition to Surrendering Control of Policing

The creation of the European Union has involved some surrender of sovereignty by individual states in order to achieve perceived greater benefits. It is, however, no surprise that several states have been resistant to moves to develop common foreign policies or common policing structures through the European Community institutional framework. Where they perceive a common interest, the states are prepared to work together on crime prevention, police co-operation and state security, but some countries are deeply opposed to any development of common police units with operational powers across national borders.

b)   Operational Powers and Europol

There are, however some moves in this direction. The Schengen Convention, for example, allows some measure of 'hot pursuit' across some borders. There is also

306

evidence that a growing number of European police officers envisage the European Drugs Unit/Europol developing in this way. Some officials working in the Schengen headquarters have said they foresee the evolution of a Europol with operational powers and this view was echoed by Colonel Fernand Diederich, Commandant of Luxembourg's *Gendarmerie*, on 14th October 1993. It was, however, made crystal clear by UK Home Office officials who were present that this vision is not shared by the United Kingdom.

c)   Gradual Evolution of Cross-Border Capabilities

It is understandable that some EU states are opposed to ceding control over any police operations within their own territory. However, the reasons for this reluctance appear to be more emotional than logical. Why should a specialist police unit, made up of officers from different states, which operates inside a particular country be seen as a threat to the political well-being of that country, as long as the rules of operation and methods of accountability are clearly drawn? If organised crime is operating across borders why should the forces of law not do the same?

It seems possible that there will be a gradual evolution of some specialist forms of European police units with some limited cross-border operational capabilities. Usually, close co-operation will enable individual countries' own specialist units to operate in their own territories in a co-ordinated manner. However, it is possible to imagine circumstances, involving dangerous criminals, where a coherent unit needs to operate across borders. Incidentally, it is worth noting that this study has received firm evidence of individual police officers operating in plain clothes in another European country, for example, following a suspect or conducting surveillance, with the full knowledge and co-operation of the local police.

7.4.9   *Future Developments in Co-operative Arrangements*

a)   Three-Speed Process

During recent years there has been considerable activity in developing macro-level and meso-level structures to facilitate various forms of police co-operation in the European Union. The most impressive progress has been made by the Schengen Group with the apparently firm commitment to introduce all the measures on 1st February 1994 for Belgium, France, Germany, Luxembourg, the Netherlands and Spain, with Portugal expected to follow soon after. The delay in implementing the provisions in Greece and Italy, and the stance of Denmark, Ireland and the UK which have so far refused to join the Group, raises the possibility of a three-speed process of development in the field of police co-operation and associated issues. The four EFTA countries, which are likely to join the EC and the European Union in the mid-1990s, have also been invited to join the Schengen Group and Austria has already made a positive response. With the accession of Finland, Norway and Sweden there would seem to be little to prevent Denmark also joining the Schengen Group, leaving only Ireland and the United Kingdom on the slow track.

There is evidence of growing discontent amongst senior UK police officers about the country's self-imposed exclusion from the Schengen Group. They are particularly concerned about the lack of access of British police to the Schengen Information System and to other means of co-operation with colleagues elsewhere in Europe. In early September 1993 a Home Office official source indicated that the UK government did not consider that the British police would be unduly disadvantaged by its exclusion from the SIS.

b)   A More Coherent Approach

It remains to be seen how the work of the Trevi Group will develop under the provisions of Title VI of the Treaty on European Union. Various initiatives are possible, building on the activities of Trevi's working groups, of which the EDU/ Europol is one of the most interesting. There is, however, a school of thought which argues that in the past Trevi has promised more than it has delivered, in terms of practical police co-operation, and there is little reason to suppose that things will change under the new structure. Others suggest that Title VI signals an energetic and coherent approach during the coming period.

The K4 Co-ordinating Committee will also have responsibility for promoting judicial co-operation and for fostering collaboration in the fields of immigration and customs. The work of MAG 92 in developing European-wide customs co-operation seems to have been particularly effective and deserves emulation by other law enforcement specialists.

c)   Rationalisation or Proliferation

Interpol has made great strides in recent years and will continue to serve as a major mechanism for micro-level police co-operation. The organisation has also become increasingly effective in promoting meso-level contacts, through its European Secretariat and regional activities. If resources are available, Interpol may be able to develop these activities yet further, by organising conferences and seminars for specialist police officers.

It is difficult to make any predictions about how the myriad of meso-level groups and networks will develop. One possibility is that a process of rationalisation will occur to create single networks in each branch of police work which requires cross-border co-operation in the European Union. Perhaps the K4 Committee and its subsidiary groups will take the initiative in rationalising this complex meso-level patchwork of structures, in order to remove duplication and confusion. However, it seems more likely that the proliferation of groups will continue, reflecting the increased professionalisation and specialisation of contemporary European policing.

7.4.10   *Much To Be Done*

Police co-operation within the European Union is most likely to be successful if it proceeds by structured evolution. It has to develop gradually if practical and effective procedures and processes are to be created, but these developments need to be structured with clear goals in mind. There is a great need for more research about what these goals should be and in which fields improved mechanisms are most required.

More attention should be devoted to accountability and scrutiny, in order to ensure that the organisations function effectively and efficiently and command widespread legitimacy. Detailed arrangements for safeguarding the rights and interests of individuals and minorities are also necessary. In order for all these things to be achieved, greater openness and transparency is required.

This Report is an attempt to make a contribution to the process of developing suitable co-operative structures for policing in the European Union. In the course of the research it has become increasingly evident that much more knowledge and understanding is needed in particular areas. It is apparent that, with a small number of exceptions, there is a widespread feeling amongst police officers and others that they lack sufficient information about police co-operation, crime and justice in Europe. There is much yet to be done to develop efficient and accountable procedures and structures in this vital field of European affairs. This Report is a contribution to this task.

APPENDIX I

SUMMMARY OF FINDINGS

CRIME, BORDER CONTROLS AND IMMIGRATION

There is a serious lack of knowledge and understanding about the extent and type of crime in Europe:

- The lack of data is recognised to be a major problem by many working in the field.

- The ignorance of the facts of crime is impeding the development of appropriate structures and strategies to combat crime in Europe.

- The vacuum is being filled with some wild and frightening predictions about the rising tide of crime in the new Europe.

It is difficult to predict with any certainty the likely effects on the levels of crime of a Europe without frontiers, but the following conclusions seem supported by the small amount of available evidence:

- International terrorism will neither increase nor decrease as a consequence of the open borders policy but increased co-operation on intelligence matters will continue to be essential.

- The relaxation of internal border controls is unlikely to see the pattern of organised drugs trafficking within the European Union change significantly, although the increased smuggling of smaller quantities of drugs is more likely. The potential for an increase in drugs trafficking from eastern Europe should not be underestimated.

- Lower-level crime, particularly acquisitive crime, is likely to increase because of greater freedom of movement.

- This is likely to be particularly true of thefts of motor vehicles.

- There is an increasing market for stolen precious art and antiques. Open borders facilitate crime involving high-value easily transportable goods.

- The free movement of capital, together with a common market for financial services, is likely to stimulate fraud and other business-related crime. Informed sources suggest that if there is one sort of crime which will probably prosper, and which might be stimulated, in the open Europe, it is fraud. Although victimisation in commercial crime is less visible than other types of crime, the extent of fraud in the European Union is substantial, including significant cross-border commercial crime, abuse of financial regulations, cheque-card and credit-card fraud and fraud against the EC itself.

- Environmental crime poses great long-term risks to the environment and ecology of the European Union.

The notion of a secure 'ring of steel' around the external frontiers of the European Union is not a wholly feasible proposition:

- There is no agreement as to what constitutes an internal and external boundary. For example, an airport may be both.

- Even with previously existing frontiers, there was already significant penetration by illegal immigration, although estimates about the precise figure vary wildly. Legal immigration is estimated to be around 10 million persons in the European Union. Illegal immigration is estimated to be in excess of 1.5 million persons.

- There are particular concerns about the permeability of the external borders and the near-impossibility of securing the external frontiers, although the nine signatories to the Schengen Agreements are optimistic that the 'ring of steel' can be made secure.

- Bilateral agreements between EU countries and non-EU states make step-by-step entry more probable.

- The disintegration of the former USSR and communist bloc countries is causing large-scale illegal immigration, particularly into Germany. Illegal immigrants may turn to crime to pay for their 'passage' into the European Union or to support themselves once they have entered.

- Extradition arrangements are in place in the European Union. Most of the states are signatories to the European Convention on Extradition although this cannot be described as a wholly effective instrument for judicial co-operation. Obstacles to extradition may be presented which are not covered by the Convention.

- Customs controls will change as a consequence of the relaxation of internal border controls and a tightening of external border controls. The use of surveillance and intelligence by customs services will increase.

The Schengen Group countries have agreed uniform conditions for entry to the nine states, which will have far-reaching implications for non-Schengen nationals from outside the European Union:

- Visa requirements will restrict the entry of non-EU nationals especially from developing countries.

- Asylum will be made more difficult, and the tightening of procedures for dealing with applicants for asylum may result in the criminalisation of asylum seekers.

- The spirit which continues to open up borders inside the European Union will make entry at the perimeter more difficult. Whilst the EU is becoming more liberal towards internal travel of its own citizens, the attitude towards those without citizenship is visibly and dramatically hardening. Of most concern is the fact that little differentiation seems to be made between the legal and the illegal groups of immigrants, and thus both are generally subject to exclusion.

- Article 100c in the EC Treaty provides for the introduction of an EC-wide scheme of visas, following ratification of the Maastricht Treaty.

A consequence of speculation about the effects of the removal of internal border controls on levels of crime in Europe has been:

- A 'moral panic' about the level of crime, exaggerating the threat posed by the removal of internal border controls.

- Worry and concern about repressive policies as part of an over-reaction to the perceived threat of crime.

POLICE FORCES IN THE EUROPEAN UNION

Numbers of Police Officers in the European Union

There are around 1.337 million police officers in the European Union. With a total population of about 344 million this means that there is approximately one police officer for every 257 people in the European Union.

However, there is considerable variation between the member states, with an estimated one police officer for every 191 citizens in Italy, and only one officer for every 499 people in Denmark.

There are 105 separate police forces in the EU, excluding agencies with primary responsibilities in areas such as customs and forestry policing. Dividing the 105 forces by the twelve member states gives an average of 8.75 forces per member state. Even if the UK with its 52 forces and the Netherlands with its 26 forces are counted as one force each, this still gives an average of just over 2 forces per member state.

The Need for a Detailed Comparative Study

The policing arrangements for the European Union are complex, given the number of forces with policing responsibilities. Before police co-operation in Europe can be promoted seriously and effectively a detailed comparative study of existing police organisations and other law enforcement agencies must be undertaken.

Without a clear outline and account of existing police structures and organisations and their responsibilities, attempts to promote co-operation are likely to be, to say the least, haphazard and inefficient.

Diversity: A Research Agenda

Even though the information obtained by this study is inevitably incomplete, one of the clear features of European policing is its diversity. This diversity is at times frustrating, but it also provides the basis for a research agenda. Areas for consideration in a comparative study of European Union policing systems would include the following:

a)   The Organisational Structures of Policing

The organisational structures of the police vary between EU states. Some forces have a dual structure, with a Gendarmerie and a state police force. Others are regionalised, like the UK and Dutch systems. In Germany, policing is organised at a national and state level. There is little uniformity between the states.

This does not preclude the possibility of conducting comparative work. On the contrary, the variation invites comparison – to tease out common denominators, where they occur; to highlight differences, including the benefits and disadvantages of one organisational structure over another; and, most importantly, to use this analysis to stimulate a more informed debate about the desirability of, and means towards, improved police co-operation across national frontiers.

The research team has been reminded constantly, primarily by senior police personnel throughout Europe, of the need for such a study.

b)   Police Powers

The powers of police officers vary between – and often within – the European Union countries. Successful co-operation between individual officers from different countries is in many ways dependent on an understanding of police powers in different countries. Comparative work which was able to map out the variations in police powers would surely assist co-operative processes.

**c)   Police Accountability, Codes of Ethics and Standards
             of Best Practice**

The accountability of law enforcement agencies and officers is of crucial importance in a democratic European Union. Institutional arrangements for ensuring accountability vary between countries. Codes of ethics and standards of best practice also vary between forces. The question *quis custodiet ipsos custodes?* is as valid today as in the past.

This is an area not covered in detail here and a full comparative account of police forces in the EU should undertake a study of these issues.

d)   Special Policing Organisations

Special police organisations exist in many countries, often operating outside the main policing structures. Examples of such police include railway police, forestry police and waterway police, police at sea ports and airports, and customs and excise. These law enforcement agencies sometimes have particular importance for international policing, especially with the continued European development of the transport infrastructure and mobility of persons.

There are also various associations and networks between some of the special policing organisations, but as yet the existence of these special police agencies in Europe is poorly charted. A detailed comparative study will need to take account of these specialist organisations.

e) Recruitment and Training

Recruitment and training practices vary between forces. This topic needs serious consideration, within a comparative framework, as part of a wider study of European policing agencies. Due to lack of space, and in some cases lack of available information, this topic is not treated in full in this Report. However, this should not be taken as an indication of the unimportance of studying police recruitment and training.

f) Cultures of Policing

A comparative study of policing in the European Union would be enhanced by an investigation into the culture of policing in the different countries. As other commentators have suggested, common functional roles exist which bind police officers together, creating a police culture (Manning 1977; Muir 1977). There is evidence to suggest that the 'cop cultures' of the police forces in the EU countries share some common features, but also have significant differences. These need elaboration as part of a comparative study.

g) Legal and Judicial Systems

The legal and judicial systems of European countries vary considerably. Besides the obvious differences between adversarial and inquisitorial systems, some countries rely on statute and case law, others have systematic codes and regulations. Rules of evidence also differ greatly. The proposed study of existing police organisations might usefully include well-researched summaries of key aspects of the legal and judicial systems in the respective European countries.

MACRO-LEVEL STRUCTURES FOR POLICE CO-OPERATION

The general view is that Interpol will continue to serve as the major channel for operational enquiries, but its capacity to promote wider police co-operation is limited:

- Despite earlier criticisms of Interpol's efficiency and security, there is a high level of support for Interpol's current activities.

- Changes at Interpol's headquarters, including the introduction of new technology, are widely appreciated.

- Although Interpol appears to discourage direct bilateral European contacts, the introduction of direct communications between the NCBs through the Automated Message Switch System (AMSS) has led to the dynamic exchange of information.

- Interpol's role in fostering collaboration in Europe is constrained by its international world role.

- Interpol must remain primarily a channel for communications at the micro level of individual cases.

316

- There is some danger that Interpol may be increasingly bypassed by new macro-level, European-wide structures for the exchange of information (the SIS and the EDU/Europol).

- Although Europol may be perceived as an alternative to Interpol this is unlikely to be the case unless one or the other undergoes fundamental change. Europol, for the present, will deal purely with *intelligence* whereas Interpol deals in *information*, although it is developing some intelligence through its Liaison and Criminal Intelligence Division.

The Schengen Agreement and Implementing Convention appear to offer a striking example of co-operation at macro, meso and micro levels of law enforcement. Schengen's role as a model or 'laboratory' for a wider European initiative is widely recognised amongst senior police officers and government officials throughout Europe, but central issues of accountability will need to be addressed:

- The history of Schengen has been characterised by a high level of commitment and resolve, and although it ran into delays and difficulties in 1992–1993 rapid progress was made after June 1993.

- It appears that at least six Schengen member states will implement the Convention from 1st February 1994.

- The Schengen working groups have made major contributions to practical police co-operation – including steps to improve compatibility in radio and computing equipment and the exchange of officers.

- The Schengen Information System provides information for police in the six countries which are initially participating, followed by Portugal, Greece and Italy at a later date.

- The Schengen Agreements include macro-level policies on policing the external borders of the member states – including the development of a common visa policy.

- Doubts remain about the effectiveness of the 'hard outer shell' at the common external borders.

- There is some concern that the so called 'ring of steel' will disadvantage nationals from developing countries.

- The common system for dealing with requests for political asylum has provoked criticisms from human rights groups.

- The Schengen Information System raises human rights, privacy and data protection issues which it is alleged have not been satisfactorily addressed, although it would appear that the data protection measures are fairly comprehensive.

- The Schengen Agreements include macro-level policies on policing the internal borders of the member states – including 'hot pursuit'.

- The complexity of the Schengen Convention raises problems of accountability and legitimacy, primarily in relation to police powers, human rights and public approval. As yet, there is no overall judicial or parliamentary accountability.

- The EFTA countries which have applied to join the EC/EU have been strongly invited to join the Schengen Group, and Austria already has observer status.

There are mixed judgements on the effectiveness of the Trevi Group:

- It has promoted the principle of increased police co-operation and given it considerable political impetus.

- It has helped to reduce national rivalries in the field of law enforcement and has promoted mutual respect and trust.
- The working groups (of all types) appear to address a wide range of matters relating to police co-operation – terrorism; technical and forensic matters; serious, international and organised crime; immigration; judicial co-operation; and the development of the EDU/Europol.

- These are macro-level initiatives which resulted in a number of meso-level, tangible benefits in practical police co-operation.

- The Trevi Group is too secretive.

- It has suffered from not being connected to the European Community institutions and political process.

- The Trevi Group operates primarily at the intergovernmental, political and senior official levels and may not be taking sufficient account of the meso- and micro-level responsibilities of law enforcement personnel 'on the ground'.

- The Trevi Group is not seen as a fully accountable, legitimate structure for policy making or executive action, and as such is treated with some suspicion by those (including police officers) whose support is needed if practical progress in police co-operation is to be achieved

- The Trevi Group's structure is regarded as inefficient and incoherent, which may in part be a function of the lack of a permanent location and secretariat, with insufficient co-ordination between the working groups and also poor 'institutional memory'.

- The creation of the EDU/Europol was in part a product of the work conducted by Trevi Working Group III.

- Even in its infancy Europol offers a 'case study' in macro, meso and micro levels of co-operation. At the macro level, the initial impetus was given by the Trevi ministerial group and then consolidated in the Treaty on European Union. The *Ad Hoc* Working Group on Europol was subsequently created to provide a meso-level constitutional framework. Project Group Europol has the micro-level task of operationalising the initiative.

- Despite the work of the *Ad Hoc* Working Group on Europol, the full development of the EDU/Europol was hindered by the failure of the Trevi ministers to agree its location until the Brussels summit of 29th October 1993 where it was agreed that the EDU/Europol should be located in The Hague.

Title VI of the Treaty on European Union marks a watershed in the development of police co-operation in Europe. For the first time there is a formal agreement to pursue co-operation in justice and home affairs:

- Although the Treaty states that member states 'shall regard' co-operation in the fields of justice and home affairs as matters of 'common interest', it is not clear what this will mean in practice. In addition, co-operation could be circumvented through the provisions of Article K.2 – where member states have a reserved right to exercise national responsibilities in maintaining law and order.

- It is not clear how the K4 Committee will relate to the European Parliament. Although the Parliament is to be consulted and its views 'duly taken into consideration', the nature of the consultation and the extent to which the Parliament's views will be taken into account remain wholly undetermined.

- Political realities have dictated that only certain matters will fall within the competence of the European Community remit – visa policy (and perhaps asylum policy) under Article 100c in the EC Treaty and Article K.9 of the Maastricht Treaty is certainly within the EC's remit, whilst judicial co-operation in criminal matters, customs co-operation and police co-operation (including Europol) are excluded. This is probably because the latter are seen as issues which remain too politically contentious to be brought within the European Community structure.

- Such an arrangement may, however, prove to be convenient for all those involved. By keeping police co-operation and associated issues outside the EC it will be possible to retain greater control and secrecy. The role of the European Parliament can be limited and – just as important – it will prove easier for some governments to prevent parliamentary scrutiny in their own countries. In the fields of judicial, home affairs and police co-operation the Commission will exercise influence at the intergovernmental level, and matters can proceed without undue 'interference' by representatives from the European or national parliaments.

- It seems likely that the Commission will play a key role in the development of co-operation in the fields of justice and home affairs under Article K of the Maastricht Treaty. The K4 Co-ordinating Committee will report to the Council and under this will be the as yet undetermined structure of subcommittees and working groups. Much of Trevi, it would appear, will be reconstituted within this structure. Article K.3 of the Treaty on European Union empowers the Council to draw up new intergovernmental conventions and to adopt joint measures.

- Although it may seem faintly ludicrous that the same ministers, advised by the same officials, at the same meetings may leap-frog between being in the European Community and being outside it, depending on the proposals they are considering, this may prove an effective device for creating the necessary momentum in the field of European police and criminal justice co-operation. The downside of this arrangement is again the lack of effective scrutiny and accountability and a possible loss of public legitimacy and consent.

- The Declaration on Police Co-operation, signed in February 1992, is strong post-Maastricht evidence for continuing political commitment in promoting police co-operation, and doing so in specific fields of police practice – such as support for criminal investigations and search operations, co-operation in forensic matters and the creation of information databases. The Declaration itself can be seen as an unambiguous attempt to translate the general political momentum for police co-operation into more specific, and more focused, concerns which have operational significance.

The effect of the Council of Europe on police co-operation has been modest, although it has played an important role in the protection of human rights:

- Under the leadership of Madame Lalumière, the Council of Europe is enjoying an enhanced reputation and with the recent accession of central European countries it now has a membership of 32 states. This number is likely to grow further in the near future.

- The Council's work in the field of human rights, and the judgements of the European Court of Human Rights, has been influential and the October 1993 decision to simplify the system may lead to increased use of the Court as a consequence of developments in police co-operation in the European Union and the tighter external border controls.

- The Council's activities in the analysis of migration, refugees and asylum have been most valuable. The renewed emphasis on safeguarding minority rights, and the agreement to launch an anti-racist campaign, is to be welcomed.

- The Pompidou Group has promoted research into various aspects of drug addiction – including the treatment and rehabilitation of offenders and criminal justice.

- The Council of Europe's 1981 Convention for the Protection of Individuals with regard to the Automatic Processing of Personal Data continues to provide the basic international framework in which the exchange of computerised information between the police forces of Europe must take place.

MESO-LEVEL GROUPS, AGREEMENTS AND NETWORKS FOR POLICE CO-OPERATION

There are several well-developed specialist police networks in Europe operating primarily at the meso and micro levels of co-operation:

Terrorism

- The Police Working Group on Terrorism (PWGOT) works well at both the meso and micro levels of co-operation, with a good deal of personal goodwill. Exchanges of personnel occur with positive results. It is generally regarded as effective in promoting collaboration and co-operation on general threats, as well as intelligence on specific incidents.

- The activities of the Police Working Group on Terrorism, and associated liaison between security services, can be regarded as successful examples of police co-operation at the meso level, bringing together police officers with responsibilities for a particular area and encouraging co-operative working practices and increased communications between forces. It is also arguable that successful meso-level co-operation will offer operational dividends at the micro level.

Drugs

- Trevi Working Group III resolved that greater use should be made of Drugs Liaison Officers (DLOs), not only in postings between European Community states but also to non-EC countries. It was subsequently decided that each Trevi Group member state should establish a National Drugs Intelligence Unit and these are now being incorporated in the member states' National Criminal Intelligence Systems.
- A further step is being taken with the establishment of the European Drugs Unit (EDU) as the first stage in the development of Europol. The EDU's major role will be to collect and analyse intelligence from member states in order to contribute to international efforts against drugs trafficking and drugs-related crime such as money laundering.

- The European Committee to Combat Drugs (ECCD), which is more commonly known by its French name and acronym *Comité Européen pour la Lutte Anti-Drogue* (CELAD), is in the process of drawing up a European-wide plan for the fight against drugs.

- There is no doubt that police efforts against drugs crime is one area where levels of co-operation are quite highly developed: drugs trafficking is a type of crime which has achieved a high level of political visibility; and the police involved in operations against drugs traffickers are mostly specialist officers who are able to deal effectively with police drugs specialists from other countries.

Football Hooliganism

- Trevi Working Group II has created a Europe-wide network of permanent correspondents for the exchange of information about football hooligans.

- The European network for the policing of football matches and associated problems has developed considerably. The network operates at the meso and micro levels and appears to have had significant and continuing success in pre-empting public disorder at international football matches.

Traffic

- Co-operation in traffic matters is developing and a number of imaginative and innovative projects are underway, some involving large-scale information exchange. These include attempts to achieve harmonisation on the maximum blood alcohol concentration for drivers, mutual disqualification from driving, and cross-national checks on vehicle index numbers and drivers' licences.

Technical Matters

• Trevi Working Group II has helped to promote a number of specialist technical networks which are fostering co-operation in relevant fields, such as computerised information systems and communications. Forensic co-operation takes place between the European laboratories and a number of specialist seminars have been held on subjects such as DNA genetic 'fingerprinting' and on firearms and ballistics.

Ports

• It is vital that co-operation occurs between the many different agencies that are involved in port and coastline security and policing. It is not clear that this occurs to any great extent at present, and further investigation of the possibilities for improvement is necessary.

Railways

• Two of the most important issues in relation to co-operation between transport police in the European Union are the increase in crime on the railways, and questions concerning the powers of transport police across internal borders. At present such matters are resolved by protocols between two or more countries, but there may be an increasing need for European-wide agreements as rail travel across Europe becomes more frequent.

Customs

• Customs co-operation appears to have succeeded in a way which co-operation in other fields has not. There is one major international network co-ordinating global operations and liaison – the Customs Co-operation Council (CCC); and one computerised information network in Europe – the Customs Information System (CIS), supported by one initiative with a primary focus on the exchange of officers between EC customs services and the organisation of joint training (the Matthaeus initiative). The degree of co-operation between the members in each group appears to be high and this has led to successful individual and joint operations.

Bilateral Co-operation: The Channel Tunnel

• Co-operation is taking place at the meso level to ensure that micro-level co-operation can occur when the Tunnel is in use. It is only then that this will be tested. Co-operation has also taken place at the macro-level with the drafting of protocols which will facilitate the meso-level and micro-level arrangements. Meso-level Memoranda of Understanding, involving Belgian, English and French police, have also proved effective.

Bilateral Co-operation: The Garda Siochana and Royal Ulster Constabulary

• There is a high level of co-operation between the two police forces, and this has been enhanced by the Anglo-Irish Agreement. The considerable political commitment at the macro level has proved an important impetus for meso-level arrangements and for the daily micro-level co-operation between operational police officers.

Bilateral Co-operation: The French – Italian Border

- Co-operation appears to occur at many different levels. The case of Bastia tends to confirm information from other sources that in many cross-border locations informal arrangements for co-operation have evolved, which may or may not be backed up by more official policies and structures. It seems reasonable to suggest that more agreement at the macro level and the meso level would help to facilitate lower-level co-operation.

Professional Organisations

- Further comparative research on the various police professional organisations, the European Network for Policewomen (ENP) and the *Union Internationale des Syndicats de Police* (UISP), needs to be undertaken in order to complement existing knowledge of police organisations in Europe.

Secret Networks

- There is no doubt that largely secret police organisations (national and international) may be essential, especially in the fight against terrorism and international organised crime. Secrecy may be a necessary condition for effective police action. Even so, it is arguable that there should be some formal mechanism to ensure accountability and public trust.

In some respects, there is a danger of an over-proliferation of unconnected European police associations and networks where similar activities are being undertaken simultaneously by different organisations:

- As policing functions become more highly differentiated the impetus to establish new international associations becomes greater.

- The most effective networks have been set up in criminal policing fields with high political visibility, such as drugs and terrorism.

- The establishment of associations and international groupings generally appears to be *ad hoc* and haphazard.

- There seems to be more than one network or association existing in some fields of specialist policing.

- There is no clear picture of existing co-operative associations and networks.

- It would appear that no single agency or institution is aware of all the existing European arrangements in specialist police fields.

- There is a danger of duplication and lack of co-ordination of co-operative arrangements.

- The proliferation of databases and mechanisms for information exchange raises questions about data protection and human rights, and also about accuracy and efficiency.

- The level of political, public and legal accountability of many of these networks appears to be woefully low.

COMMUNICATIONS AND INFORMATION EXCHANGE

Good communications are a necessary condition for efficient and effective police co-operation. However, a number of different legal issues must be considered:

- Data protection and the rights of data subjects.

- The distinction between 'hard' criminal information and 'soft' criminal intelligence.

- The legality of some sorts of information exchange.

- Compatibility with the 1981 Council of Europe Convention for the Protection of Individuals with regard to Automatic Processing of Personal Data and with the Council of Europe 1987 Recommendation (R(87)15) on the use of personal data in the police sector.

Paradoxically, as Interpol is showing a new-found technological confidence, a fresh set of information-exchange problems are beginning to emerge – legal issues in relation to data protection:

- Whatever the validity of past criticisms, in recent years Interpol has invested and is continuing to invest heavily in sophisticated telecommunications and computer systems (AMSS and ASF). If Interpol is to maintain and enhance its world-wide role in criminal information it will need to be at the cutting edge of communications technology. The recent evidence suggests that this is in fact the case.

- Although Interpol data subjects have a right of representation to the independent supervisory board to seek to rectify or erase inaccurate information, the extent to which they can exercise this right is open to question.

- Interpol is constitutionally constrained to act only in accordance with the national laws of member states. This causes a particular problem with the transmission of data between NCBs, using the AMSS, when one country has a high standard of data protection and another country has a lower standard or no protection at all, and vice versa.

- Interpol is constrained to use information submitted only if it leads to the conclusion that a person is 'liable' to engage in international criminal activity, but there is a degree of 'interpretational latitude' over how this criterion could be used.

- Interpol is committed to developing analytical techniques on criminal intelligence through the Analytical Criminal Intelligence Unit (ACIU) in its Liaison and Criminal Intelligence Division. This represents a significant change of emphasis. It is certainly a long way from the traditional Interpol role of acting as a conduit for 'hard facts'.

Despite new initiatives and the continuing importance of specialist networks, Interpol continues to be by far the most important structure for the transmission of basic criminal investigative information between European Union countries, and between EU countries and further afield:

- In 1992 some 400,000 communications through Interpol involved European Union states, representing some 40 per cent of the total. The wider European region of 44 countries was responsible for some 80 per cent of all Interpol communications.

- Most information exchange between European police forces concerns local 'ordinary' crime and the revamped Interpol service appears to handle this function efficiently and effectively.

The Schengen Information System is the most highly developed European system of information exchange for practical police co-operation. As such it stands as a role model for future developments or, perhaps, as the model for the future. It is likely that the SIS has an unstoppable political momentum and that it could force its standards (technical and otherwise) on those European Union countries which have not joined and on the wider Europe:

- The Schengen Information System has successfully bypassed the problems of incompatibility between national police computer systems by creating a series of stand-alone national databases (NSISs) feeding a central unit (CSIS) which then acts as a resource for all member states.

- The Schengen Information System through the Schengen Implementing Convention offers a mechanism for information exchange with formal instruments of governance. Previously, mutual assistance in information exchange between police forces has taken place in a largely unstructured fashion through micro-level, informal contacts on a case-by-case basis.

- The Schengen Information System has well worked out data protection regulations. Information exchange is subject to national laws, and to oversight by three supervisory bodies; and data subjects have rights of access, including those of rectification and erasure.

- There appears to be considerable political will and commitment behind the Schengen Information System. With nine participating members and a target date of 1st February 1994 for operationalising the provisions of the Schengen Implementing Convention, for six of the countries, a European system for police co-operation on the exchange of information is substantially in place.

- There is evidence that EFTA countries which are negotiating entry to the European Union have been strongly invited to join the Schengen Group and Austria already has observer status.

325

The Supplementary Information Request at the National Entry system (SIReNE) is an innovative infrastructure which enables the participating Schengen states to exchange information on particular entries in the main Schengen Information System:

- The SIReNE is a rapid information exchange structure based on an electronic mail system on which standardised messages are sent from one participating country to another.

- A national SIReNE (N-SIReNE) office is being established in each country which will have round-the-clock staffing, translation services, and access to competent authorities, in order to respond quickly to requests which are sent.

- The supplementary requests which will be handled by the SIReNE include further information about extradition and ten categories of information about entries on, and the functioning of, the main Schengen Information System (SIS).

- Although technically separate from the SIS, the SIReNE is closely attached to it. It will have its own dedicated communication lines and is scheduled to be fully operational between the initial six participating countries by 1st February 1994.

- The proposed Visa Inquiry Open-Border Network (VISION) will probably operate through the SIReNE network. This will enable the relevant authorities in the Schengen countries to consult each other about the issue of visas to individuals (in accordance with Article 17 of the Schengen Implementing Convention). VISION is expected to become operational during 1994.

The major contribution of the Trevi Group to international police communications has been in providing the macro-level political impetus to facilitate meso-level and micro-level information exchange. Much of the practical progress has been made at the operational level of face-to-face dialogue between police officers with a common interest in a particular type of crime:

- Working Group I has undoubtedly been successful in promoting co-operation against terrorism through its liaison network of specialist officers, but it is not possible to offer an informed assessment of its activities or of its dedicated secure facsimile information network (TSFN).

- Working Group II has facilitated information exchange between officers on public order offences, including football hooliganism. The Group has also been working on a directory of police training in Europe and on the exchange of information about technical and scientific advances. It has apparently been examining the development of a communications system for all European Union member states.

- Working Group III has instituted a European-wide network for the exchange of drugs trafficking information, and this was instrumental in providing the impetus for the EDU/Europol. Trevi Working Group III has also promoted the exchange of information on money-laundering, armed robbery, stolen vehicles and stolen works of art, and is currently exploring environmental crime and the development of comparative crime analysis in the EU.

• These initiatives have clear operational significance, and they relate to highly-focused police activities in restricted, discrete, specialist areas, such as drugs, terrorism and disorder. A good deal of the contact is face-to-face liaison.

The creation of the European Drugs Unit/Europol is the most recent example of developments in European police communications and information exchange, and is arguably of long-term importance, but there are difficulties:

• At present data protection safeguards exist only at the level of working 'agreements', although the *Ad Hoc* Working Group on Europol will seek to incorporate data protection regulations in the draft Convention for the Establishment of Europol. This is not expected to be approved until 1994 or 1995 at the earliest.

• The EDU/Europol databases will contain intelligence or 'soft', unverifiable information. This raises questions about the purposes for which such information may be used and how it is controlled.

• The relationships between Europol and Interpol and between Europol and the Schengen Information System have yet to be resolved. There is potential for duplication of effort; and attempts to rationalise activities may prove to be politically contentious.

• Some police officers and officials in Europe expect Europol to develop specialist operational policing capabilities and tasks, but this view is not shared by UK officials.

APPENDIX II

PRINCIPAL PROPOSALS

CRIME, BORDER CONTROLS AND IMMIGRATION

Research and discussion on crime in Europe needs to move beyond predictable concerns about terrorism and drugs trafficking. In addition, new research should concentrate on acquisitive crimes related to the free movement of people and also investigate business crime related to the free movement of capital, especially fraud.

Too much attention has been given to the crimes which cause most anxiety but where the risk of victimisation is low, and too little attention has been paid to offences which receive little publicity but where the risks are real and the harm considerable. There is an imbalance which needs rectifying. For example, much more attention could be paid to firearms control and availability. There are differences between the European Union states which will remain until a recent EC Directive takes effect.

Consideration should be given, as a matter of priority, to the establishment of a European unit for the co-ordination of activities against fraud and the policing of fraud.

This would need to have operational capabilities. There are enormous difficulties in tracking down international business crime and divorcing 'intelligence' and 'operations' will be counter-productive. This may need legislation and will certainly need resourcing properly. This unit should be developed with the benefit of the experience of UCLAF.

Environmental crime threatens the health of the European Union's ecosystem, and research is urgently needed into the levels and implications of environmental crime.

Environmental crime threatens everyone, including those who perpetrate it. It poses great risks to the health of the planet, and the long-term costs are incalculable.

Europe as a whole, and at the highest level, needs to re-think its position with respect to conditions of entry for non-European Union nationals. There is evidence of an inner-Europe excluding non-Union nationals.

The price of freedom of movement within Europe may be to restrict the right of entry for people from outside Europe. This would seem incompatible with the spirit of 'open borders', although some degree of control is essential. There is a subtle balance to be struck.

Policing policies must not be made in the absence of high-quality research. Fear of crime is easily generated by unsubstantiated claims from so-called experts. A consequence of this may be repressive social policies.

Policing the European Union needs to be well-organised, but the structure of collaborative efforts needs to be based on fact not scaremongering fantasy. Policy makers should pay attention to the warnings of the civil liberties lobby on the dangers of a policing policy constructed on the basis of moral panics.

In order for high-quality research to be undertaken a European Centre for Research into Crime should be established.

Such a Centre would need to be adequately funded. Contributions could come from European Union governments or from EC institutions. The research undertaken should be European in nature and benefit from the wealth of experience available across Europe. Academics and practitioners from all European countries should be actively involved in the programme.

A pan-European, strategic approach to police co-operation can only be effective if it is premised on high-quality information about types and levels of crime, and trends in crime over time. These point to the need for a European Centre for Research into Crime. To avoid disagreement over its location the Centre should be federal in nature with one or two sites in each European Union country.

POLICE FORCES IN THE EUROPEAN UNION

A comprehensive comparative study of existing police organisations and other law enforcement agencies in European Union member states should be undertaken.

The study should outline key national, administrative and cultural features that bear on policing, describe the legal and judicial systems in each country and its effects on policing, and chart in detail the functions and structures of the police and other law enforcement organisations, including special police agencies.

The investigation should also outline police powers and mechanisms for accountability. The study should not rely solely on police organisations' accounts of their activities, but should consult and interview other knowledgeable sources.

The research should also examine the mechanisms for police recruitment and training, as well as the ways in which 'performance indicators' are used to monitor and evaluate the ways in which police officers discharge their responsibilities.

A conceptually-sound comparative framework would be needed in order to give such a study coherence and credibility.

MACRO-LEVEL STRUCTURES FOR POLICE CO-OPERATION

Interpol, Schengen and the Trevi Group (or its successor) should follow the Council of Europe's lead and commission serious research.

It is remarkable that the intergovernmental agencies with the prime responsibility for promoting police co-operation do not undertake, or commission, more detailed research of the problems with which they are dealing. Proper research is a necessary condition for developing appropriate responses. This should certainly be an integral part of the development of 'Europol',

Suitable mechanisms to ensure the satisfactory accountability of the Schengen structures should be established.

Although experiences and expectations of levels of accountability for law enforcement bodies appear to vary considerably between European countries, it is essential that proper arrangements are made to ensure high levels of legitimacy and support throughout the Schengen sphere of influence – including macro-level policies on borders; data protection and safeguards for the SIS; and micro-level police practices, such as 'hot pursuit'.

Whilst the advent of the K4 Committee will address some of the criticisms levelled at the Trevi Group, a detailed appraisal should be undertaken to ensure that the failings of Trevi are avoided from the outset.

The historical separation of the Trevi Group and the EC has not been satisfactory. There is a clear democratic deficit. Although Title VI of the Treaty on European Union states explicitly that progress on co-operation in judicial and home affairs will be subject to oversight by the European Commission (Article K.4) and subject to scrutiny by the European Parliament (Article K.6), it is essential that the rather weak and vague provisions in the Treaty are met in full. Failure to secure proper accountability of the K4 Committee, and the work of sub-committees responsible to it, will only serve to perpetuate the development of police co-operation under a Trevi-type, intergovernmental veil of secrecy.

A European Union Police Forum should be established at which those involved in developing the structures for police co-operation would make an annual report on the progress achieved and future plans. This would enable police officers, those involved in human rights groups and others to engage in constructive criticism and comment.

The post-Maastricht momentum for greater police co-operation is most clear at the level of political commitment, but the evolving structures and mechanisms for securing co-operation (particularly the work of the K4 Committee under Article 100d of the EC Treaty and Article K of the Treaty on European Union) are less clear, as are the lines of accountability to both the European Commission and the European Parliament.

What is required is an ongoing review of developments rather than a post hoc historical assessment of what has been achieved. This is necessary to secure the proper degree of accountability which is required for legitimacy and consent in police co-operation. It is also necessary in order to avoid confusion and a wasteful duplication of effort. In the complex web of evolving structures for police co-operation the central point is at the macro level of government ministers and their senior officials.

It would be extremely useful if an annual report were to be made to a specially convened group of interested parties (including senior police officers from EU member states, representatives from police forces' trades unions, human rights groups, academics and others). This could take the form of a conference – a European Union Policing Forum.

The purpose would be both to report on progress made and to engage senior officials, senior police officers and others in a dialogue which would then inform the next stage in the process. This would certainly promote accountability and legitimacy. It would also offer a real mechanism for promoting co-operation through 'structured feedback' from police officers who would comment with the benefit of practical experience and operational responsibilities.

MESO-LEVEL GROUPS, AGREEMENTS AND NETWORKS FOR POLICE CO-OPERATION

There is a distinct need for a clear and comprehensive account of existing networks and associations.

The present *ad hoc* and haphazard growth of associations and groupings is clearly not the best way to proceed. However, without a detailed account of which networks function well and which areas of specialist policing require further developments, it will not prove possible to promote efficient and effective means of European police co-operation, or proper accountability.

Areas of specialist and technical police activity which would benefit from increased European co-operation should be identified.

The most effective police networks are in fields such as terrorism and drugs: those with high status and visibility. There would appear to be other areas of criminal police work, such as stolen vehicles, fraud and technical activities, including forensic work, which would benefit from more effective European police networks.

The changing nature of informal intelligence exchanges requires further study.

In the light of rapidly changing technology and substantial expansion in the number of specialist networks, the status of informal information exchange needs consideration. Such an investigation should be placed within the context of current debates about the role of the police in economically developed democratic societies, and informed by contemporary theories of social control.

COMMUNICATIONS AND INFORMATION EXCHANGE

A study should be mounted to explore officers' perceptions of pan-European police communications and exchanges of information, drawing a sample from officers with specialist policing responsibilities (such as terrorism, drugs or fraud).

There are clear differences in the types of police communication: for example, face-to-face contacts, specialist networks or Interpol-type communication. It would prove most useful to undertake a study to ascertain which forms of information exchange and communication are seen to be the most effective in different fields of police work.

An information systems compatibility audit should be commissioned in order to identify the points of similarity and difference throughout Europe.

There is an unacceptable lack of information about the compatibility of police information systems throughout Europe. Only a painstaking investigation will reveal the current position and suggest how progress might be made.

A major initiative is required to bring together police officers, academics and information technology specialists in order to examine the range of practical and legal problems concerning the use of information technology for international police co-operation.

The practical problems include: secure networks (for voice, data, image and video); communications standards, including open systems; command and control systems; co-operation in major international investigations; and contingency planning (security and disaster planning). The legal problems include the governance of systems for information exchange with a particular emphasis on data protection regulations.

At present the three major organisations (Interpol, the Schengen Group and the EDU/Europol) are addressing these difficulties in different ways and at different levels.

POLICE CO-OPERATION IN EUROPE: TOWARDS THE FUTURE

A European Centre for Research into Crime should be established.

Much of the contemporary discussion about the effects on crime of abolishing internal border controls, the potential for large-scale immigration and the need for improved police co-operation, is founded on the shifting sands of ignorance, half-truth and prejudice. Discussion needs to be grounded on a firmer foundation as a result of detailed research into different sorts of crime in Europe.

Crime *is* a growing problem for the people of Europe, and much of it could profitably be tackled at a pan-European level, but first greater knowledge and understanding is needed. New crimes, such as environmental offences, also need investigation. For these reasons, a major proposal of this study is that a European Centre for Research into Crime should be established. This could be federal in nature, with different parts of the Centre located in different European Union states. Such a Centre would enable the governments and police of Europe to draw on a great array of knowledge and understanding amongst experts in various institutions.

A comparative study of police forces and other law enforcement organisations in the countries of the European Union should be undertaken.

This investigation has found a widespread lack of comparative knowledge of the policing structures and organisations in different European Union countries. Without a clear outline and account of the existing police forces, and their responsibilities and ways of operating, attempts to promote increased cross-national co-operation are likely to be haphazard and ill-conceived. There would appear to be a strong case for a detailed comparative study of policing in the different countries of the European Union.

The key word to characterise policing in Europe is diversity. There are variations in responsibilities and powers, and in structures and methods of operation. There are differences in recruitment and training, and in conditions of service. The legal and judicial systems are different and so, too, are the traditions and cultures within which policing takes place. The arrangements for accountability, and supervision and monitoring, vary and so do relations with local government and community structures. There are also noticeable differences in the use of civilians in police forces and in the development of specialist units and groups.

There is thus a need for a comprehensive comparative study of the police and other law enforcement organisations with responsibilities in the countries of the European Union. Such a study would provide the basis for a more coherent and efficient approach to cross-national police co-operation structures and procedures.

There is a need for an investigation into police networks and associations in Europe.

There is also a distinct lack of knowledge and understanding about the various specialist groups, networks and associations which exist to promote different kinds of police co-operation. There is a complex patchwork of these networks and groups, with some overlapping activities and membership. Some have a narrow remit, others take a broader approach; some are relatively inactive, whereas others appear to have a range of activities; the membership of some is drawn from only a few EU countries, while others are genuinely pan-European. In some specialist fields there seem to be only a few groups, while in others there appear to be more. Some networks involve quite high-ranking police, while others draw their membership from a lower level.

At present this is uncharted territory. No one seems to know how many such groups there are or what they achieve. There is evidence of considerable duplication and confusion. A detailed investigation to provide an account of these European police networks and groups would clear the way for a more efficient and coherent approach.

A European Fraud Squad should be established to undertake concerted action against serious fraud within the European Union.

One of the major crime problems in the European Union is fraud, and yet it does not seem to have received the attention it merits. The removal of internal frontier checks and the development of the Single Market and the European Union may lead to an increase in certain types of fraud. The evidence that is available shows that the extent of fraud is already enormous but much of it is relatively invisible, publicly unacknowledged and often highly complex.

For a number of reasons, fraud is notoriously difficult to police. The technological developments that have made business fraud so much simpler have also made its investigation much harder. There is also evidence of a growing problem with credit-card and cheque-book fraud, which seems to be increasingly organised by criminal gangs. Defrauding the EC itself is also a major problem.

There are strong arguments in favour of creating a European Fraud Squad (EFS). Member states already have local or regional fraud squads and, increasingly, more centralised units, in addition to the support provided by the EC's own anti-fraud unit UCLAF. It would be a logical progression to use these developments as the basis for a European-wide agency.

A European Fraud Squad would have to meet three criteria. First, it would require staffing by police and customs officers, accountants, lawyers and information technology (IT) specialists. They would need to act in partnership. Secondly, the EFS would need an operational arm. Although this is contentious, without genuine powers of investigation the European Fraud Squad would be unable to operate in the concerted and vigorous way that is necessary. Thirdly, a proper career structure would need to be developed for both officers and non-police personnel, in order to attract high-quality staff.

The European Fraud Squad proposal merits serious and overdue consideration. The proposal may succeed because it is in each individual country's interests. Commercial crime is a specialist field where co-ordinated international action is needed. The European Fraud Squad would have to be properly accountable and should make annual reports to the European Parliament. How such a force could be established with executive, operational functions should be investigated. The research team emphasise this proposal as a central conclusion of the research project.

A European Police University should be established.

There is a great need to undertake teaching and training for police, customs and other law enforcement officers who are charged with preventing crime, protecting safety and security and catching offenders in the new Europe. Appropriate research into detailed areas is also required.

One single institute would not be capable of co-ordinating all the training, research and information needed on police co-operation in Europe. A number of designated centres throughout Europe would be needed, and together they would constitute the federal European Police University. It would be important for each college in the University to be principally devoted to teaching and research in *European* policing matters, although the work could also embrace wider international policing issues.

The proposed European Police University would obviously need adequate funding to enable it to undertake the necessary teaching, training and research. One arrangement could be the mechanism which will be used to finance the European Drugs Unit/Europol or the sliding scale of contributions by which Interpol is funded. Funding could also come from the budget of the European Community, as provided for in Article K.8(2) of Title VI of the Treaty on European Union. The EPU would draw on a range of teaching and research resources. Police and customs officers themselves would be involved as would experts from specialist organisations and groups and other universities and research centres. The European Police University would work closely with the proposed European Centre for Research into Crime.

APPENDIX III

BIBLIOGRAPHY

Association of Chief Police Officers and Metropolitan Police European Unit, (1989), *Rabies*, Briefing Note 8/90, London: Joint ACPO Metropolitan Police European Unit.

Agelink, M. and van Gestel, G. (1989), 'Comparative information on police systems', in Netherlands Police Academy, *Report of the European Police Summer Course 1989*, Apeldoorn and Warnsveld, Netherlands: Police Academy and Police Studies Centre, pp.33–52.

Agelink, M., van Gestel, G. and Lommen, Y. (1990), 'Comparative information on police systems', in Netherlands Police Academy, *Report of the Second European Police Summer Course 1990*, Apeldoorn and Warnsveld, Netherlands: Police Academy and Police Studies Centre, pp.29–58.

Alderson, J. (1989), 'Are border controls necessary?', *Police Journal*, Vol.62, (July – September), pp.238–242.

Alexander, Y. and Myers, K. (1982), *Terrorism in Europe*, London: Croom Helm.

Anderson, M. (1989), *Policing the World*, Oxford: Clarendon Press.

Anderson, M. (1991), *The French Police and European Co-operation*, Working Paper I, Edinburgh: Department of Politics, University of Edinburgh.

Andrade, J. (1985), *World Police and Paramilitary Forces*, London: Macmillan.

Bal, P. (1993), 'Dutch drugs policy: a mistaken fear of European integration', paper presented to a colloquium 'Schengen: A First Assessment After the Opening of the Frontiers', Luxembourg, 14–15th October 1993.

Bayley, D.H. (1985), *Patterns of Policing: A Comparative International Analysis*, New Brunswick: Rutgers University Press.

Benyon, J. (1992), *Issues in European Police Co-operation*, Leicester University Discussion Papers in Politics No.P92/11, Leicester: Department of Politics, University of Leicester.

Benyon, J. (ed.) (1984), *Scarman and After*, Oxford: Pergamon.

Bethell, Lord (1990a), 'Crime knows no frontiers', *Police*, Vol.22, No.6, pp.14–16.

Bethell, Lord (1990b), 'All the time the thieves were one step ahead of us', *Police*, Vol.23, No.9, June, p.8.

Bigo, D. (1992), 'The European internal security field', paper presented to 'ECPR Workshop on European Police Co-operation', Limerick, April 1992.

Birch, R. (1989), 'Policing Europe in 1992', *Police Review*, Vol.97, No.5010, 5th May, pp.918–919.

Birch, R. (1992a), 'Policing Europe – current issues', *PRSU Bulletin*, No.42, January, pp.4–6.

Birch, R. (1992b), 'Why Europe needs Interpol', *Police Review*, 17th January, p.121.

Blessmann, K. (1993), 'Practical questions regarding border controls', paper presented to a European Institute of Public Administration colloquium 'Schengen: A First Assessment After the Opening of the Frontiers', Luxembourg, 14–15th October 1993.

Boer, M. Den, (1991), *The Police in the Netherlands and European Police Co-operation*, Working Paper IV, Edinburgh: Department of Politics, University of Edinburgh.

Boer, M. Den, (1992a), 'The quest for international policing: rhetoric and justification in a disorderly debate', paper presented to 'ECPR Workshop on European Police Co-operation', Limerick, April 1992.

Boer, M. Den, (1992b), *Police Co-operation After Maastricht*, Research Paper No. 2/92, Hull: University of Hull. EC Research Unit.

Boer, M. Den, and Walker, N. (1993), 'European policing after 1992', *Journal of Common Market Studies*, Vol.31, pp.3–28.

Borghini, E. (1992), 'Italy', in Netherlands Police Academy, *Report of the Fourth European Police Summer Course 1992*, Apeldoorn and Warnsveld, Netherlands: Police Academy and Police Studies Centre.

Bossard, A. (1988), 'Interpol and law enforcement: response to transnational crime', *Police Studies*, Vol.11, No.4, pp.177–182.

Boye, I. (1990), 'Law enforcement initiatives in Denmark', *The Police Chief*, July, p.17.

Bresler, F. (1992), *Interpol*, London: Sinclair Stevenson.

Brug H. van der and Meijs, J. (1991), 'Dutch high risk supporters at the World Football Championships in Italy' quoted in Williams, J. (1992), *Football Spectators and Italia 90: A Report on the Behaviour and Control of European Football Fans at the World Cup Finals 1990*, unpublished report for the Council of Europe: University of Leicester, Sir Norman Chester Centre for Football Research.

Busch, N. (1992), 'German crime prevention and policing policies: a model for Europol', paper presented at 'Platform Fortress Europe Workshop, European Civic Forum Conference', Limans, August 1992; updated November 1992.

Butler, A.J. (1982), 'Effectiveness, accountability and management: the challenge of contemporary police work', in Jones, C. and Stevenson, J. (eds.), (1982), *Yearbook of Social Policy in Britain 1980–81*, London: Routledge.

Butt Philip, A. (1989), *European Border Controls: Who Needs Them?*, Royal Institute of International Affairs Paper 19, London: RIIA.

Cameron-Waller, S. (1993a), 'Organised crime - criminal intelligence: the future role of Interpol in Europe', paper presented to International Chiefs of Police, 10th Regional Executive Conference.

Cameron-Waller, S. (1993b), 'Interpol's point of view', paper presented to a European Institute of Public Administration colloquium 'Schengen: A First Assessment After the Opening of the Frontiers', Luxembourg, 14–15th October 1993.

Carvel, J. (1993a), 'Fortress Europe prepares to wall in its racism', *The Guardian* , 27th May.

Carvel, J. (1993b), 'Changing face of EC refugees', *The Guardian*, 1st June.

Castle, T. and Sutton, H. (1990), 'How enforcers target the drug money launderers', *The European*, 29th June–1st July.

Clark, J. and Sanctuary, C. (1992), 'Anti-drug smuggling operational research in HM Customs and Excise', *Public Administration*, pp.577–589.

Cohen, S. (1972), *Folk Devils and Moral Panics: The Creation of the Mods and Rockers*, London: Paladin.

Collier, A. (1993), *The Problems of Measuring International Cross-Frontier Crime and their Relationship to Decision Making on Police Resource Allocation*, Bramshill Fellowship Paper, Bramshill: Police Staff College.

Colvin, M. (1992), 'The criminal record and information system in England and Wales', *International Yearbook of Law, Computers and Technology*, Vol.6, pp.139–156.

Commission of the European Communities, (1989), *Europe Without Frontiers – Completing the Internal Market*, Luxembourg: Office for Official Publications of the European Communities.

Commission of the European Communities, (1992), *Eurobarometer: Public Opinion in the European Community*, No.37, June, Brussels: European Commission.

Commission of the European Communities, (1993a), *Report on the Fight Against Fraud: Report on 1992 and Action Programme for 1993*, Brussels: European Commission.

Commission of the European Communities, (1993b), 'Road safety background report', *The Week in Europe*, ISEC/B24/93, 17th August, Brussels: European Commission.

Council of Europe, (1990), *Report on the New Countries of Immigration*, Document 6211, Strasbourg: Council of Europe.

Crossick, S. (1988), 'Mrs Thatcher and the single market', *New Law Journal*, Vol.138, No.6385, December, pp.881–882.

Cruz, A. (1993), *Schengen, Ad Hoc Immigration Group and Other European Inter-Governmental Bodies in View of a Europe Without Borders*, Briefing Paper No.12, Brussels: Churches Committee for Migrants in Europe.

Cullen, P. (1992), *The German Police and European Police Co-operation*, Working Paper II, Edinburgh: Department of Politics, University of Edinburgh.

Customs News, (1992), 'Anti-smuggling controls', *Customs News*, No.5, p.3.

Dahrendorf, R. (1980), 'Effectiveness and legitimacy: on the "governability" of democracies', *Political Quarterly*, Vol.51, No.4, pp. 393–410.

Danish Ministry of Justice and Ministry of the Interior, (1993), *Press Release: Meeting of Justice and Interior Ministers of the EC Member States*, 6–7th May 1993, Copenhagen: Ministry of Justice.

Dashko, G.V. (1992), 'Quantitative and qualitative changes in crime in the USSR', *British Journal of Criminology*, Vol.32, No.2, pp.160–166.

Devon and Cornwall Constabulary, (1990), *The Channel Tunnel and Devon and Cornwall*, Exeter: Devon and Cornwall Constabulary.

Diederich, F. (1993), 'Police co-operation', paper presented to a European Institute of Public Administration colloquium 'Schengen: A First Assessment After the Opening of the Frontiers', Luxembourg, 14-15th October 1993.

Dijk, J. van, (1993), 'Crime in Europe: trends and prospects', paper presented to a conference 'Crime in Europe: Patterns and Prospects for the 1990s', 23rd September 1993, Leicester: University of Leicester, Centre for the Study of Public Order.

Dijk, J. van and Mayhew, P. (1993), 'Criminal victimisation in the industrial world', a report to the NICRI conference 'Understanding Crime: Experiences of Crime and Crime Control', 18–20th November 1992.

Dijk, J. van, Mayhew, P. and Killias, M. (1990), *Experiences of Crime Across the World: Key Findings from the 1989 International Crime Survey*, Daventer, Netherlands: Kluwer/Law and Taxation.

Dorn, N. (1992), 'Drug enforcement within Europe: police co-operation in the age of free movement for EC nationals', unpublished paper, London: Howard League for Penal Reform.

Drüke, L. (1993), 'Asylum seekers and refugees in the turmoil after the opening (or closing) of the frontiers', paper presented to a European Institute of Public Administration colloquium 'Schengen: A First Assessment After the Opening of the Frontiers', Luxembourg, 14-15th October 1993.

Duyne, P.C. van (1993), 'Organised crime markets in a turbulent Europe', *European Journal on Criminal Policy and Research*, Vol.1, No.3, pp.10–30.

Eastwood, A. (1989), 'On to 1992', *Police*, Vol.22, No.1, September–October, pp.24–26.

Elsen, C. (1993), 'Institutional mechanisms: Trevi, Schengen, Dublin, Maastricht', paper presented to a European Institute of Public Administration colloquium 'Schengen: A First Assessment After the Opening of the Frontiers', Luxembourg, 14-15th October 1993.

European Network for Policewomen, (1992a), *Facts, Figures and General Information*, report prepared for the European conference 'Quality Through Equality', 23rd–27th March 1992, Amersfoort: ENP.

European Network for Policewomen, (1992b), *Unite to Succeed: Policy Plan of the European Network for Policewomen 1992–1997*, Amersfoort: ENP.

European Network for Policewomen, (1992c), *Newsletter*, December, Amersfoort: ENP.

Erbes, J.M., Monet, J.C., Funk, A., Reinke, H., Ponsaers, P., Janssens, C., Cartuyvels, Y., Dauge, M., Gleizal, J.J., Journes, C. and Palidda, S. (1992), *Polices d'Europe*, Paris: Institut des Hautes Études de Sécurité Intérieure / L'Harmattan.

Ericson, R. (1982), *Reproducing Order*, Toronto: University of Toronto Press.

Esterow, M. (1967), *The Art Stealers*, London: Wiedenfeld and Nicolson.

European Community Information Technology Task Force, (1984), *The Vulnerability of the Information Conscious Society: European Situation*, unpublished research monograph.

European Parliament, (1992), *Report Drawn Up by the Committe of Enquiry Into the Spread of Organised Crime Linked to Drugs Trafficking in the Member States of the European Community*, PE152.380/fin, Luxembourg: European Parliament.

European Parliamentary Labour Party, (1991), *Drug Trafficking and Organised Crime*, press release, December 1991.

Fijnaut, C. (1987), 'The internationalization of criminal investigation in western Europe', in Fijnaut, C. and Hermans, R. (eds.), *Police Co-operation in Europe: Lectures at the International Symposium on Surveillance*, Lochem: Van den Brink.

Focus, (1992), 'Policespeak', *Focus*, No.1, December, p.16.

Follain, M. (1989), 'On the trail of a simple international language', *The Financial Times*, 28th June.

Fooner, M. (1989), *Interpol: Issues in World Crime and International Criminal Justice*, New York: Plenum Press.

Frontier-free Europe, (1993), No.4, p.2.

Gallagher, F. (1992), 'Kent County Constabulary: its European perspective', *PRSU Bulletin*, No.42, January, pp.18–24.

Gal-Or, N. (1985), *International Co-operation to Suppress Terrorism*, London: Croom Helm.

Garrison, O. (1976), *The Secret World of Interpol*, Glasgow: Machellan Press.

Gregory, F. (1993), 'Issues in European police co-operation', paper presented to a conference 'European Police C-operation: Current Arrangements and Future Developments', 16th September 1993, Leicester: University of Leicester, Centre for the Study of Public Order.

Greilsamer, L. (1986), *Interpol: Le Seige du Soupcon*, Paris: A. Moreau.

Groenendijk, C. (1989), 'Schengen, refugees and human rights,' *Race and Immigration*, No.227, July – August, pp.10–15.

Grundy, S. (1990), 'Kent's French connection', *Police Review*, 5th January, pp.26–27.

Guarda Civil, (1993), *Yearbook of the Guarda Civil*, Barcelona: *Guarda Civil.*

Hadfield, R. (1993), '*Crime in Europe: The Role of the Police*', paper presented to the conference 'Crime in Europe: Patterns and Prospects for the 1990s', 23rd September 1993, Centre for the Study of Public Order, Leicester.

Hall, S., Critcher, C., Jefferson, T., Clarke, J. and Roberts, B. (1978), *Policing the Crisis*, London: Macmillan.

Hantrais, L., Mangen, S. and O'Brien, M. (1992), *Doing Cross-National Research*, Cross-National Research Paper No. 1, Birmingham: Aston University, Aston Modern Languages Club.

Harring, S. (1983), *Policing a Class Society*, New Brunswick, N.J.: Rutgers University Press.

Heard, C. (1990), 'The great disappearing act', *Leicester Mercury*, 25th July.

Heidensohn, F. and Farrell, M. (1991), *Crime in Europe*, London: Routledge.

HM Customs and Excise, (1992), *Changes for Customs Checks on Intra-EC Traffic After 1992*, unpublished briefing paper, London: HM Customs and Excise.

Home Office, (1977), Home Office Circular 153/77, London: Home Office.

Hough, M. and Mayhew, P. (1983), *The British Crime Survey: First Report*, Home Office Research Study No. 76, London: HMSO.

Hough, M. and Mayhew, P. (1985), *Taking Account of Crime: Key Findings from the 1984 British Crime Survey*, Home Office Research Study No. 85, London: HMSO.

House of Commons, (1989), *Session 1988–89, Seventh Report into Drug Trafficking and Related Serious Crime*, London: HMSO.

House of Commons, (1990a), *Session 1989–90, Home Affairs Committee Seventh Report on Practical Police Co-operation in the European Community, Volume I, Report together with the Proceedings of the Committee*, London: HMSO.

House of Commons, (1990b), *Session 1989–90, Home Affairs Committee Seventh Report Practical Police Co-operation in the European Community, Volume II Memoranda of Evidence, Minutes of Evidence and Appendices*, London: HMSO.

House of Commons, (1991), *Session 1990–91, Policing Football Hooliganism*, Second Report, *Volume I, Report together with Proceedings of the Committee*, London: HMSO.

House of Lords, (1989), *Report of the Select Committee on the European Communities – 1992: Border Control of People*, Paper 90, London: HMSO.

Imbert, P. (1989), 'Crimes without frontiers', *Police Review*, Vol.97, p.1174.

Jamieson, A. (1992), *Drug Trafficking After 1992: A Special Report*, Conflict Studies, No.250, London: Research Institute for the Study of Conflict and Terrorism.

Jepson, J. (1986), 'Moral panics and the spread of control models in Europe – seen from Denmark', paper prepared for the European Group for the Study of Deviance and Social Control, Madrid, September.

Joutsen, M. (1993), 'The potential for the growth of organized crime in central and eastern Europe', *European Journal on Criminal Policy and Research*, Vol. 1, No. 3, pp. 76–86.

Keraudren, P. (1993), 'New French reservations regarding Schengen', paper presented to a European Institute of Public Administration colloquium 'Schengen: A First Assessment After the Opening of the Frontiers', Luxembourg, 14–15th October 1993.

Killias, M. (1993), 'Will open borders result in more crime? A criminological statement', *European Journal on Criminal Policy and Research*, Vol. 1, No. 3, pp. 7–9.

King, M. (1993), 'Europol: a model for convergence of policing systems', paper presented to the *Centro Nazionale di Studi e Ricerche sulla Polizia* and SIULP conference 'Europol', Bolanzo, Italy, 13th March.

Kniper, A. (1993), *The Reorganisation of the Dutch Police*, unpublished paper, Leicester: University of Leicester, Centre for the Study of Public Order.

Kondogiannis, A. (1990), 'The control of international crime', paper presented to the '12th Annual Convention of the Chiefs of Police from the Capital Cities of Europe', Athens: Hellenic Police.

Kube, E. and Kuckuck, W. (1992), 'Research and technological development in the police: requirements from the western European point of view', *Police Studies*, Vol. 15, No. 1.

Kühne, H. (1993), *Control at Internal Borders and National Security*, paper presented to a European Institute of Public Administration colloquium on 'Schengen: A First Assessment After the Opening of the Frontiers', Luxembourg, 14–15th October 1993.

Kuijvenhoven, A. (1992), 'The police in the Netherlands', *Focus*, December, p. 42.

Kurian, G.T. (1989), *World Encyclopaedia of Police Forces and Penal Systems*, London and New York: Facts on File.

Kury, H. (1992), 'Victim surveys in Germany', paper prepared for the United Nations Interregional Crime and Justice Research Institute 'Preparatory Seminar of the International Conference on Understanding Crime: Experiences of Crime and Crime Control', Rome, 17-18th March.

Larnaude, F. and Roux, J. (eds.) (1926), *Premier Congres de Police Judiciaire Internationale (Monaco 1914) – Actes du Congres*, Paris.

Latter, R. (1990), *Crime and the European Community After 1992*, Wilton Park Papers 3, London: HMSO.

Latter, R. (1991), *Terrorism in the 1990s*, Wilton Park Papers No. 44, London: HMSO.

Layton-Henry, Z. (1992), *The Politics of Immigration: Immigration, Race and Race Relations in Post-War Britain*, Oxford: Blackwell.

Levi, M. (1986) *The Incidence, Reporting and Prevention of Commercial Fraud*, unpublished monograph prepared for the Home Office Crime Prevention Unit, London: Home Office.

Levi, M. (1987), *Regulating Fraud: White Collar Crime and the Criminal Process*, London: Tavistock.

Levi, M. (1993), 'The extent of cross-border crime in Europe: the view from Britain', *European Journal on Criminal Policy and Research*, Vol.1, No.3, pp.57–76.

Lewis, R. (1976), *A Force for the Future*, London: Temple Smith.

Lindop, N. (1978), *Report of the Committee on Data Protection*, London: HMSO (Cmnd 7341).

Lodge, J. (1991), *Frontier Problems and the Single Market in Counter Terrorism in Europe: Implications of 1992*, Conflict Studies, No.238, London: Research Institute for the Study of Conflict and Terrorism.

Lowenthal, R. (1984), *Social Change and Cultural Crisis*, New York: Columbia University Press.

Manning, P. (1977), *Police Work: The Social Organization of Policing*, Cambridge, Massachusetts: Massachusetts Institute of Technology.

Marrinan, J. (1988), 'Challenge and threat of 1992', *Garda Review*, Vol.16, No.8, September, pp.16–18.

Marshall, A. (1993), 'Citizens of the thirteenth country', *The Independent on Sunday*, 6th June.

Mason, G. (1991), 'Kendall's kingdom', *Police Review*, 4th January, p.19.

Mattera, P. (1985), *Off the Books*, London: Pluto Press.

Mawby, R. (1992), 'Comparative police systems: searching for a continental model', in Bottomley, K, Fowles, T and Reiner, R. (eds.), *Criminal Justice: Theory and Practice*, British Criminology Conference 1991, Selected Papers Vol.2, London: Wright, pp.108-132.

Mayhew, P. (1990), 'Experiences of crime across the world in 1988', *Home Office Research and Statistics Bulletin*, No.28, London: Home Office Research and Planning Unit.

Meldal-Johnsen, T. and Young, V. (1979), *The Interpol Connection: An Enquiry into the International Criminal Police Organisation*, New York.

Middlemass, K. (1975), *The Double Market: Art Theft and Art Thieves*, Hampshire: Saxon House DC-Heath.

Migration News Sheet, (1993), 'Strong hopes of the Convention being implemented in December', *Migration News Sheet*, August, pp.23.

Monjardet, D. (1992), '*Le modèle français de police*', paper presented at *Institut des Hautes Études de la Sécurité Intérieure* conference 'Les Systèmes de Police et la Cooperation Policière en Europe: Comparaisons, Tendances, Defis', Paris, 1st–4th December.

Muir, W. (1977), *Police: Streetcorner Politicians*, Chicago: University of Chicago Press.

Muncie, J. (1987), 'Much ado about nothing? The sociology of moral panics', *Social Studies Review*, Vol.3, No.2, pp.42–46.

National Commissioner's Office, (1992), *The Police in Denmark*, Copenhagen: National Commissioner's Office.

National Union of Civil and Public Servants and Civil and Public Services Association, (1992), *Drugs: Destination Europe – The Case for Strengthening Customs Checks after 1993*, London: NUCPS and CPSA.

New Statesman and Society, (1992), 'No room for them', *New Statesman and Society*, 4th December, p.5.

Nundy, J. and Doyle, L. (1993), 'France retains frontier controls', *The Independent*, 1st May.

O'Keefe, D. (1993a), 'Non-adherence to the Schengen Conventions: the case of the United Kingdom and Ireland', paper presented to a European Institute of Public Administration colloquium 'Schengen: A First Assessment After the Opening of the Frontiers', Luxembourg, 14–15th October 1993.

O'Keefe, D. (1993b), 'The Schengen agreements and community law', paper presented to a European Institute of Public Administration colloquium 'Schengen: A First Assessment After the Opening of the Frontiers', Luxembourg, 14–15th October 1993.

Office for Official Publications of the European Communities, (1990), *Europe – A Fresh Start: The Schumann Declaration 1950-1990*, Luxembourg: Office for Official Publications of the European Communities.

Osmond, J. (ed.), (1992), *German Reunification; A Reference Guide and Commentary*, Essex: Longman Group.

Outrive, L. van, (1992a), *Second Report of the Committee on Civil Liberties and Internal Affairs on the Entry into Force of the Schengen Agreements*, European Parliament Session Documents, A3–0336/92, Luxembourg: European Parliament.

Outrive, L. van, (1992b), *Report to the Committee on Civil Liberties and Internal Affairs on the Setting Up of Europol*, European Parliament Session Documents, A3–0382/92, Luxembourg: European Parliament.

Owen, R. and Dynes, M. (1989), *The Times Guide to 1992: Britain in a Europe Without Frontiers*, London: Times Books Ltd.

Pinder, J. (1991), *The European Community*, Oxford: Oxford University Press.

Platform Fortress Europe, (1992–93), 'Germany and Bulgaria co-operate on return of refused asylum seekers', *Platform Fortress Europe*, No.11, p.3.

Police Review, (1993), 'Kent joins Euro-traffic computer network', *Police Review*, 18th June, p.9.

PoliceSpeak, (1993), *Police Communications and Language and the Channel Tunnel: Report*, Cambridge: PoliceSpeak Publications.

Police Requirements Support Unit, (1992), 'From morse to email in a decade: communications at Interpol London', *PRSU Bulletin*, No.42, January, pp.58–60.

Rae, S. (1993), 'Nationwide squads to be based in the Park', *Garda Review*, Vol.21, No.1, January, p.7.

Reiner, R. and Spencer, S. (eds.) (1993), *Accountable Policing: Effectiveness, Empowerment and Equity*, London: Institute for Public Policy Research.

Reinke, S. (1992), 'The EC Commission's anti-fraud activity', in Anderson, M. and Den Boer, M. (eds.) *European Police Co-operation: Proceedings of a Seminar*, Edinburgh: Department of Politics, University of Edinburgh.

Reiss, A.J. (1971), *The Police and the Public*, New Haven: Yale University Press.

Roberts, A. (1993), 'London is smuggling capital of art world', *The Times*, 24th February.

Robertson, K. (1992), 'Police intelligence co-operation: problems and prospects', paper presented to 'ECPR Workshop on European Police Co-operation', Limerick, April 1992.

Ruimchotel, D. (1993), 'Ambiguities between criminal policy and scientific research: the case of fraud against the EC', *European Journal on Criminal Policy and Research*, Vol.1, No.3, pp.101–122.

Russell, A. (1993), 'Cross border crime and the changing role of customs in Europe', paper presented to a conference 'Crime in Europe: Patterns and Prospects for the 1990s', 23rd September 1993, Leicester: University of Leicester, Centre for the Study of Public Order.

Sage, A. (1993), 'Croatian war refugees face deportation today', *The Independent*, 21st April.

Savona, E.U. (1993), 'Mafia money-laundering versus Italian legislation', *European Journal on Criminal Policy and Research*, Vol.1, No.3, pp.31–56.

Schmidt-Nothen, R. (1989), 'Police co-operation in Europe in the context of the abolition of border controls', *International Criminal Police Review*, No.420, September – October, pp.5–9.

Scottish Home and Health Department, (1990), 'The UK Government's view – the Scottish dimension', paper presented to the Scottish Lawyers' European Group and the Scottish Police Service Conference, 'Europe Post-1992: What Price Free Movement?', Tulliallan: Scottish Police College.

Sicot, M. (1961), *A la Barre de l'Interpol*, Paris: Les Productions de Paris.

Smart, V. (1993), 'Passport checks to be abolished at last', *The European*, 1st–4th June.

Statewatch (1991), 'The Kilowatt network', *Statewatch*, No.1, March – April, p.2.

Statewatch (1992a), 'EURO police glossary', *Statewatch* Vol.2, No.1, January – February, p.3.

Statewatch (1992b), 'Forgery course', *Statewatch*, Vol.2, No.6, November – December, p.1.

Stein, T. (undated), *Abolition of Control of Persons at Intra-Community Borders*, Heidelberg: University of Heidelberg.

Stewart-Clark, Sir J. (1989), 'Drugs – Europe's biggest business?', *House Magazine*, 13th November, p.23.

Surrey Constabulary, (1992), *Surrey Sans Frontières: The Implications of the Single European State on the Policing of Surrey*, Surrey Constabulary: Policy Analysis Unit.

Target 92, (1992), 'Cross-border training for customs officers', *Target 92*, No.9, p.2.

The Guardian, (1990), 'Dutch police break IRA cell with fourth arrest', 20th June.

The Guardian, (1993), 'Germany tops the migrants table', 22nd June.

The Independent on Sunday, (1991), 'Tourists tricked into smuggling drugs', 21st April.

Tiedemann, K. (1985), 'International research tasks in the field of economic crime' in Magnusson, D. (ed.), *Economic Crime – Programs for Future Research*, Stockholm: National Council for Crime Prevention.

Trevi Group, (1990), *Programme of Action Relating to the Reinforcement of Police Co-operation and of the Endeavours to Combat Terrorism or Other Forms of Organised Crime* (The Dublin Programme of Action), Trevi Group, June.

Union Internationale des Syndicates de Polices, (1987), *Union Internationale des Syndicates de Polices: Statutes and Standing Orders*, Hildon: UISP.

Union Internationale des Syndicates de Polices, (1992), *Union Internationale des Syndicates de Polices: Report of Activity*, unpublished briefing paper, Hildon: UISP.

Verraes, J. (1993), 'Schengen: an agreement to co-operate', paper presented to a conference 'European Police Co-operation: Current Arrangements and Future Developments', 16th September 1993, Leicester: University of Leicester, Centre for the Study of Public Order.

Walker, N. (1992), 'Models of European integration and models of European police co-operation', paper presented to 'ECPR Workshop on European Police Co-operation', Limerick, April 1992.

Wilkinson, P. (1989), *The Lessons of Lockerbie*, Conflict Studies, No.226, London: Research Institute for the Study of Conflict and Terrorism.

Wilkinson, P. (1990), 'Internal market for terror?', *The Times*, 5th May.

Williams, J. (1992), *Football Spectators and Italia 90: A Report on the Behaviour and Control of European Football Fans at the World Cup Finals 1990*, unpublished report for the Council of Europe: University of Leicester, Sir Norman Chester Centre for Football Research.

Wilzing, J. (1987), 'Welcome speech', in Fijnaut, C. and Hermans, R. (eds.) *Police Co-operation in Europe: Lectures at the International Symposium on Surveillance*, Lochem: Van den Brink, pp.11–15.

Wohlfart, G. (1993), 'Opening speech', paper presented to a European Institute of Public Administration colloquium 'Schengen: A First Assessment After the Opening of the Frontiers', Luxembourg, 14–15th October 1993.

Wood, J. (1990), 'Biting the city's rotten apples', *Police Review*, 27th July, pp.1492–1493.

Woodward, R. (1993), 'The establishment of Europol: a critique', paper presented to the Cyprus Police Academy International Seminar 'Co-operation with the Police Forces of the Community and with Europol', Nicosia, Cyprus, 20th–23rd April 1993.